DEMOCRACY

BY THE SAME ARTISTS

LOGICOMIX: AN EPIC SEARCH FOR TRUTH

DEMOCRACY

CONCEPT
ALECOS PAPADATOS

STORY
ALECOS PAPADATOS & ABRAHAM KAWA

SCRIPT
ABRAHAM KAWA

ART DIRECTION & DRAWINGS
ALECOS PAPADATOS

COLOURING
ANNIE DI DONNA

BLOOMSBURY
NEW YORK · LONDON · OXFORD · NEW DELHI · SYDNEY

Bloomsbury USA
An imprint of Bloomsbury Publishing Plc

1385 Broadway, New York, NY 10018, USA
50 Bedford Square, London, WC1B 3DP, UK
www.bloomsbury.com

US ISBN: TPB: 978-1-60819-719-4
UK ISBN: TPB: 978-1-4088-2017-9
ebook: 978-1-63286-317-1

Library of Congress Cataloging-in-Publication Data
has been applied for.

British Library Cataloguing-in-Publication Data
A catalogue record for this book is available from the British Library.

2 4 6 8 10 9 7 5 3 1

Printed and bound in China by C&C Offset Printing Co. Ltd

To find out more about our authors and books visit www.bloomsbury.com. Here you will find extracts,
author interviews, details of forthcoming events and the option to sign up for our newsletters.

Bloomsbury books may be purchased for business or promotional use. For information on bulk pur-
chases please contact Macmillan Corporate and Premium Sales Department at
specialmarkets@macmillan.com.

A novel, some say, is like a child.
This one is for our fathers,
Nikos, Sinica, and René,
and the values they gave us.

SUMMER'S END

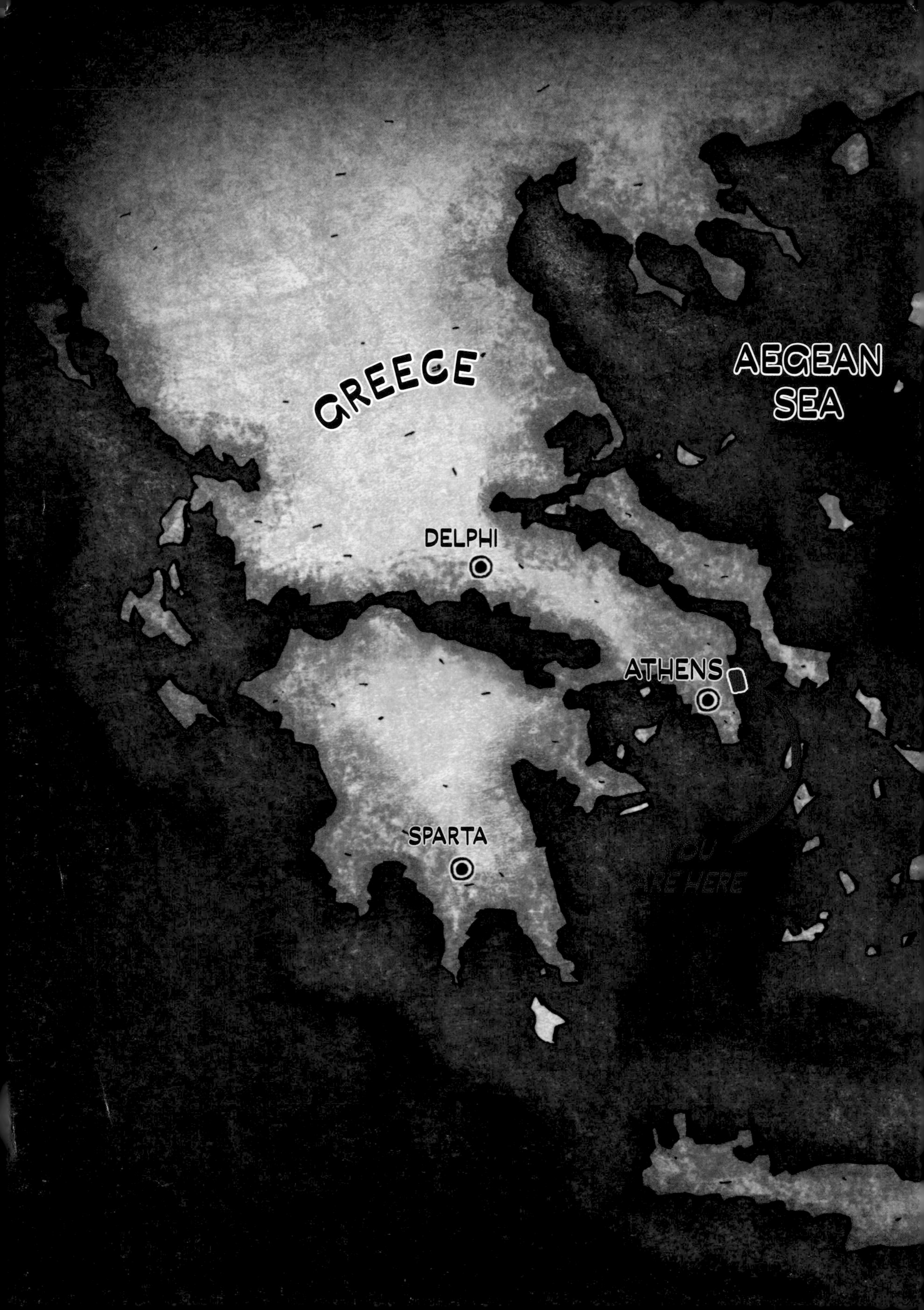
GREECE
AEGEAN SEA
DELPHI
ATHENS
SPARTA
YOU ARE HERE

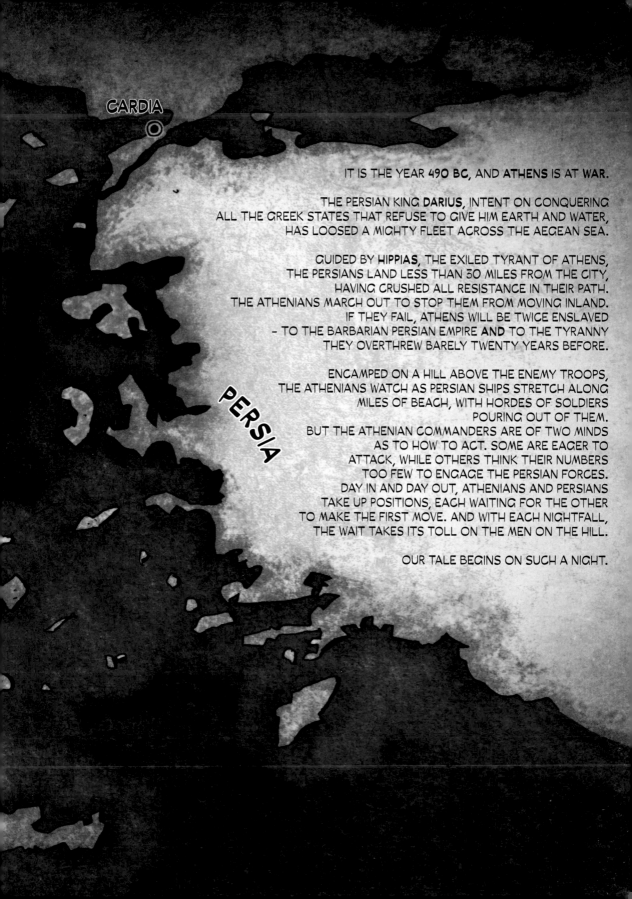

CARDIA

PERSIA

IT IS THE YEAR **490 BC**, AND **ATHENS** IS AT WAR.

THE PERSIAN KING **DARIUS**, INTENT ON CONQUERING
ALL THE GREEK STATES THAT REFUSE TO GIVE HIM EARTH AND WATER,
HAS LOOSED A MIGHTY FLEET ACROSS THE AEGEAN SEA.

GUIDED BY **HIPPIAS**, THE EXILED TYRANT OF ATHENS,
THE PERSIANS LAND LESS THAN 30 MILES FROM THE CITY,
HAVING CRUSHED ALL RESISTANCE IN THEIR PATH.
THE ATHENIANS MARCH OUT TO STOP THEM FROM MOVING INLAND.
IF THEY FAIL, ATHENS WILL BE TWICE ENSLAVED
– TO THE BARBARIAN PERSIAN EMPIRE **AND** TO THE TYRANNY
THEY OVERTHREW BARELY TWENTY YEARS BEFORE.

ENCAMPED ON A HILL ABOVE THE ENEMY TROOPS,
THE ATHENIANS WATCH AS PERSIAN SHIPS STRETCH ALONG
MILES OF BEACH, WITH HORDES OF SOLDIERS
POURING OUT OF THEM.
BUT THE ATHENIAN COMMANDERS ARE OF TWO MINDS
AS TO HOW TO ACT. SOME ARE EAGER TO
ATTACK, WHILE OTHERS THINK THEIR NUMBERS
TOO FEW TO ENGAGE THE PERSIAN FORCES.
DAY IN AND DAY OUT, ATHENIANS AND PERSIANS
TAKE UP POSITIONS, EACH WAITING FOR THE OTHER
TO MAKE THE FIRST MOVE. AND WITH EACH NIGHTFALL,
THE WAIT TAKES ITS TOLL ON THE MEN ON THE HILL.

OUR TALE BEGINS ON SUCH A NIGHT.

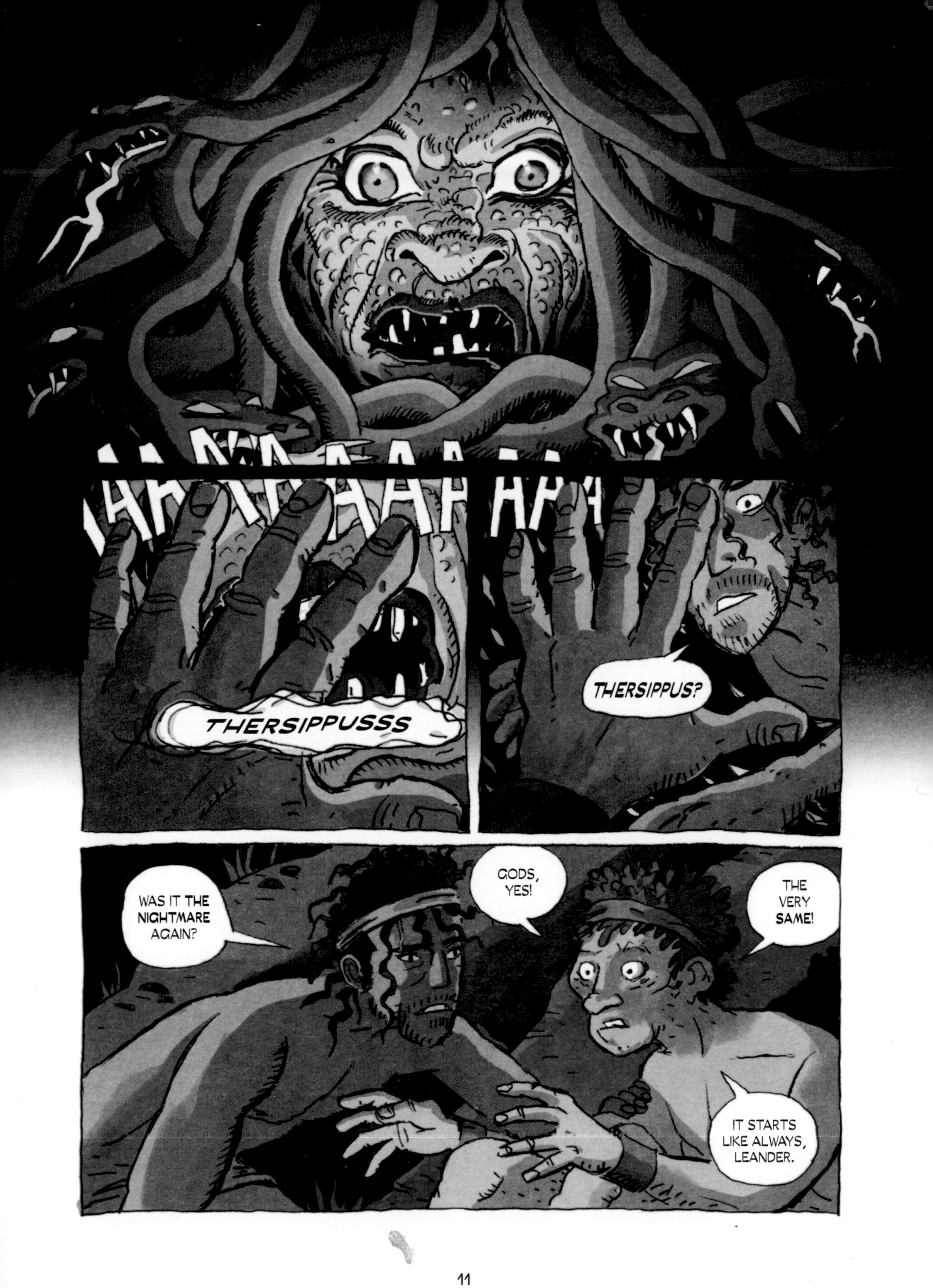
AAAAAAAAAAAA
THERSIPPUSSS
THERSIPPUS?
WAS IT THE NIGHTMARE AGAIN?
GODS, YES!
THE VERY SAME!
IT STARTS LIKE ALWAYS, LEANDER.

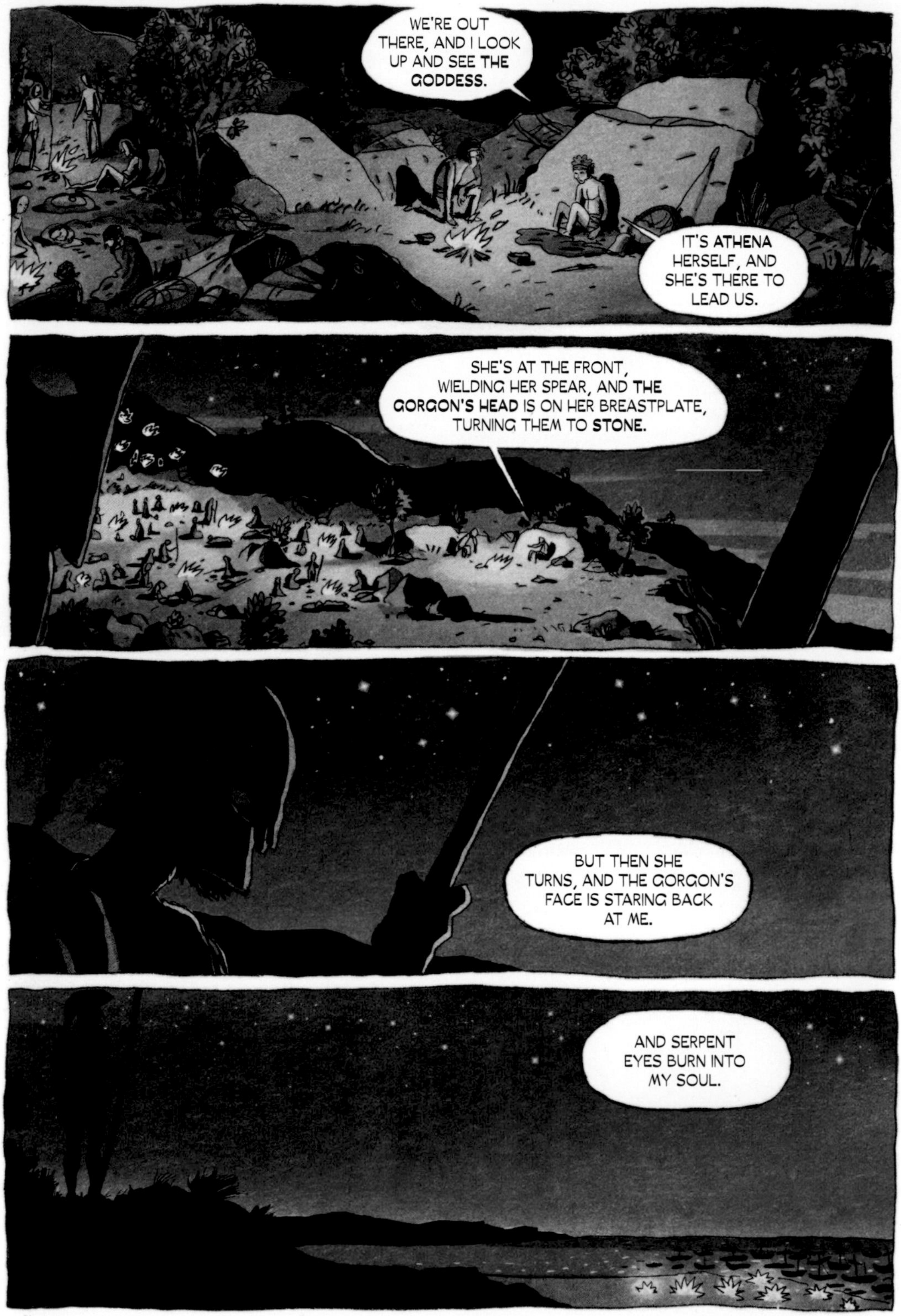
WE'RE OUT THERE, AND I LOOK UP AND SEE THE GODDESS.
IT'S ATHENA HERSELF, AND SHE'S THERE TO LEAD US.
SHE'S AT THE FRONT, WIELDING HER SPEAR, AND THE GORGON'S HEAD IS ON HER BREASTPLATE, TURNING THEM TO STONE.
BUT THEN SHE TURNS, AND THE GORGON'S FACE IS STARING BACK AT ME.
AND SERPENT EYES BURN INTO MY SOUL.

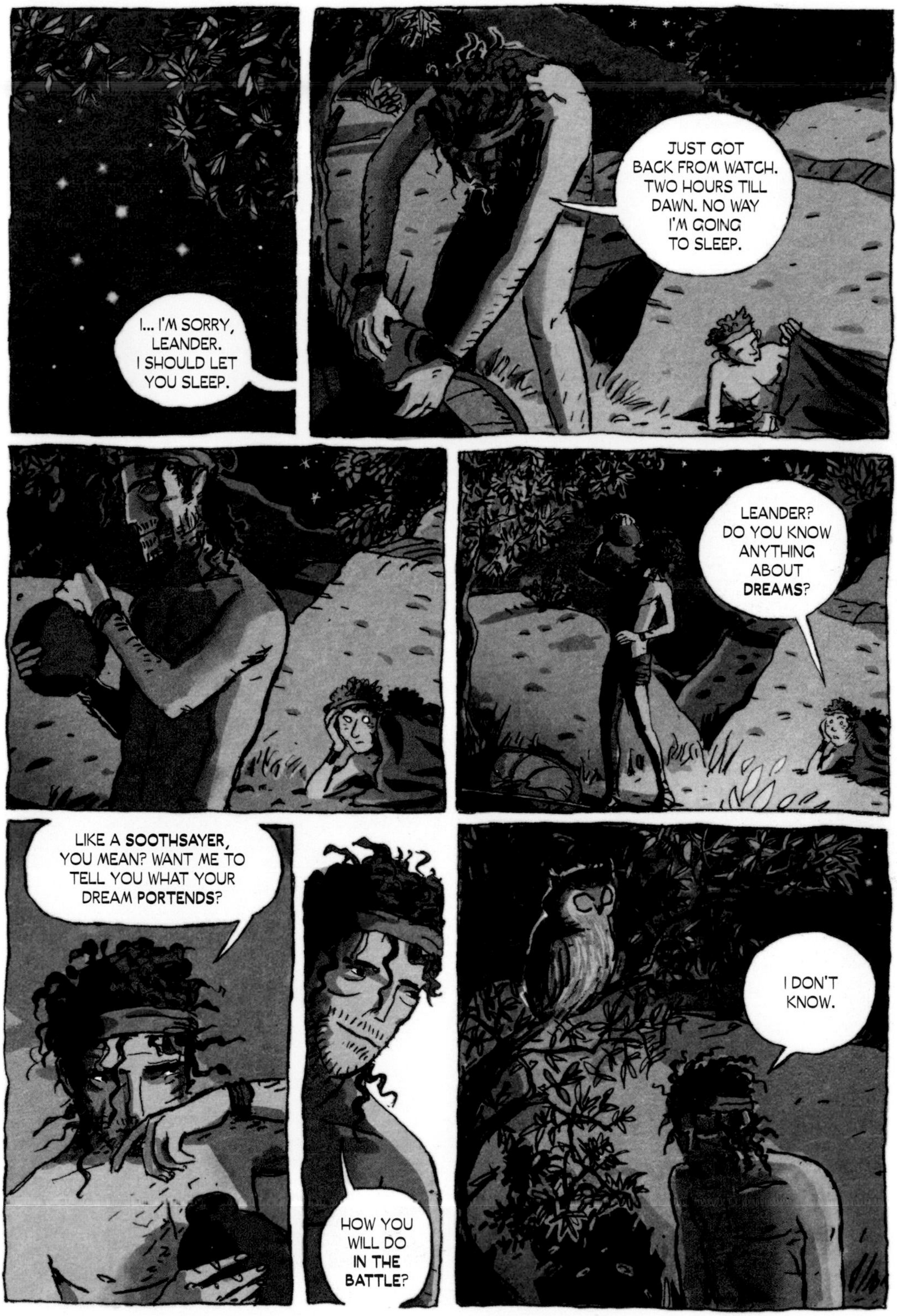
I... I'M SORRY, LEANDER. I SHOULD LET YOU SLEEP.
JUST GOT BACK FROM WATCH. TWO HOURS TILL DAWN. NO WAY I'M GOING TO SLEEP.
LEANDER? DO YOU KNOW ANYTHING ABOUT DREAMS?
LIKE A SOOTHSAYER, YOU MEAN? WANT ME TO TELL YOU WHAT YOUR DREAM PORTENDS?
HOW YOU WILL DO IN THE BATTLE?
I DON'T KNOW.

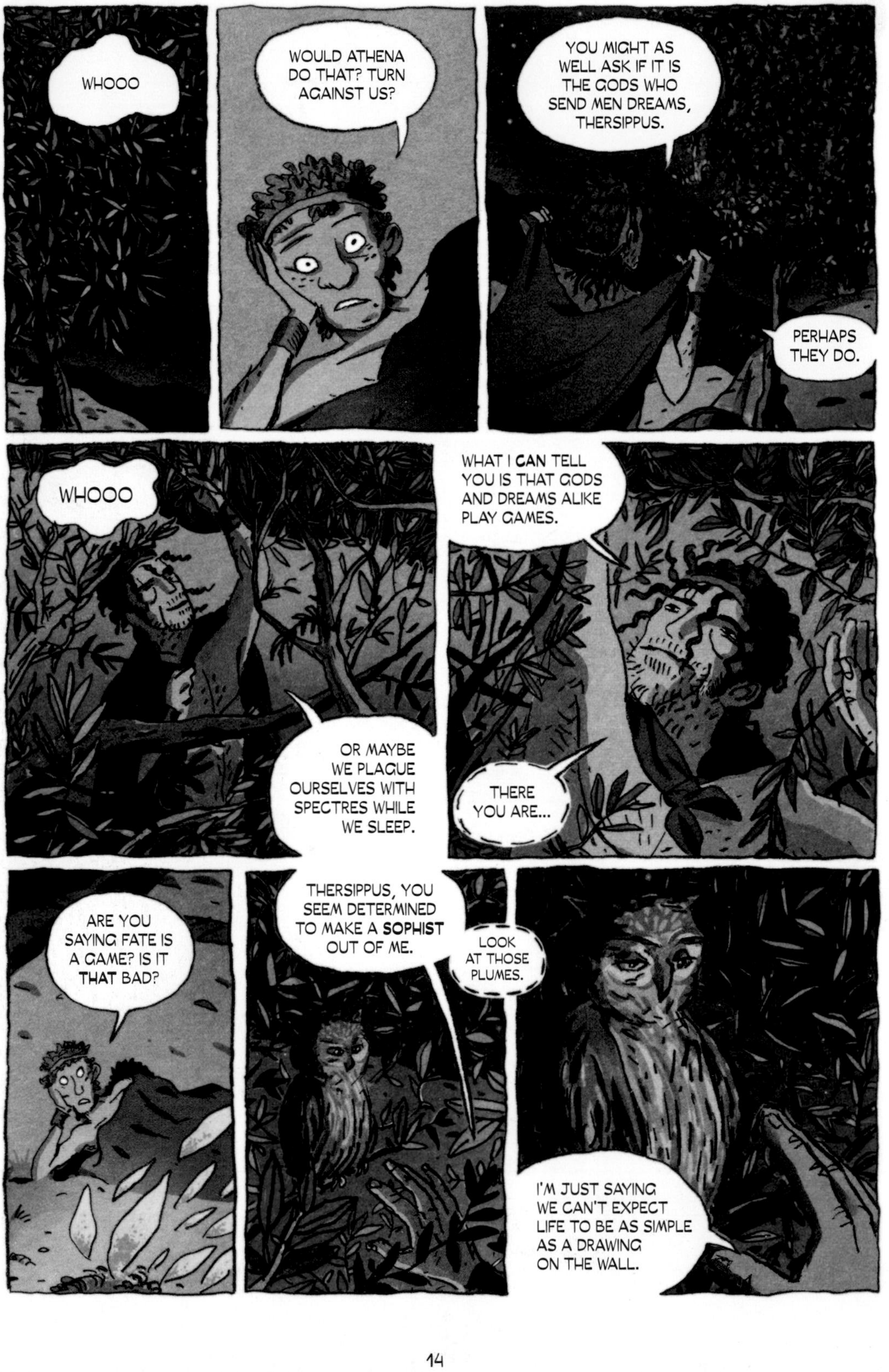

WHOOO
WOULD ATHENA DO THAT? TURN AGAINST US?
YOU MIGHT AS WELL ASK IF IT IS THE GODS WHO SEND MEN DREAMS, THERSIPPUS.
PERHAPS THEY DO.
WHOOO
WHAT I CAN TELL YOU IS THAT GODS AND DREAMS ALIKE PLAY GAMES.
OR MAYBE WE PLAGUE OURSELVES WITH SPECTRES WHILE WE SLEEP.
THERE YOU ARE...
ARE YOU SAYING FATE IS A GAME? IS IT THAT BAD?
THERSIPPUS, YOU SEEM DETERMINED TO MAKE A SOPHIST OUT OF ME.
LOOK AT THOSE PLUMES.
I'M JUST SAYING WE CAN'T EXPECT LIFE TO BE AS SIMPLE AS A DRAWING ON THE WALL.

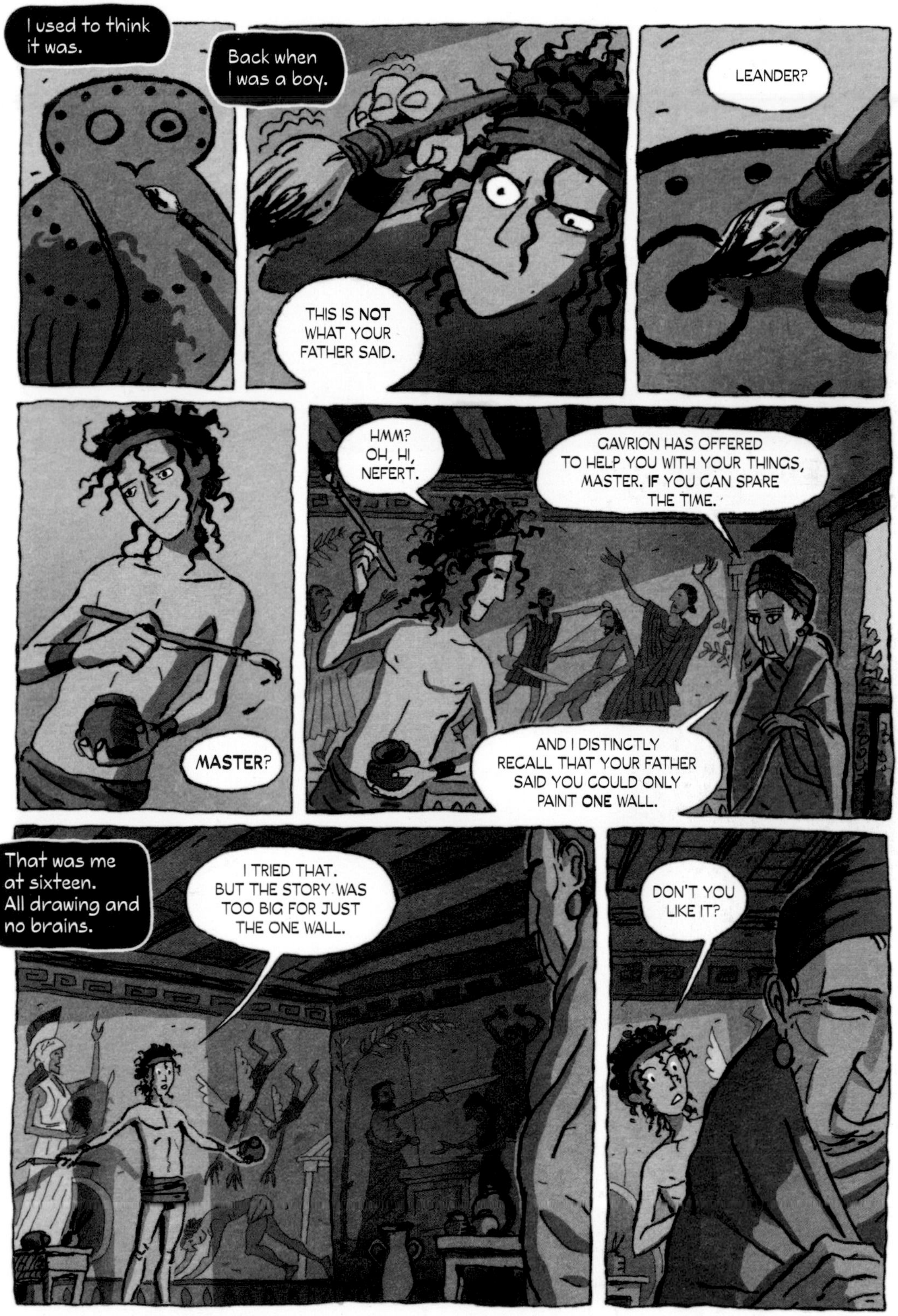
I used to think it was.
Back when I was a boy.
THIS IS NOT WHAT YOUR FATHER SAID.
LEANDER?
MASTER?
HMM? OH, HI, NEFERT.
GAVRION HAS OFFERED TO HELP YOU WITH YOUR THINGS, MASTER. IF YOU CAN SPARE THE TIME.
AND I DISTINCTLY RECALL THAT YOUR FATHER SAID YOU COULD ONLY PAINT ONE WALL.
That was me at sixteen. All drawing and no brains.
I TRIED THAT. BUT THE STORY WAS TOO BIG FOR JUST THE ONE WALL.
DON'T YOU LIKE IT?

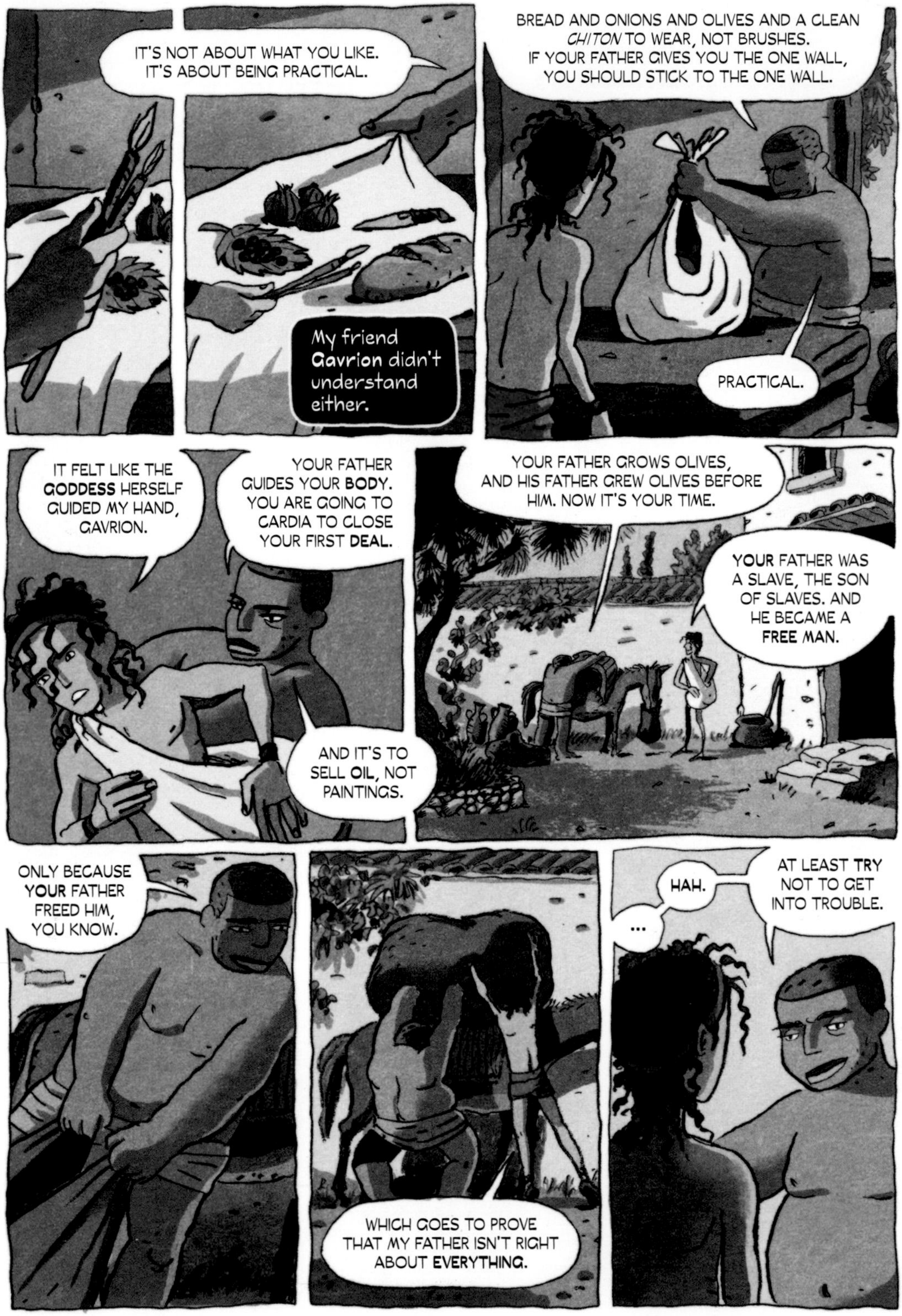
IT'S NOT ABOUT WHAT YOU LIKE. IT'S ABOUT BEING PRACTICAL.
My friend Gavrion didn't understand either.
BREAD AND ONIONS AND OLIVES AND A CLEAN *CHITON* TO WEAR, NOT BRUSHES. IF YOUR FATHER GIVES YOU THE ONE WALL, YOU SHOULD STICK TO THE ONE WALL.
PRACTICAL.
IT FELT LIKE THE **GODDESS** HERSELF GUIDED MY HAND, GAVRION.
YOUR FATHER GUIDES YOUR **BODY**. YOU ARE GOING TO CARDIA TO CLOSE YOUR FIRST **DEAL**.
AND IT'S TO SELL **OIL**, NOT PAINTINGS.
YOUR FATHER GROWS OLIVES, AND HIS FATHER GREW OLIVES BEFORE HIM. NOW IT'S YOUR TIME.
YOUR FATHER WAS A SLAVE, THE SON OF SLAVES. AND HE BECAME A **FREE MAN**.
ONLY BECAUSE **YOUR** FATHER FREED HIM, YOU KNOW.
WHICH GOES TO PROVE THAT MY FATHER ISN'T RIGHT ABOUT **EVERYTHING**.
HAH.
...
AT LEAST **TRY** NOT TO GET INTO TROUBLE.

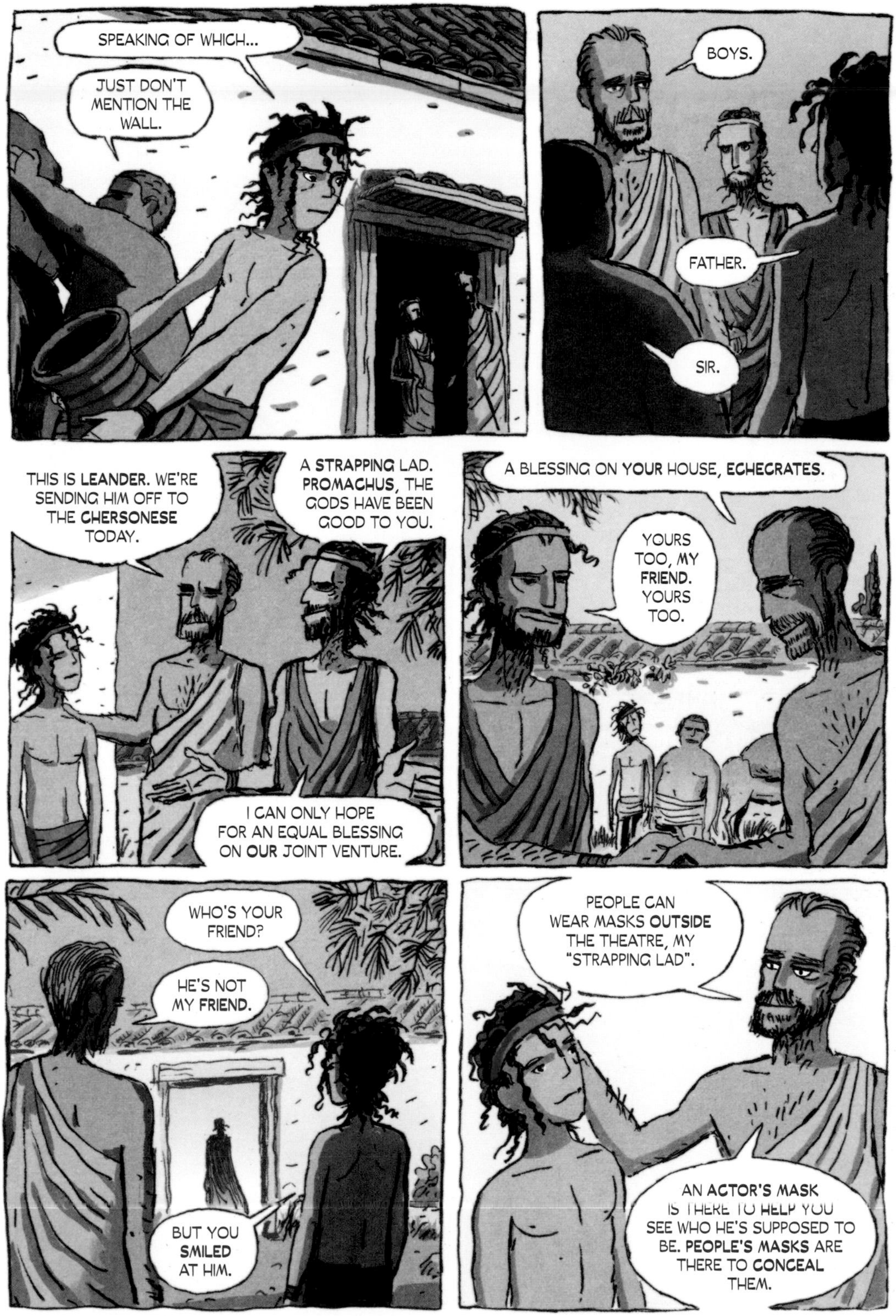
SPEAKING OF WHICH...
JUST DON'T MENTION THE WALL.
BOYS.
FATHER.
SIR.
THIS IS LEANDER. WE'RE SENDING HIM OFF TO THE CHERSONESE TODAY.
A STRAPPING LAD. PROMACHUS, THE GODS HAVE BEEN GOOD TO YOU.
I CAN ONLY HOPE FOR AN EQUAL BLESSING ON OUR JOINT VENTURE.
A BLESSING ON YOUR HOUSE, ECHECRATES.
YOURS TOO, MY FRIEND. YOURS TOO.
WHO'S YOUR FRIEND?
HE'S NOT MY FRIEND.
BUT YOU SMILED AT HIM.
PEOPLE CAN WEAR MASKS OUTSIDE THE THEATRE, MY "STRAPPING LAD".
AN ACTOR'S MASK IS THERE TO HELP YOU SEE WHO HE'S SUPPOSED TO BE. PEOPLE'S MASKS ARE THERE TO CONCEAL THEM.

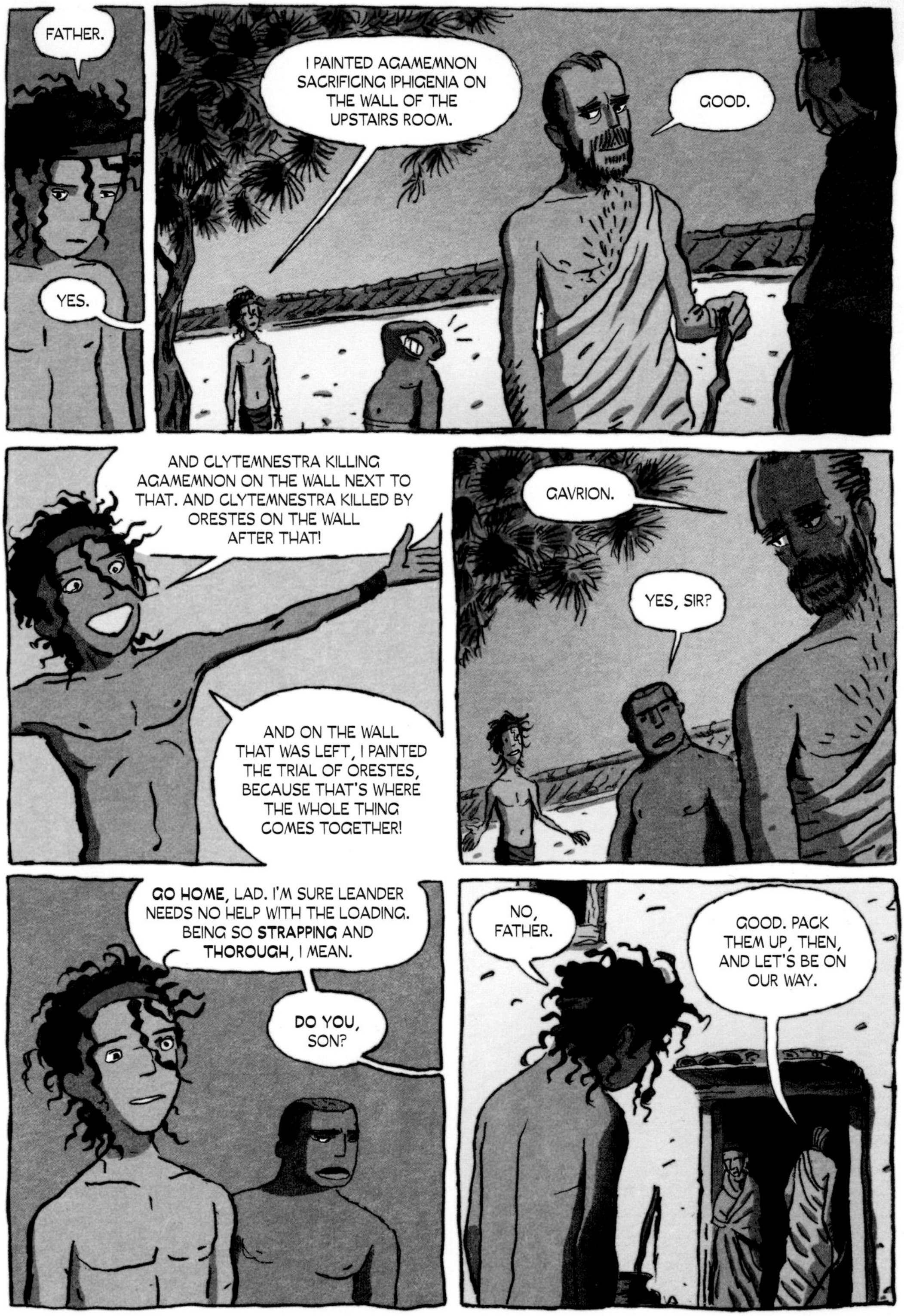

FATHER.
YES.
I PAINTED AGAMEMNON SACRIFICING IPHIGENIA ON THE WALL OF THE UPSTAIRS ROOM.
GOOD.
AND CLYTEMNESTRA KILLING AGAMEMNON ON THE WALL NEXT TO THAT. AND CLYTEMNESTRA KILLED BY ORESTES ON THE WALL AFTER THAT!
AND ON THE WALL THAT WAS LEFT, I PAINTED THE TRIAL OF ORESTES, BECAUSE THAT'S WHERE THE WHOLE THING COMES TOGETHER!
GAVRION.
YES, SIR?
GO HOME, LAD. I'M SURE LEANDER NEEDS NO HELP WITH THE LOADING. BEING SO STRAPPING AND THOROUGH, I MEAN.
DO YOU, SON?
NO, FATHER.
GOOD. PACK THEM UP, THEN, AND LET'S BE ON OUR WAY.

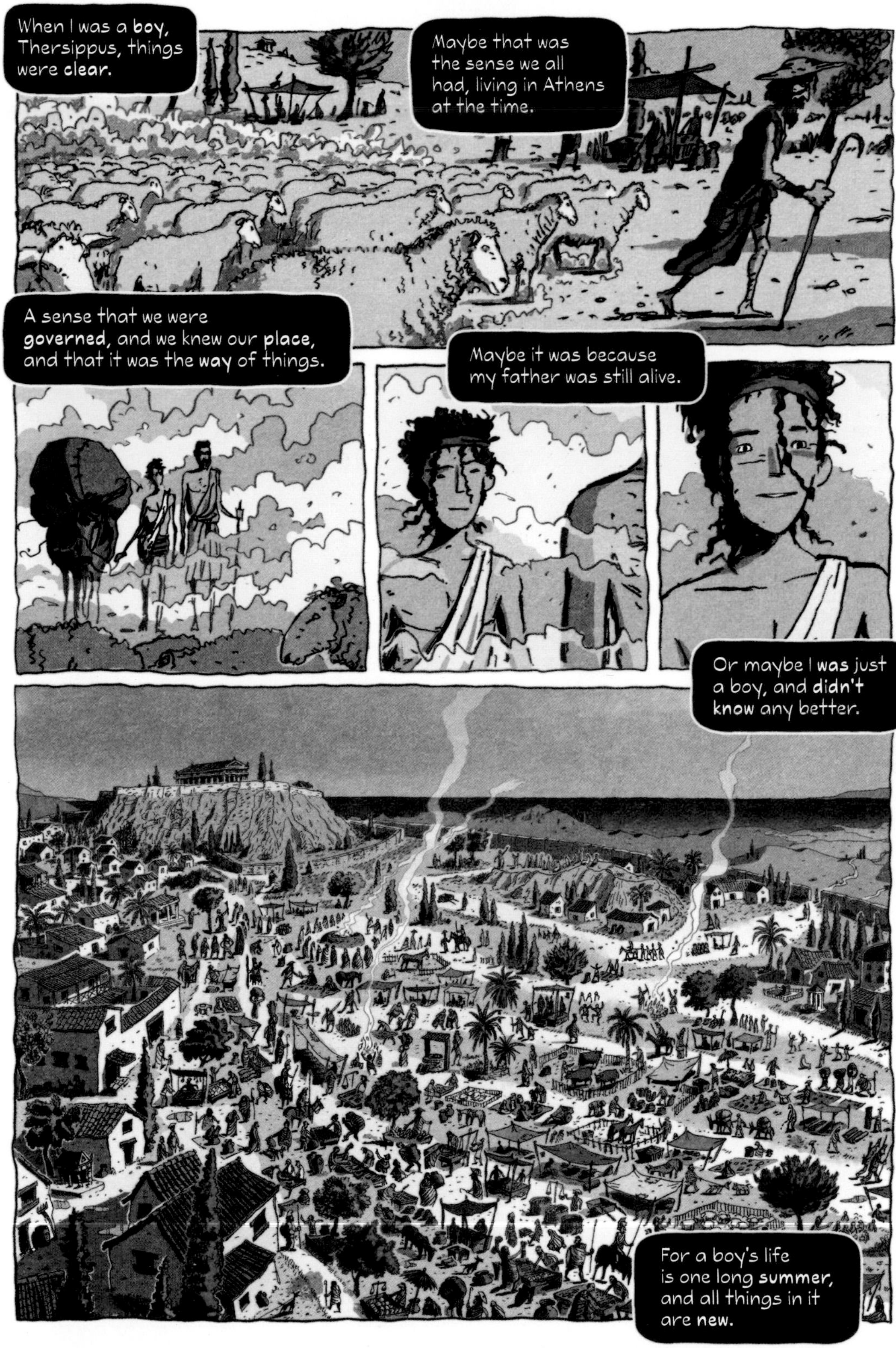

When I was a **boy**, Thersippus, things were **clear**.
Maybe that was the sense we all had, living in Athens at the time.
A sense that we were **governed**, and we knew our **place**, and that it was the **way** of things.
Maybe it was because my father was still alive.
Or maybe I **was** just a boy, and **didn't know** any better.
For a boy's life is one long **summer**, and all things in it are **new**.

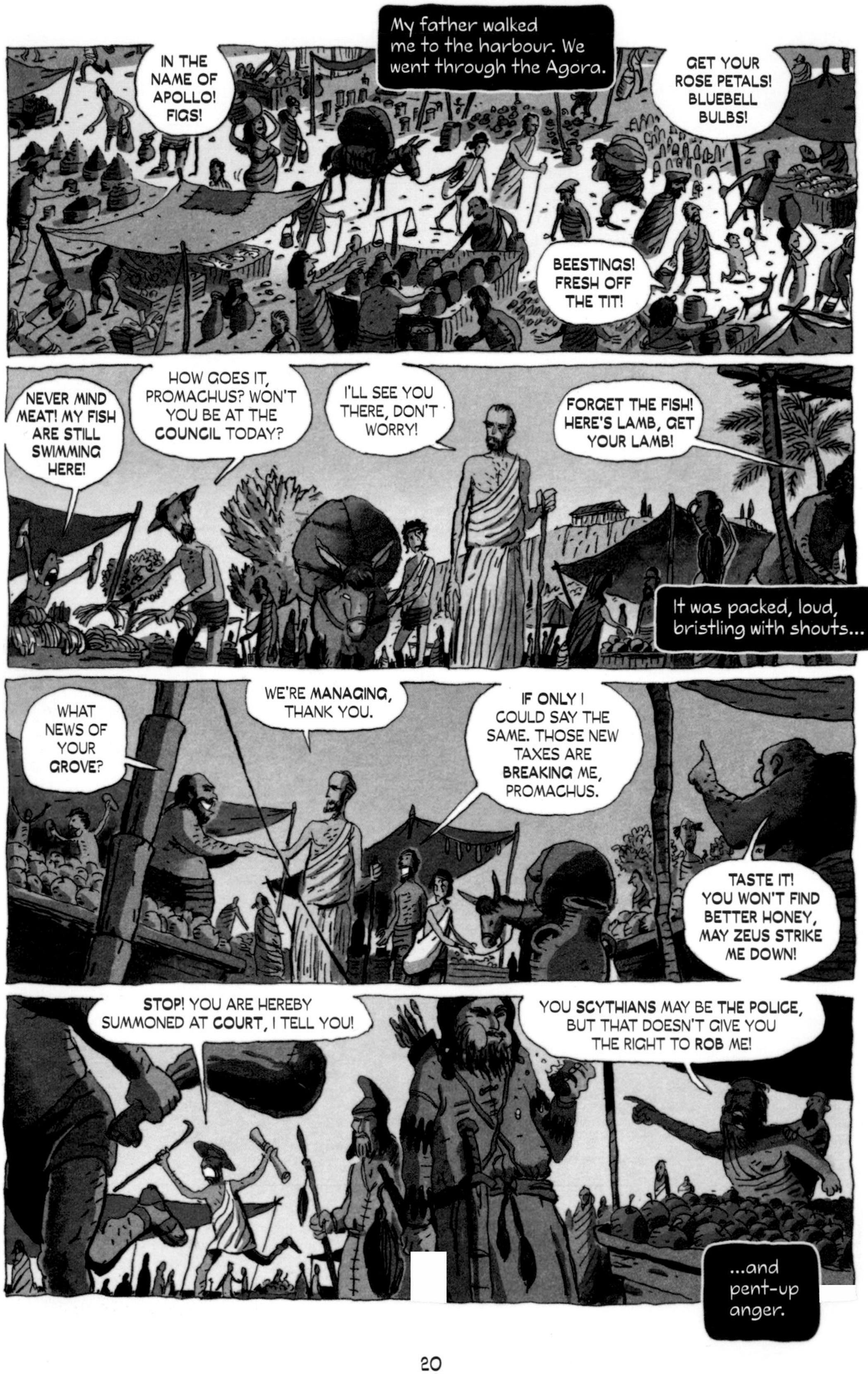
My father walked me to the harbour. We went through the Agora.
IN THE NAME OF APOLLO! FIGS!
GET YOUR ROSE PETALS! BLUEBELL BULBS!
BEESTINGS! FRESH OFF THE TIT!
NEVER MIND MEAT! MY FISH ARE STILL SWIMMING HERE!
HOW GOES IT, PROMACHUS? WON'T YOU BE AT THE COUNCIL TODAY?
I'LL SEE YOU THERE, DON'T WORRY!
FORGET THE FISH! HERE'S LAMB, GET YOUR LAMB!
It was packed, loud, bristling with shouts...
WHAT NEWS OF YOUR GROVE?
WE'RE MANAGING, THANK YOU.
IF ONLY I COULD SAY THE SAME. THOSE NEW TAXES ARE BREAKING ME, PROMACHUS.
TASTE IT! YOU WON'T FIND BETTER HONEY, MAY ZEUS STRIKE ME DOWN!
STOP! YOU ARE HEREBY SUMMONED AT COURT, I TELL YOU!
YOU SCYTHIANS MAY BE THE POLICE, BUT THAT DOESN'T GIVE YOU THE RIGHT TO ROB ME!
...and pent-up anger.

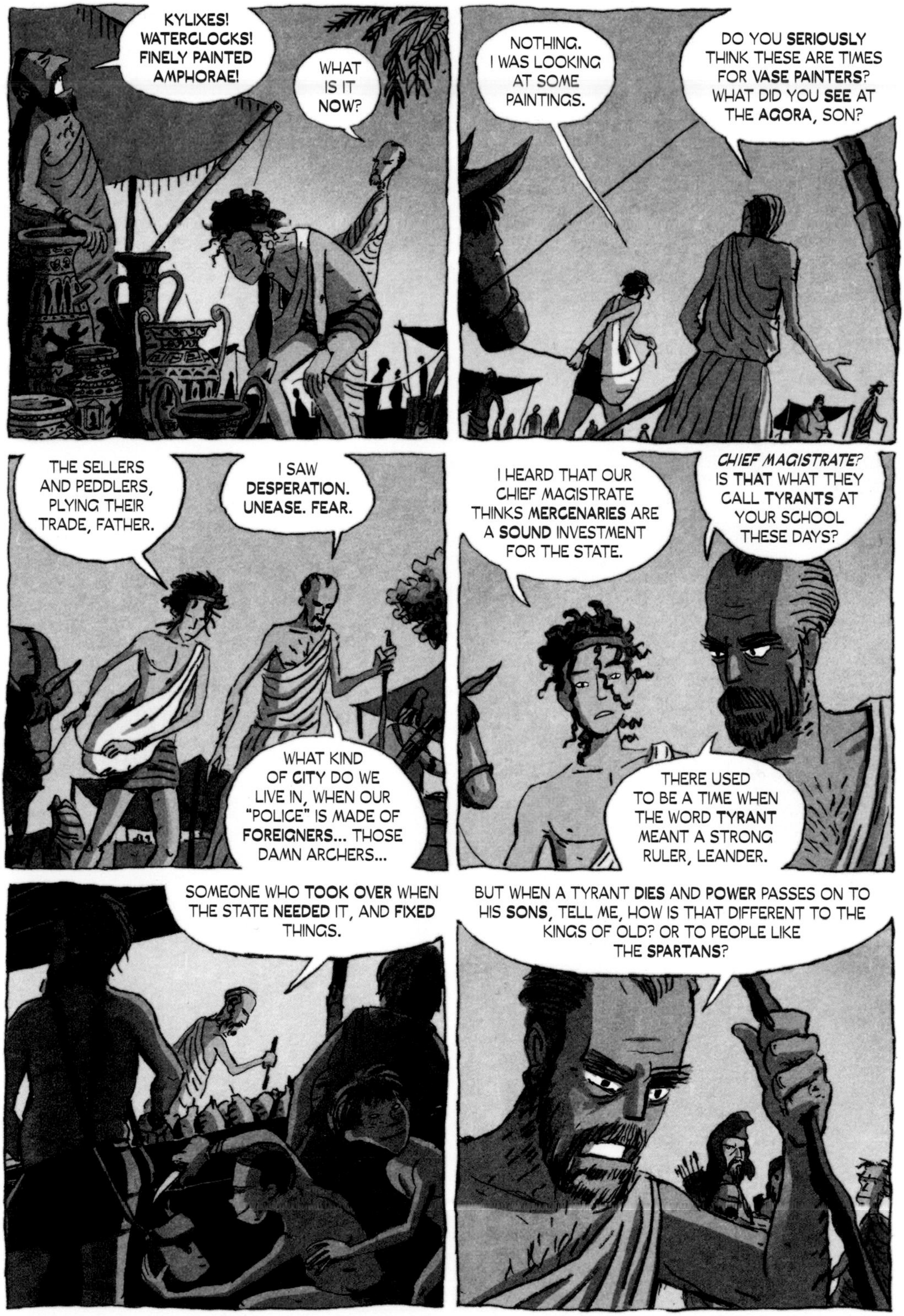
KYLIXES! WATERCLOCKS! FINELY PAINTED AMPHORAE!
WHAT IS IT NOW?
NOTHING. I WAS LOOKING AT SOME PAINTINGS.
DO YOU SERIOUSLY THINK THESE ARE TIMES FOR VASE PAINTERS? WHAT DID YOU SEE AT THE AGORA, SON?
THE SELLERS AND PEDDLERS, PLYING THEIR TRADE, FATHER.
I SAW DESPERATION. UNEASE. FEAR.
WHAT KIND OF CITY DO WE LIVE IN, WHEN OUR "POLICE" IS MADE OF FOREIGNERS... THOSE DAMN ARCHERS...
I HEARD THAT OUR CHIEF MAGISTRATE THINKS MERCENARIES ARE A SOUND INVESTMENT FOR THE STATE.
CHIEF MAGISTRATE? IS THAT WHAT THEY CALL TYRANTS AT YOUR SCHOOL THESE DAYS?
THERE USED TO BE A TIME WHEN THE WORD TYRANT MEANT A STRONG RULER, LEANDER.
SOMEONE WHO TOOK OVER WHEN THE STATE NEEDED IT, AND FIXED THINGS.
BUT WHEN A TYRANT DIES AND POWER PASSES ON TO HIS SONS, TELL ME, HOW IS THAT DIFFERENT TO THE KINGS OF OLD? OR TO PEOPLE LIKE THE SPARTANS?

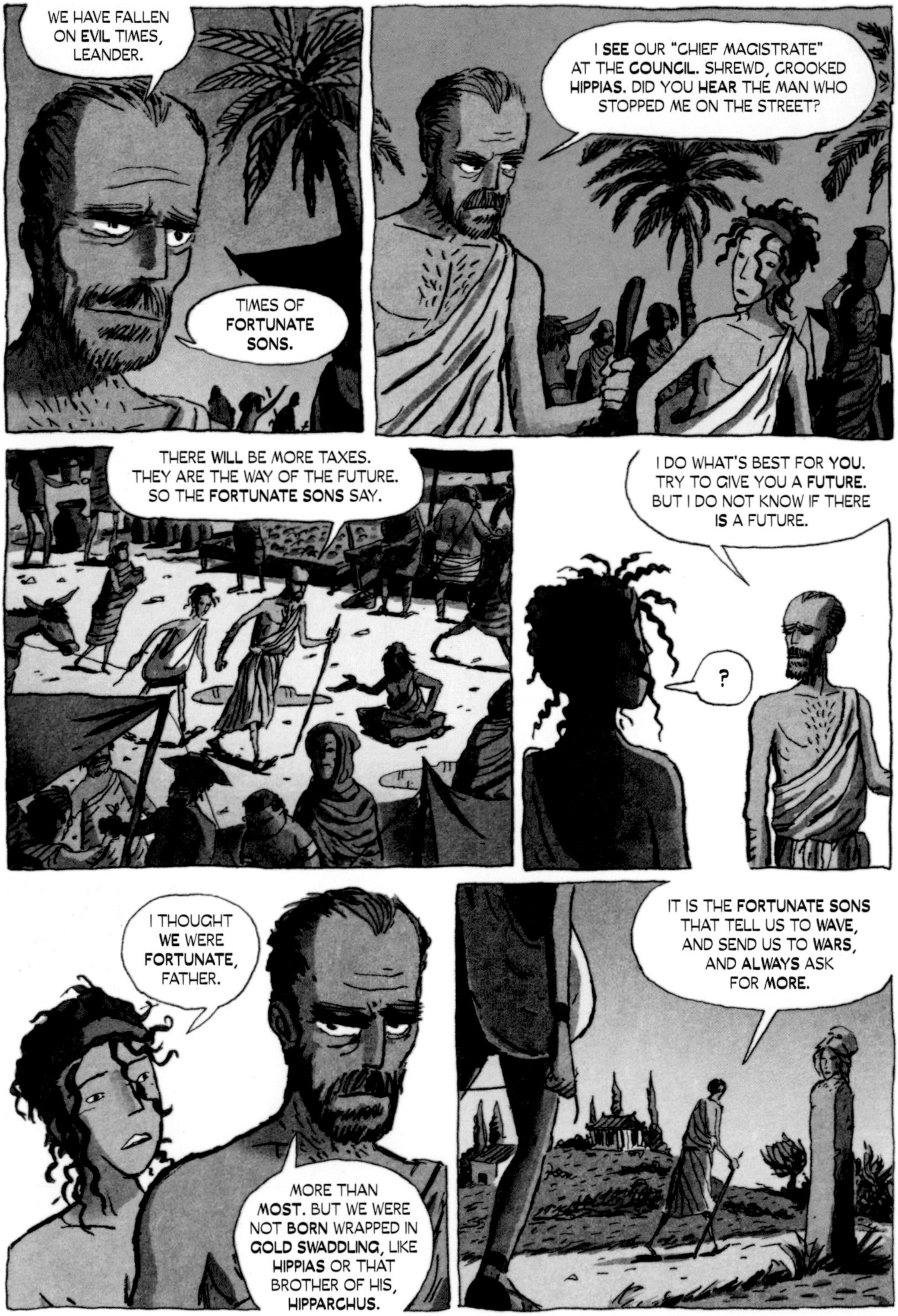
WE HAVE FALLEN ON **EVIL** TIMES, LEANDER.
TIMES OF **FORTUNATE SONS.**
I **SEE** OUR "CHIEF MAGISTRATE" AT THE **COUNCIL.** SHREWD, CROOKED **HIPPIAS.** DID YOU **HEAR** THE MAN WHO STOPPED ME ON THE STREET?
THERE **WILL** BE MORE TAXES. THEY ARE THE WAY OF THE FUTURE. SO THE **FORTUNATE SONS** SAY.
I DO WHAT'S BEST FOR **YOU.** TRY TO GIVE YOU A **FUTURE.** BUT I DO NOT KNOW IF THERE **IS** A FUTURE.
?
I THOUGHT **WE** WERE **FORTUNATE,** FATHER.
MORE THAN **MOST.** BUT WE WERE NOT **BORN** WRAPPED IN **GOLD SWADDLING,** LIKE **HIPPIAS** OR THAT BROTHER OF HIS, **HIPPARCHUS.**
IT IS THE **FORTUNATE SONS** THAT TELL US TO **WAVE,** AND SEND US TO **WARS,** AND **ALWAYS** ASK FOR **MORE.**

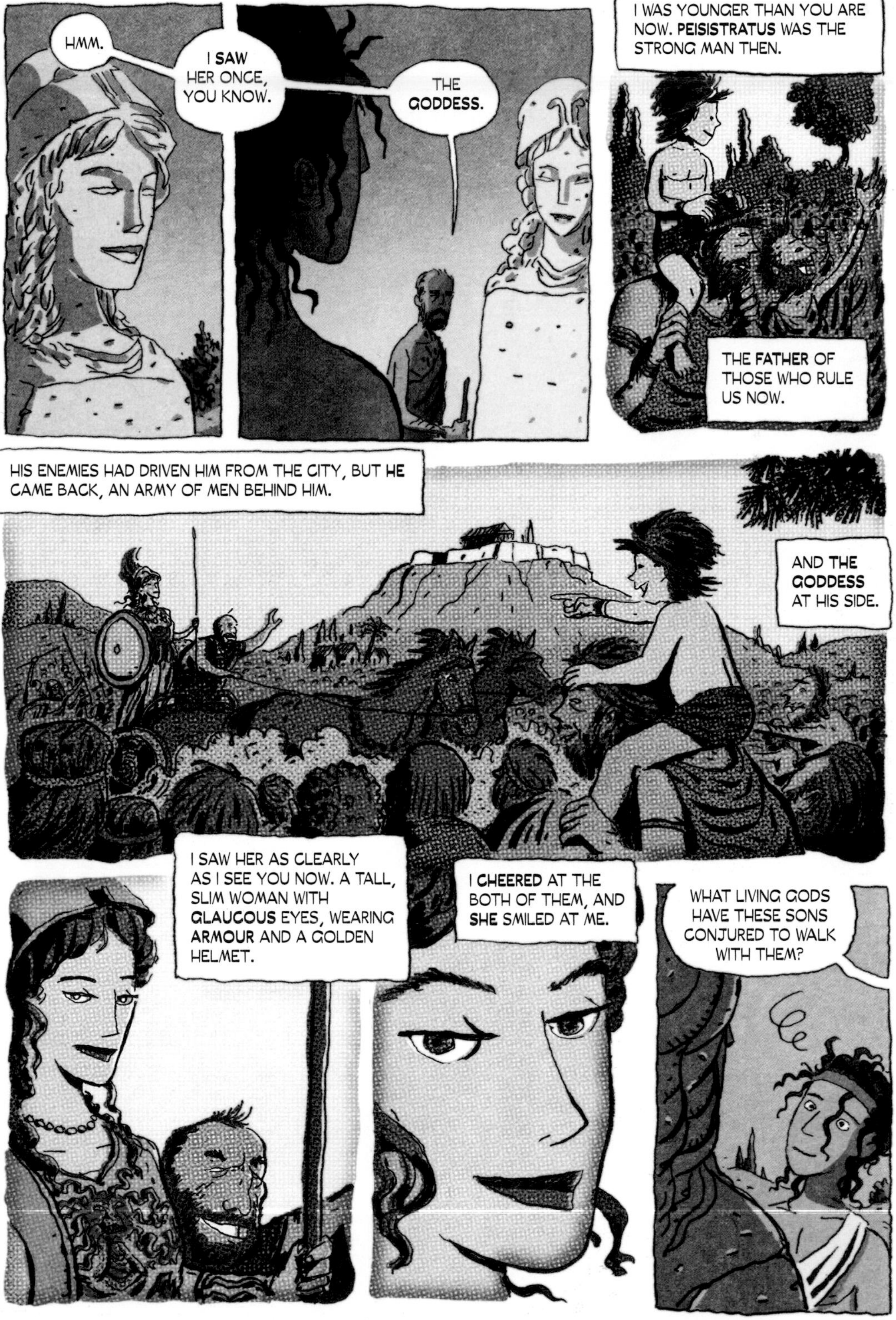
HMM.
I SAW HER ONCE, YOU KNOW.
THE GODDESS.
I WAS YOUNGER THAN YOU ARE NOW. PEISISTRATUS WAS THE STRONG MAN THEN.
THE FATHER OF THOSE WHO RULE US NOW.
HIS ENEMIES HAD DRIVEN HIM FROM THE CITY, BUT HE CAME BACK, AN ARMY OF MEN BEHIND HIM.
AND THE GODDESS AT HIS SIDE.
I SAW HER AS CLEARLY AS I SEE YOU NOW. A TALL, SLIM WOMAN WITH GLAUCOUS EYES, WEARING ARMOUR AND A GOLDEN HELMET.
I CHEERED AT THE BOTH OF THEM, AND SHE SMILED AT ME.
WHAT LIVING GODS HAVE THESE SONS CONJURED TO WALK WITH THEM?

SOME SAY THE RULE OF **PEISISTRATUS** WAS AN **AGE OF GOLD.**

I DON'T KNOW ABOUT **THAT.**

BUT THOSE **WERE** BETTER DAYS.

PEISISTRATUS WAS A HERO OF THE COLONY WARS. HE RULED LIKE A **GENERAL.**

EVERYBODY WAS TO MIND THEIR **OWN** BUSINESS AND LET HIM BEAR THE **BURDEN** OF THE STATE.

HE WAS THE **FIRST** TO REPRESENT THE INTERESTS OF THE PENNILESS FARMERS OF THE HILLS.

TRUE, HE KEPT THE STATE'S ASSETS FOR **HIMSELF,** BUT HE WAS GENEROUS, EVEN TO HIS RIVALS.

THIS WAY, HE HELD THE **ARISTOS** IN CHECK.

THAT'S **ALSO** WHY HE CREATED A **POLICE FORCE.**

THE **SCYTHIAN** ARCHERS.

BY SENDING SOME OF HIS RIVALS TO THE **CHERSONESE** TO ESTABLISH A NEW **COLONY** THERE, HE OPENED NEW, VITAL ROUTES FOR **COMMERCE,** AND PUT FOOD ON OUR TABLES.

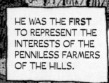

THE **TYRANT** SOUGHT THE APPROVAL OF THE PEOPLE.

HE TOURED THE **COUNTRYSIDE,** SHAKING **HANDS** WITH OUR POOREST, SERVING **JUSTICE** SO THAT PEOPLE HAVING COURT TROUBLES WOULD BE **SPARED** THE TRIP TO ATHENS.

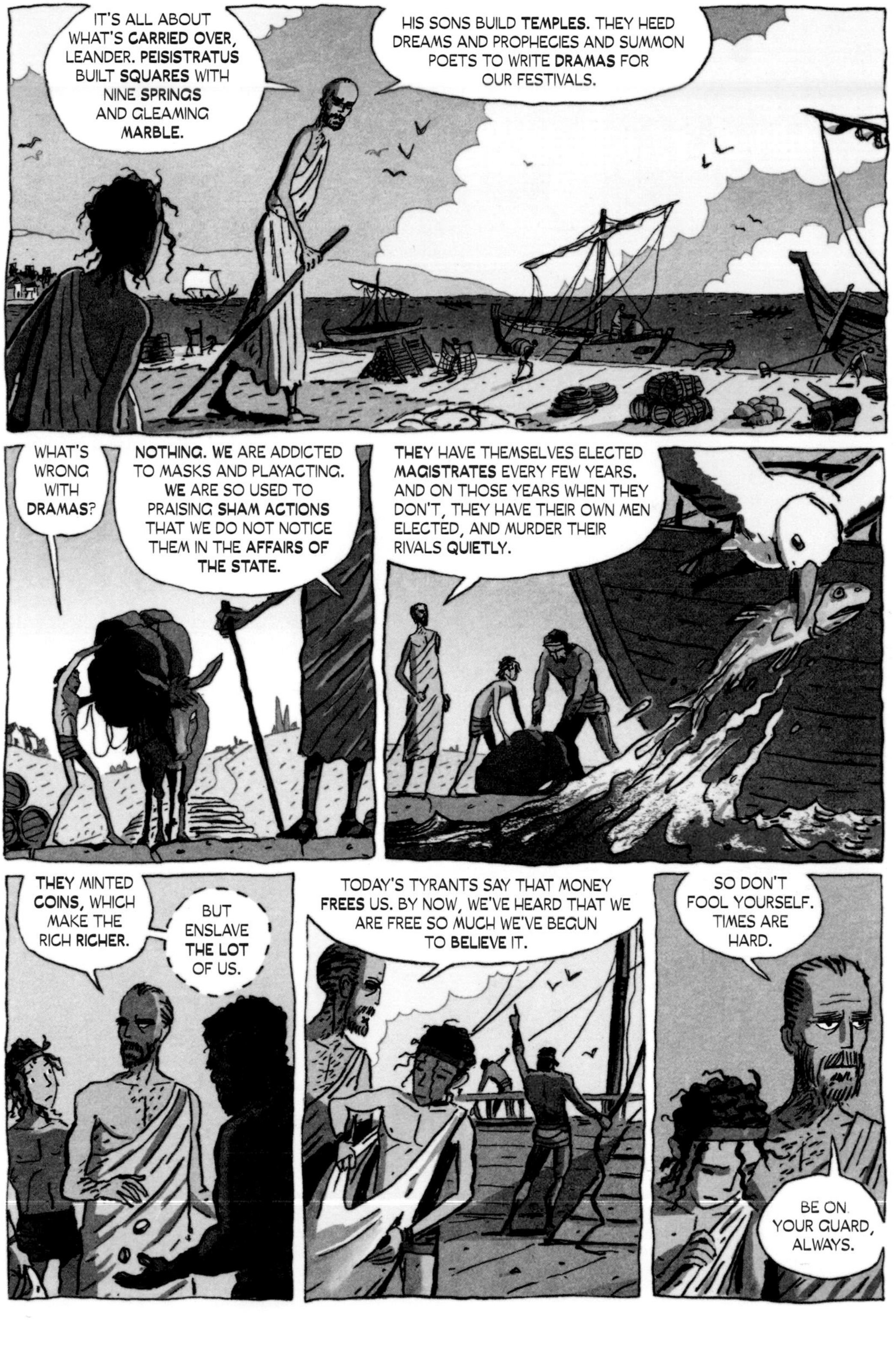
IT'S ALL ABOUT WHAT'S CARRIED OVER, LEANDER. PEISISTRATUS BUILT SQUARES WITH NINE SPRINGS AND GLEAMING MARBLE.
HIS SONS BUILD TEMPLES. THEY HEED DREAMS AND PROPHECIES AND SUMMON POETS TO WRITE DRAMAS FOR OUR FESTIVALS.
WHAT'S WRONG WITH DRAMAS?
NOTHING. WE ARE ADDICTED TO MASKS AND PLAYACTING. WE ARE SO USED TO PRAISING SHAM ACTIONS THAT WE DO NOT NOTICE THEM IN THE AFFAIRS OF THE STATE.
THEY HAVE THEMSELVES ELECTED MAGISTRATES EVERY FEW YEARS. AND ON THOSE YEARS WHEN THEY DON'T, THEY HAVE THEIR OWN MEN ELECTED, AND MURDER THEIR RIVALS QUIETLY.
THEY MINTED COINS, WHICH MAKE THE RICH RICHER.
BUT ENSLAVE THE LOT OF US.
TODAY'S TYRANTS SAY THAT MONEY FREES US. BY NOW, WE'VE HEARD THAT WE ARE FREE SO MUCH WE'VE BEGUN TO BELIEVE IT.
SO DON'T FOOL YOURSELF. TIMES ARE HARD.
BE ON YOUR GUARD, ALWAYS.

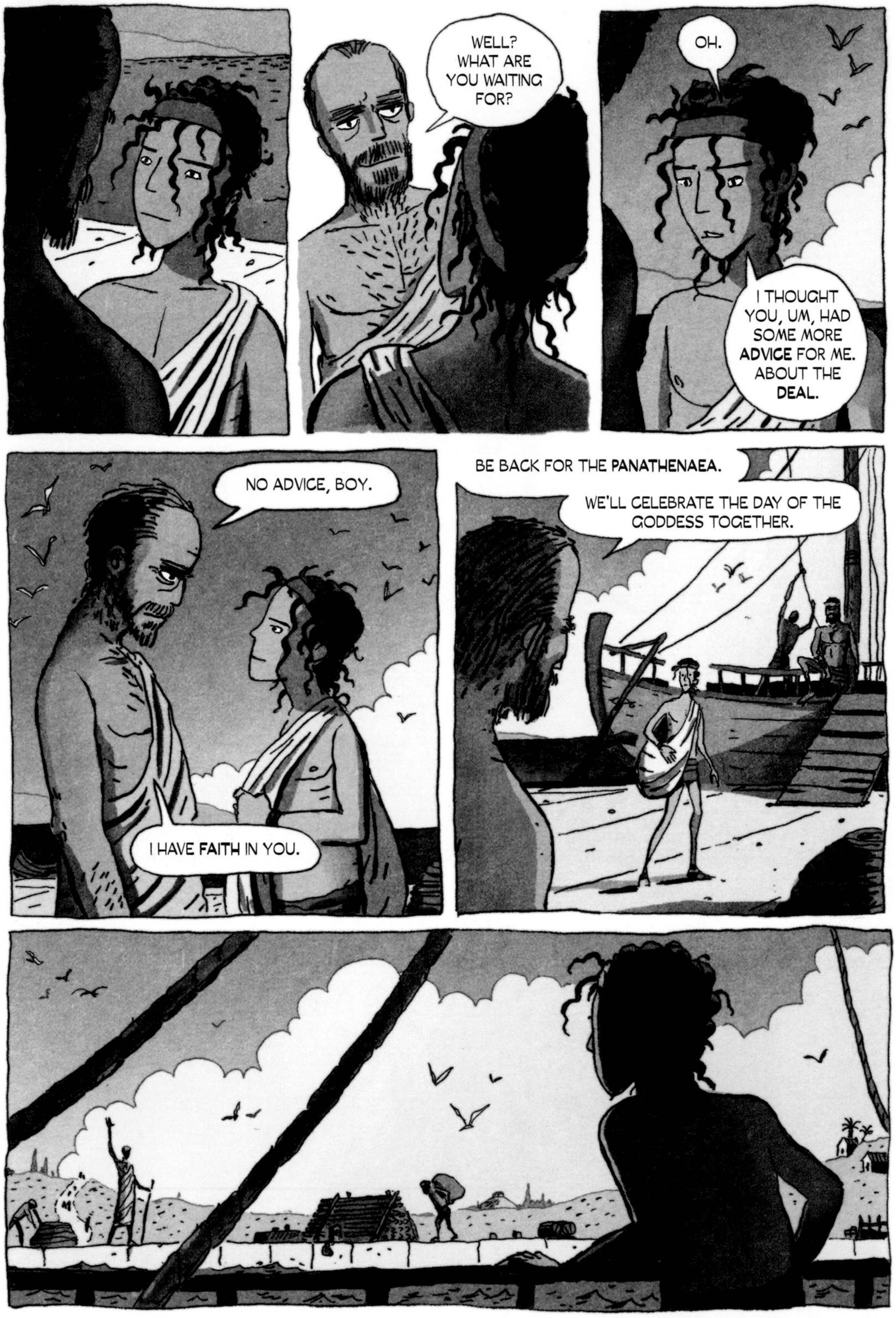
WELL? WHAT ARE YOU WAITING FOR?
OH.
I THOUGHT YOU, UM, HAD SOME MORE ADVICE FOR ME. ABOUT THE DEAL.
NO ADVICE, BOY.
I HAVE FAITH IN YOU.
BE BACK FOR THE PANATHENAEA.
WE'LL CELEBRATE THE DAY OF THE GODDESS TOGETHER.

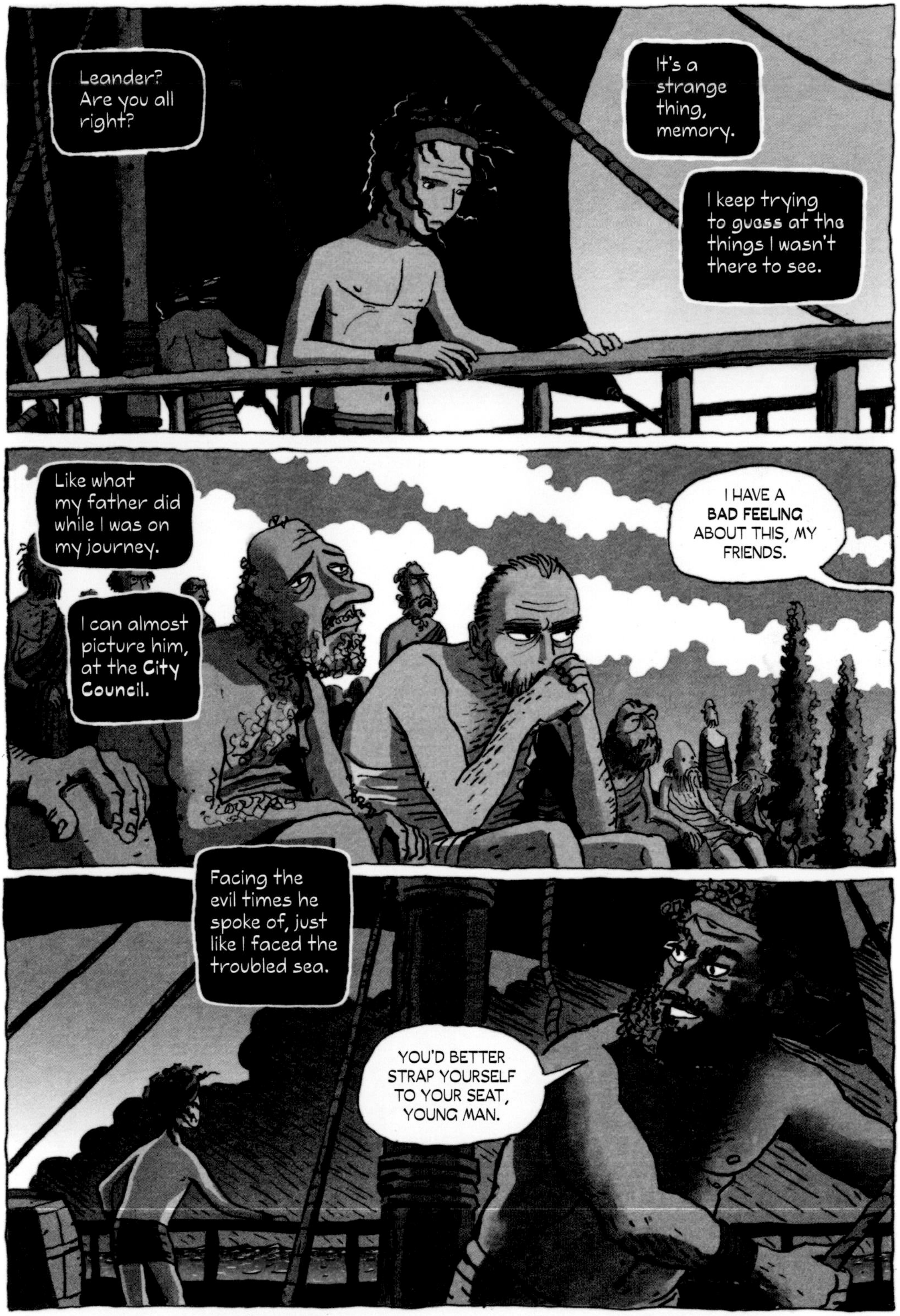

Leander? Are you all right?
It's a strange thing, memory.
I keep trying to guess at the things I wasn't there to see.
Like what my father did while I was on my journey.
I can almost picture him, at the City Council.
I HAVE A BAD FEELING ABOUT THIS, MY FRIENDS.
Facing the evil times he spoke of, just like I faced the troubled sea.
YOU'D BETTER STRAP YOURSELF TO YOUR SEAT, YOUNG MAN.

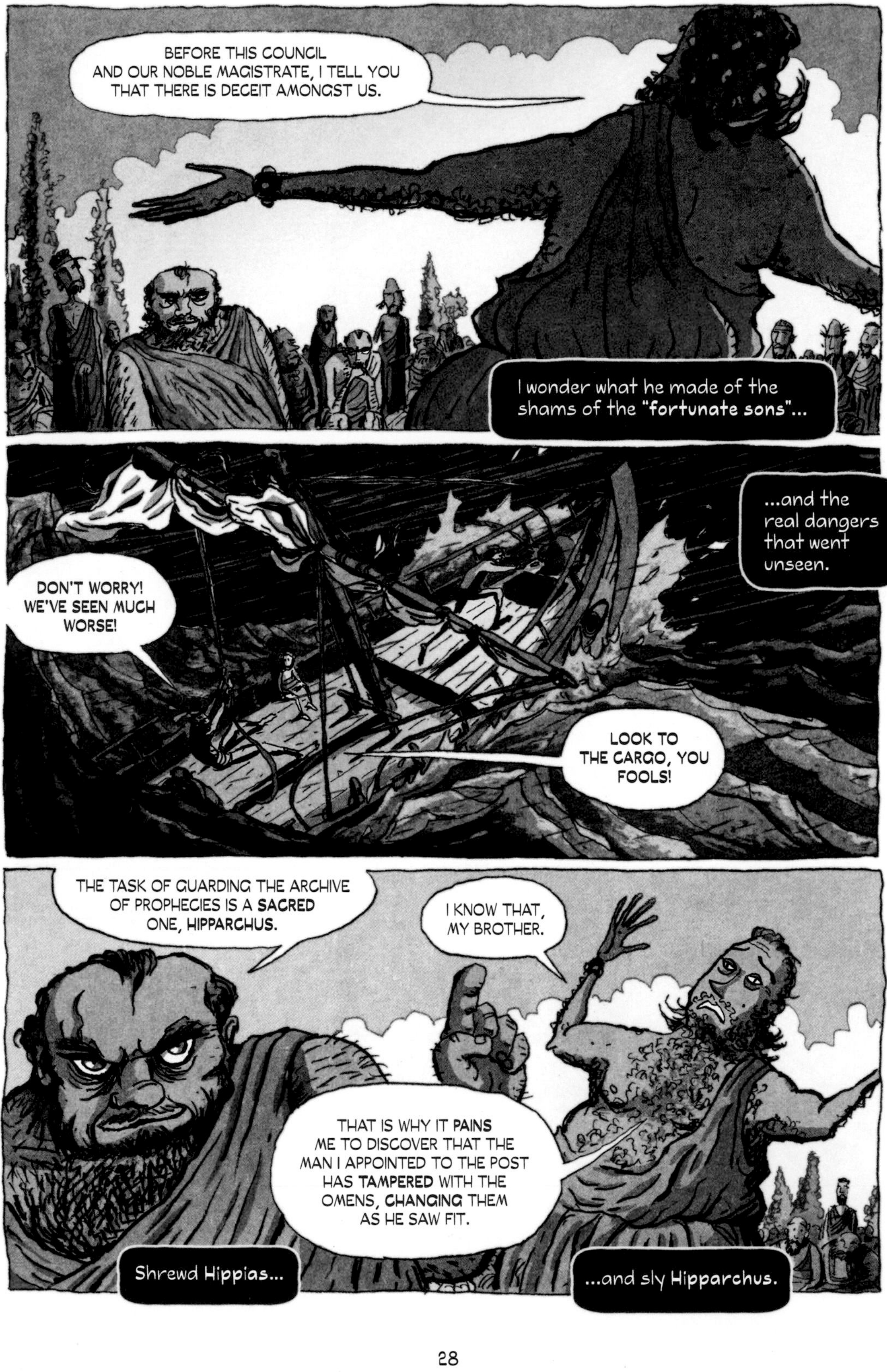
BEFORE THIS COUNCIL AND OUR NOBLE MAGISTRATE, I TELL YOU THAT THERE IS DECEIT AMONGST US.
I wonder what he made of the shams of the "fortunate sons"...
...and the real dangers that went unseen.
DON'T WORRY! WE'VE SEEN MUCH WORSE!
LOOK TO THE CARGO, YOU FOOLS!
THE TASK OF GUARDING THE ARCHIVE OF PROPHECIES IS A SACRED ONE, HIPPARCHUS.
I KNOW THAT, MY BROTHER.
THAT IS WHY IT PAINS ME TO DISCOVER THAT THE MAN I APPOINTED TO THE POST HAS TAMPERED WITH THE OMENS, CHANGING THEM AS HE SAW FIT.
Shrewd Hippias...
...and sly Hipparchus.

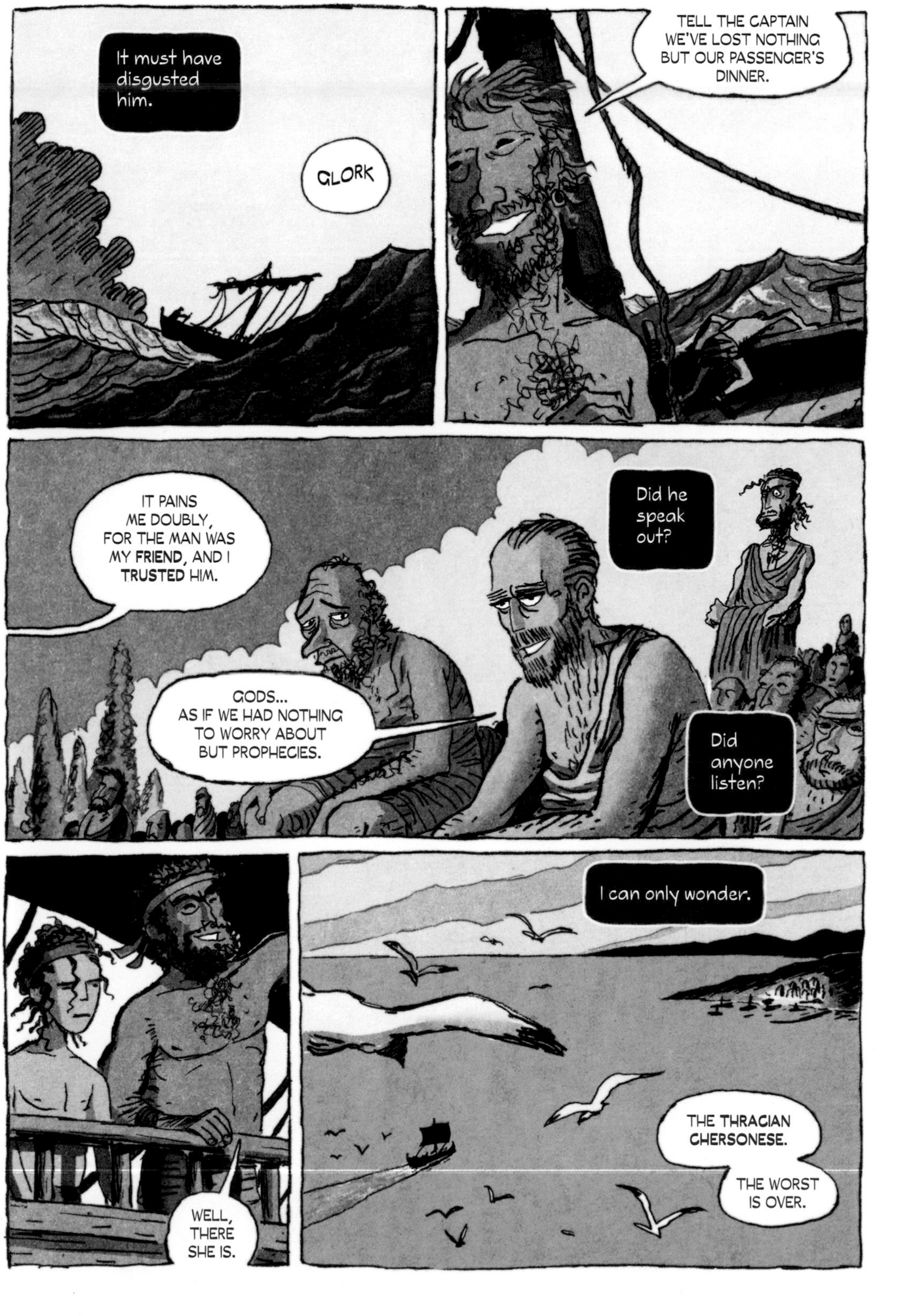
It must have disgusted him.
GLORK
TELL THE CAPTAIN WE'VE LOST NOTHING BUT OUR PASSENGER'S DINNER.
IT PAINS ME DOUBLY, FOR THE MAN WAS MY FRIEND, AND I TRUSTED HIM.
GODS... AS IF WE HAD NOTHING TO WORRY ABOUT BUT PROPHECIES.
Did he speak out?
Did anyone listen?
WELL, THERE SHE IS.
I can only wonder.
THE THRACIAN CHERSONESE.
THE WORST IS OVER.

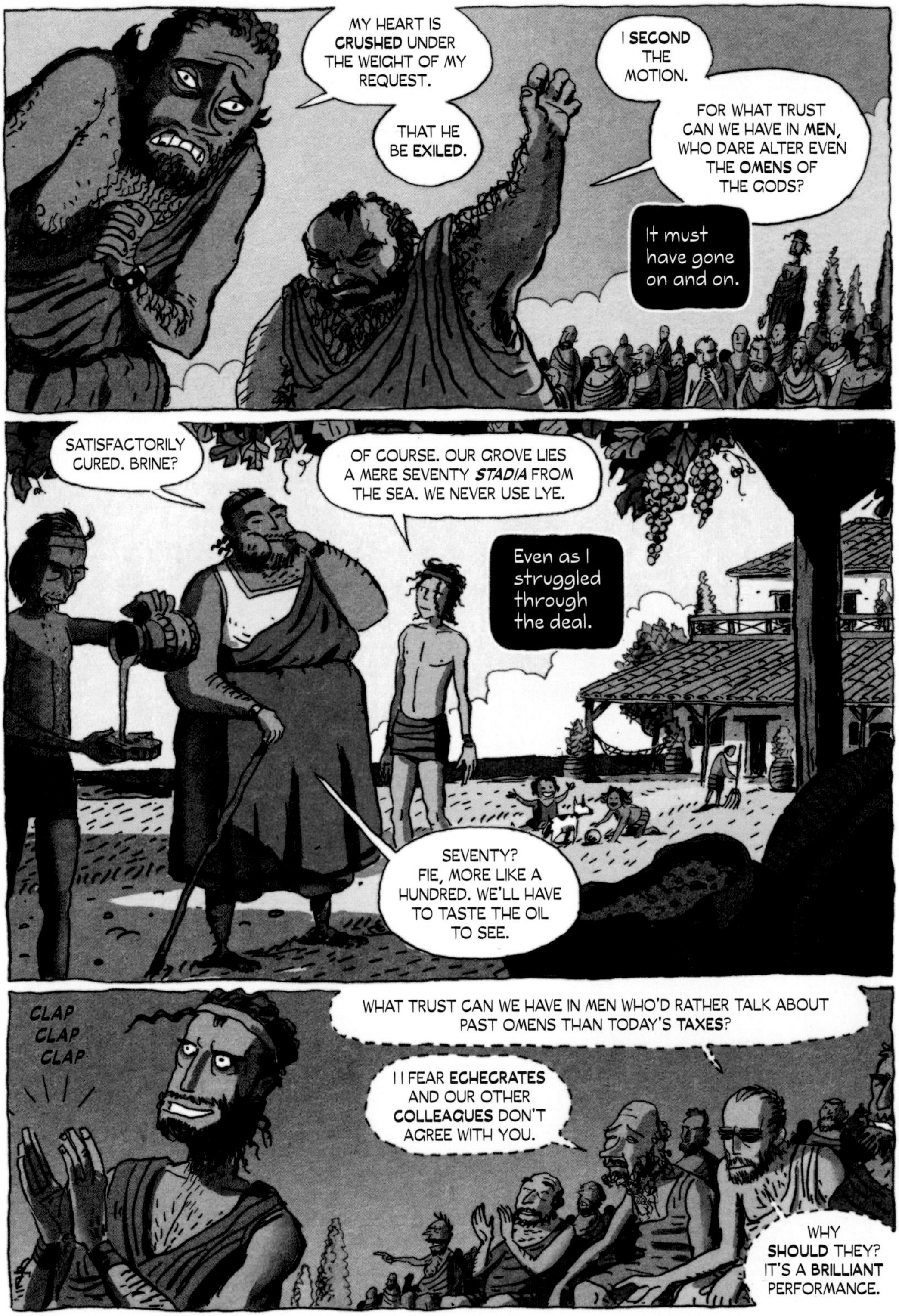
MY HEART IS **CRUSHED** UNDER THE WEIGHT OF MY REQUEST.
THAT HE BE **EXILED.**
I **SECOND** THE MOTION.
FOR WHAT TRUST CAN WE HAVE IN **MEN,** WHO DARE ALTER EVEN THE **OMENS** OF THE GODS?
It must have gone on and on.
SATISFACTORILY CURED. BRINE?
OF COURSE. OUR GROVE LIES A MERE SEVENTY *STADIA* FROM THE SEA. WE NEVER USE LYE.
Even as I struggled through the deal.
SEVENTY? FIE, MORE LIKE A HUNDRED. WE'LL HAVE TO TASTE THE OIL TO SEE.
CLAP CLAP CLAP
WHAT TRUST CAN WE HAVE IN MEN WHO'D RATHER TALK ABOUT PAST OMENS THAN TODAY'S **TAXES**?
I I FEAR **ECHECRATES** AND OUR OTHER **COLLEAGUES** DON'T AGREE WITH YOU.
WHY **SHOULD** THEY? IT'S A **BRILLIANT** PERFORMANCE.

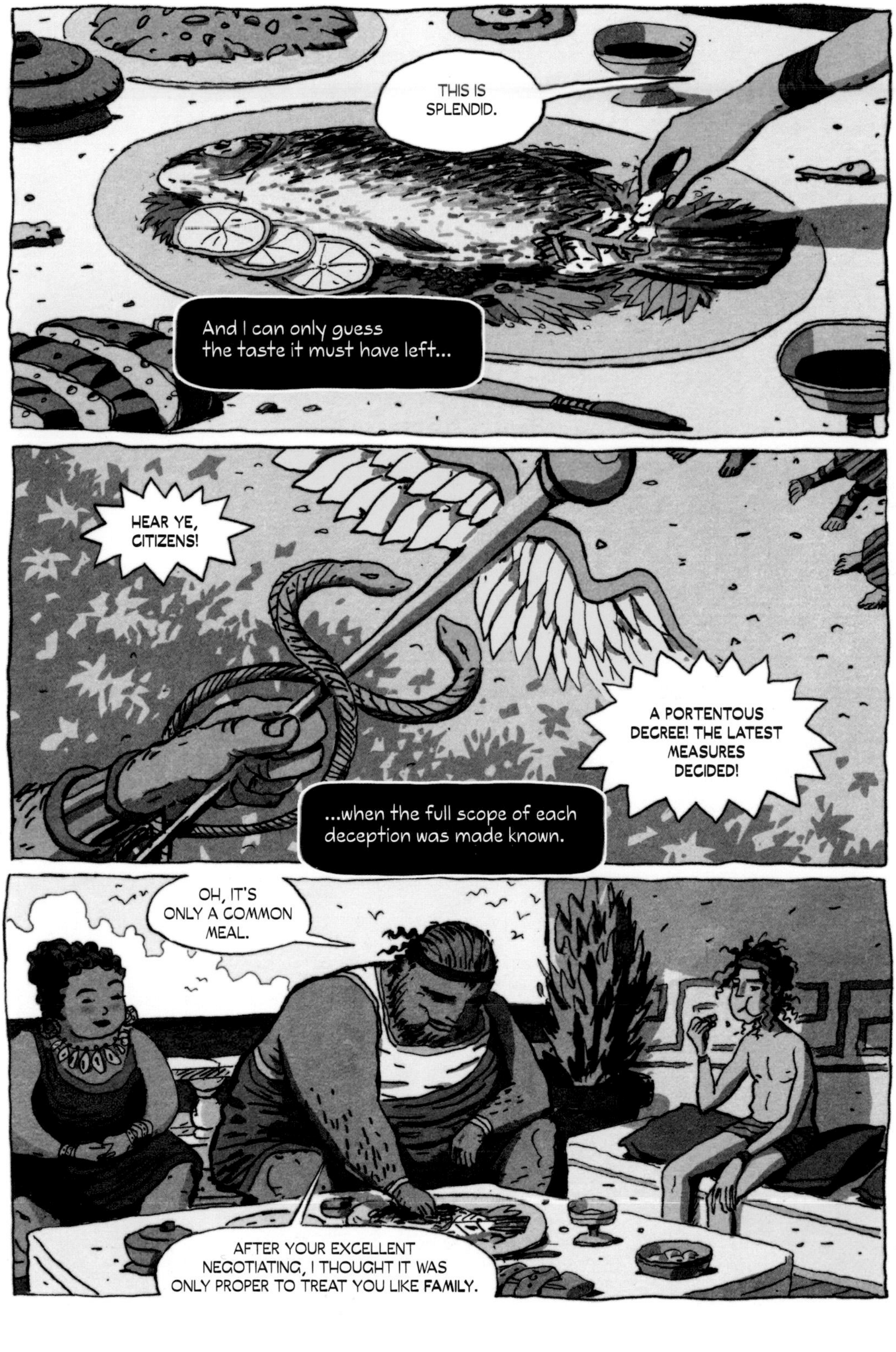

THIS IS SPLENDID.
And I can only guess the taste it must have left...
HEAR YE, CITIZENS!
A PORTENTOUS DECREE! THE LATEST MEASURES DECIDED!
...when the full scope of each deception was made known.
OH, IT'S ONLY A COMMON MEAL.
AFTER YOUR EXCELLENT NEGOTIATING, I THOUGHT IT WAS ONLY PROPER TO TREAT YOU LIKE **FAMILY**.

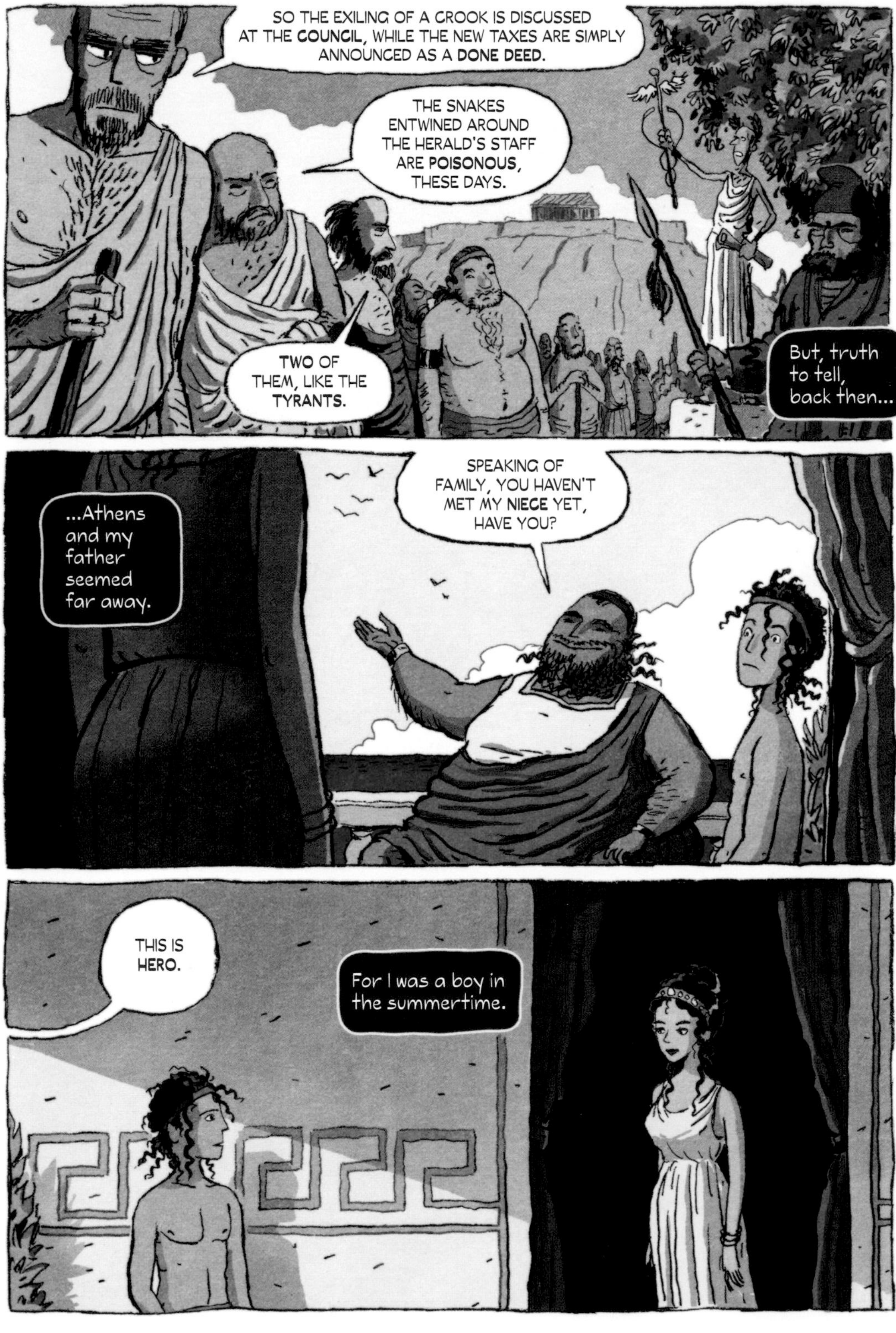

SO THE EXILING OF A CROOK IS DISCUSSED AT THE **COUNCIL**, WHILE THE NEW TAXES ARE SIMPLY ANNOUNCED AS A **DONE DEED**.
THE SNAKES ENTWINED AROUND THE HERALD'S STAFF ARE **POISONOUS**, THESE DAYS.
TWO OF THEM, LIKE THE **TYRANTS**.
But, truth to tell, back then...
...Athens and my father seemed far away.
SPEAKING OF FAMILY, YOU HAVEN'T MET MY **NIECE** YET, HAVE YOU?
THIS IS **HERO**.
For I was a boy in the summertime.

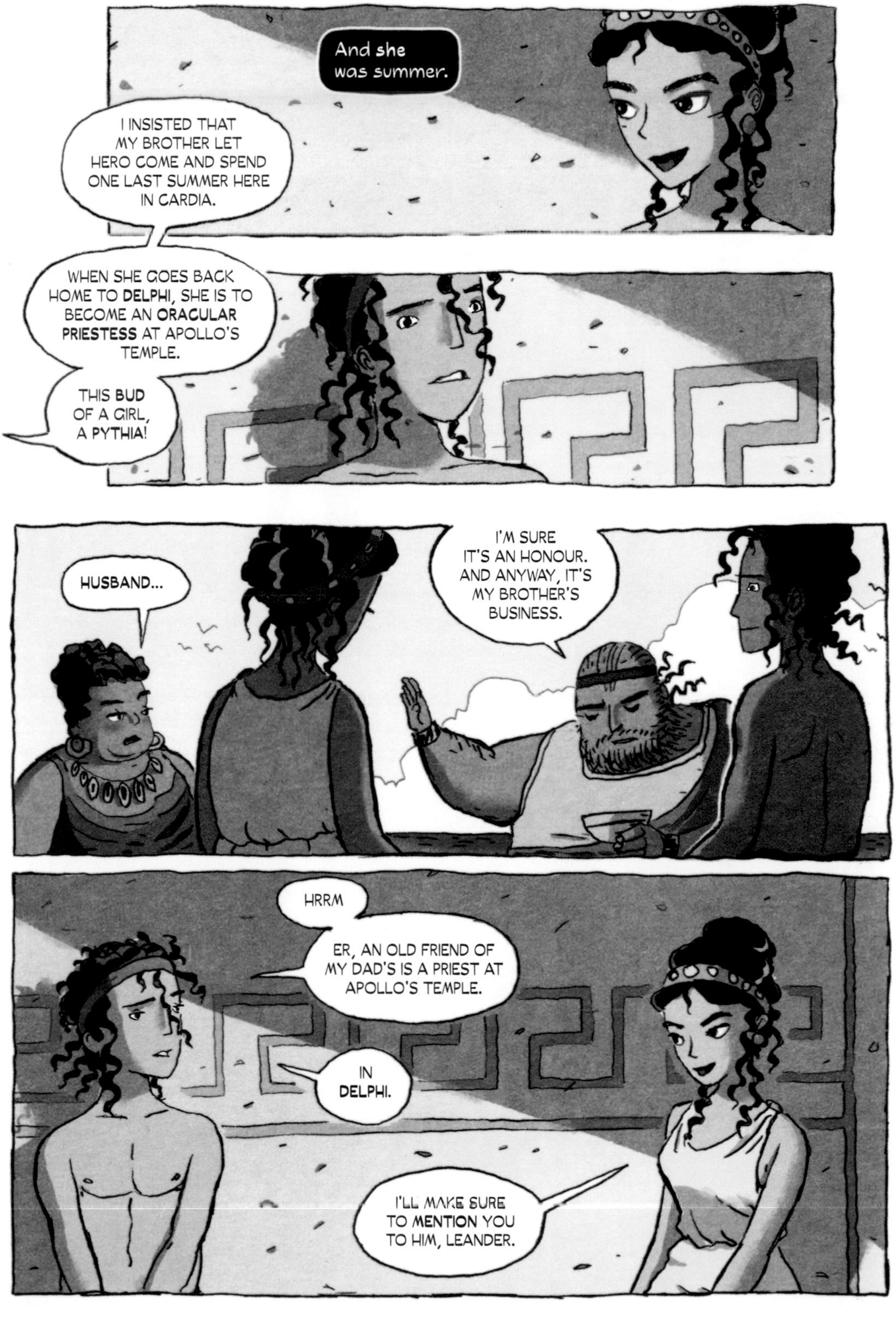
And she was summer.
I INSISTED THAT MY BROTHER LET HERO COME AND SPEND ONE LAST SUMMER HERE IN CARDIA.
WHEN SHE GOES BACK HOME TO DELPHI, SHE IS TO BECOME AN ORACULAR PRIESTESS AT APOLLO'S TEMPLE.
THIS BUD OF A GIRL, A PYTHIA!
HUSBAND...
I'M SURE IT'S AN HONOUR. AND ANYWAY, IT'S MY BROTHER'S BUSINESS.
HRRM
ER, AN OLD FRIEND OF MY DAD'S IS A PRIEST AT APOLLO'S TEMPLE.
IN DELPHI.
I'LL MAKE SURE TO MENTION YOU TO HIM, LEANDER.

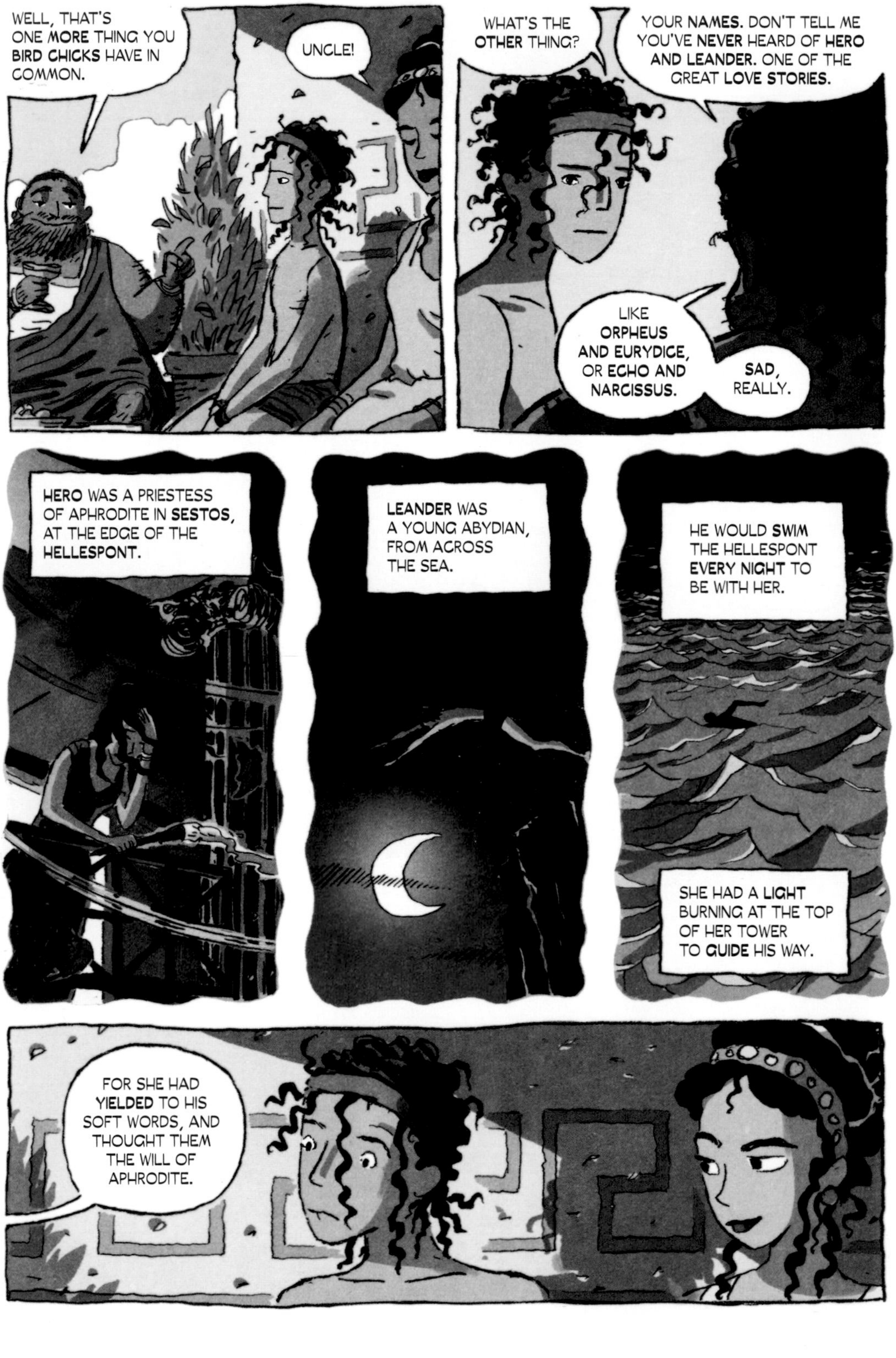
WELL, THAT'S ONE MORE THING YOU BIRD CHICKS HAVE IN COMMON.
UNCLE!
WHAT'S THE OTHER THING?
YOUR NAMES. DON'T TELL ME YOU'VE NEVER HEARD OF HERO AND LEANDER. ONE OF THE GREAT LOVE STORIES.
LIKE ORPHEUS AND EURYDICE, OR ECHO AND NARCISSUS.
SAD, REALLY.
HERO WAS A PRIESTESS OF APHRODITE IN SESTOS, AT THE EDGE OF THE HELLESPONT.
LEANDER WAS A YOUNG ABYDIAN, FROM ACROSS THE SEA.
HE WOULD SWIM THE HELLESPONT EVERY NIGHT TO BE WITH HER.
SHE HAD A LIGHT BURNING AT THE TOP OF HER TOWER TO GUIDE HIS WAY.
FOR SHE HAD YIELDED TO HIS SOFT WORDS, AND THOUGHT THEM THE WILL OF APHRODITE.

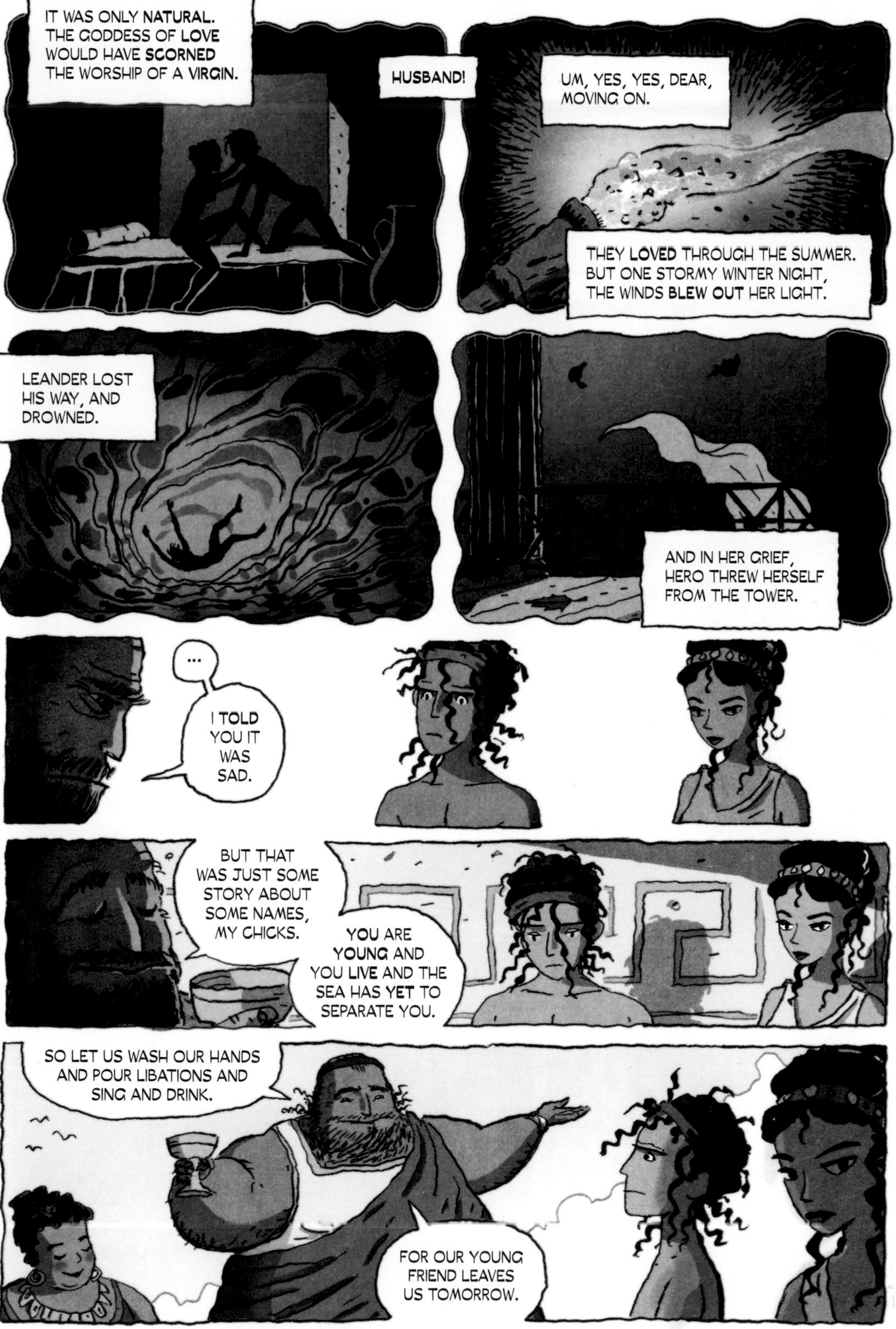

IT WAS ONLY NATURAL. THE GODDESS OF LOVE WOULD HAVE SCORNED THE WORSHIP OF A VIRGIN.
HUSBAND!
UM, YES, YES, DEAR, MOVING ON.
THEY LOVED THROUGH THE SUMMER. BUT ONE STORMY WINTER NIGHT, THE WINDS BLEW OUT HER LIGHT.
LEANDER LOST HIS WAY, AND DROWNED.
AND IN HER GRIEF, HERO THREW HERSELF FROM THE TOWER.
...
I TOLD YOU IT WAS SAD.
BUT THAT WAS JUST SOME STORY ABOUT SOME NAMES, MY CHICKS.
YOU ARE YOUNG AND YOU LIVE AND THE SEA HAS YET TO SEPARATE YOU.
SO LET US WASH OUR HANDS AND POUR LIBATIONS AND SING AND DRINK.
FOR OUR YOUNG FRIEND LEAVES US TOMORROW.

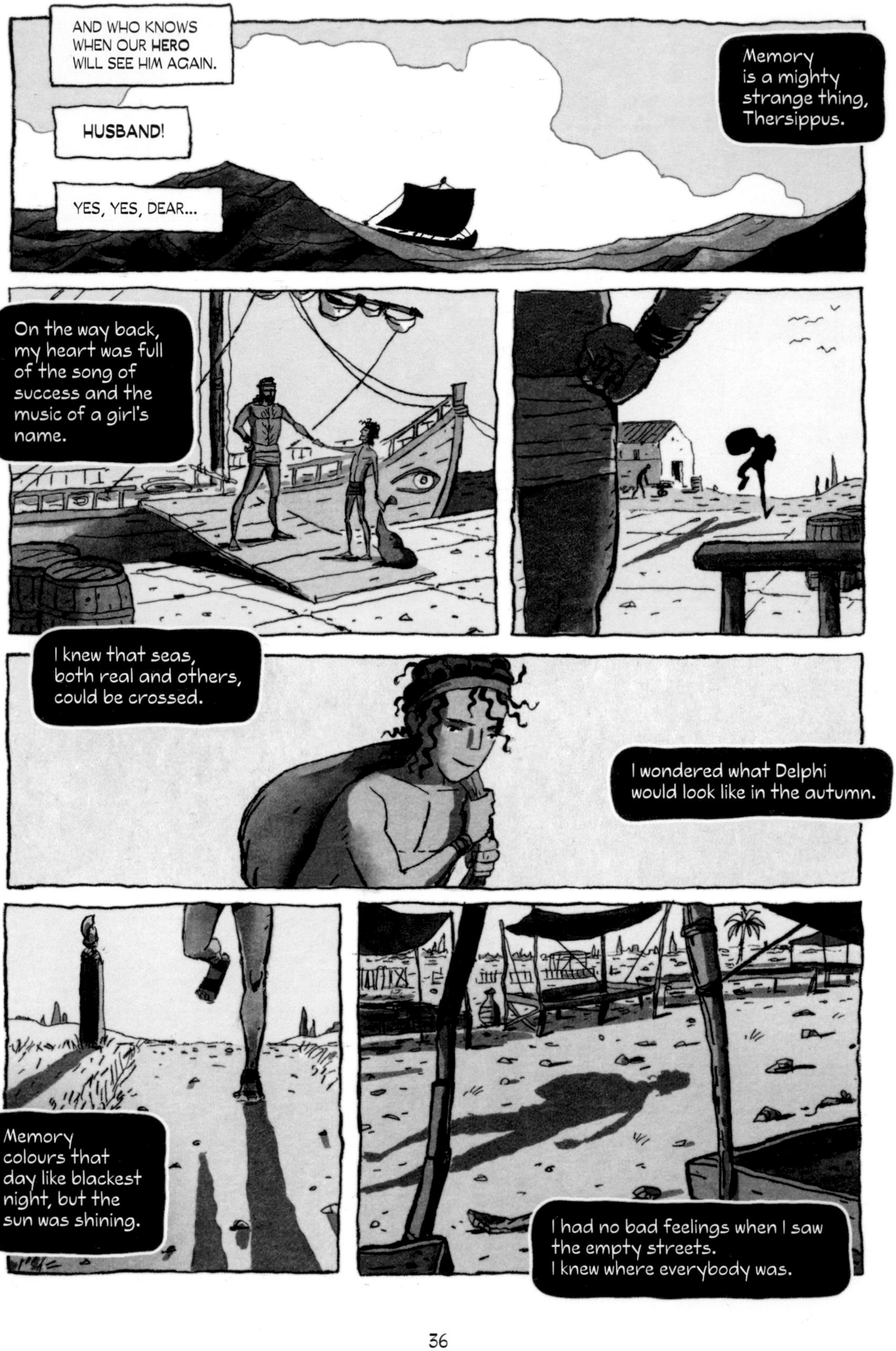

AND WHO KNOWS WHEN OUR HERO WILL SEE HIM AGAIN.
HUSBAND!
YES, YES, DEAR...
Memory is a mighty strange thing, Thersippus.
On the way back, my heart was full of the song of success and the music of a girl's name.
I knew that seas, both real and others, could be crossed.
I wondered what Delphi would look like in the autumn.
Memory colours that day like blackest night, but the sun was shining.
I had no bad feelings when I saw the empty streets.
I knew where everybody was.

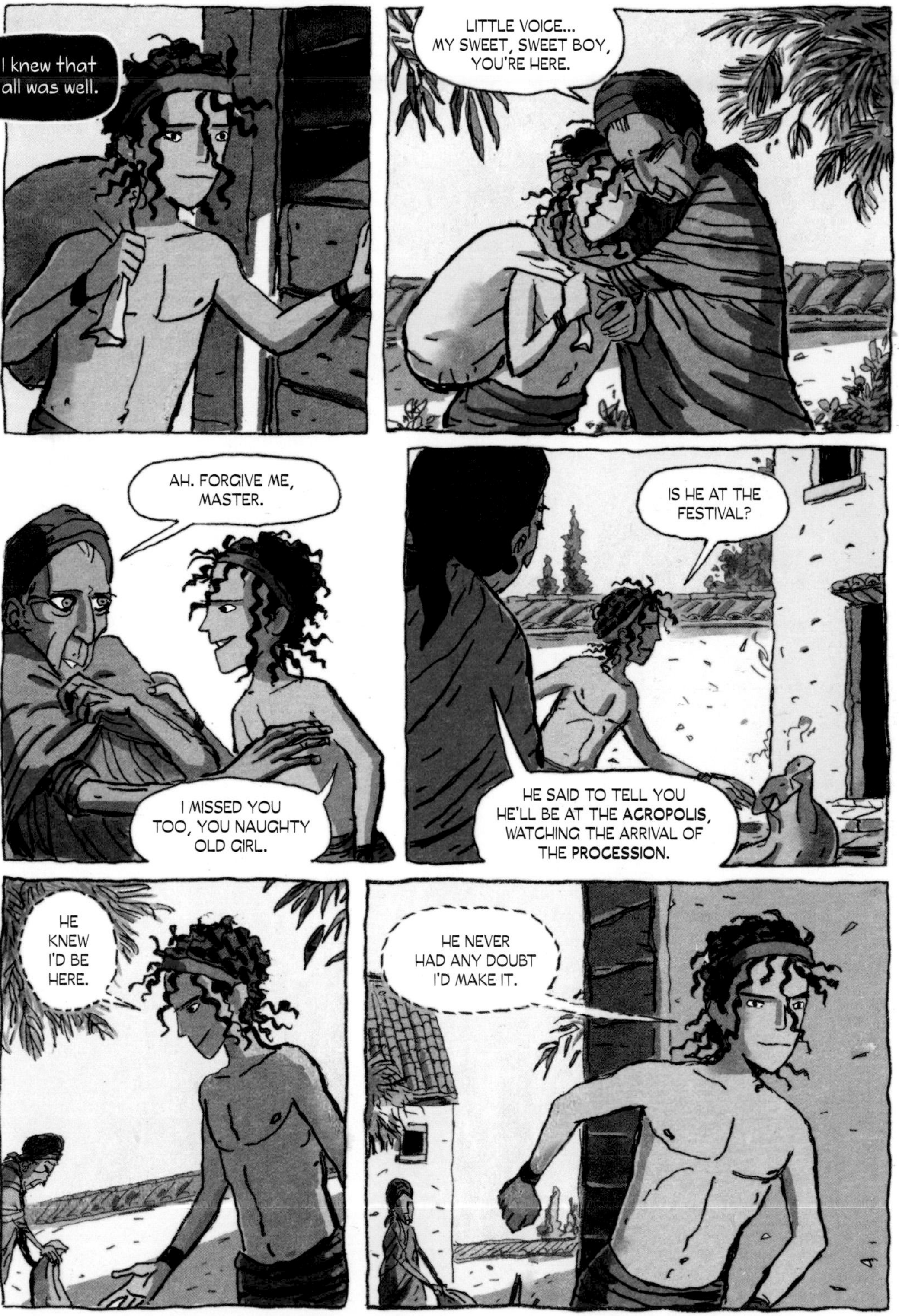

I knew that all was well.
LITTLE VOICE... MY SWEET, SWEET BOY, YOU'RE HERE.
AH. FORGIVE ME, MASTER.
I MISSED YOU TOO, YOU NAUGHTY OLD GIRL.
IS HE AT THE FESTIVAL?
HE SAID TO TELL YOU HE'LL BE AT THE ACROPOLIS, WATCHING THE ARRIVAL OF THE PROCESSION.
HE KNEW I'D BE HERE.
HE NEVER HAD ANY DOUBT I'D MAKE IT.

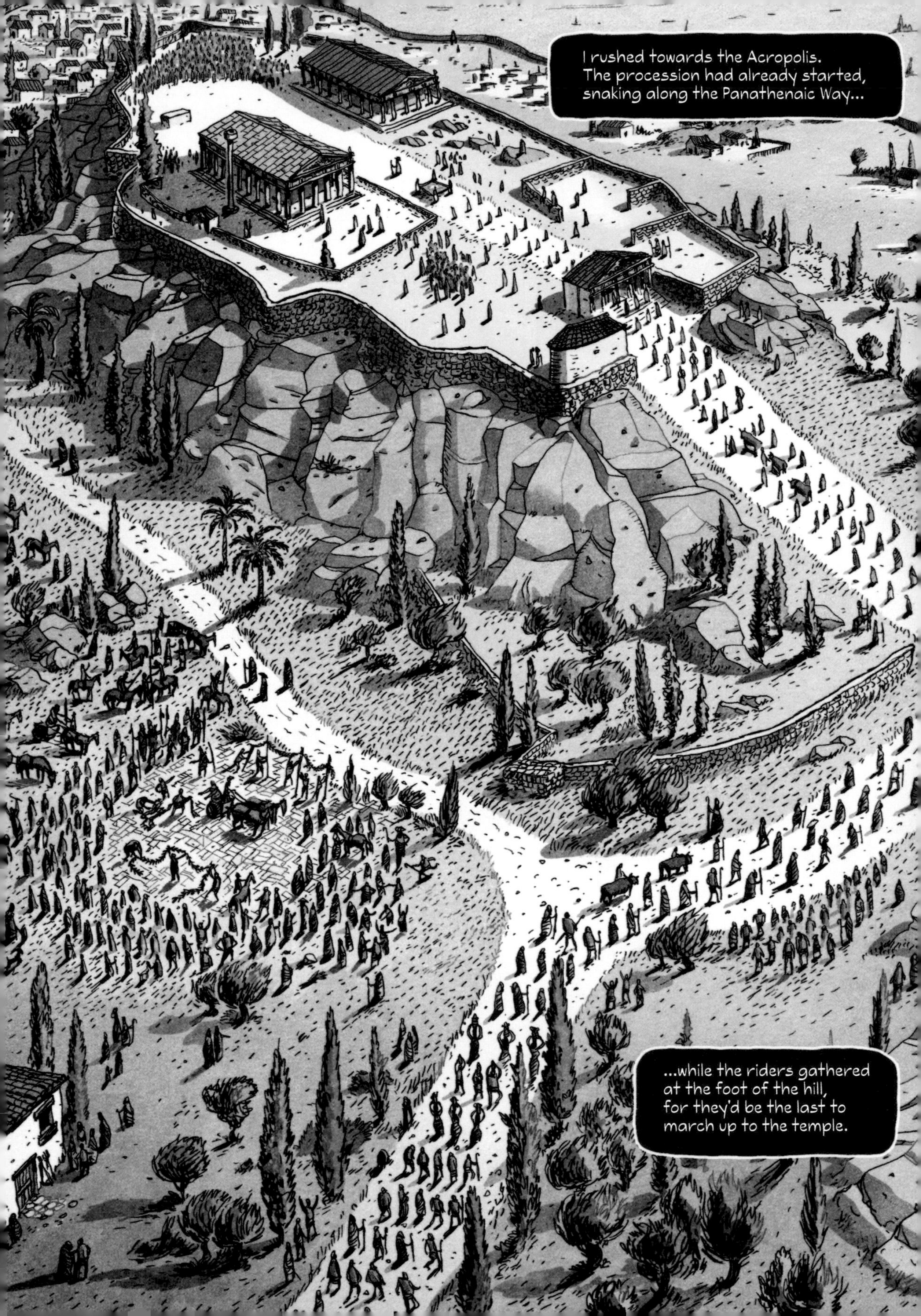
I rushed towards the Acropolis. The procession had already started, snaking along the Panathenaic Way...
...while the riders gathered at the foot of the hill, for they'd be the last to march up to the temple.

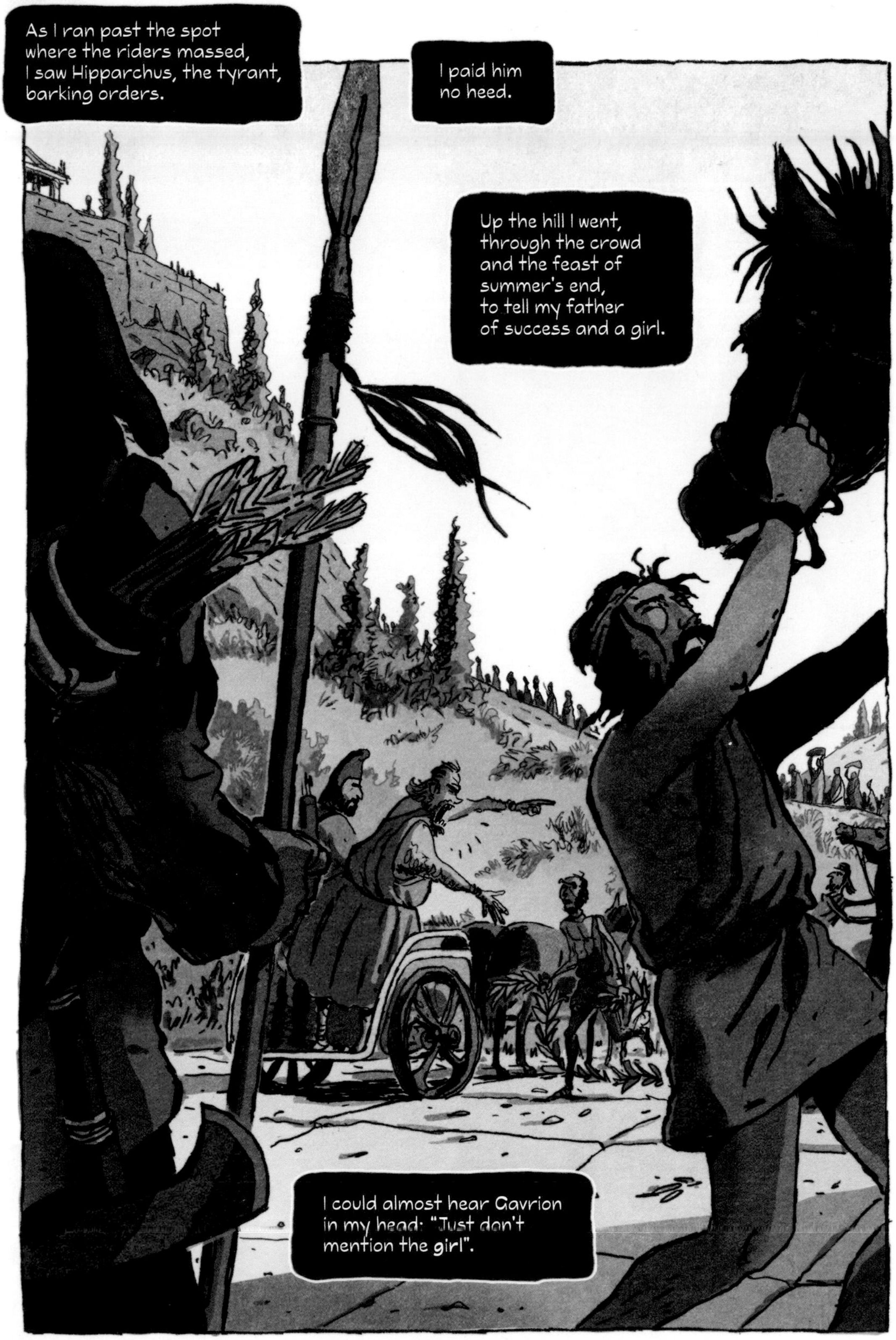
As I ran past the spot where the riders massed, I saw Hipparchus, the tyrant, barking orders.
I paid him no heed.
Up the hill I went, through the crowd and the feast of summer's end, to tell my father of success and a girl.
I could almost hear Gavrion in my head: "Just don't mention the girl".

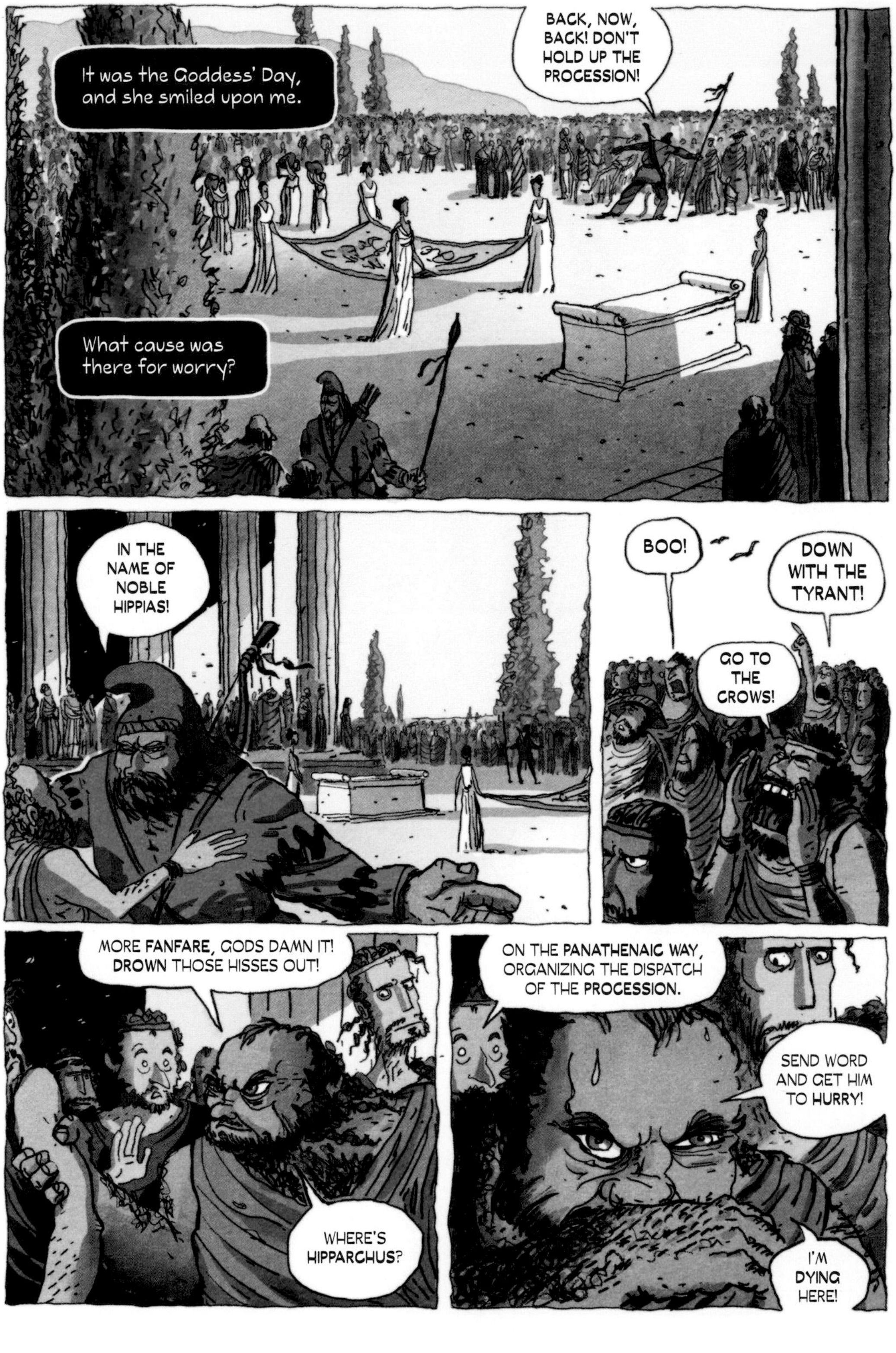
It was the Goddess' Day, and she smiled upon me.
BACK, NOW, BACK! DON'T HOLD UP THE PROCESSION!
What cause was there for worry?
IN THE NAME OF NOBLE HIPPIAS!
BOO!
DOWN WITH THE TYRANT!
GO TO THE CROWS!
MORE **FANFARE**, GODS DAMN IT! **DROWN** THOSE HISSES OUT!
WHERE'S **HIPPARCHUS**?
ON THE **PANATHENAIC WAY**, ORGANIZING THE DISPATCH OF THE **PROCESSION**.
SEND WORD AND GET HIM TO **HURRY**!
I'M **DYING** HERE!

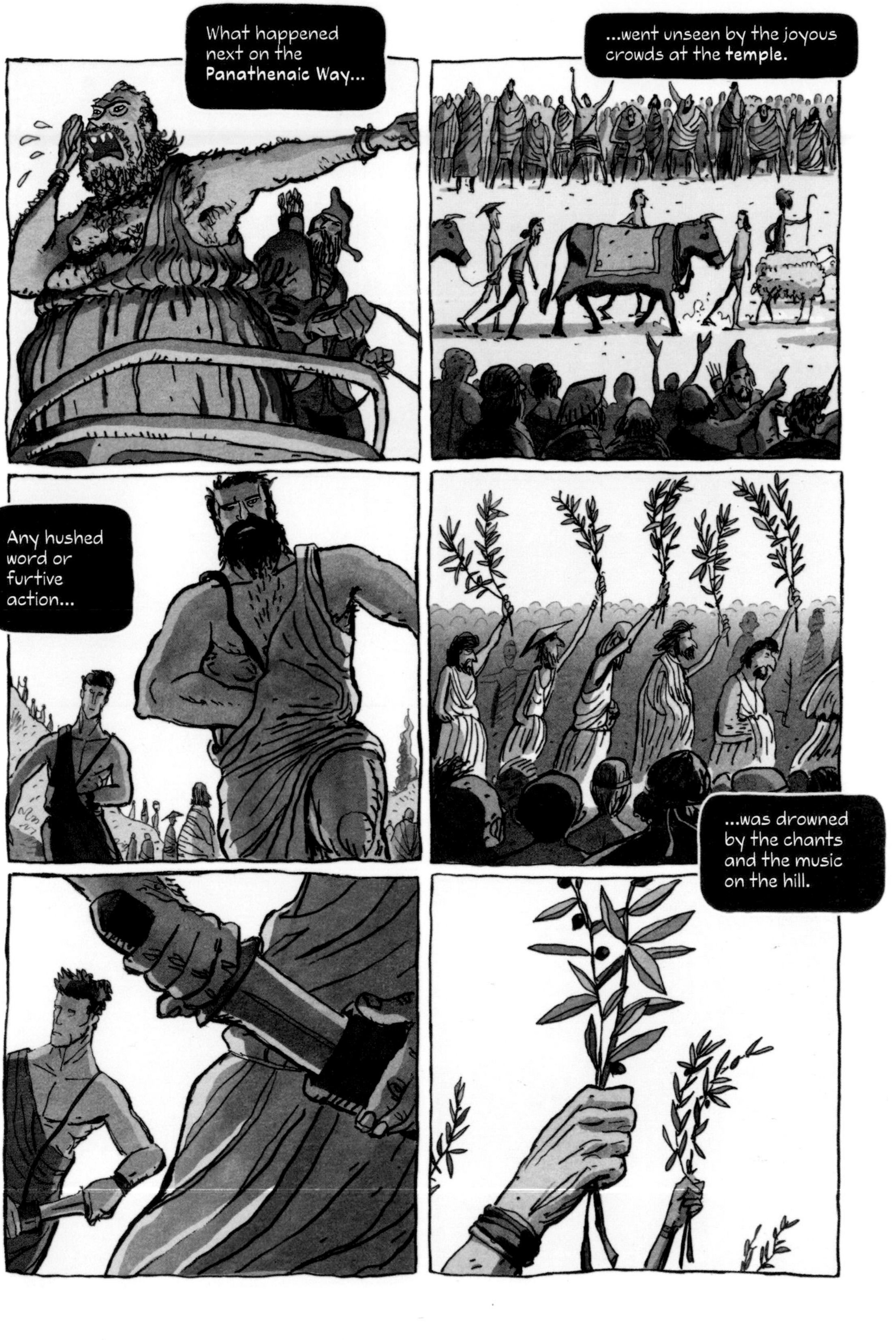
What happened next on the Panathenaic Way...
...went unseen by the joyous crowds at the temple.
Any hushed word or furtive action...
...was drowned by the chants and the music on the hill.

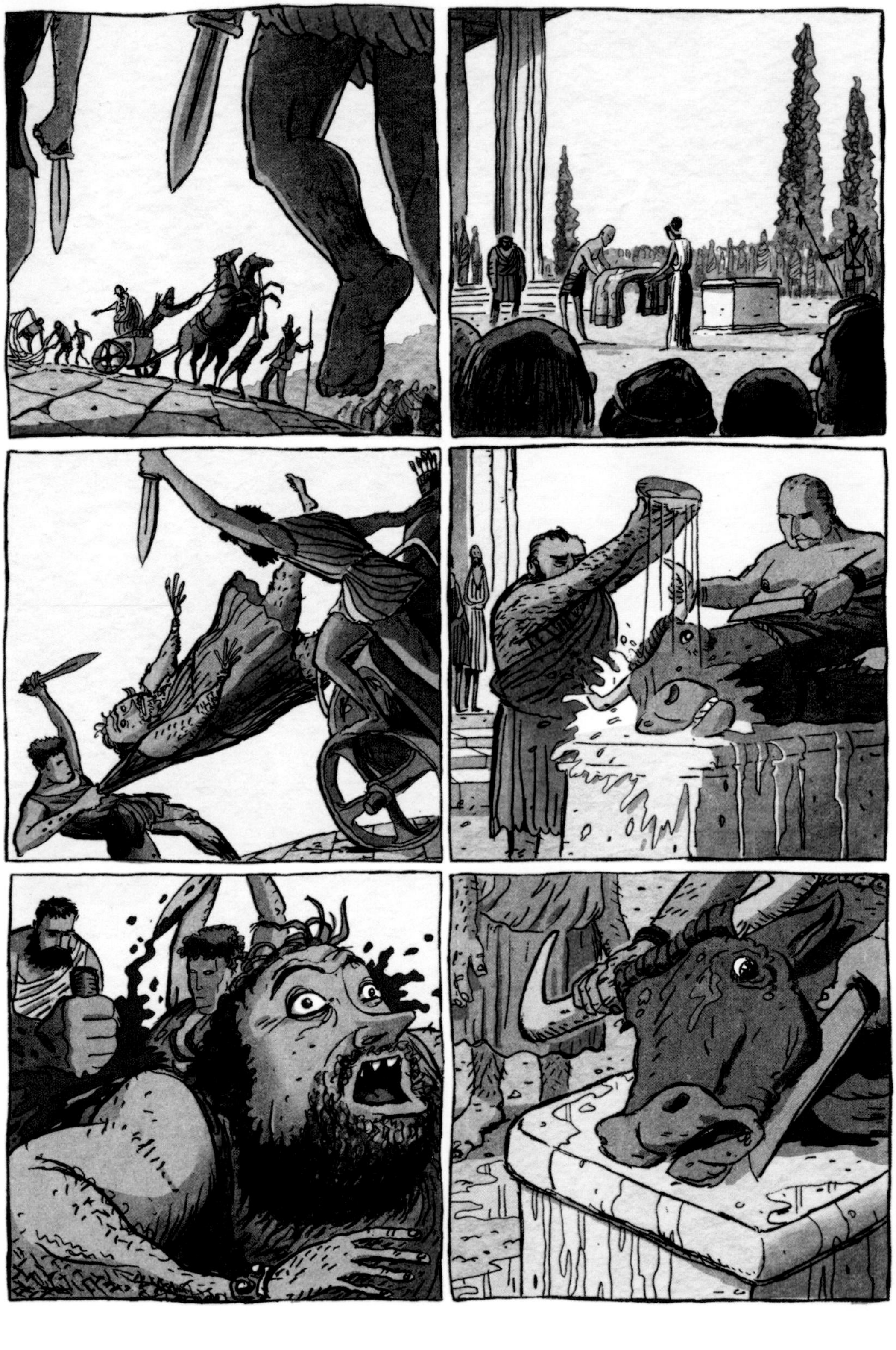

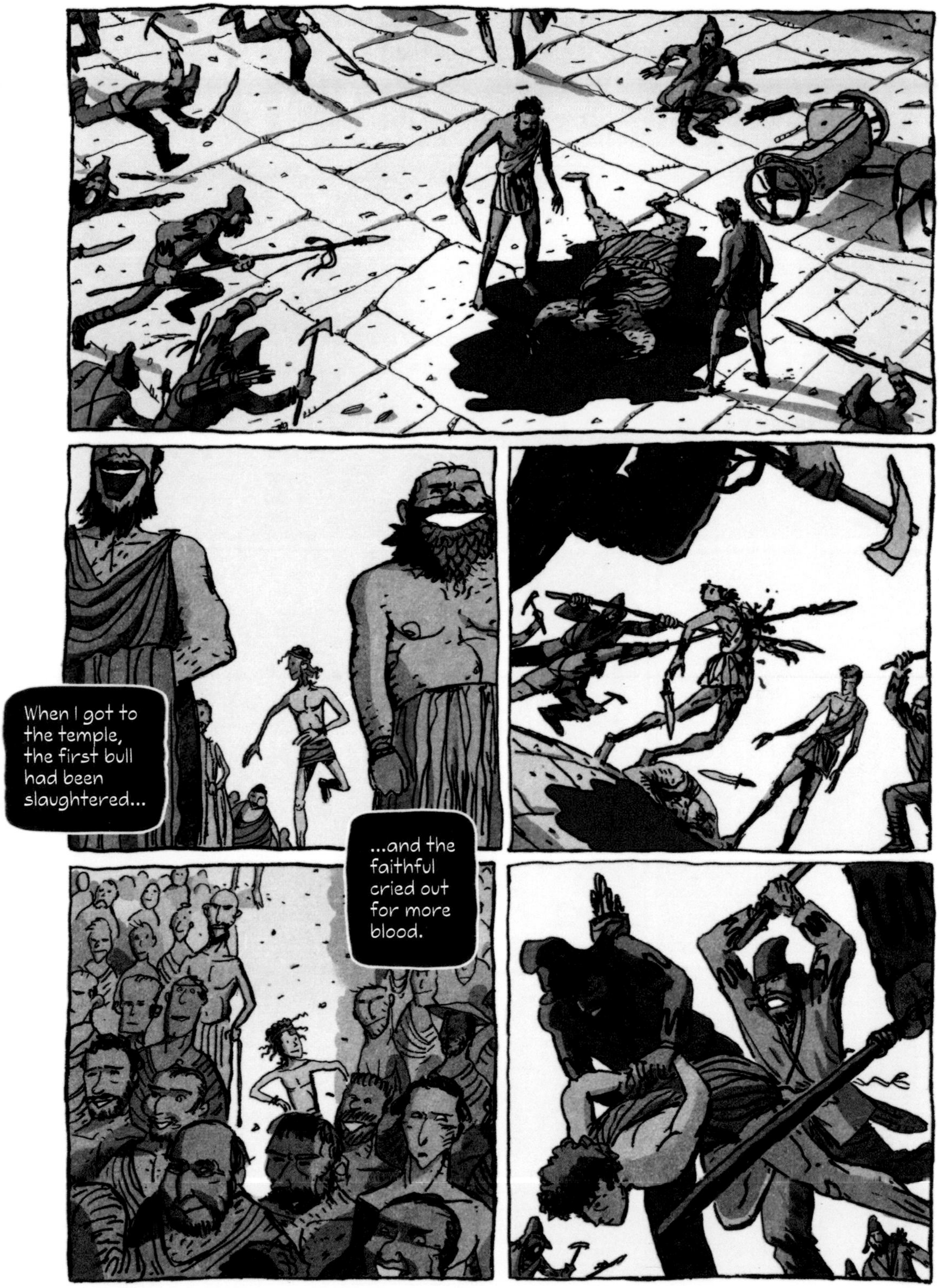
When I got to the temple, the first bull had been slaughtered...
...and the faithful cried out for more blood.

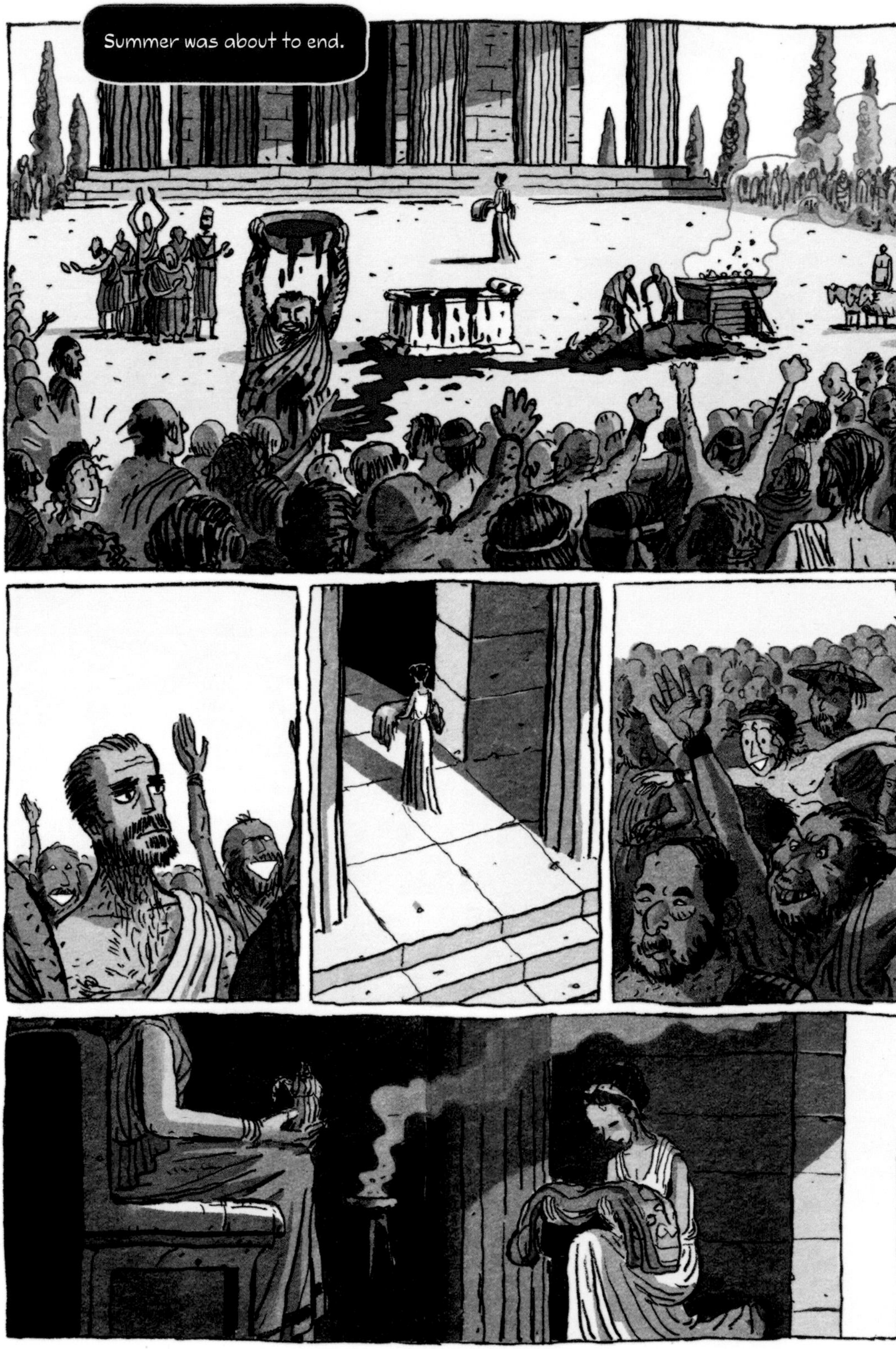
Summer was about to end.

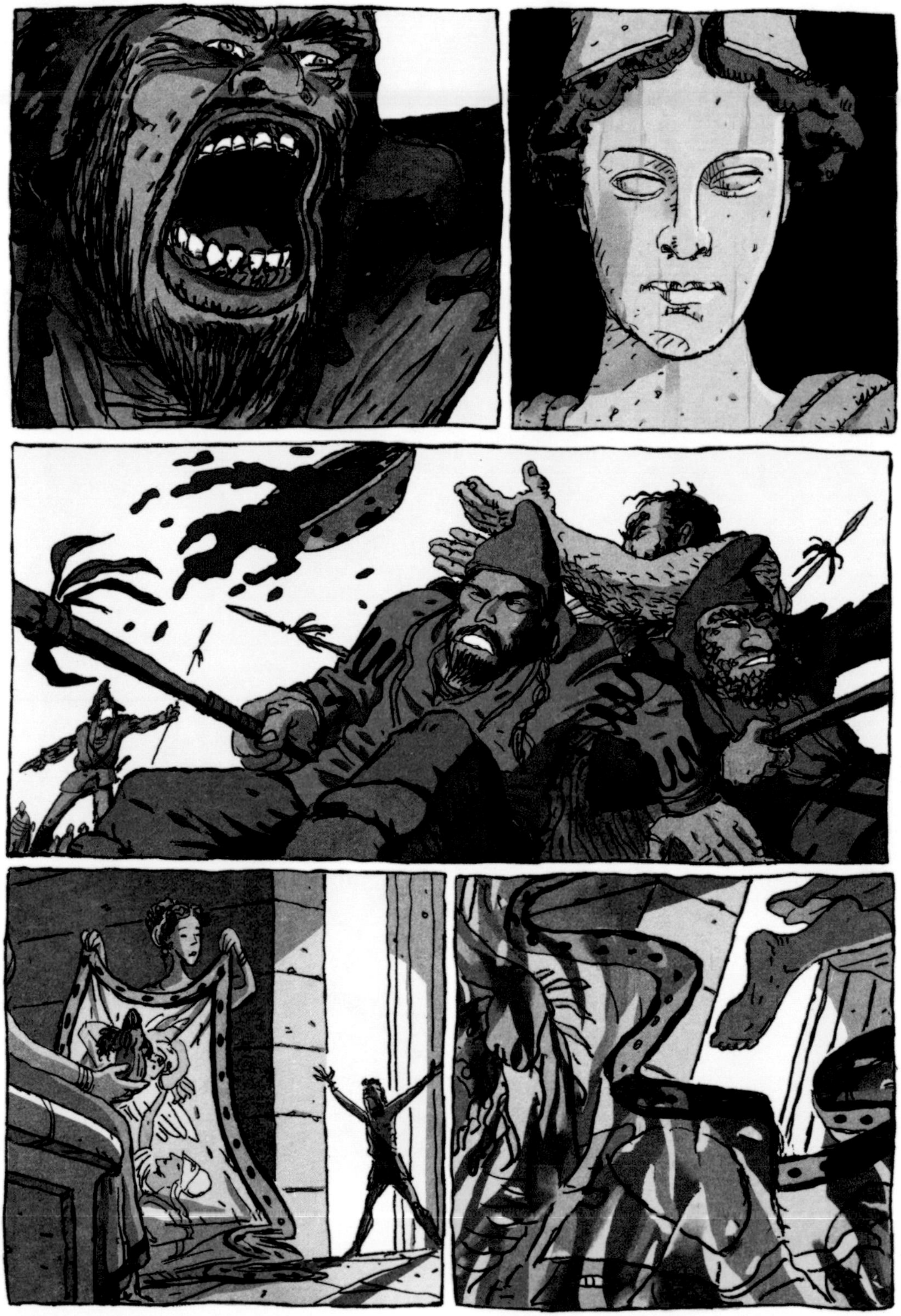

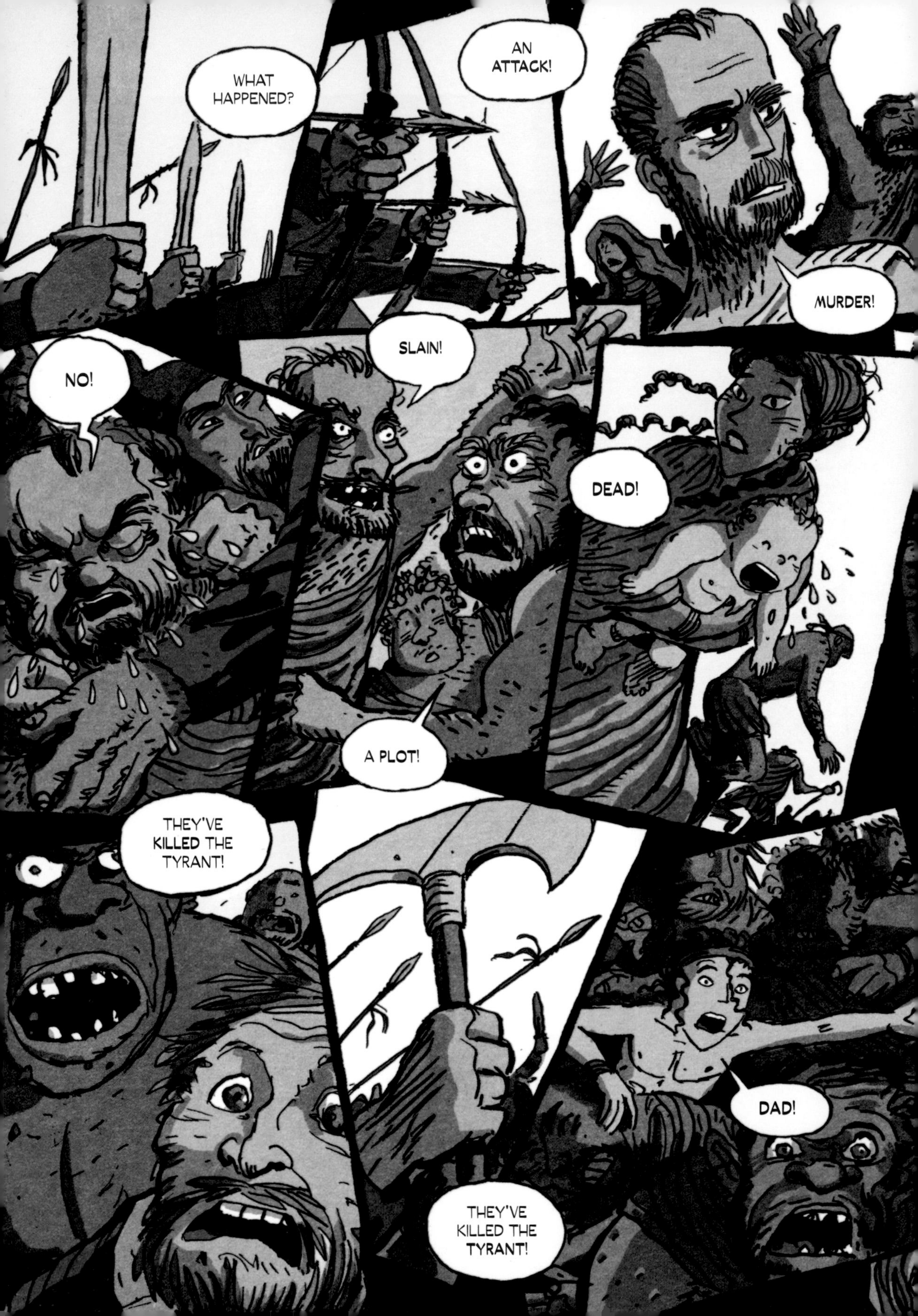
WHAT HAPPENED?
AN ATTACK!
MURDER!
NO!
SLAIN!
DEAD!
A PLOT!
THEY'VE KILLED THE TYRANT!
DAD!
THEY'VE KILLED THE TYRANT!

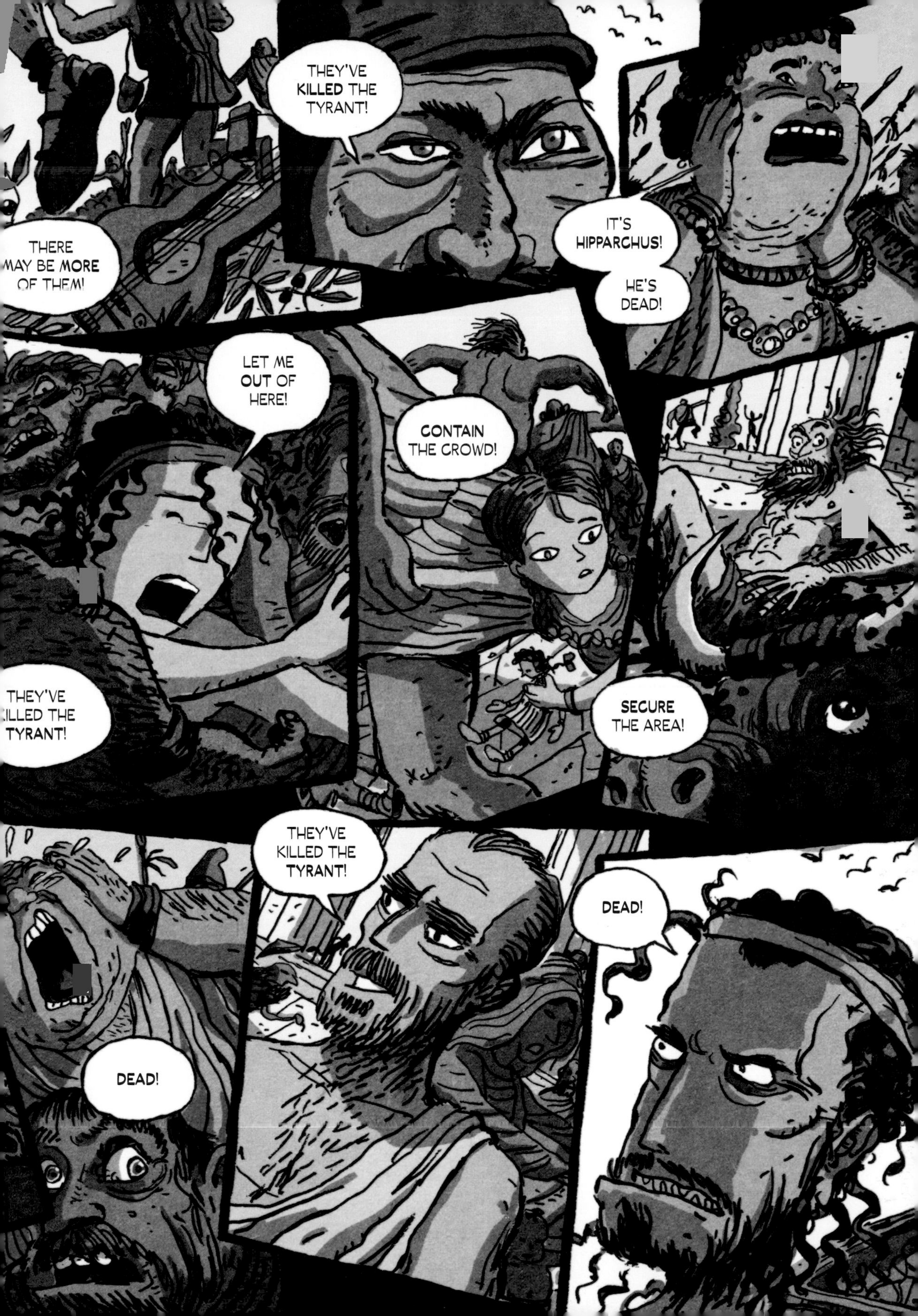

THERE MAY BE MORE OF THEM!
THEY'VE KILLED THE TYRANT!
IT'S HIPPARCHUS!
HE'S DEAD!
LET ME OUT OF HERE!
THEY'VE ILLED THE TYRANT!
CONTAIN THE CROWD!
SECURE THE AREA!
DEAD!
THEY'VE KILLED THE TYRANT!
DEAD!

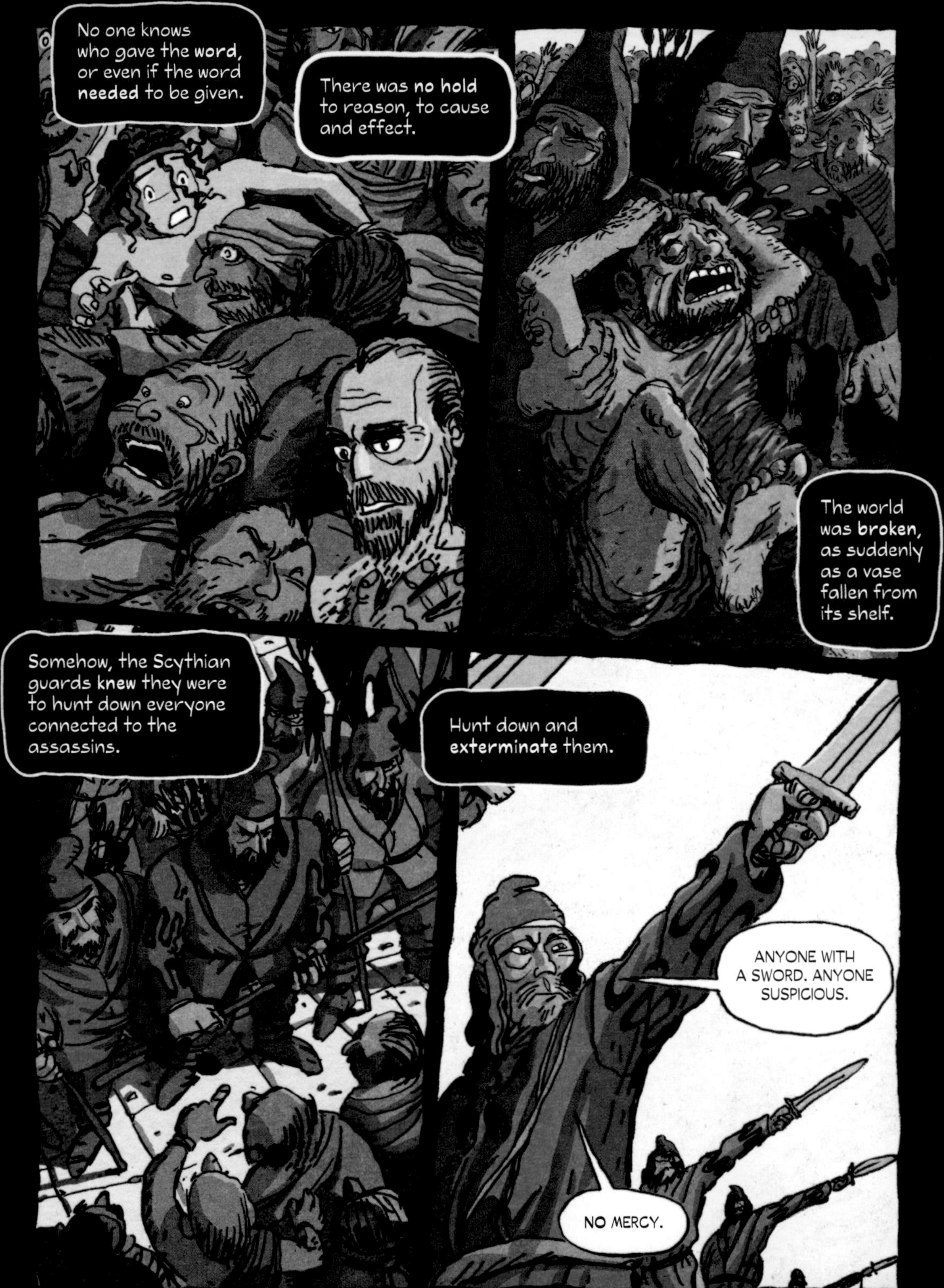

No one knows who gave the **word**, or even if the word **needed** to be given.
There was **no hold** to reason, to cause and effect.
The world was **broken**, as suddenly as a vase fallen from its shelf.
Somehow, the Scythian guards **knew** they were to hunt down everyone connected to the assassins.
Hunt down and **exterminate** them.
ANYONE WITH A SWORD. ANYONE SUSPICIOUS.
NO MERCY.

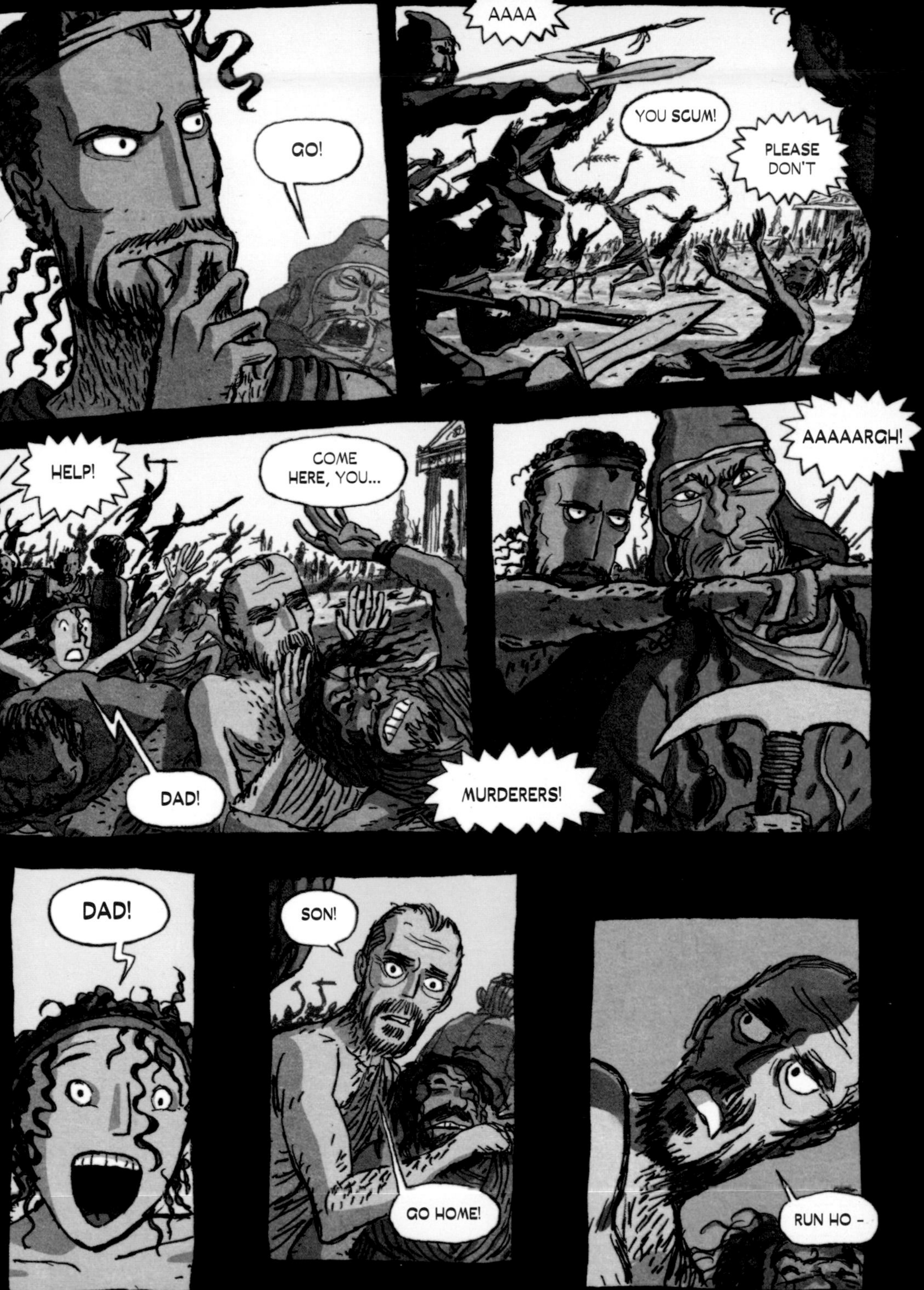
GO!
AAAA
YOU SCUM!
PLEASE DON'T
HELP!
COME HERE, YOU...
DAD!
MURDERERS!
AAAAARGH!
DAD!
SON!
GO HOME!
RUN HO -

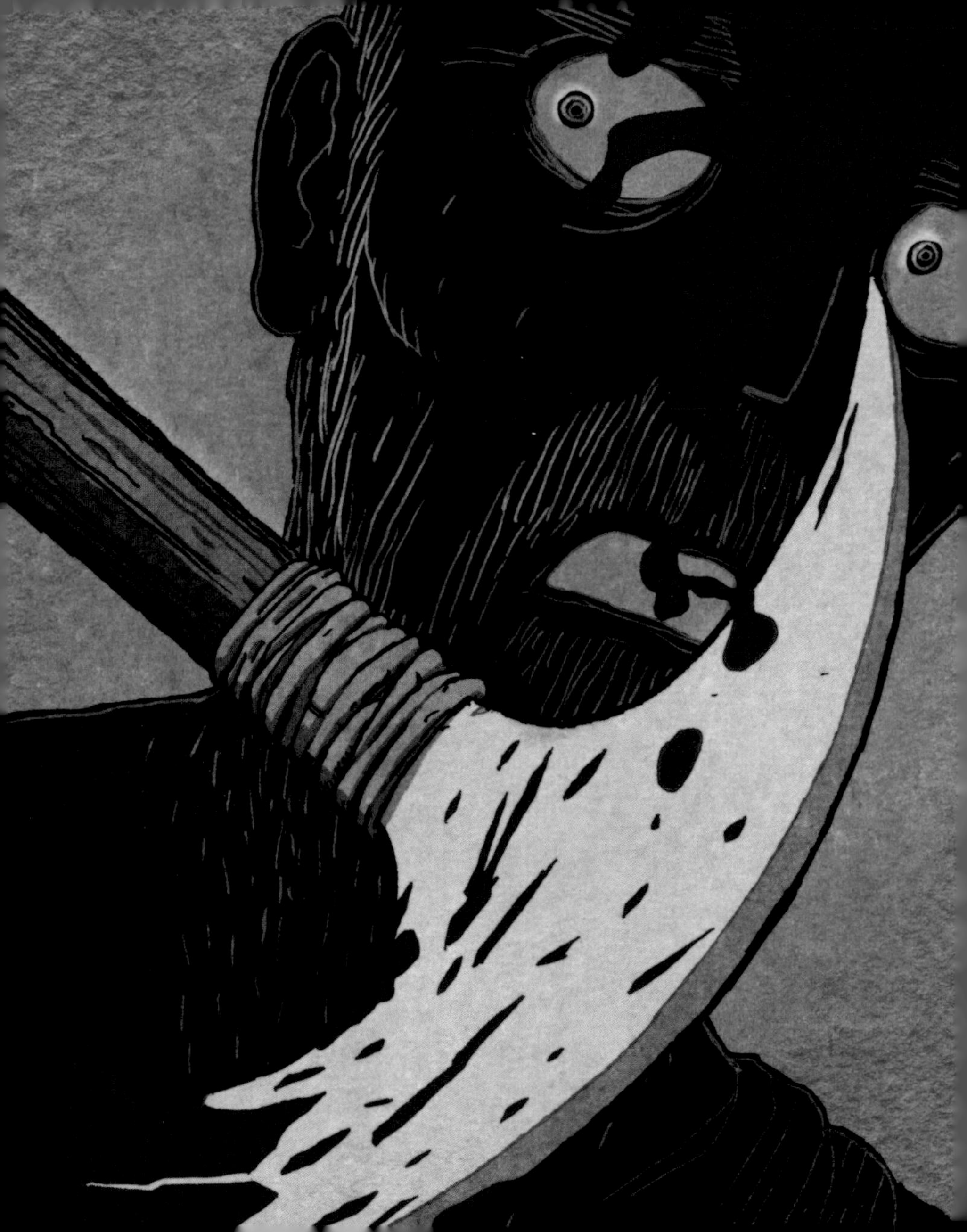

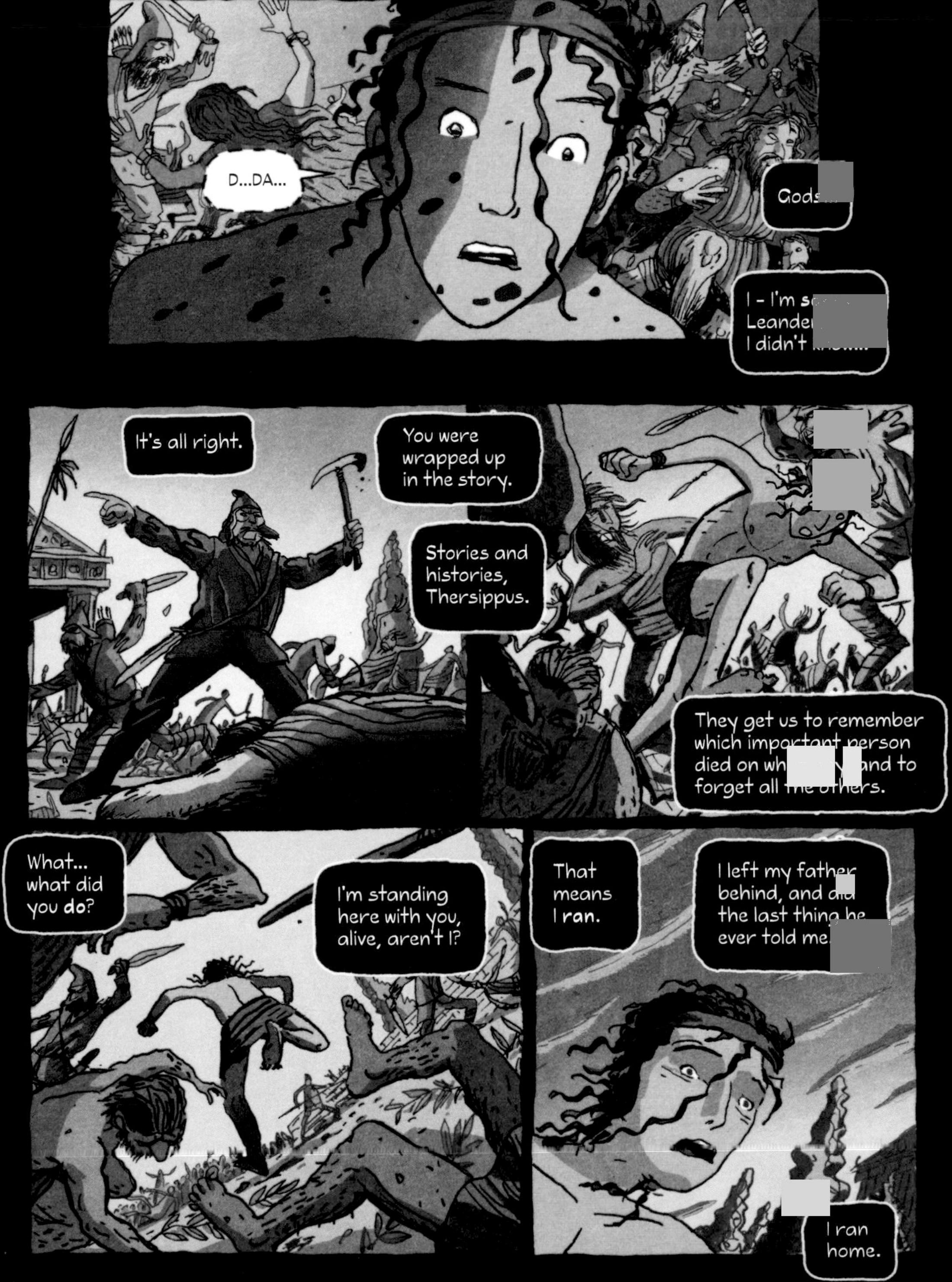
D...DA...
Gods
I – I'm
I didn't
It's all right.
You were wrapped up in the story.
Stories and histories, Thersippus.
They get us to remember which important person died on
and to forget all the others.
What... what did you do?
I'm standing here with you, alive, aren't I?
That means I ran.
I left my father behind, and
the last thing he ever told me.
I ran home.

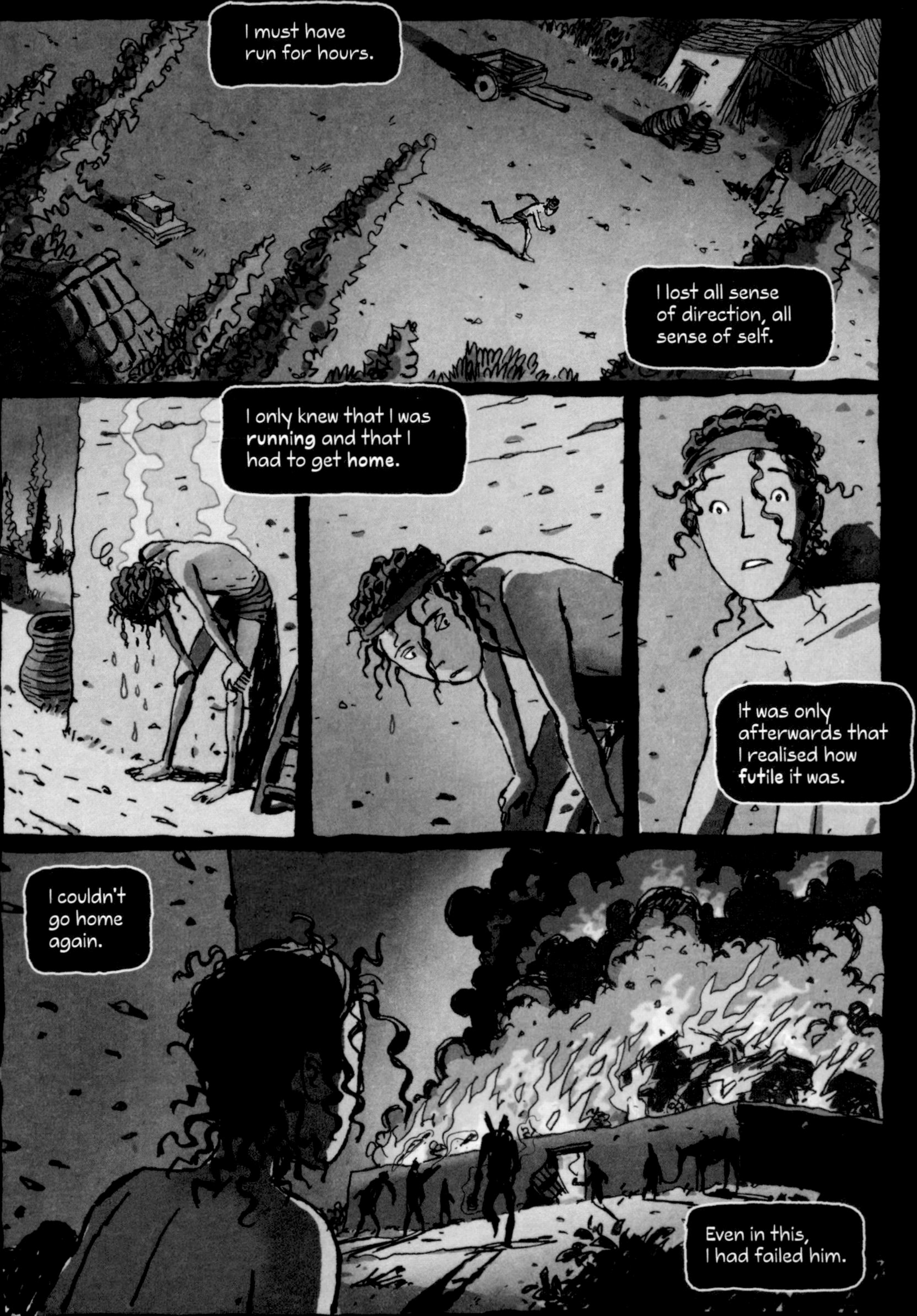
I must have run for hours.
I lost all sense of direction, all sense of self.
I only knew that I was **running** and that I had to get **home**.
It was only afterwards that I realised how **futile** it was.
I couldn't go home again.
Even in this, I had failed him.

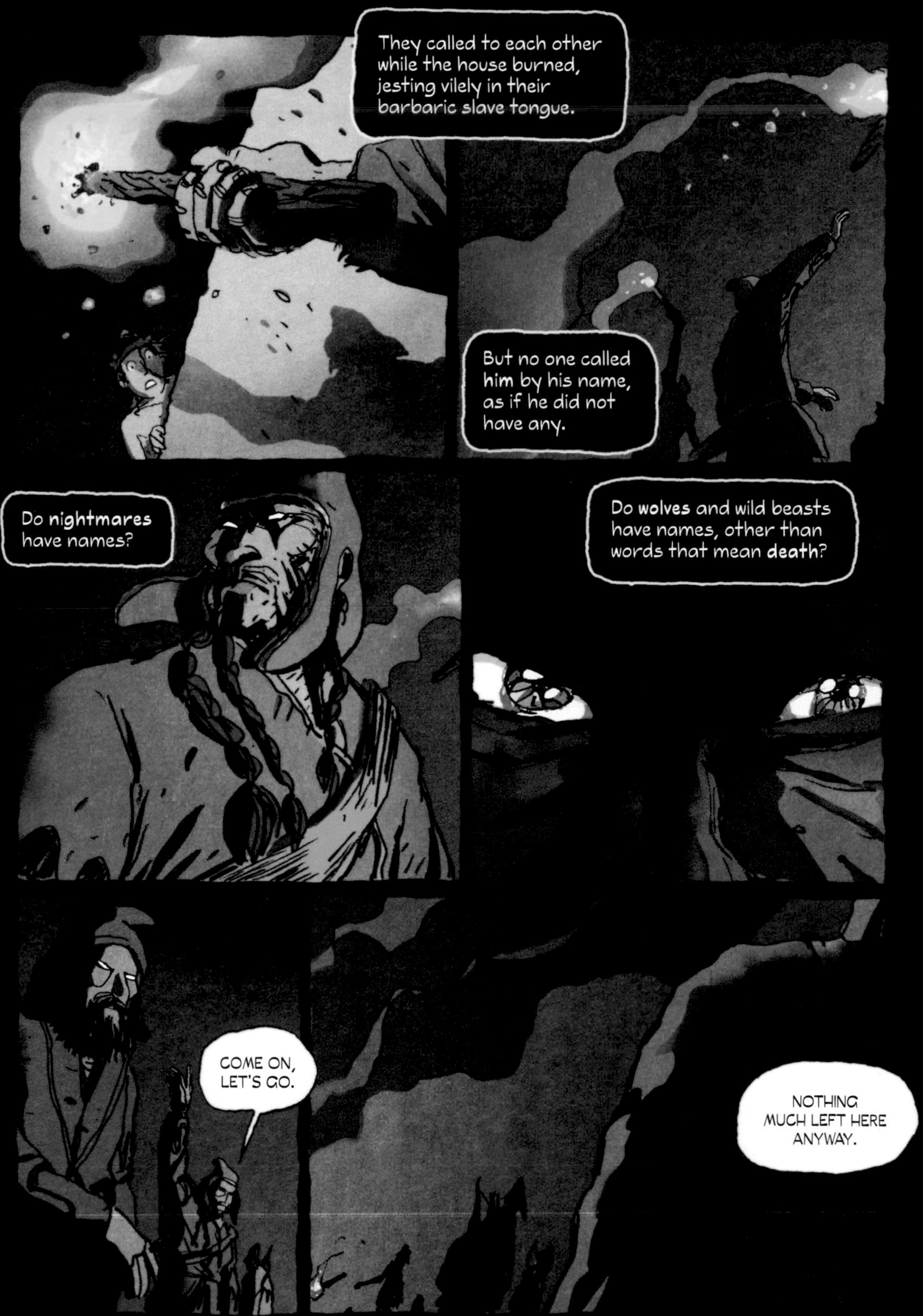
They called to each other while the house burned, jesting vilely in their barbaric slave tongue.
But no one called **him** by his name, as if he did not have any.
Do **nightmares** have names?
Do **wolves** and wild beasts have names, other than words that mean **death**?
COME ON, LET'S GO.
NOTHING MUCH LEFT HERE ANYWAY.

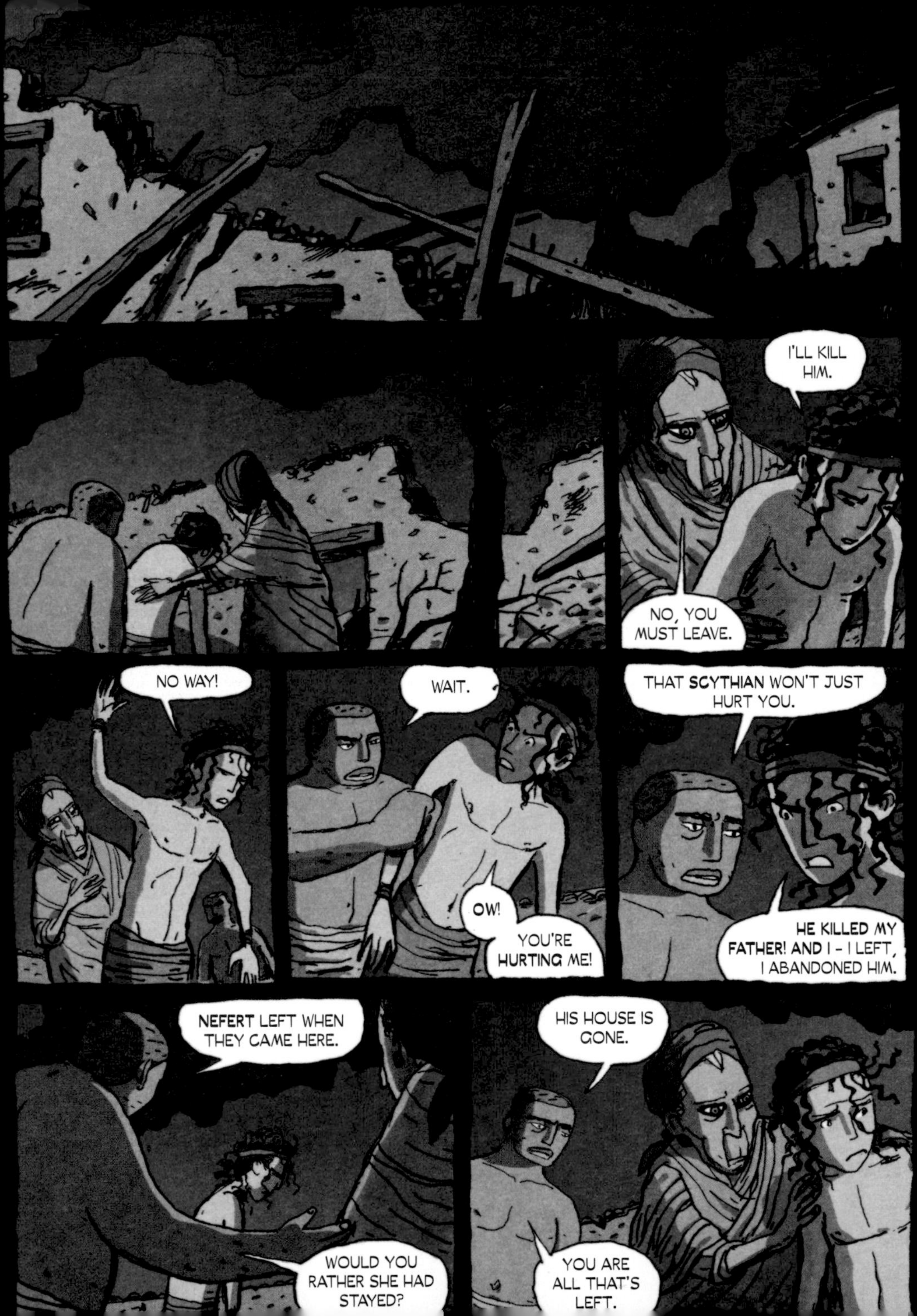
I'LL KILL HIM.
NO, YOU MUST LEAVE.
NO WAY!
WAIT.
OW!
YOU'RE HURTING ME!
THAT SCYTHIAN WON'T JUST HURT YOU.
HE KILLED MY FATHER! AND I - I LEFT, I ABANDONED HIM.
NEFERT LEFT WHEN THEY CAME HERE.
WOULD YOU RATHER SHE HAD STAYED?
HIS HOUSE IS GONE.
YOU ARE ALL THAT'S LEFT.

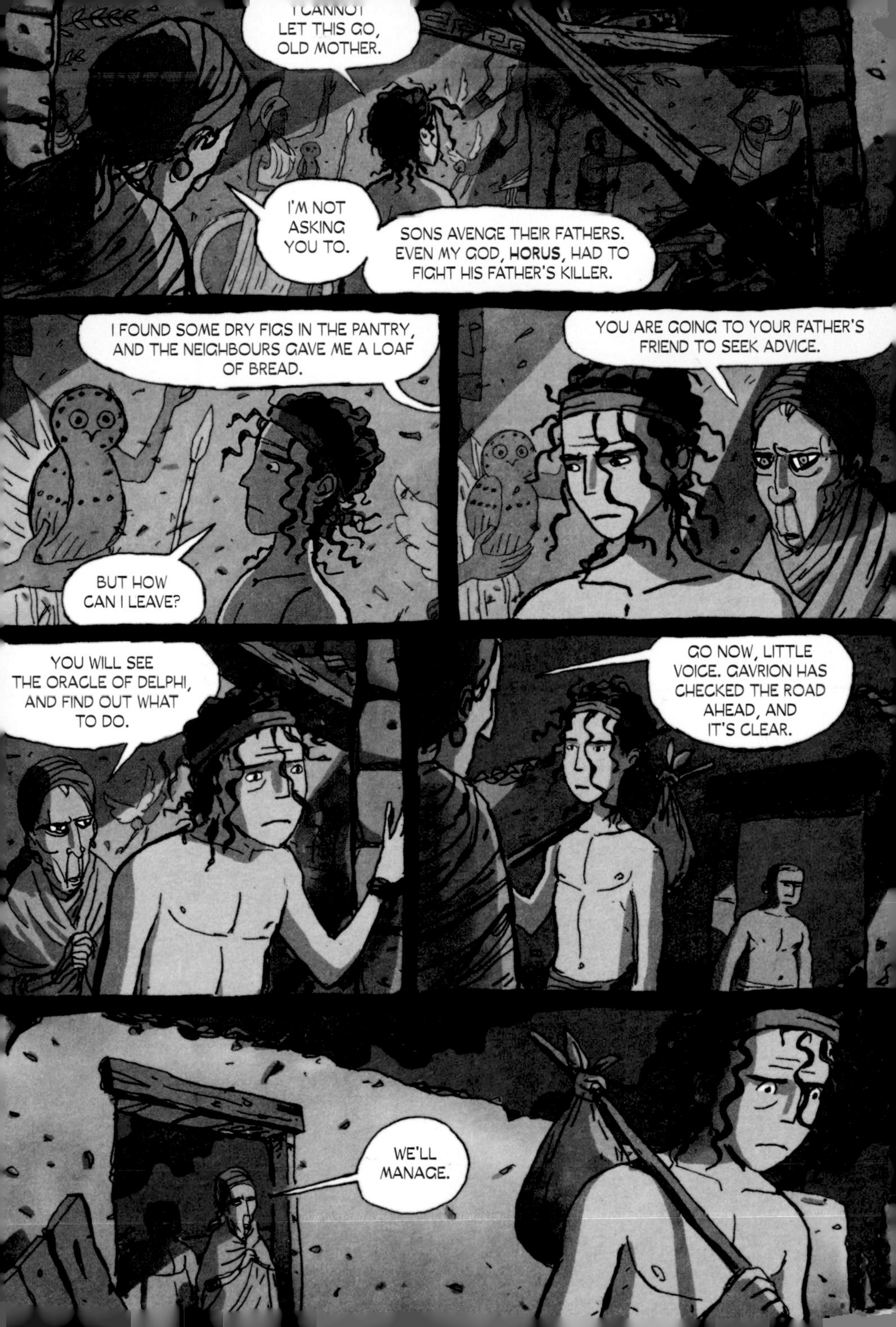
I CANNOT LET THIS GO, OLD MOTHER.
I'M NOT ASKING YOU TO.
SONS AVENGE THEIR FATHERS. EVEN MY GOD, **HORUS**, HAD TO FIGHT HIS FATHER'S KILLER.
I FOUND SOME DRY FIGS IN THE PANTRY, AND THE NEIGHBOURS GAVE ME A LOAF OF BREAD.
BUT HOW CAN I LEAVE?
YOU ARE GOING TO YOUR FATHER'S FRIEND TO SEEK ADVICE.
YOU WILL SEE THE ORACLE OF DELPHI, AND FIND OUT WHAT TO DO.
GO NOW, LITTLE VOICE. GAVRION HAS CHECKED THE ROAD AHEAD, AND IT'S CLEAR.
WE'LL MANAGE.

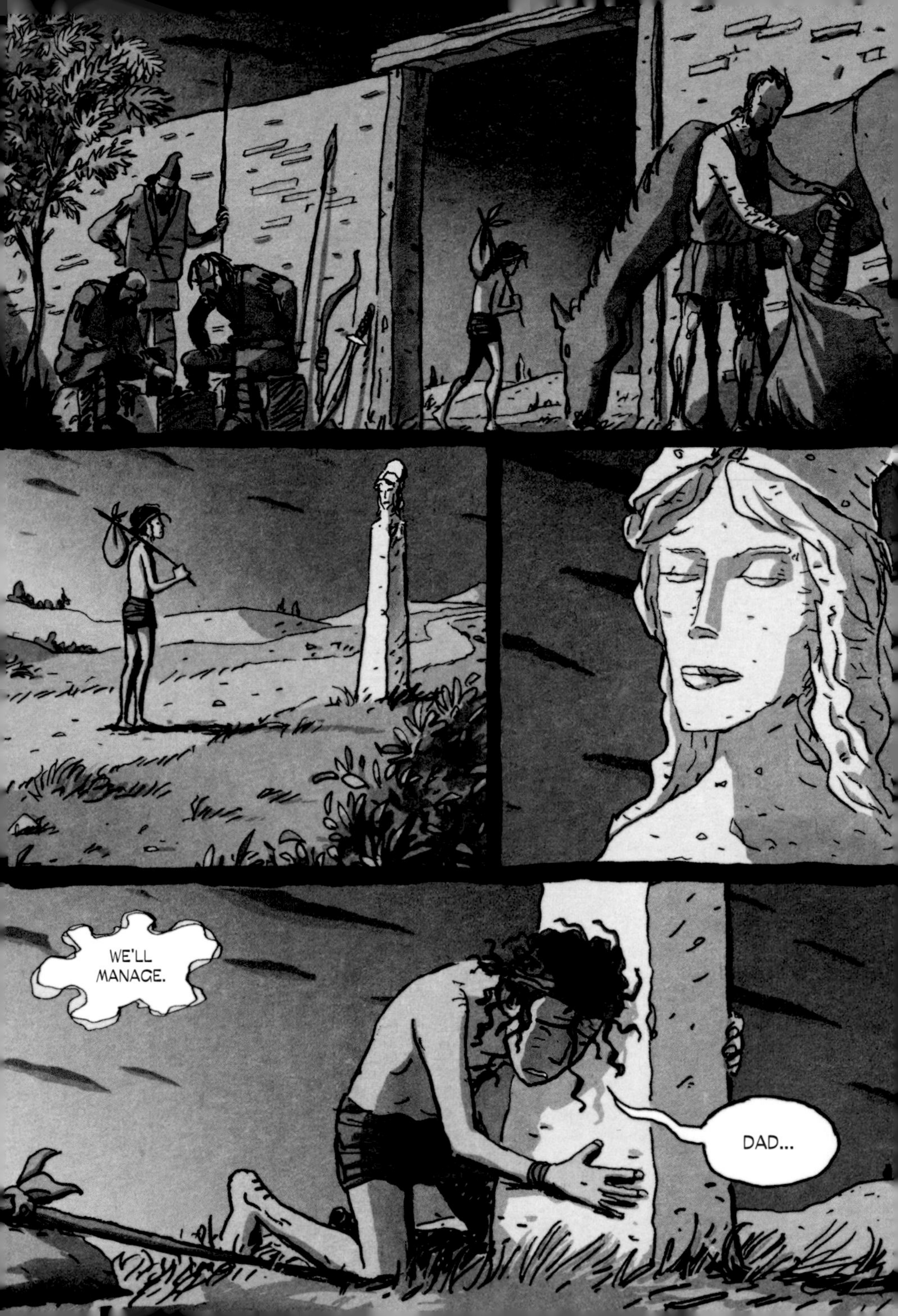
WE'LL MANAGE.
DAD...

THE SECRET WORLD

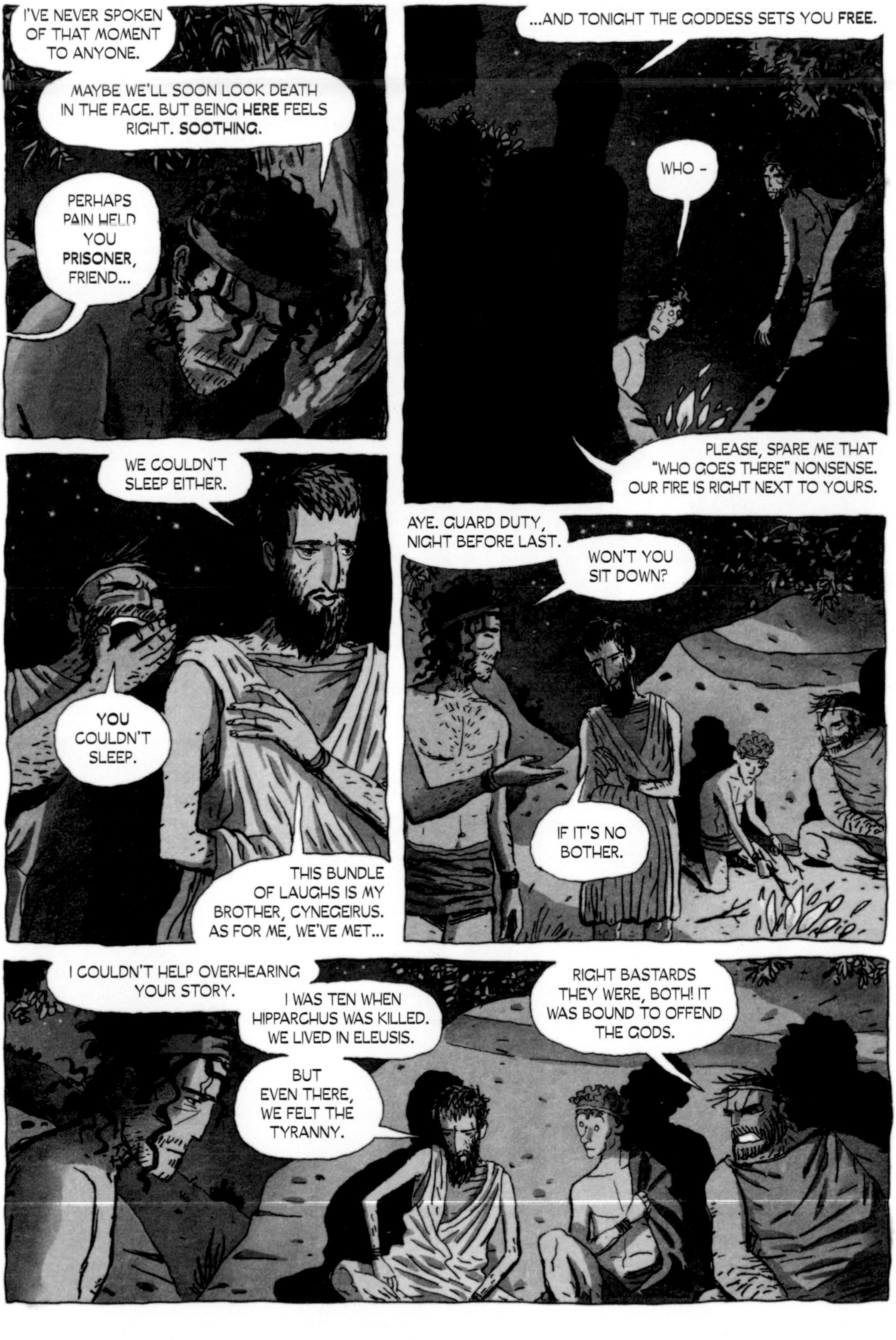
I'VE NEVER SPOKEN OF THAT MOMENT TO ANYONE.
MAYBE WE'LL SOON LOOK DEATH IN THE FACE. BUT BEING **HERE** FEELS RIGHT. **SOOTHING.**
PERHAPS PAIN HELD YOU **PRISONER,** FRIEND...
...AND TONIGHT THE GODDESS SETS YOU **FREE.**
WHO -
PLEASE, SPARE ME THAT "WHO GOES THERE" NONSENSE. OUR FIRE IS RIGHT NEXT TO YOURS.
WE COULDN'T SLEEP EITHER.
YOU COULDN'T SLEEP.
THIS BUNDLE OF LAUGHS IS MY BROTHER, CYNEGEIRUS. AS FOR ME, WE'VE MET...
AYE. GUARD DUTY, NIGHT BEFORE LAST.
WON'T YOU SIT DOWN?
IF IT'S NO BOTHER.
I COULDN'T HELP OVERHEARING YOUR STORY.
I WAS TEN WHEN HIPPARCHUS WAS KILLED. WE LIVED IN ELEUSIS.
BUT EVEN THERE, WE FELT THE TYRANNY.
RIGHT BASTARDS THEY WERE, BOTH! IT WAS BOUND TO OFFEND THE GODS.

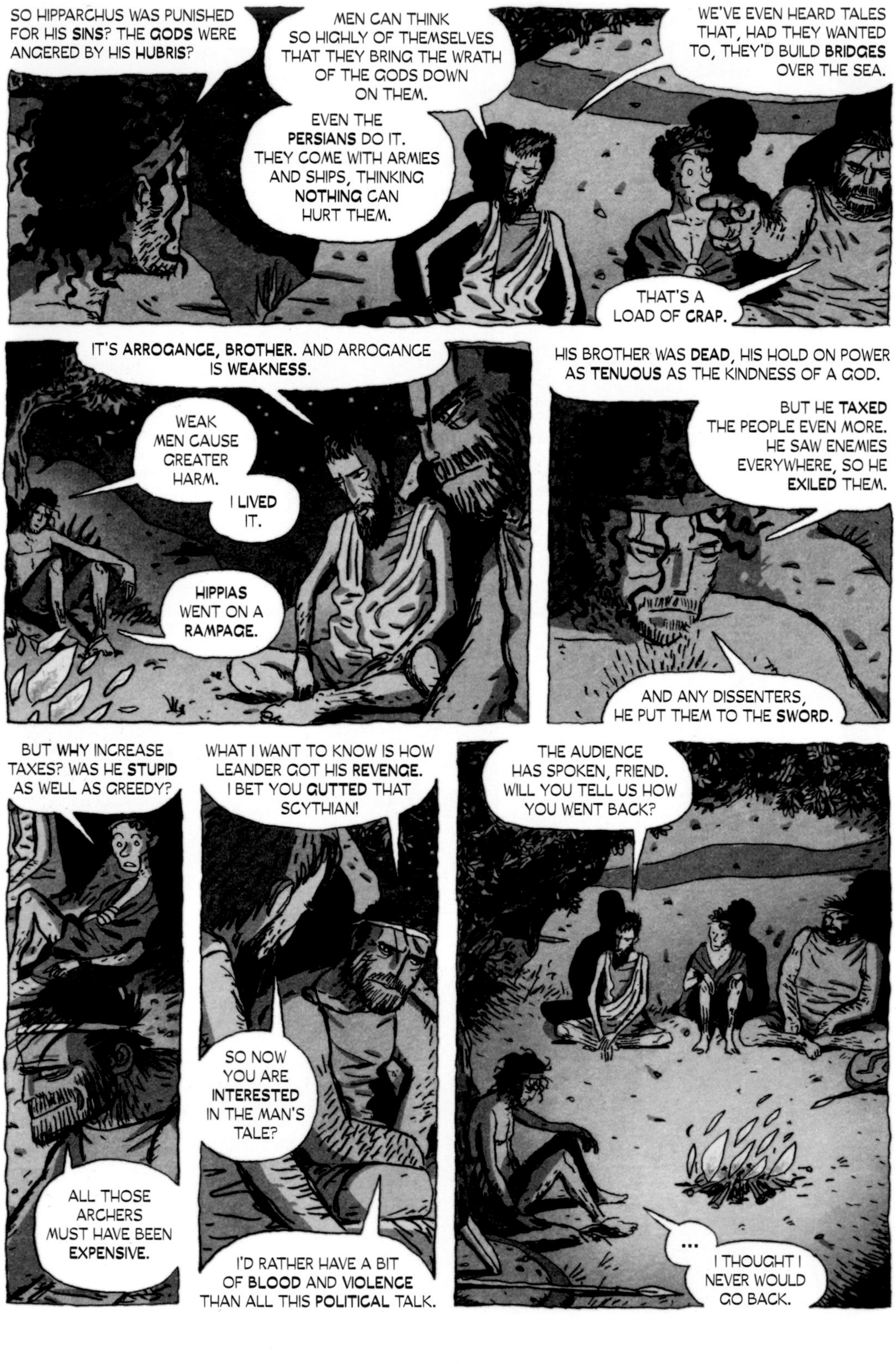
SO HIPPARCHUS WAS PUNISHED FOR HIS **SINS**? THE **GODS** WERE ANGERED BY HIS **HUBRIS**?
MEN CAN THINK SO HIGHLY OF THEMSELVES THAT THEY BRING THE WRATH OF THE GODS DOWN ON THEM.
EVEN THE **PERSIANS** DO IT. THEY COME WITH ARMIES AND SHIPS, THINKING **NOTHING** CAN HURT THEM.
WE'VE EVEN HEARD TALES THAT, HAD THEY WANTED TO, THEY'D BUILD **BRIDGES** OVER THE SEA.
THAT'S A LOAD OF **CRAP**.
IT'S **ARROGANCE, BROTHER.** AND ARROGANCE IS **WEAKNESS.**
WEAK MEN CAUSE GREATER HARM.
I **LIVED** IT.
HIPPIAS WENT ON A **RAMPAGE.**
HIS BROTHER WAS **DEAD**, HIS HOLD ON POWER AS **TENUOUS** AS THE KINDNESS OF A GOD.
BUT HE **TAXED** THE PEOPLE EVEN MORE. HE SAW ENEMIES EVERYWHERE, SO HE **EXILED** THEM.
AND ANY DISSENTERS, HE PUT THEM TO THE **SWORD.**
BUT **WHY** INCREASE TAXES? WAS HE **STUPID** AS WELL AS GREEDY?
ALL THOSE ARCHERS MUST HAVE BEEN **EXPENSIVE.**
WHAT I WANT TO KNOW IS HOW LEANDER GOT HIS **REVENGE.** I BET YOU **GUTTED** THAT SCYTHIAN!
SO NOW YOU ARE **INTERESTED** IN THE MAN'S TALE?
I'D RATHER HAVE A BIT OF **BLOOD** AND **VIOLENCE** THAN ALL THIS **POLITICAL** TALK.
THE AUDIENCE HAS SPOKEN, FRIEND. WILL YOU TELL US HOW YOU WENT BACK?
...
I THOUGHT I NEVER WOULD GO BACK.

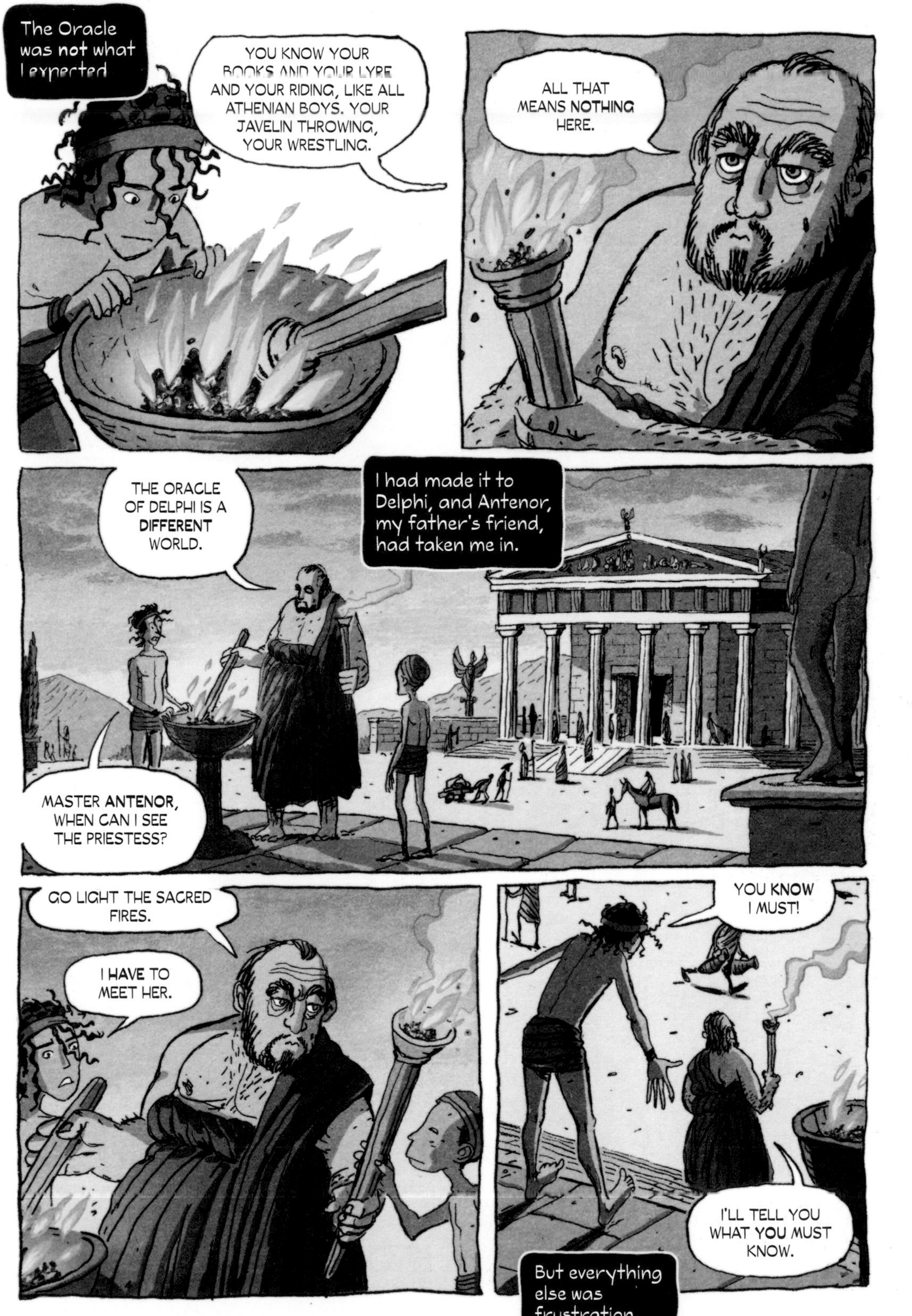

The Oracle was not what I expected.
YOU KNOW YOUR BOOKS AND YOUR LYRE AND YOUR RIDING, LIKE ALL ATHENIAN BOYS. YOUR JAVELIN THROWING, YOUR WRESTLING.
ALL THAT MEANS NOTHING HERE.
THE ORACLE OF DELPHI IS A DIFFERENT WORLD.
I had made it to Delphi, and Antenor, my father's friend, had taken me in.
MASTER ANTENOR, WHEN CAN I SEE THE PRIESTESS?
GO LIGHT THE SACRED FIRES.
I HAVE TO MEET HER.
YOU KNOW I MUST!
I'LL TELL YOU WHAT YOU MUST KNOW.
But everything else was frustration.

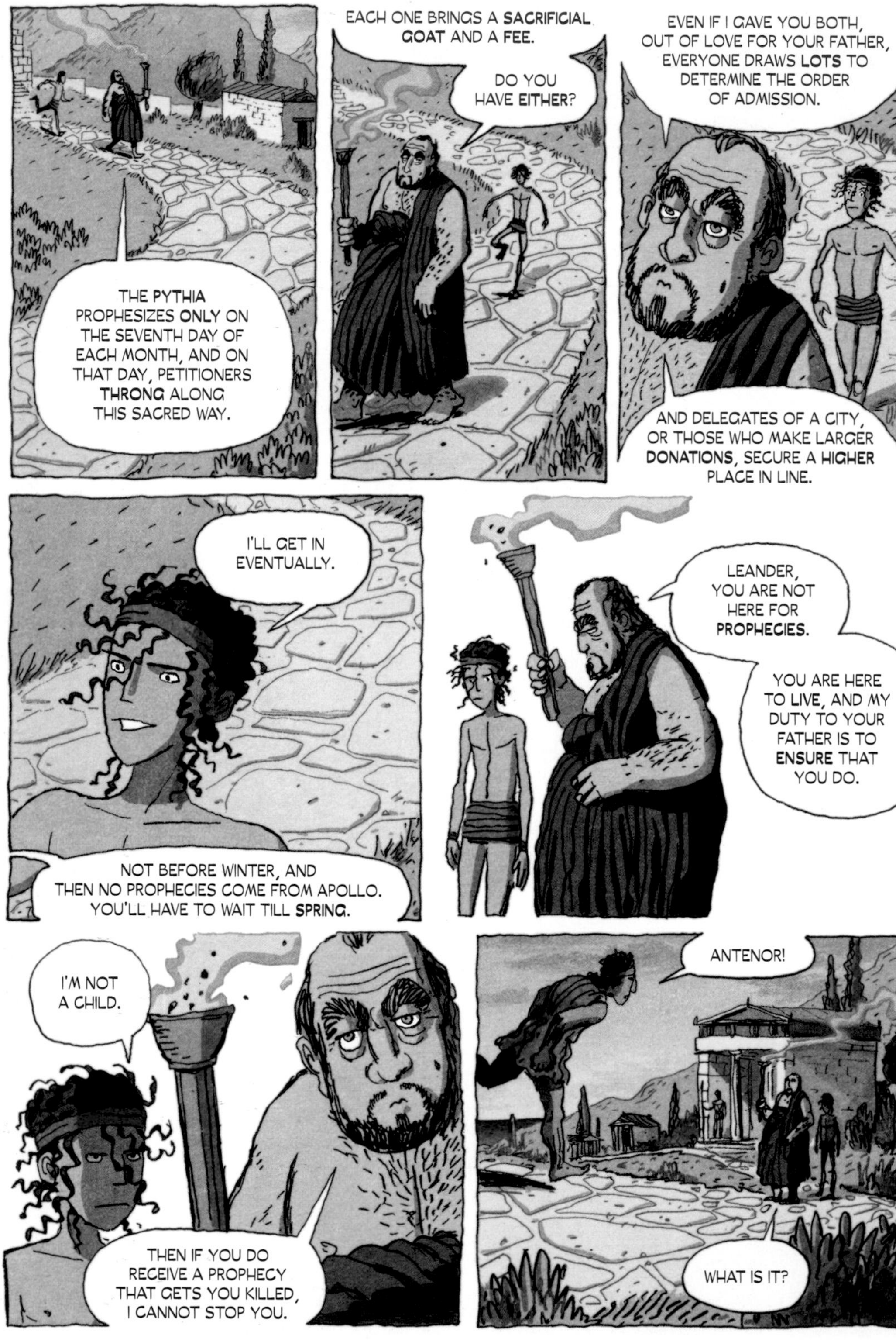
THE PYTHIA PROPHESIZES ONLY ON THE SEVENTH DAY OF EACH MONTH, AND ON THAT DAY, PETITIONERS THRONG ALONG THIS SACRED WAY.
EACH ONE BRINGS A SACRIFICIAL GOAT AND A FEE.
DO YOU HAVE EITHER?
EVEN IF I GAVE YOU BOTH, OUT OF LOVE FOR YOUR FATHER, EVERYONE DRAWS LOTS TO DETERMINE THE ORDER OF ADMISSION.
AND DELEGATES OF A CITY, OR THOSE WHO MAKE LARGER DONATIONS, SECURE A HIGHER PLACE IN LINE.
I'LL GET IN EVENTUALLY.
NOT BEFORE WINTER, AND THEN NO PROPHECIES COME FROM APOLLO. YOU'LL HAVE TO WAIT TILL SPRING.
LEANDER, YOU ARE NOT HERE FOR PROPHECIES.
YOU ARE HERE TO LIVE, AND MY DUTY TO YOUR FATHER IS TO ENSURE THAT YOU DO.
I'M NOT A CHILD.
THEN IF YOU DO RECEIVE A PROPHECY THAT GETS YOU KILLED, I CANNOT STOP YOU.
ANTENOR!
WHAT IS IT?

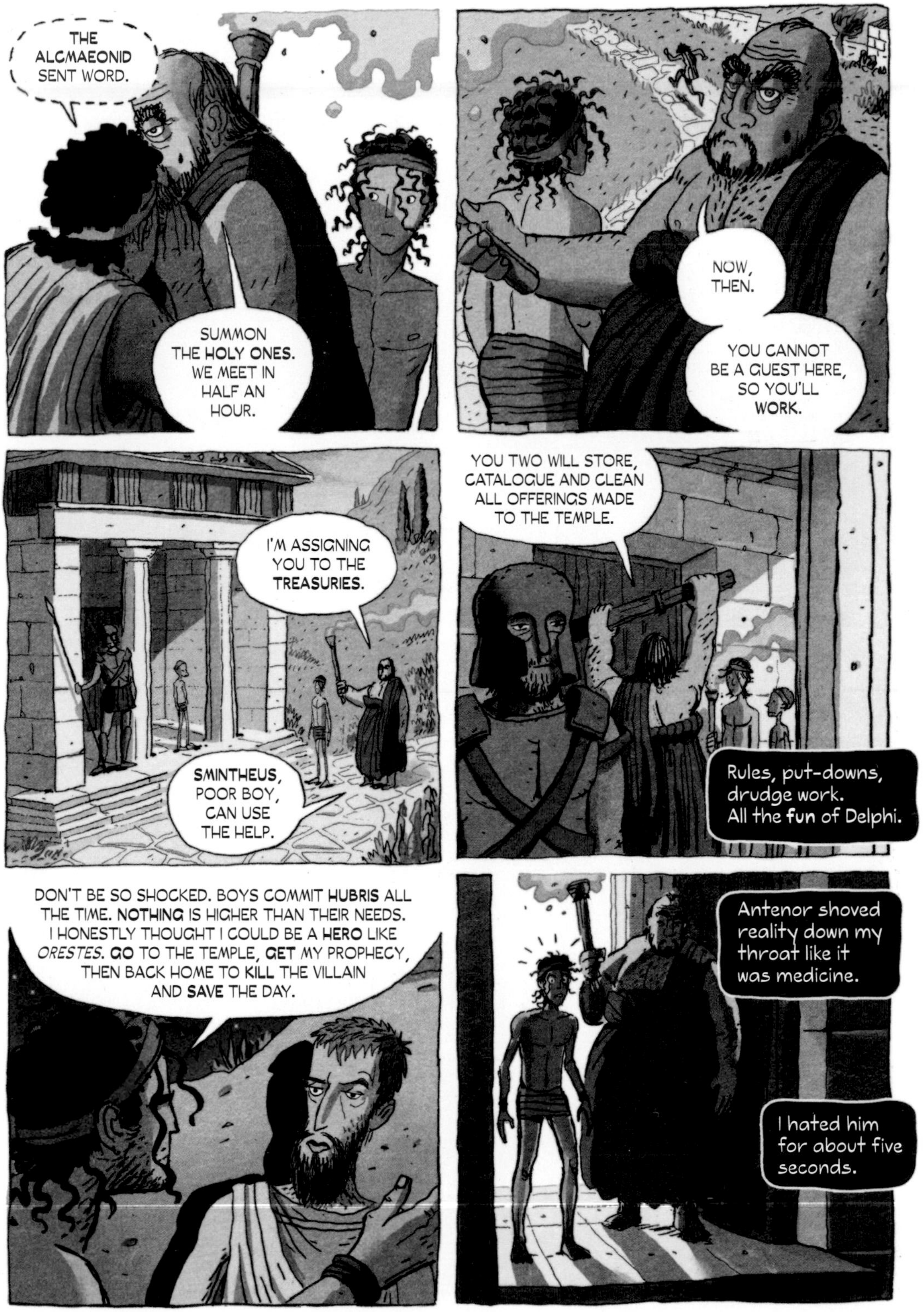
THE ALCMAEONID SENT WORD.
SUMMON THE HOLY ONES. WE MEET IN HALF AN HOUR.
NOW, THEN.
YOU CANNOT BE A GUEST HERE, SO YOU'LL WORK.
I'M ASSIGNING YOU TO THE TREASURIES.
SMINTHEUS, POOR BOY, CAN USE THE HELP.
YOU TWO WILL STORE, CATALOGUE AND CLEAN ALL OFFERINGS MADE TO THE TEMPLE.
Rules, put-downs, drudge work. All the fun of Delphi.
DON'T BE SO SHOCKED. BOYS COMMIT HUBRIS ALL THE TIME. NOTHING IS HIGHER THAN THEIR NEEDS. I HONESTLY THOUGHT I COULD BE A HERO LIKE ORESTES. GO TO THE TEMPLE, GET MY PROPHECY, THEN BACK HOME TO KILL THE VILLAIN AND SAVE THE DAY.
Antenor shoved reality down my throat like it was medicine.
I hated him for about five seconds.

And then my eyes were filled with images of everything.

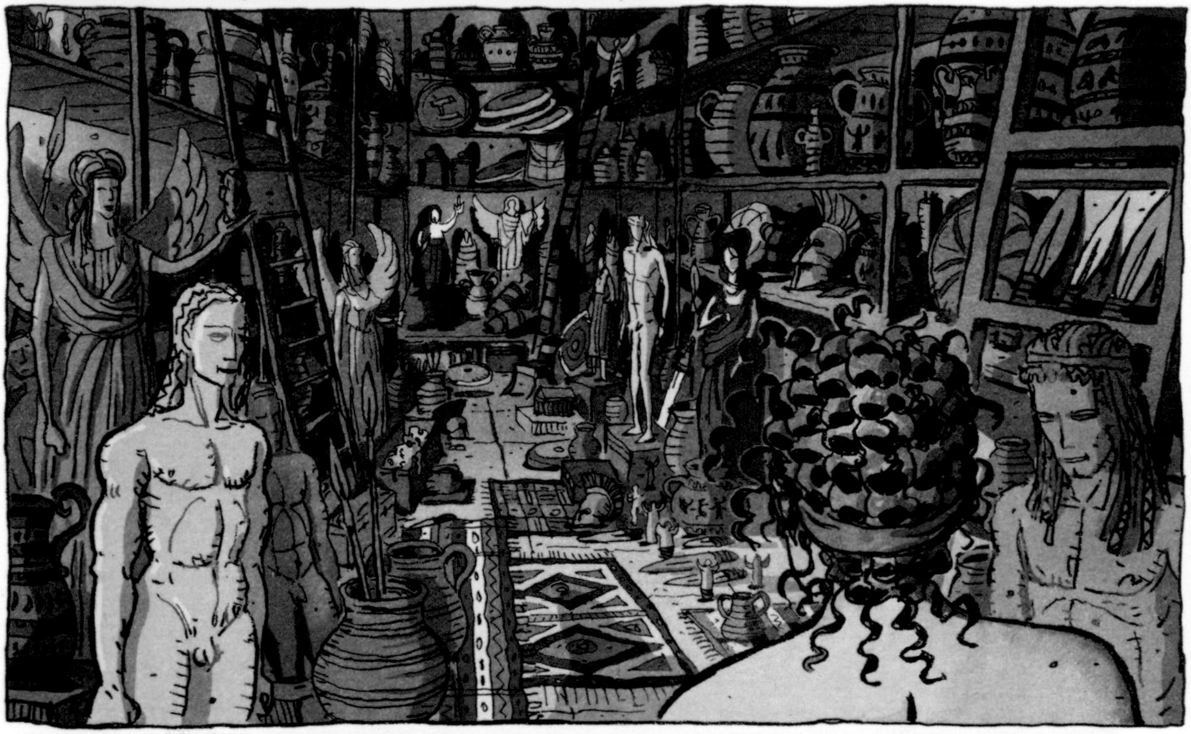

It was as if the world, the little I knew of it and the vast wealth I never hoped to see, had been condensed and fitted inside a palace at the navel of the earth, in the shape of all the things ever made by man.

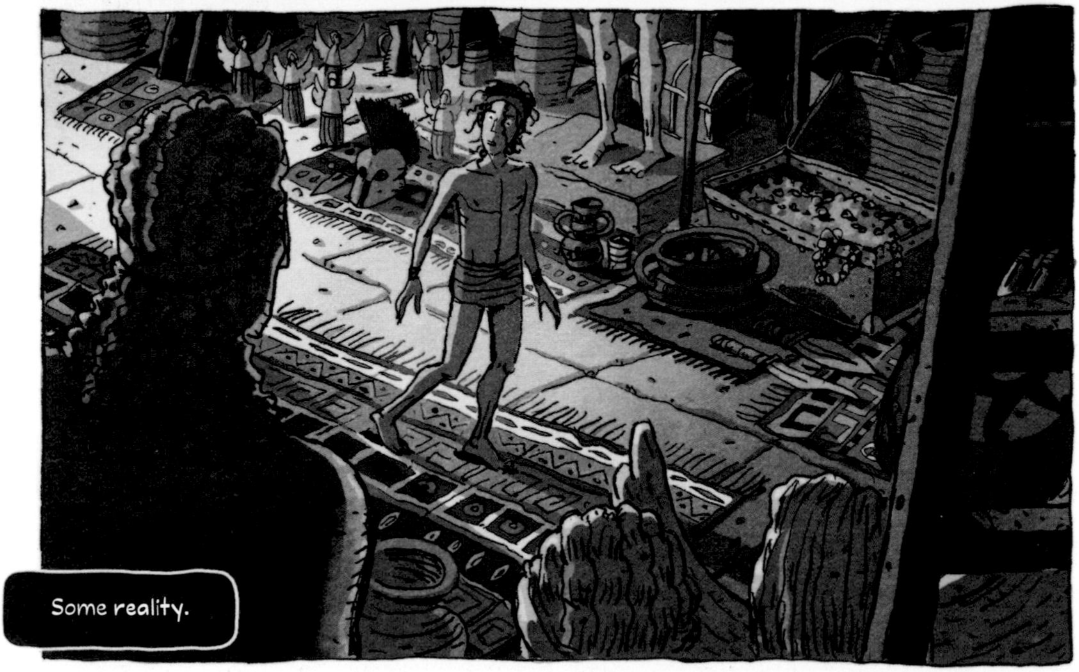
Some reality.

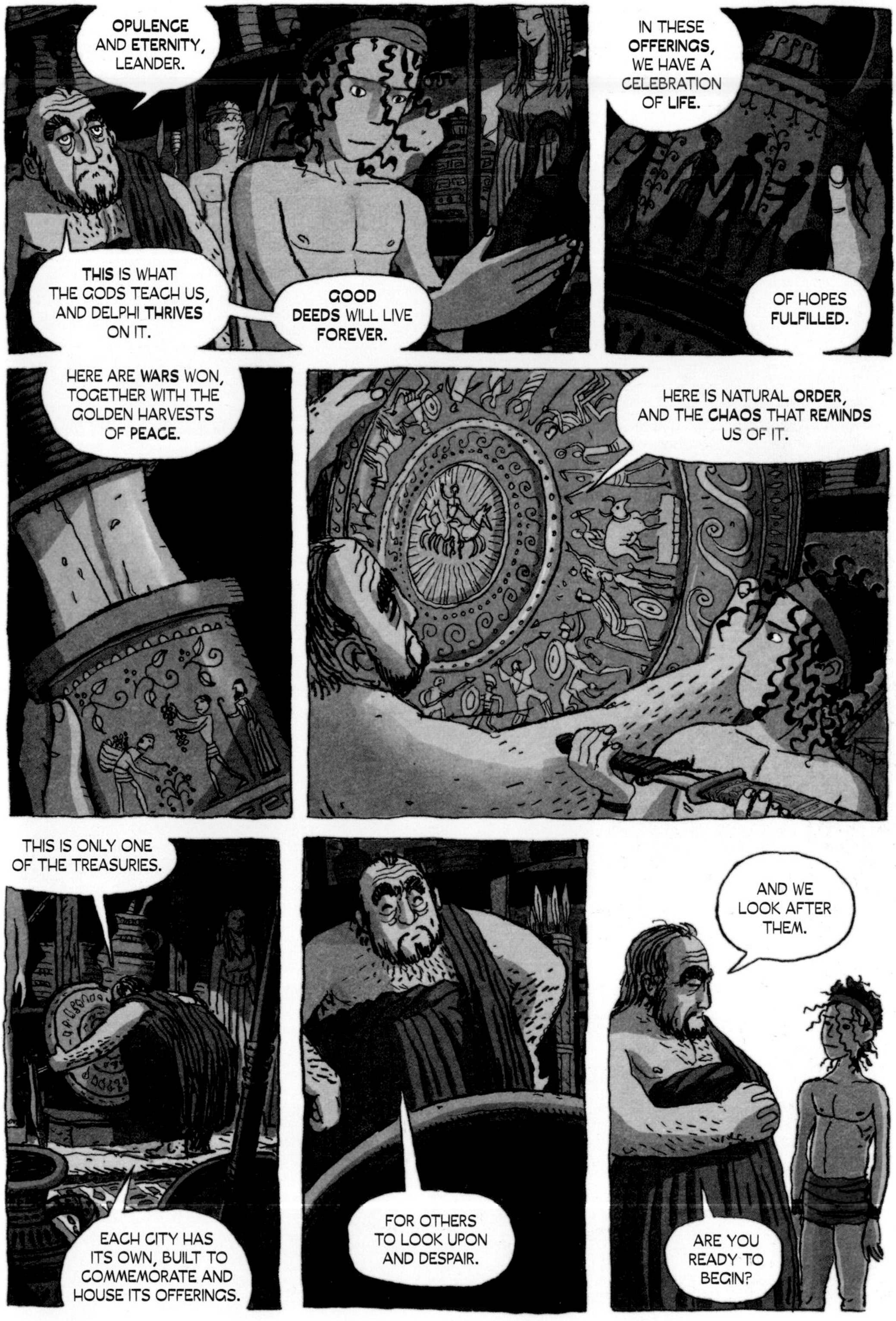
OPULENCE AND ETERNITY, LEANDER.
THIS IS WHAT THE GODS TEACH US, AND DELPHI THRIVES ON IT.
GOOD DEEDS WILL LIVE FOREVER.
IN THESE OFFERINGS, WE HAVE A CELEBRATION OF LIFE.
OF HOPES FULFILLED.
HERE ARE WARS WON, TOGETHER WITH THE GOLDEN HARVESTS OF PEACE.
HERE IS NATURAL ORDER, AND THE CHAOS THAT REMINDS US OF IT.
THIS IS ONLY ONE OF THE TREASURIES.
EACH CITY HAS ITS OWN, BUILT TO COMMEMORATE AND HOUSE ITS OFFERINGS.
FOR OTHERS TO LOOK UPON AND DESPAIR.
AND WE LOOK AFTER THEM.
ARE YOU READY TO BEGIN?

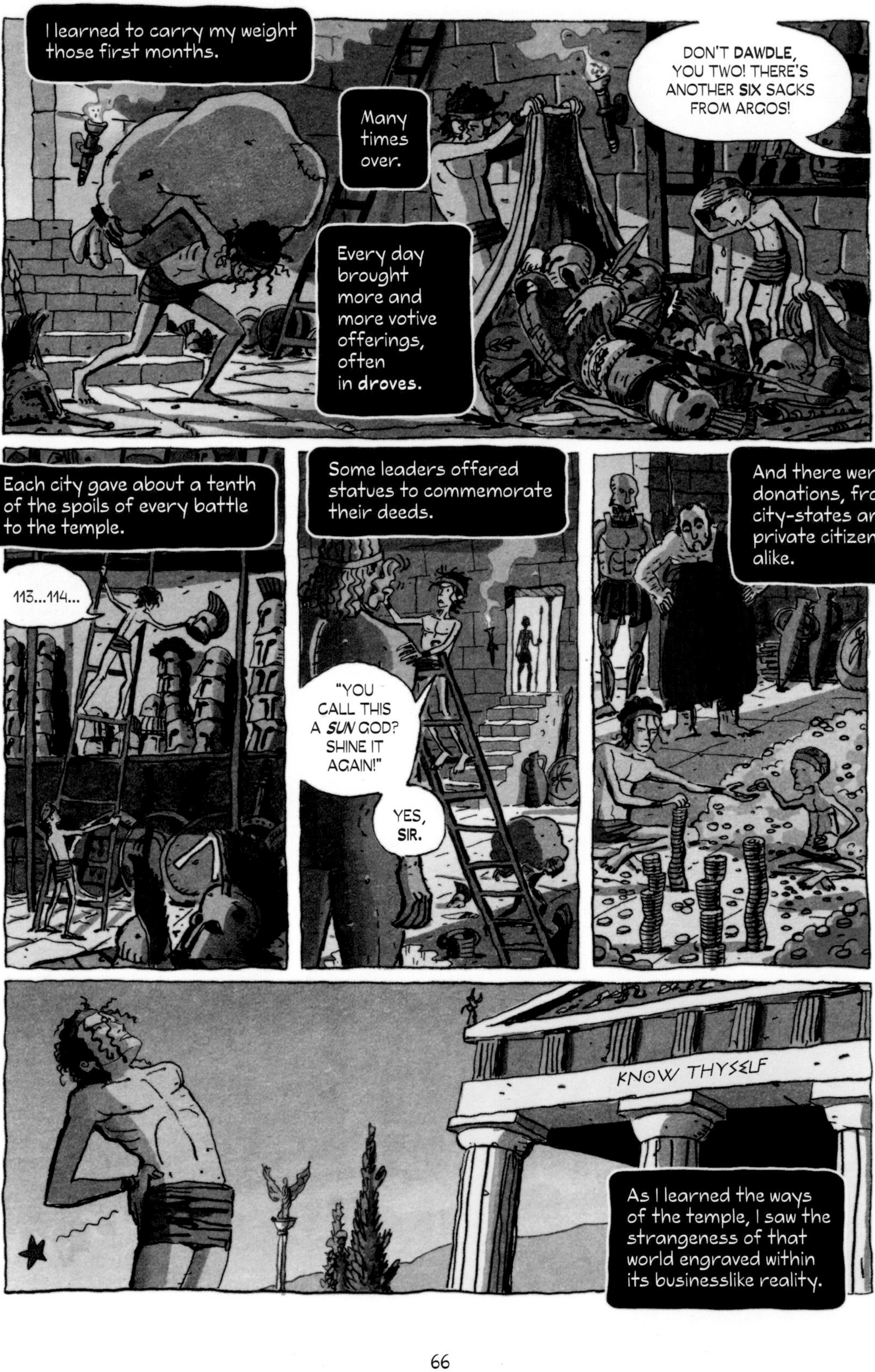

I learned to carry my weight those first months.
Many times over.
DON'T DAWDLE, YOU TWO! THERE'S ANOTHER SIX SACKS FROM ARGOS!
Every day brought more and more votive offerings, often in droves.
Each city gave about a tenth of the spoils of every battle to the temple.
113...114...
Some leaders offered statues to commemorate their deeds.
"YOU CALL THIS A *SUN* GOD? SHINE IT AGAIN!"
YES, SIR.
And there were donations, from city-states and private citizens alike.
KNOW THYSELF
As I learned the ways of the temple, I saw the strangeness of that world engraved within its businesslike reality.

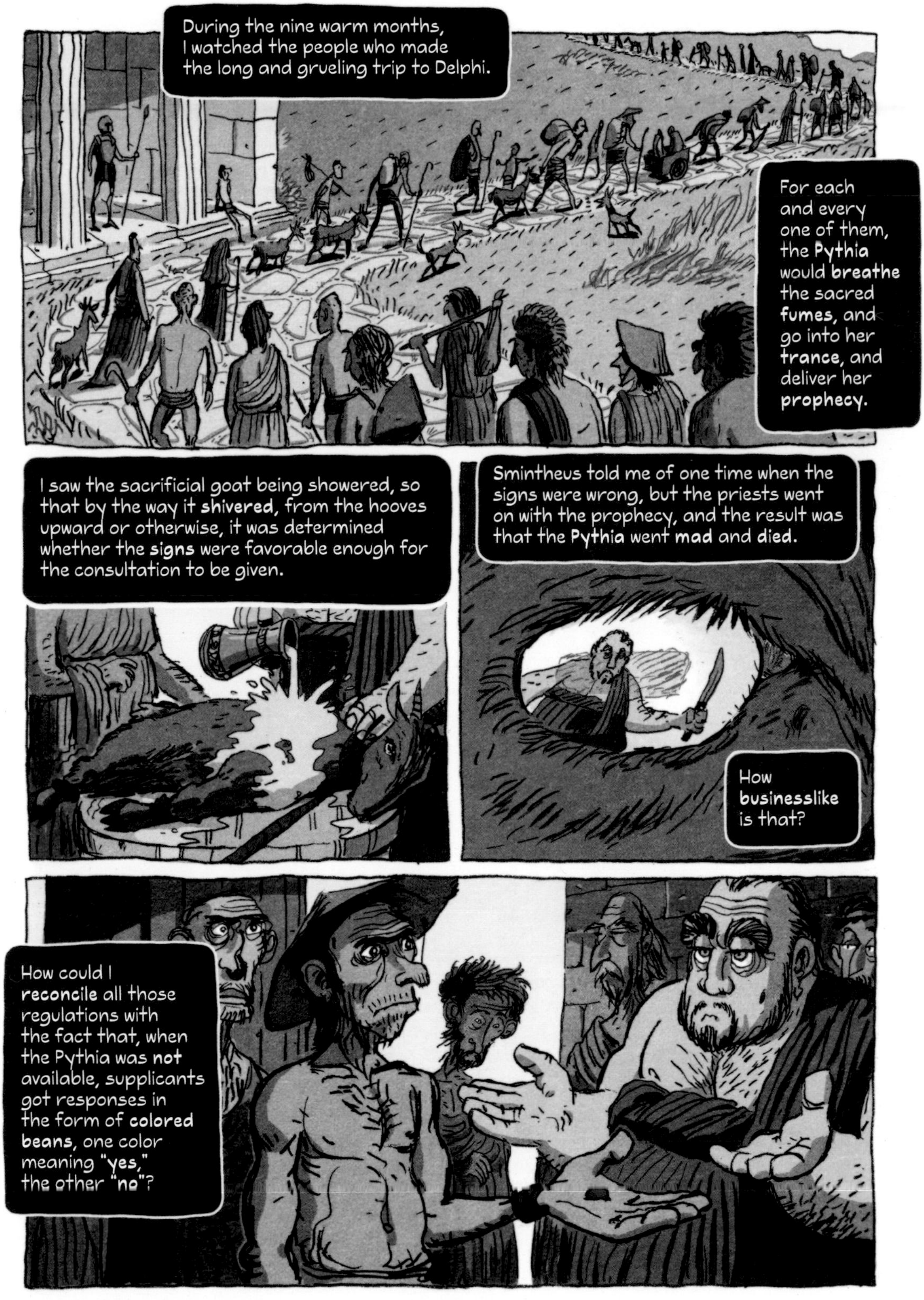

During the nine warm months, I watched the people who made the long and grueling trip to Delphi.
For each and every one of them, the **Pythia** would **breathe** the sacred **fumes,** and go into her **trance,** and deliver her **prophecy.**
I saw the sacrificial goat being showered, so that by the way it **shivered,** from the hooves upward or otherwise, it was determined whether the **signs** were favorable enough for the consultation to be given.
Smintheus told me of one time when the signs were wrong, but the priests went on with the prophecy, and the result was that the **Pythia** went **mad** and **died.**
How **businesslike** is that?
How could I **reconcile** all those regulations with the fact that, when the Pythia was **not** available, supplicants got responses in the form of **colored beans,** one color meaning "**yes,**" the other "**no**"?

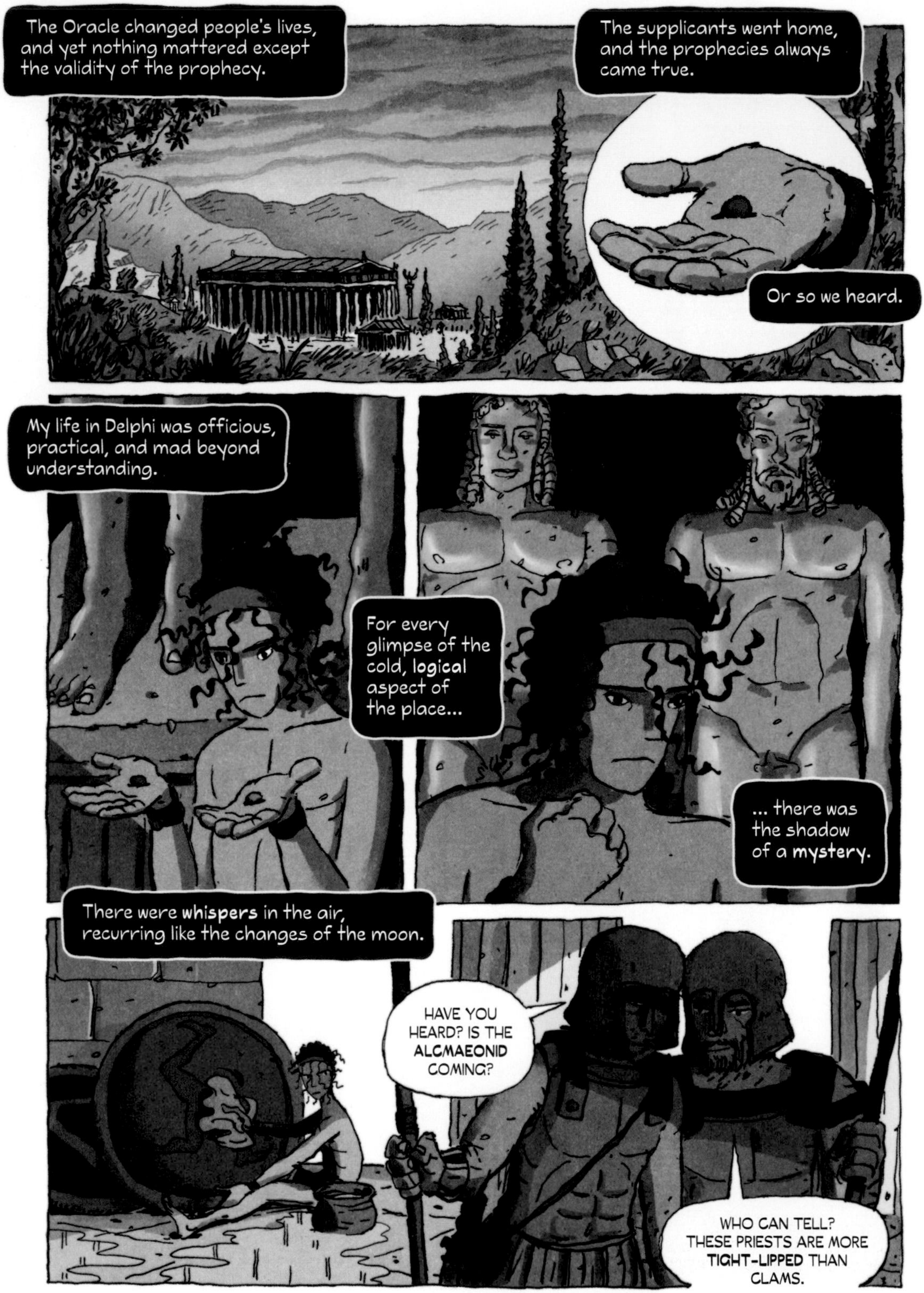
The Oracle changed people's lives, and yet nothing mattered except the validity of the prophecy.
The supplicants went home, and the prophecies always came true.
Or so we heard.
My life in Delphi was officious, practical, and mad beyond understanding.
For every glimpse of the cold, **logical** aspect of the place...
... there was the shadow of a **mystery**.
There were **whispers** in the air, recurring like the changes of the moon.
HAVE YOU HEARD? IS THE **ALCMAEONID** COMING?
WHO CAN TELL? THESE PRIESTS ARE MORE **TIGHT-LIPPED** THAN CLAMS.

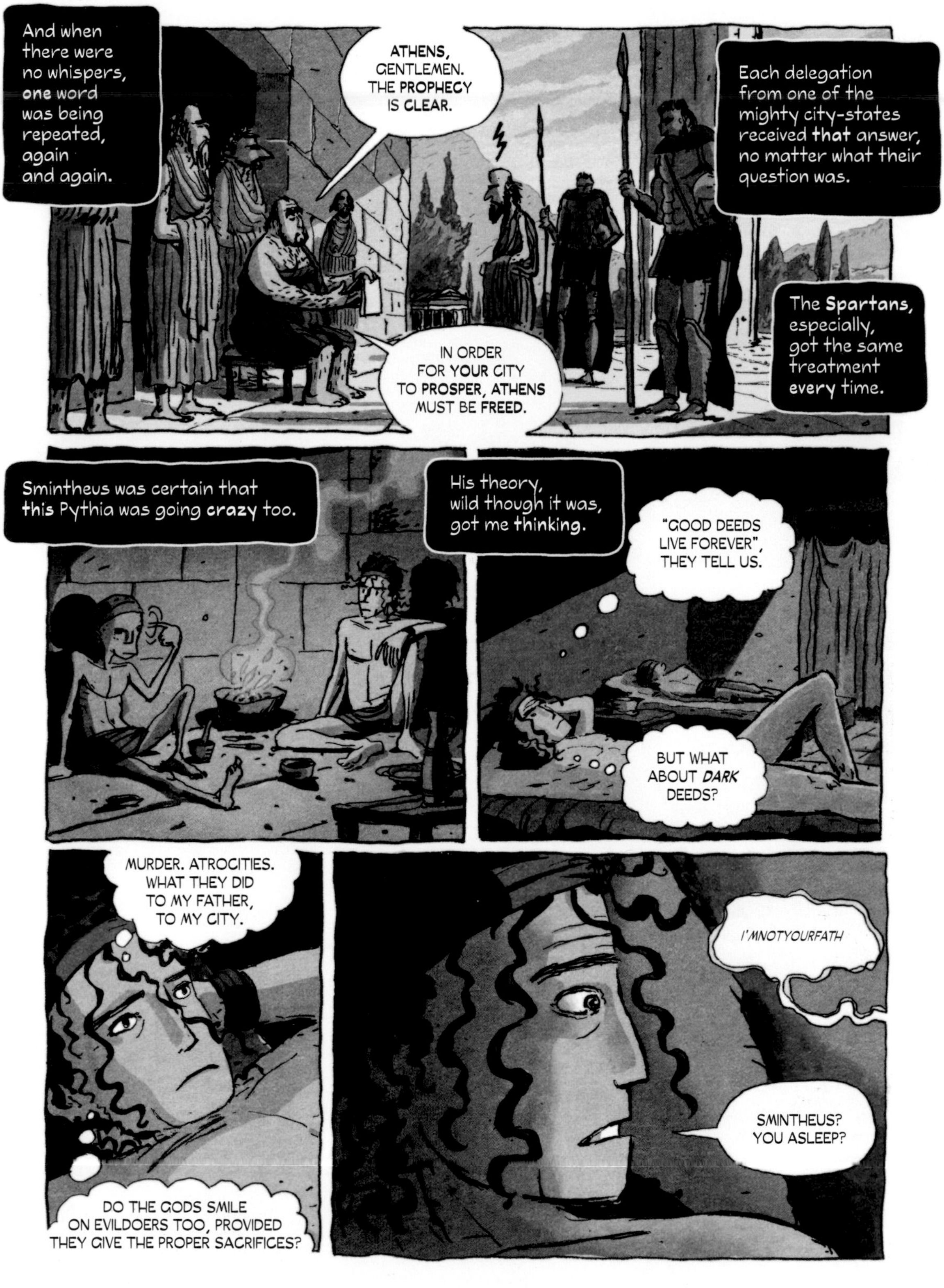

And when there were no whispers, **one** word was being repeated, again and again.
ATHENS, GENTLEMEN. THE **PROPHECY** IS **CLEAR.**
Each delegation from one of the mighty city-states received **that** answer, no matter what their question was.
IN ORDER FOR **YOUR** CITY TO **PROSPER, ATHENS** MUST BE **FREED.**
The **Spartans,** especially, got the same treatment **every** time.
Smintheus was certain that **this** Pythia was going **crazy** too.
His theory, wild though it was, got me **thinking.**
"GOOD DEEDS LIVE FOREVER", THEY TELL US.
BUT WHAT ABOUT ***DARK*** DEEDS?
MURDER. ATROCITIES. WHAT THEY DID TO MY FATHER, TO MY CITY.
DO THE GODS SMILE ON EVILDOERS TOO, PROVIDED THEY GIVE THE PROPER SACRIFICES?
I'MNOTYOURFATH
SMINTHEUS? YOU ASLEEP?

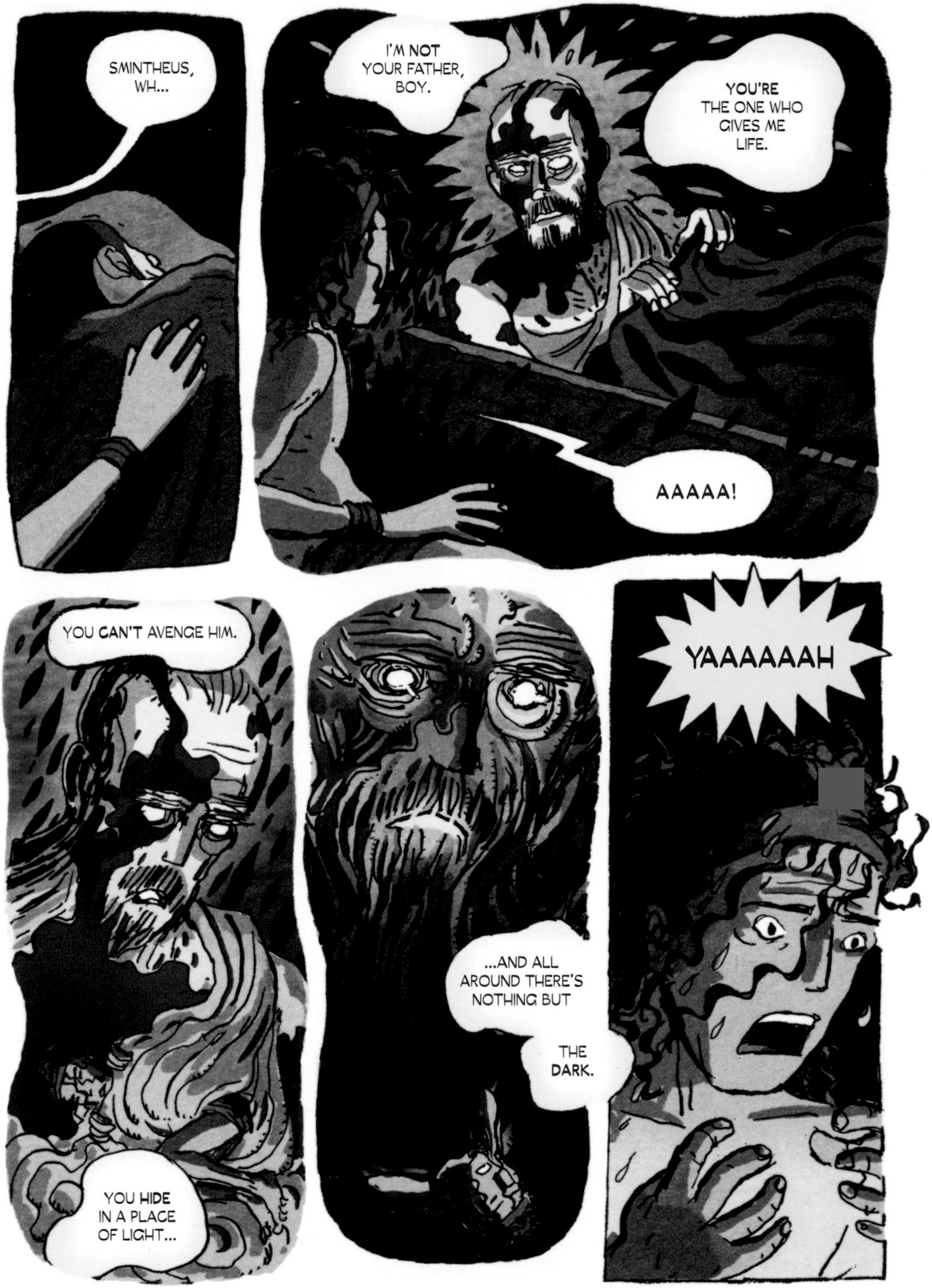
SMINTHEUS, WH...
I'M NOT YOUR FATHER, BOY.
YOU'RE THE ONE WHO GIVES ME LIFE.
AAAAA!
YOU CAN'T AVENGE HIM.
YOU HIDE IN A PLACE OF LIGHT...
...AND ALL AROUND THERE'S NOTHING BUT
THE DARK.
YAAAAAAH

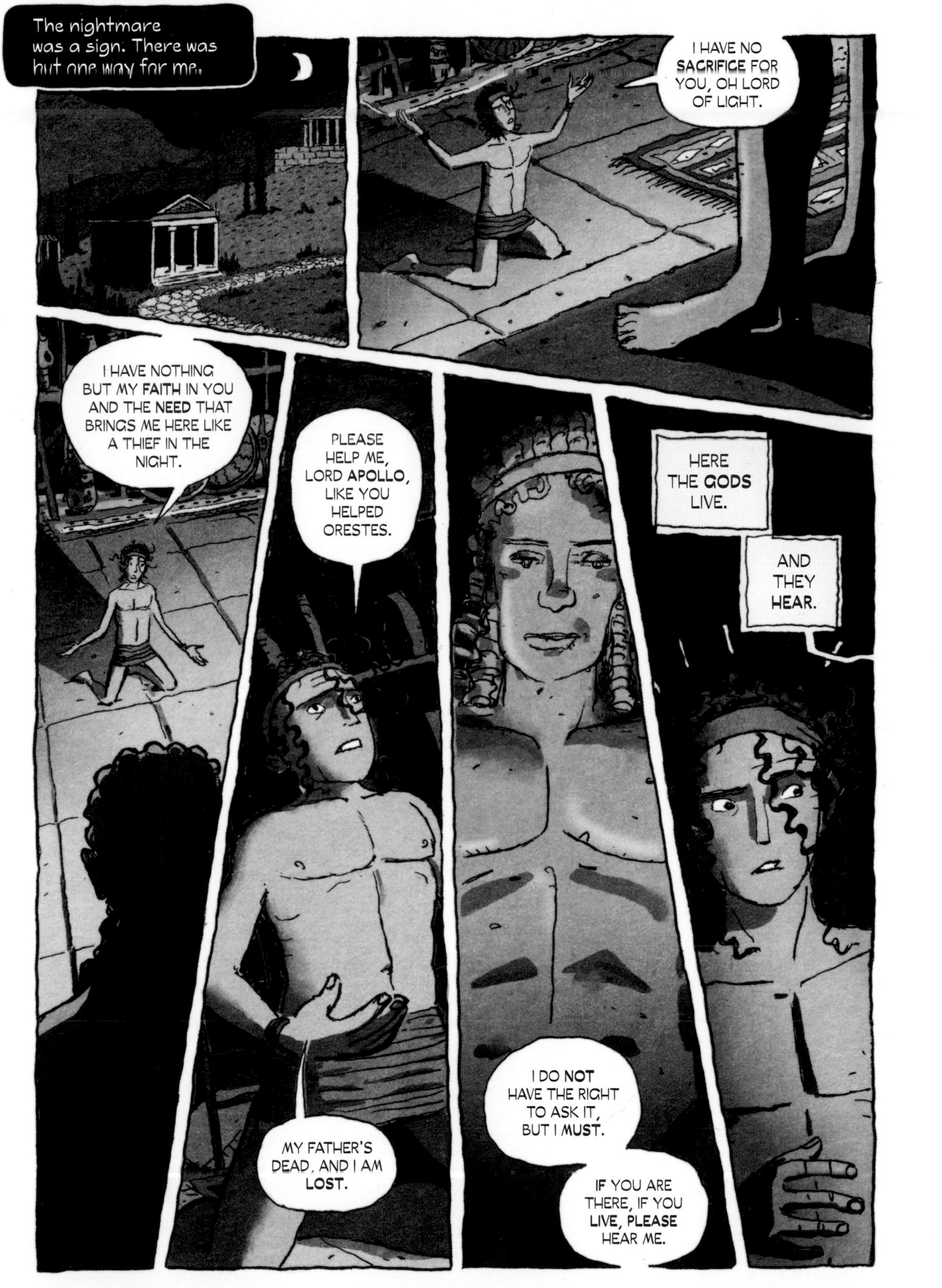
The nightmare was a sign. There was but one way for me.
I HAVE NO SACRIFICE FOR YOU, OH LORD OF LIGHT.
I HAVE NOTHING BUT MY FAITH IN YOU AND THE NEED THAT BRINGS ME HERE LIKE A THIEF IN THE NIGHT.
PLEASE HELP ME, LORD APOLLO, LIKE YOU HELPED ORESTES.
MY FATHER'S DEAD, AND I AM LOST.
I DO NOT HAVE THE RIGHT TO ASK IT, BUT I MUST.
IF YOU ARE THERE, IF YOU LIVE, PLEASE HEAR ME.
HERE THE GODS LIVE.
AND THEY HEAR.

WELL?
HAVE YOU FORGOTTEN ME?
...
N-NO, BY THE GODS, YOUR KIN.
WHO AM I?
YOU...
YOU ARE THE *PALLAS.*
SLAYER... OF **GIANTS** AND **UNREASON.**
MOTHER... OF **ART**, DAUGHTER OF **WISDOM.**
YOU ARE TH-THE *POLIAS,* PROTECTRESS OF OUR CITY.
YOU ARE **ATHENA.**

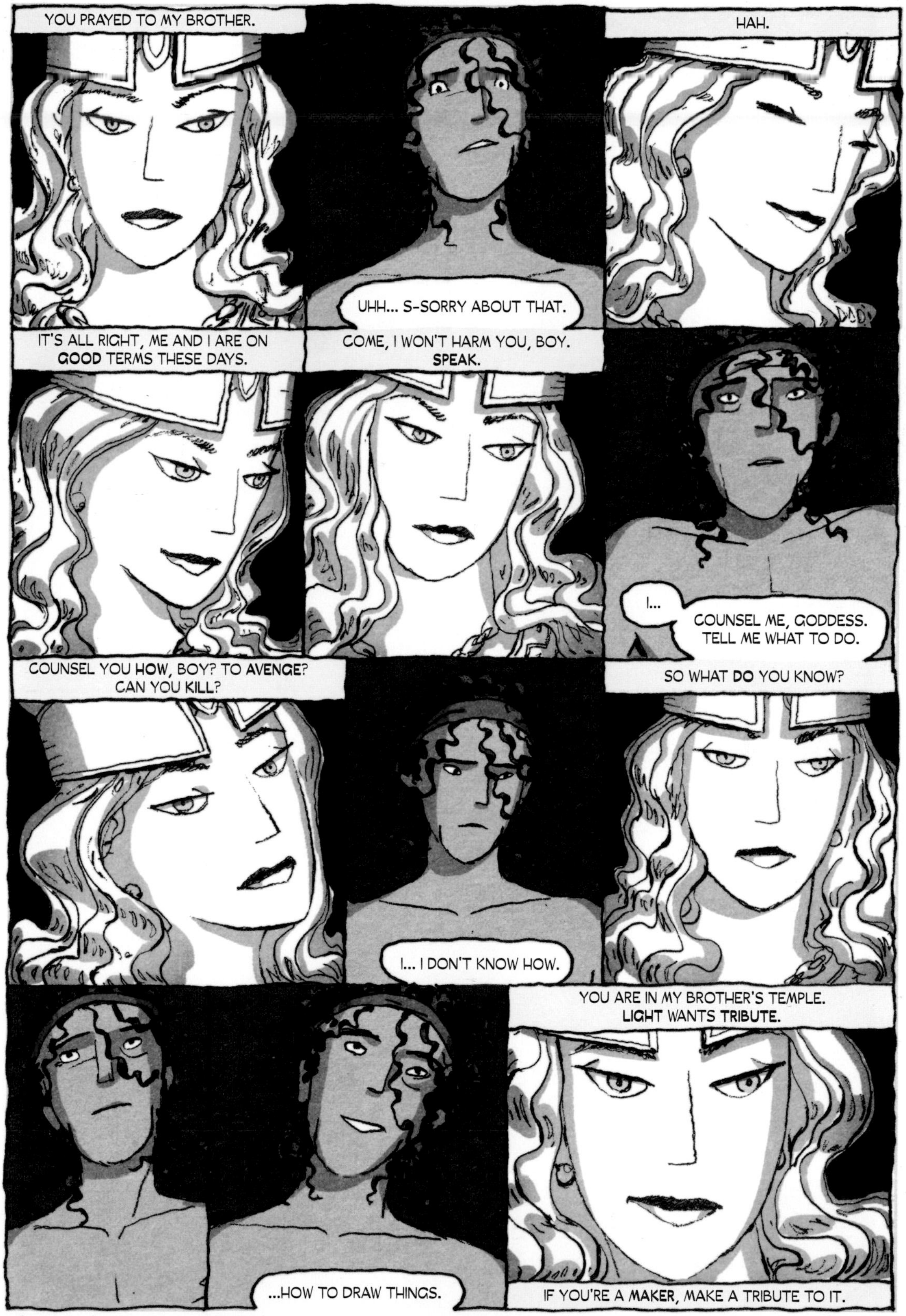
YOU PRAYED TO MY BROTHER.
UHH... S-SORRY ABOUT THAT.
HAH.
IT'S ALL RIGHT, ME AND I ARE ON GOOD TERMS THESE DAYS.
COME, I WON'T HARM YOU, BOY. SPEAK.
I...
COUNSEL ME, GODDESS. TELL ME WHAT TO DO.
COUNSEL YOU HOW, BOY? TO AVENGE? CAN YOU KILL?
I... I DON'T KNOW HOW.
SO WHAT DO YOU KNOW?
...HOW TO DRAW THINGS.
YOU ARE IN MY BROTHER'S TEMPLE. LIGHT WANTS TRIBUTE.
IF YOU'RE A MAKER, MAKE A TRIBUTE TO IT.

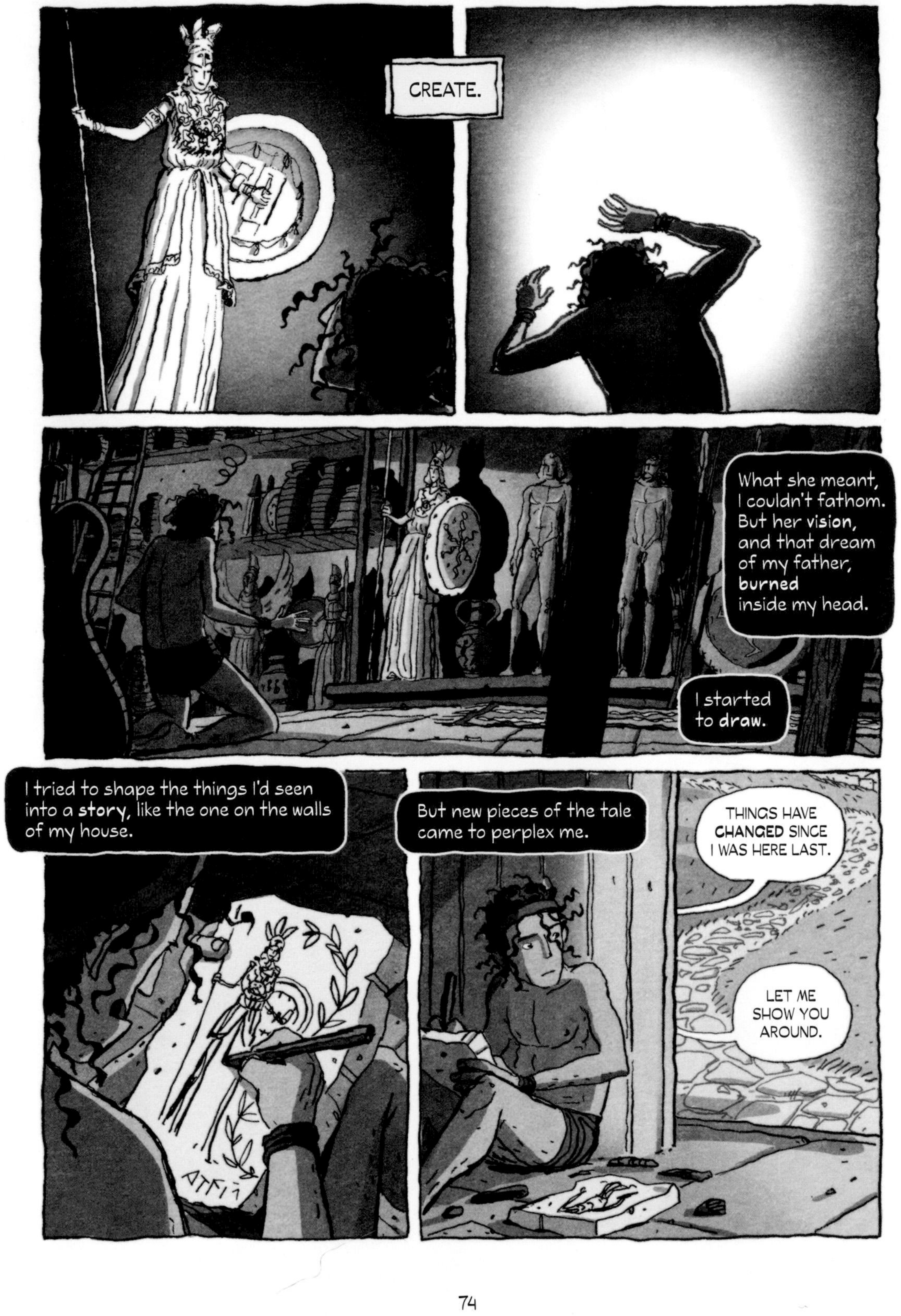
CREATE.
What she meant, I couldn't fathom. But her **vision**, and that dream of my father, **burned** inside my head.
I started to **draw.**
I tried to shape the things I'd seen into a **story**, like the one on the walls of my house.
But new pieces of the tale came to perplex me.
THINGS HAVE **CHANGED** SINCE I WAS HERE LAST.
LET ME SHOW YOU AROUND.

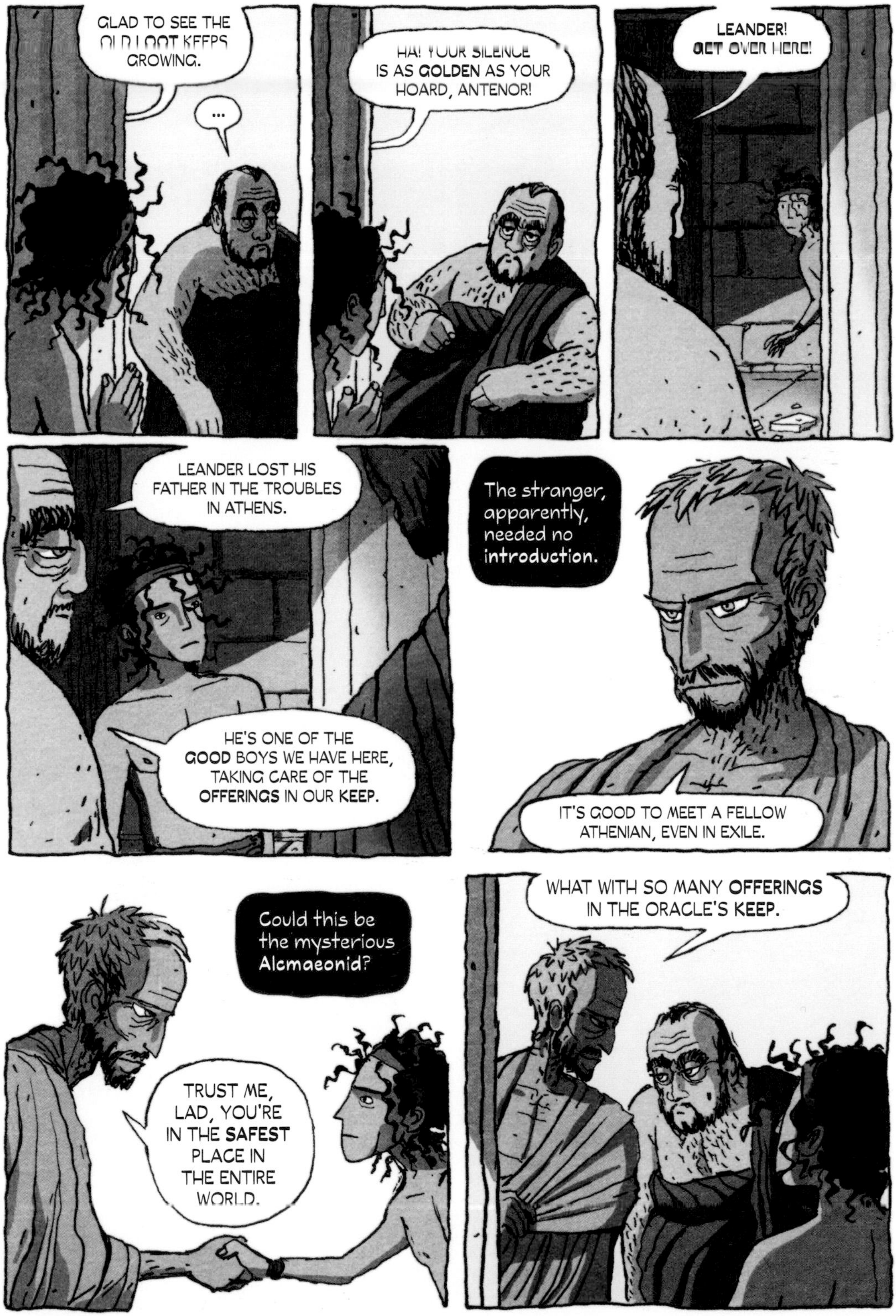
GLAD TO SEE THE OLD LOOT KEEPS GROWING.
...
HA! YOUR SILENCE IS AS GOLDEN AS YOUR HOARD, ANTENOR!
LEANDER! GET OVER HERE!
LEANDER LOST HIS FATHER IN THE TROUBLES IN ATHENS.
HE'S ONE OF THE GOOD BOYS WE HAVE HERE, TAKING CARE OF THE OFFERINGS IN OUR KEEP.
The stranger, apparently, needed no introduction.
IT'S GOOD TO MEET A FELLOW ATHENIAN, EVEN IN EXILE.
Could this be the mysterious Alcmaeonid?
TRUST ME, LAD, YOU'RE IN THE SAFEST PLACE IN THE ENTIRE WORLD.
WHAT WITH SO MANY OFFERINGS IN THE ORACLE'S KEEP.

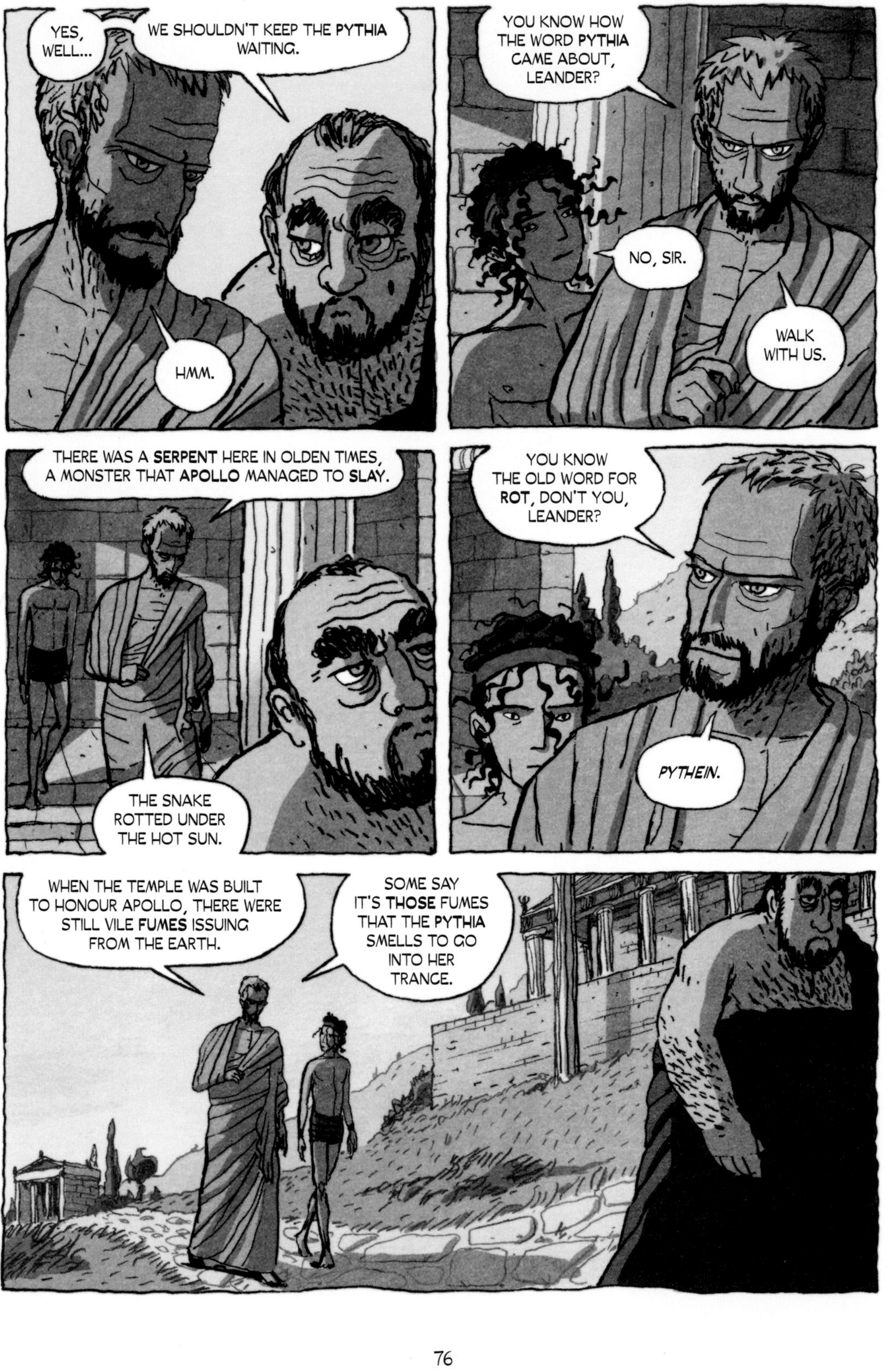
YES, WELL...
WE SHOULDN'T KEEP THE **PYTHIA** WAITING.
HMM.
YOU KNOW HOW THE WORD **PYTHIA** CAME ABOUT, LEANDER?
NO, SIR.
WALK WITH US.
THERE WAS A **SERPENT** HERE IN OLDEN TIMES, A MONSTER THAT **APOLLO** MANAGED TO **SLAY**.
THE SNAKE ROTTED UNDER THE HOT SUN.
YOU KNOW THE OLD WORD FOR **ROT**, DON'T YOU, LEANDER?
PYTHEIN.
WHEN THE TEMPLE WAS BUILT TO HONOUR APOLLO, THERE WERE STILL VILE **FUMES** ISSUING FROM THE EARTH.
SOME SAY IT'S **THOSE** FUMES THAT THE **PYTHIA** SMELLS TO GO INTO HER TRANCE.

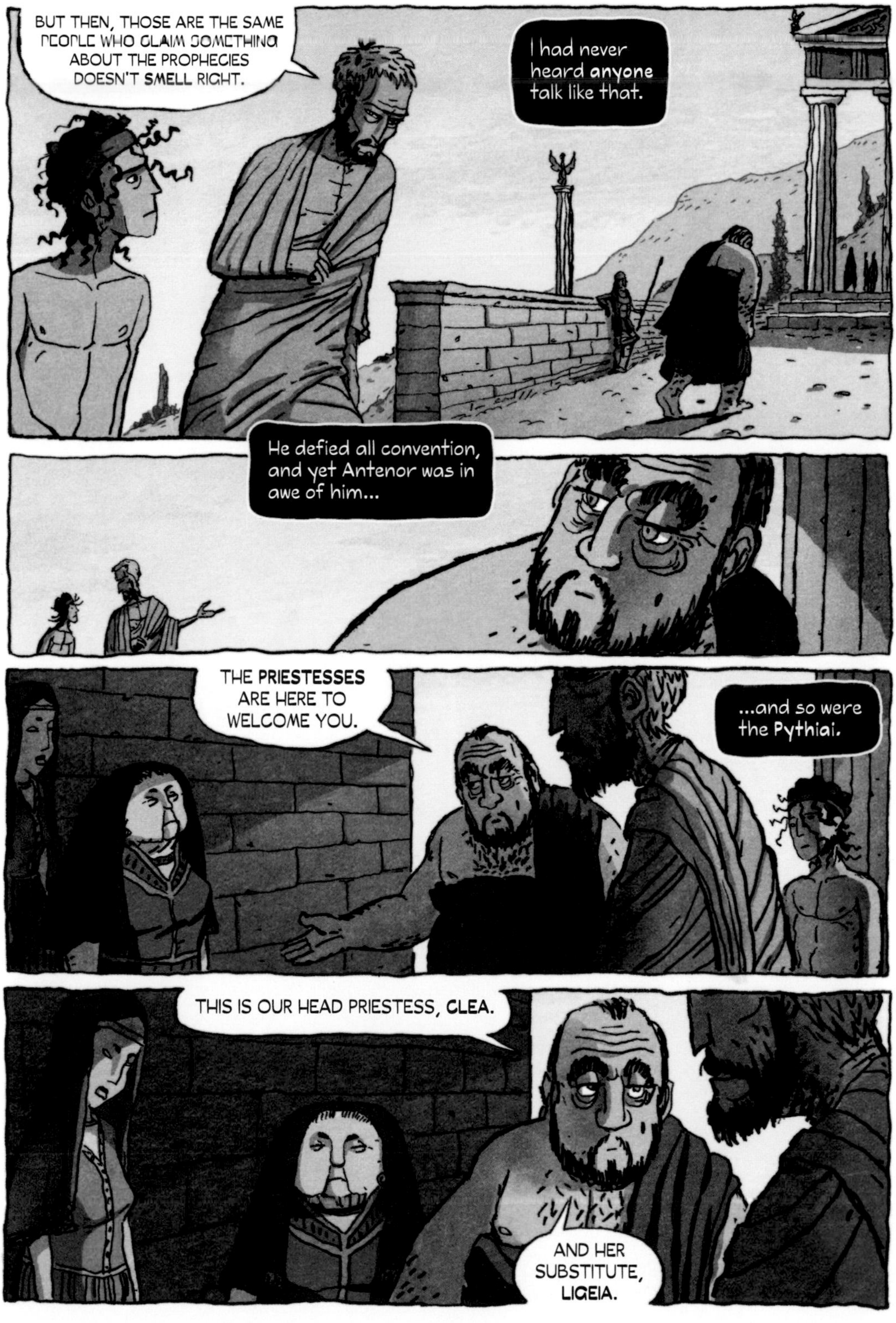
BUT THEN, THOSE ARE THE SAME PEOPLE WHO CLAIM SOMETHING ABOUT THE PROPHECIES DOESN'T SMELL RIGHT.
I had never heard anyone talk like that.
He defied all convention, and yet Antenor was in awe of him...
THE PRIESTESSES ARE HERE TO WELCOME YOU.
...and so were the Pythiai.
THIS IS OUR HEAD PRIESTESS, CLEA.
AND HER SUBSTITUTE, LIGEIA.

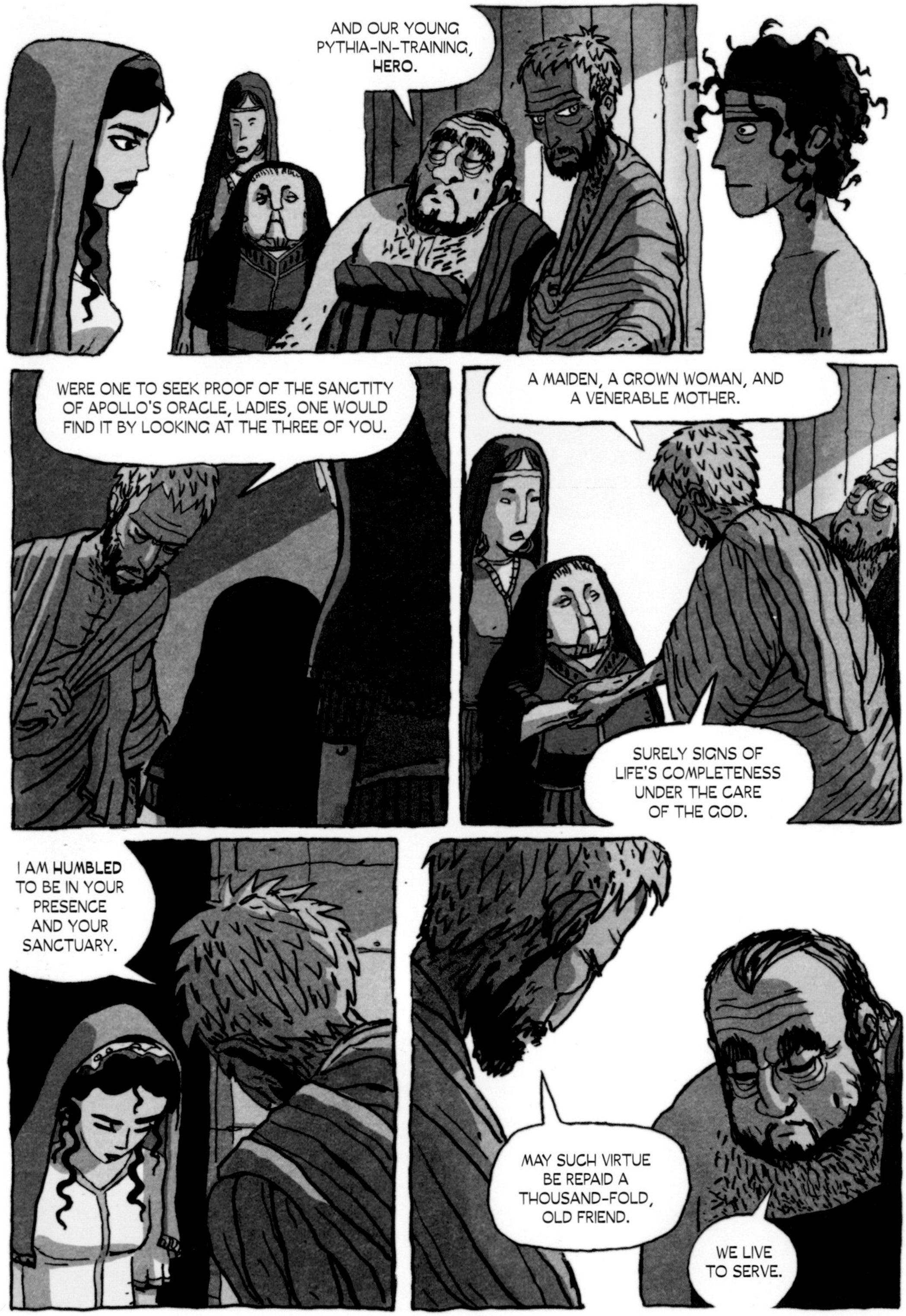
AND OUR YOUNG PYTHIA-IN-TRAINING, HERO.
WERE ONE TO SEEK PROOF OF THE SANCTITY OF APOLLO'S ORACLE, LADIES, ONE WOULD FIND IT BY LOOKING AT THE THREE OF YOU.
A MAIDEN, A GROWN WOMAN, AND A VENERABLE MOTHER.
SURELY SIGNS OF LIFE'S COMPLETENESS UNDER THE CARE OF THE GOD.
I AM HUMBLED TO BE IN YOUR PRESENCE AND YOUR SANCTUARY.
MAY SUCH VIRTUE BE REPAID A THOUSAND-FOLD, OLD FRIEND.
WE LIVE TO SERVE.

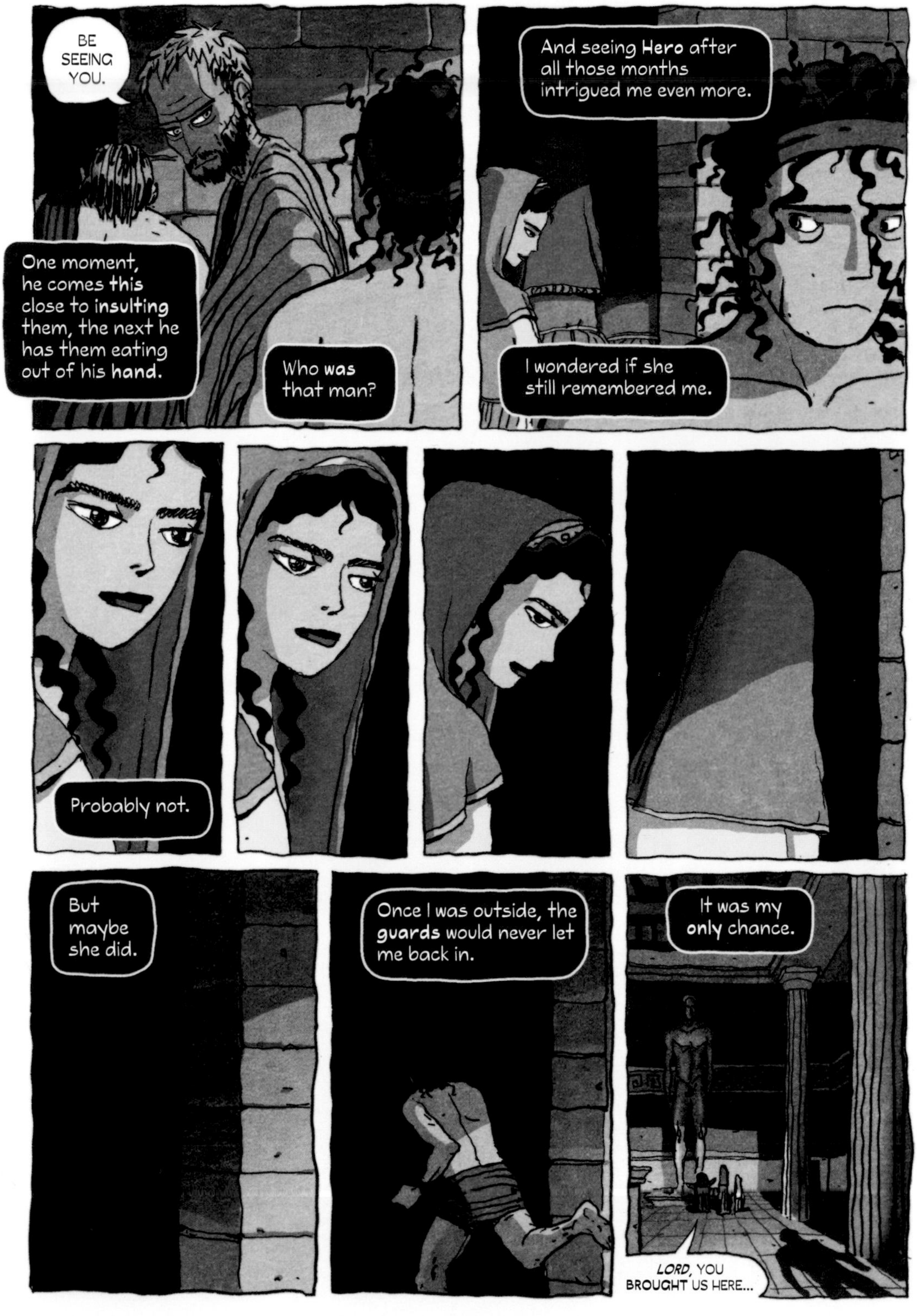

BE SEEING YOU.
One moment, he comes **this** close to **insulting** them, the next he has them eating out of his **hand**.
Who **was** that man?
And seeing **Hero** after all those months intrigued me even more.
I wondered if she still remembered me.
Probably not.
But maybe she did.
Once I was outside, the **guards** would never let me back in.
It was my **only** chance.
LORD, YOU **BROUGHT** US HERE...

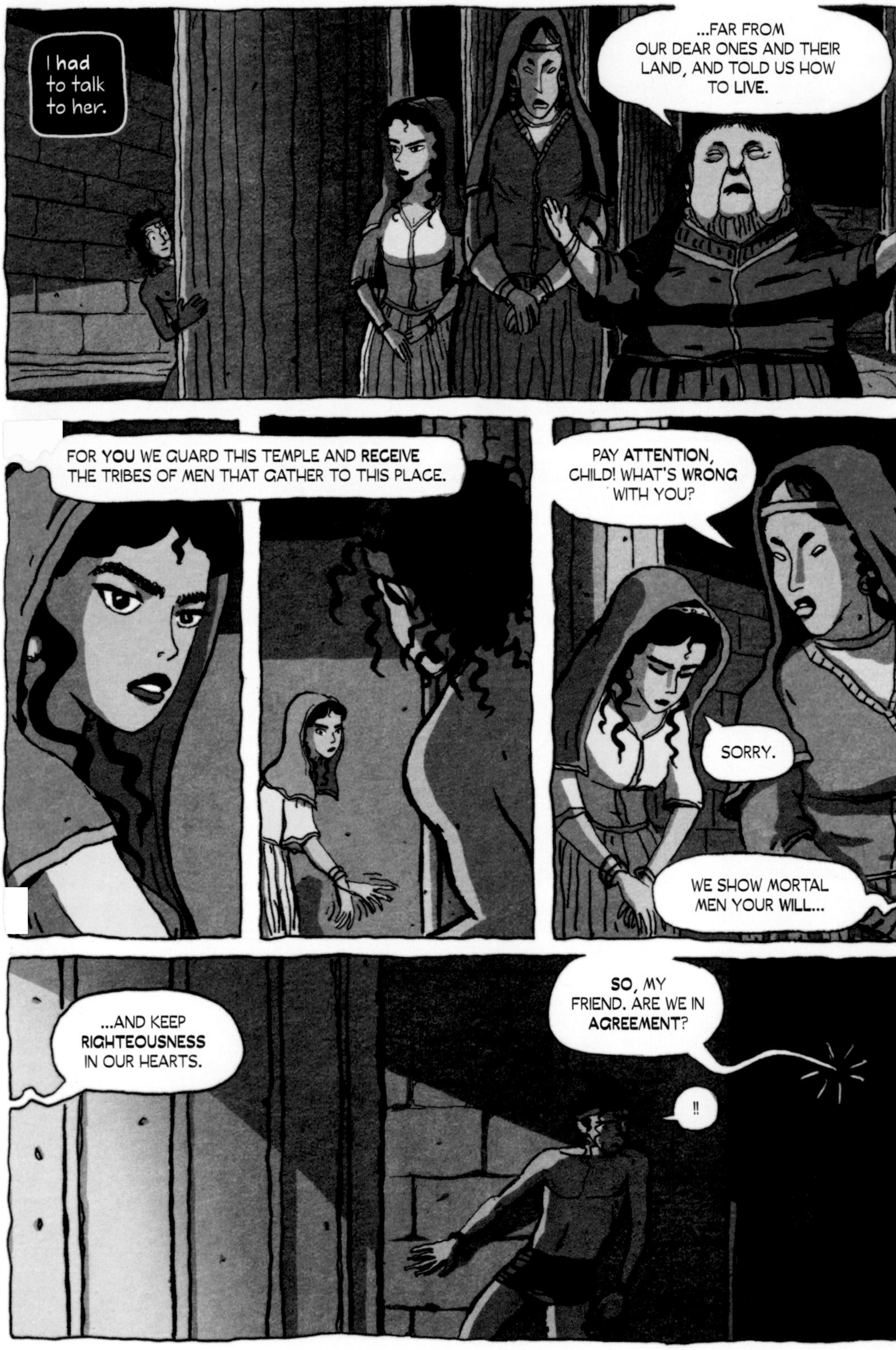
I had to talk to her.
...FAR FROM OUR DEAR ONES AND THEIR LAND, AND TOLD US HOW TO LIVE.
FOR YOU WE GUARD THIS TEMPLE AND RECEIVE THE TRIBES OF MEN THAT GATHER TO THIS PLACE.
PAY ATTENTION, CHILD! WHAT'S WRONG WITH YOU?
SORRY.
WE SHOW MORTAL MEN YOUR WILL...
...AND KEEP RIGHTEOUSNESS IN OUR HEARTS.
SO, MY FRIEND. ARE WE IN AGREEMENT?
!!

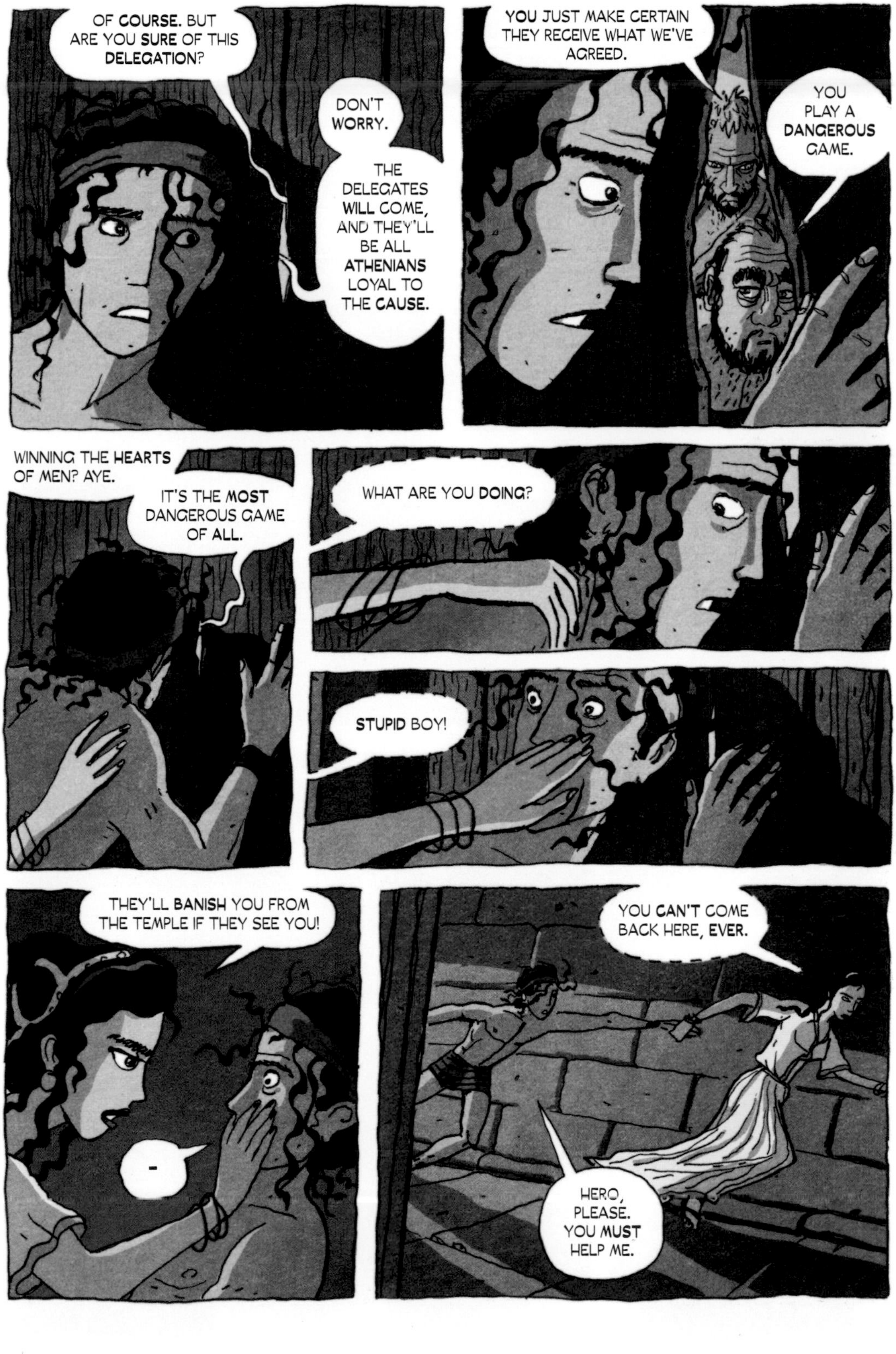
OF COURSE. BUT ARE YOU SURE OF THIS DELEGATION?
DON'T WORRY.
THE DELEGATES WILL COME, AND THEY'LL BE ALL ATHENIANS LOYAL TO THE CAUSE.
YOU JUST MAKE CERTAIN THEY RECEIVE WHAT WE'VE AGREED.
YOU PLAY A DANGEROUS GAME.
WINNING THE HEARTS OF MEN? AYE.
IT'S THE MOST DANGEROUS GAME OF ALL.
WHAT ARE YOU DOING?
STUPID BOY!
THEY'LL BANISH YOU FROM THE TEMPLE IF THEY SEE YOU!
-
YOU CAN'T COME BACK HERE, EVER.
HERO, PLEASE. YOU MUST HELP ME.

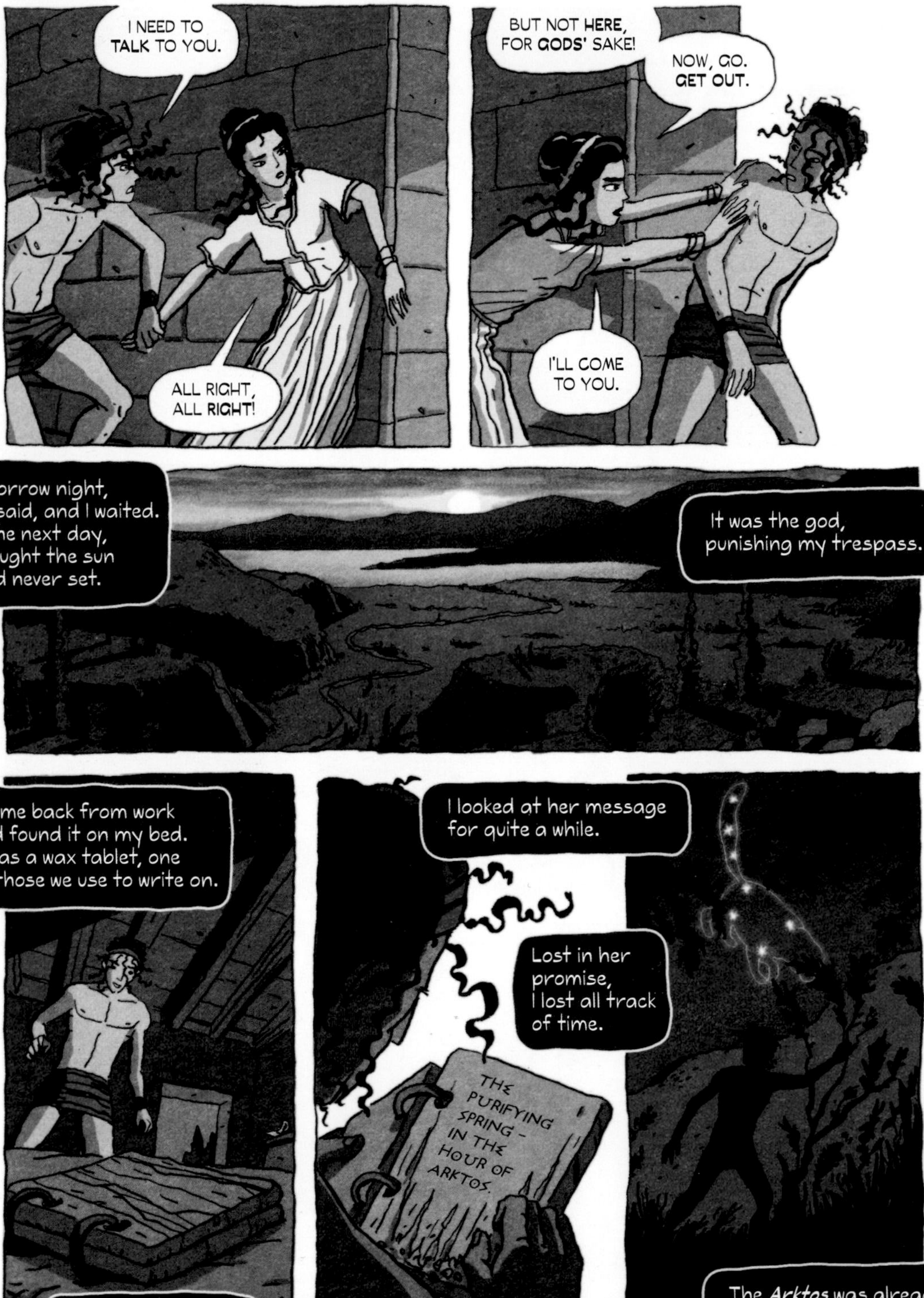

I NEED TO TALK TO YOU.
ALL RIGHT, ALL RIGHT!
BUT NOT HERE, FOR GODS' SAKE!
NOW, GO. GET OUT.
I'LL COME TO YOU.
Tomorrow night, she said, and I waited. All the next day, I thought the sun would never set.
It was the god, punishing my trespass.
I came back from work and found it on my bed. It was a wax tablet, one of those we use to write on.
This one was blank, unwritten, and not one of mine.
I looked at her message for quite a while.
Lost in her promise, I lost all track of time.
THE PURIFYING SPRING - IN THE HOUR OF ARKTOS.
The *Arktos* was already hunting in the sky by the time I reached the purifying spring.

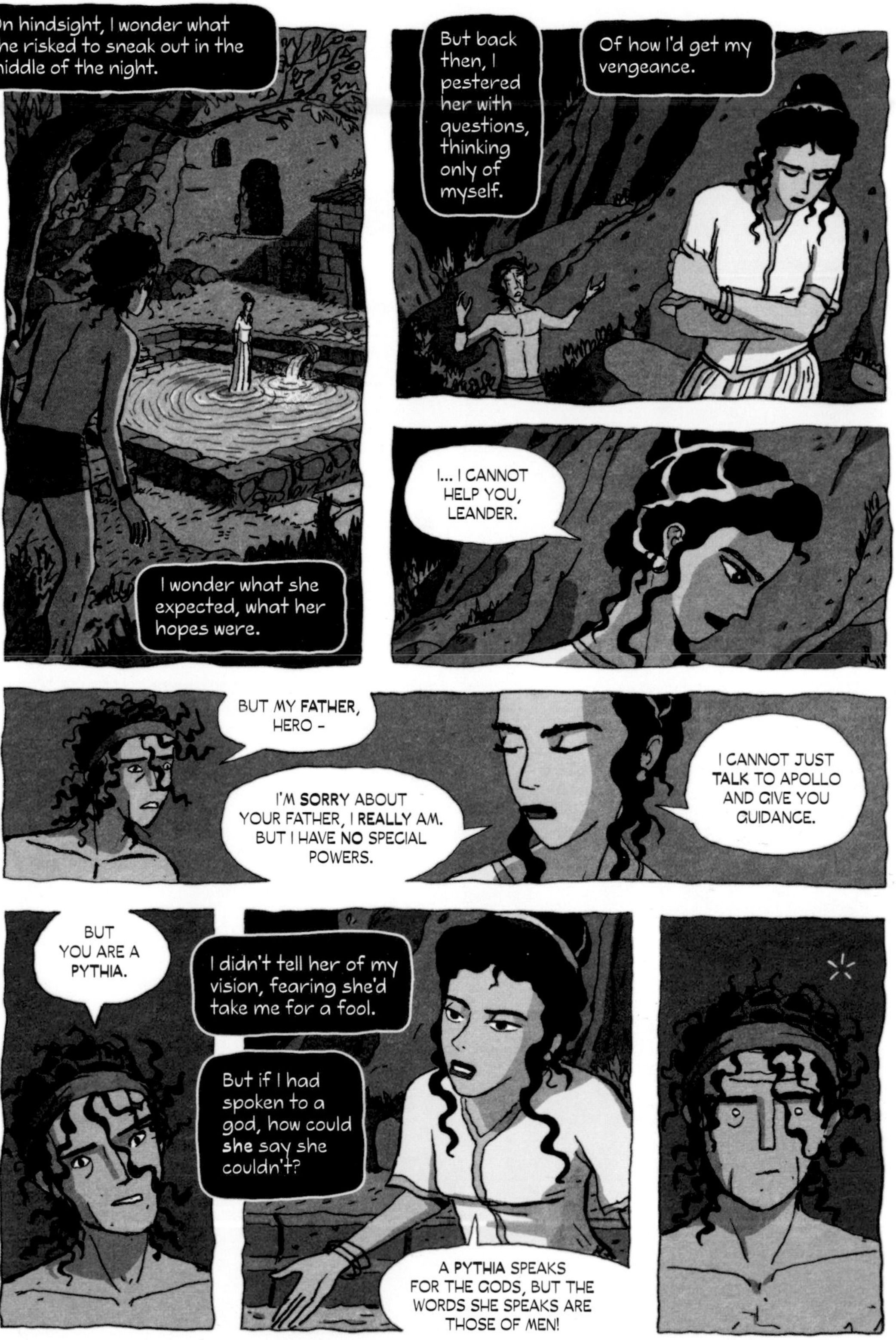
On hindsight, I wonder what she risked to sneak out in the middle of the night.
I wonder what she expected, what her hopes were.
But back then, I pestered her with questions, thinking only of myself.
Of how I'd get my vengeance.
I... I CANNOT HELP YOU, LEANDER.
BUT MY FATHER, HERO –
I'M SORRY ABOUT YOUR FATHER, I REALLY AM. BUT I HAVE NO SPECIAL POWERS.
I CANNOT JUST TALK TO APOLLO AND GIVE YOU GUIDANCE.
BUT YOU ARE A PYTHIA.
I didn't tell her of my vision, fearing she'd take me for a fool.
But if I had spoken to a god, how could she say she couldn't?
A PYTHIA SPEAKS FOR THE GODS, BUT THE WORDS SHE SPEAKS ARE THOSE OF MEN!

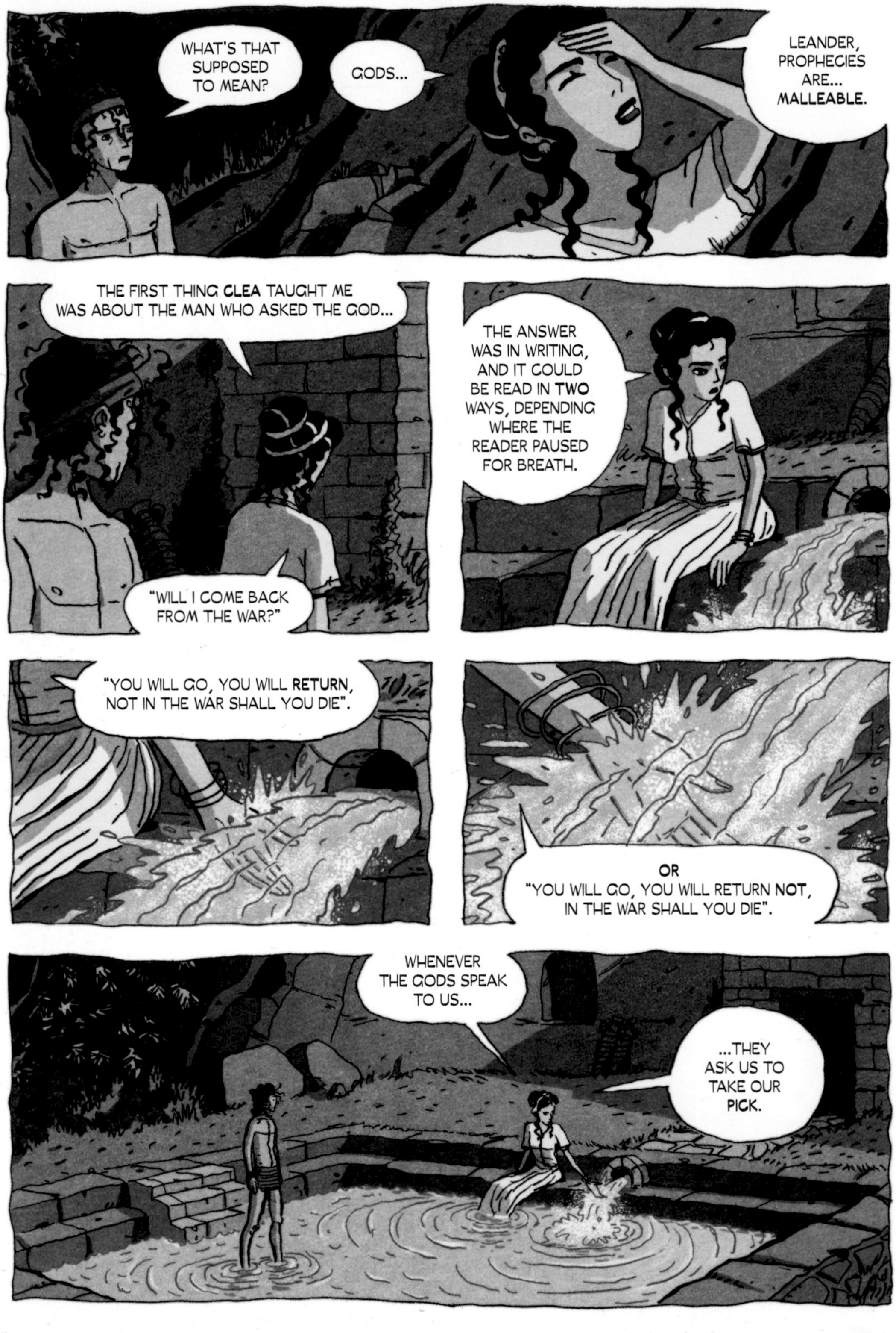

WHAT'S THAT SUPPOSED TO MEAN?
GODS...
LEANDER, PROPHECIES ARE... MALLEABLE.
THE FIRST THING CLEA TAUGHT ME WAS ABOUT THE MAN WHO ASKED THE GOD...
"WILL I COME BACK FROM THE WAR?"
THE ANSWER WAS IN WRITING, AND IT COULD BE READ IN TWO WAYS, DEPENDING WHERE THE READER PAUSED FOR BREATH.
"YOU WILL GO, YOU WILL RETURN, NOT IN THE WAR SHALL YOU DIE".
OR "YOU WILL GO, YOU WILL RETURN NOT, IN THE WAR SHALL YOU DIE".
WHENEVER THE GODS SPEAK TO US...
...THEY ASK US TO TAKE OUR PICK.

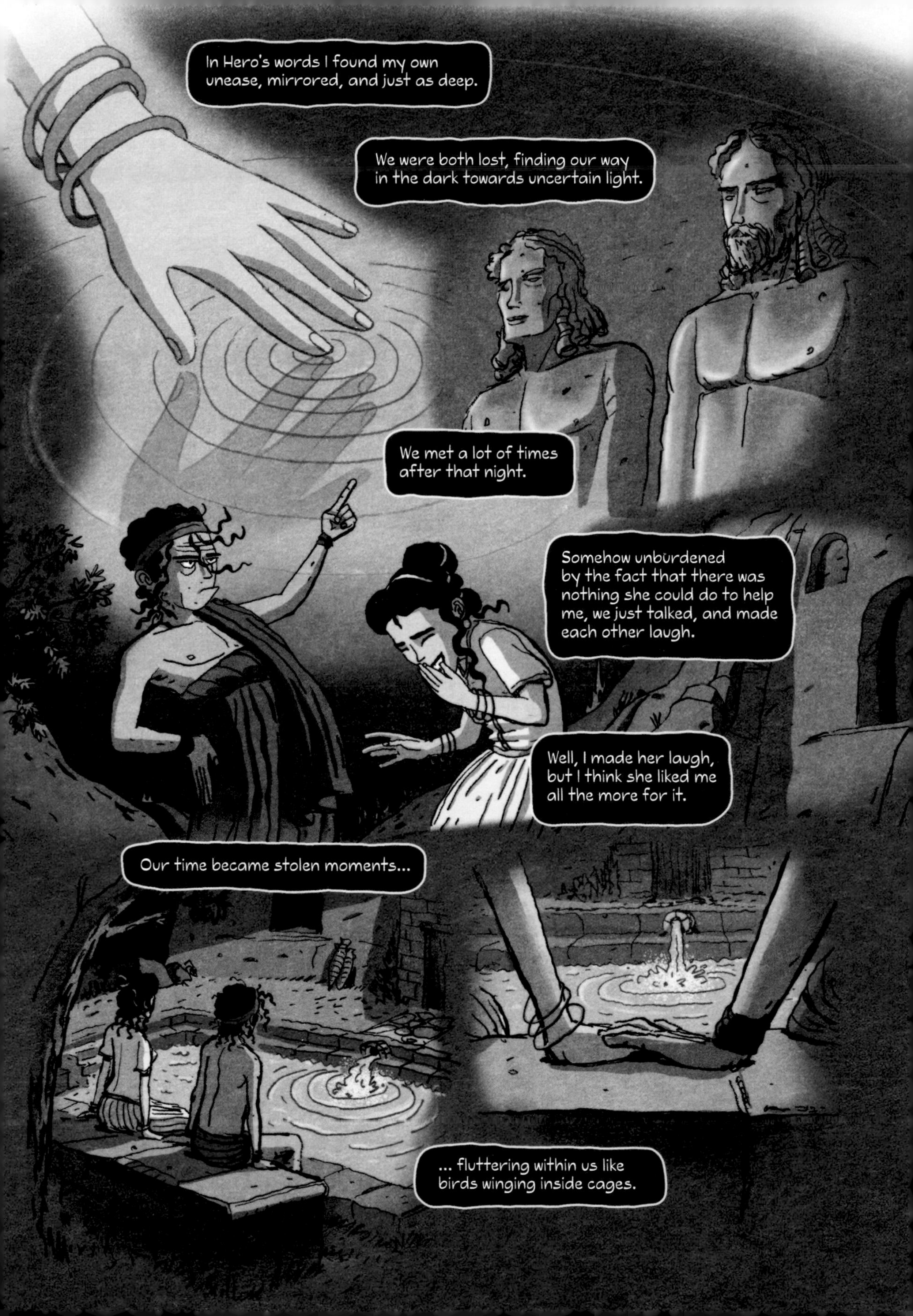
In Hero's words I found my own unease, mirrored, and just as deep.
We were both lost, finding our way in the dark towards uncertain light.
We met a lot of times after that night.
Somehow unburdened by the fact that there was nothing she could do to help me, we just talked, and made each other laugh.
Well, I made her laugh, but I think she liked me all the more for it.
Our time became stolen moments...
... fluttering within us like birds winging inside cages.

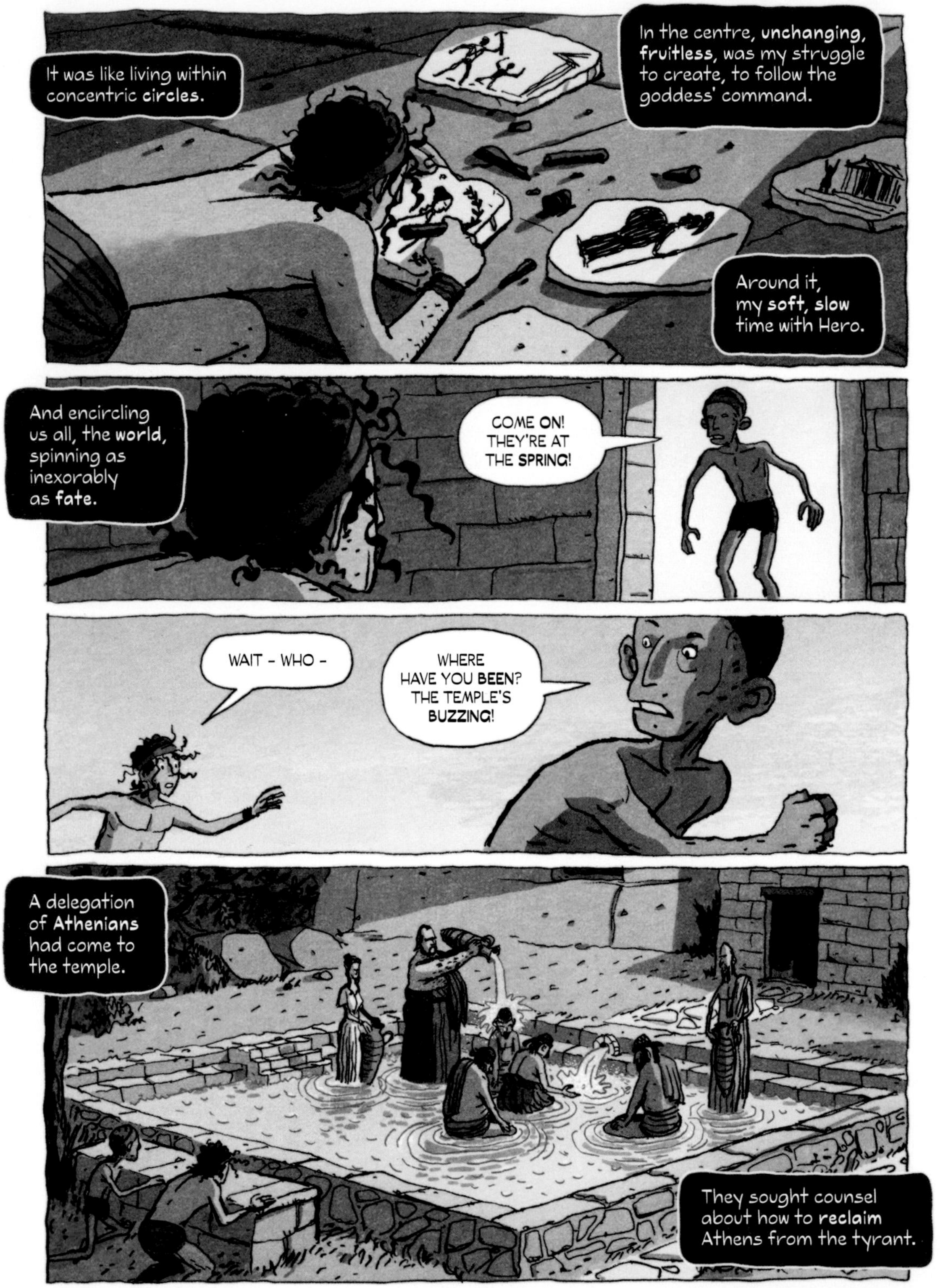
It was like living within concentric circles.
In the centre, unchanging, fruitless, was my struggle to create, to follow the goddess' command.
Around it, my soft, slow time with Hero.
And encircling us all, the world, spinning as inexorably as fate.
COME ON! THEY'RE AT THE SPRING!
WAIT - WHO -
WHERE HAVE YOU BEEN? THE TEMPLE'S BUZZING!
A delegation of Athenians had come to the temple.
They sought counsel about how to reclaim Athens from the tyrant.

WHO WILL SPEAK FOR YOU?

WHO WILL ASK THE GOD?

I WILL.

YOUR **NAME**, ATHENIAN?

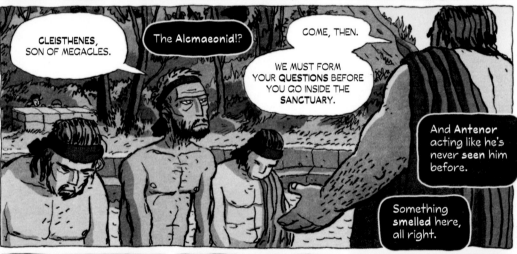

CLEISTHENES, SON OF MEGACLES.

The Alcmaeonid!?

COME, THEN.

WE MUST FORM YOUR **QUESTIONS** BEFORE YOU GO INSIDE THE **SANCTUARY**.

And **Antenor** acting like he's never **seen** him before.

Something **smelled** here, all right.

We got back before them and circled to the back of the temple.

There were no guards there...

...because there was no door connecting the back room with the temple.

Smintheus had told **no** one about the **loose** block in the wall.

That's how he knew about that other Pythia's...

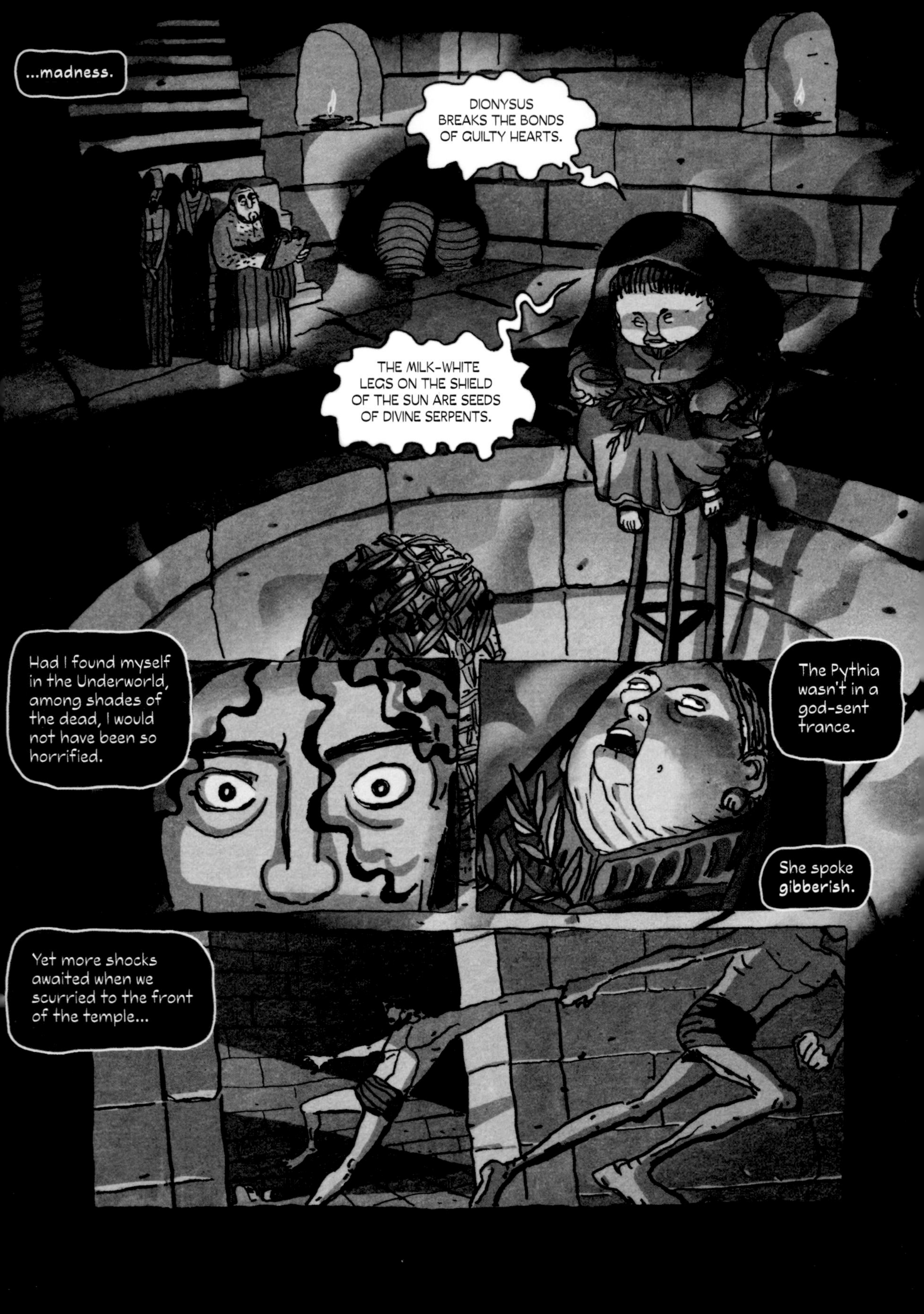
...madness.
DIONYSUS BREAKS THE BONDS OF GUILTY HEARTS.
THE MILK-WHITE LEGS ON THE SHIELD OF THE SUN ARE SEEDS OF DIVINE SERPENTS.
Had I found myself in the Underworld, among shades of the dead, I would not have been so horrified.
The Pythia wasn't in a god-sent trance.
She spoke gibberish.
Yet more shocks awaited when we scurried to the front of the temple...

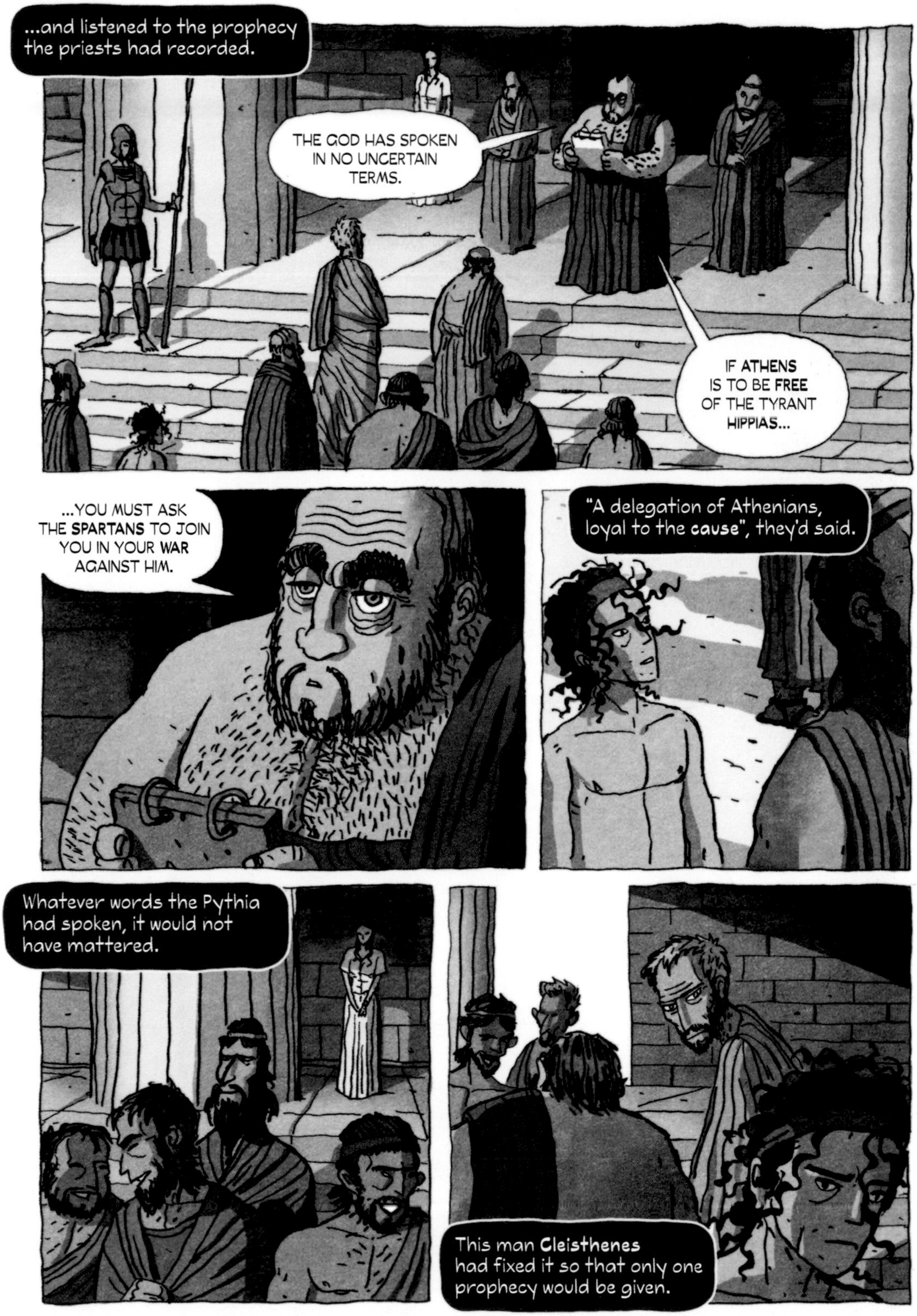
...and listened to the prophecy the priests had recorded.
THE GOD HAS SPOKEN IN NO UNCERTAIN TERMS.
IF ATHENS IS TO BE FREE OF THE TYRANT HIPPIAS...
...YOU MUST ASK THE SPARTANS TO JOIN YOU IN YOUR WAR AGAINST HIM.
"A delegation of Athenians, loyal to the cause", they'd said.
Whatever words the Pythia had spoken, it would not have mattered.
This man Cleisthenes had fixed it so that only one prophecy would be given.

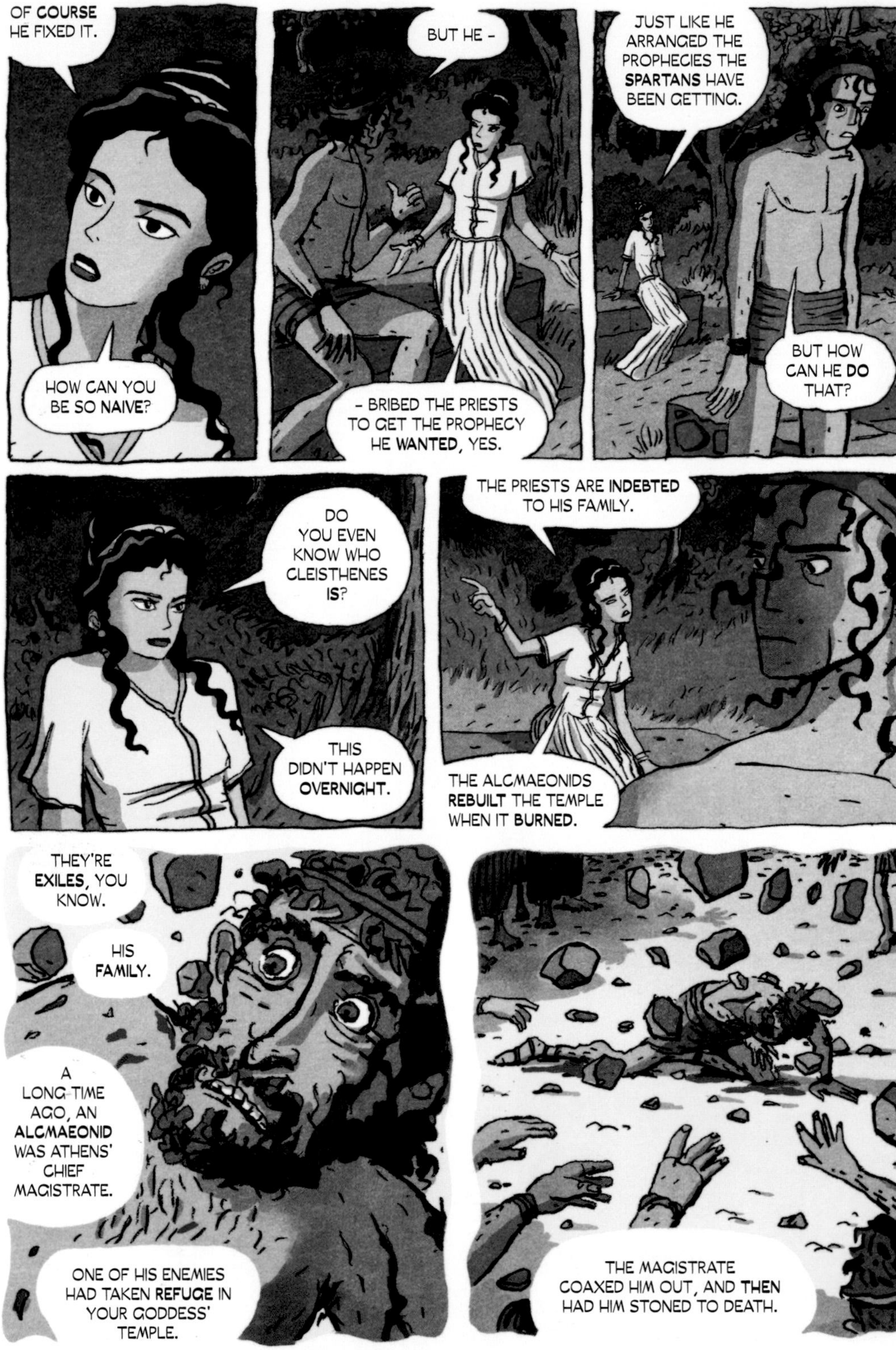
OF COURSE HE FIXED IT.
HOW CAN YOU BE SO NAIVE?
BUT HE -
- BRIBED THE PRIESTS TO GET THE PROPHECY HE WANTED, YES.
JUST LIKE HE ARRANGED THE PROPHECIES THE SPARTANS HAVE BEEN GETTING.
BUT HOW CAN HE DO THAT?
DO YOU EVEN KNOW WHO CLEISTHENES IS?
THIS DIDN'T HAPPEN OVERNIGHT.
THE PRIESTS ARE INDEBTED TO HIS FAMILY.
THE ALCMAEONIDS REBUILT THE TEMPLE WHEN IT BURNED.
THEY'RE EXILES, YOU KNOW.
HIS FAMILY.
A LONG TIME AGO, AN ALCMAEONID WAS ATHENS' CHIEF MAGISTRATE.
ONE OF HIS ENEMIES HAD TAKEN REFUGE IN YOUR GODDESS' TEMPLE.
THE MAGISTRATE COAXED HIM OUT, AND THEN HAD HIM STONED TO DEATH.

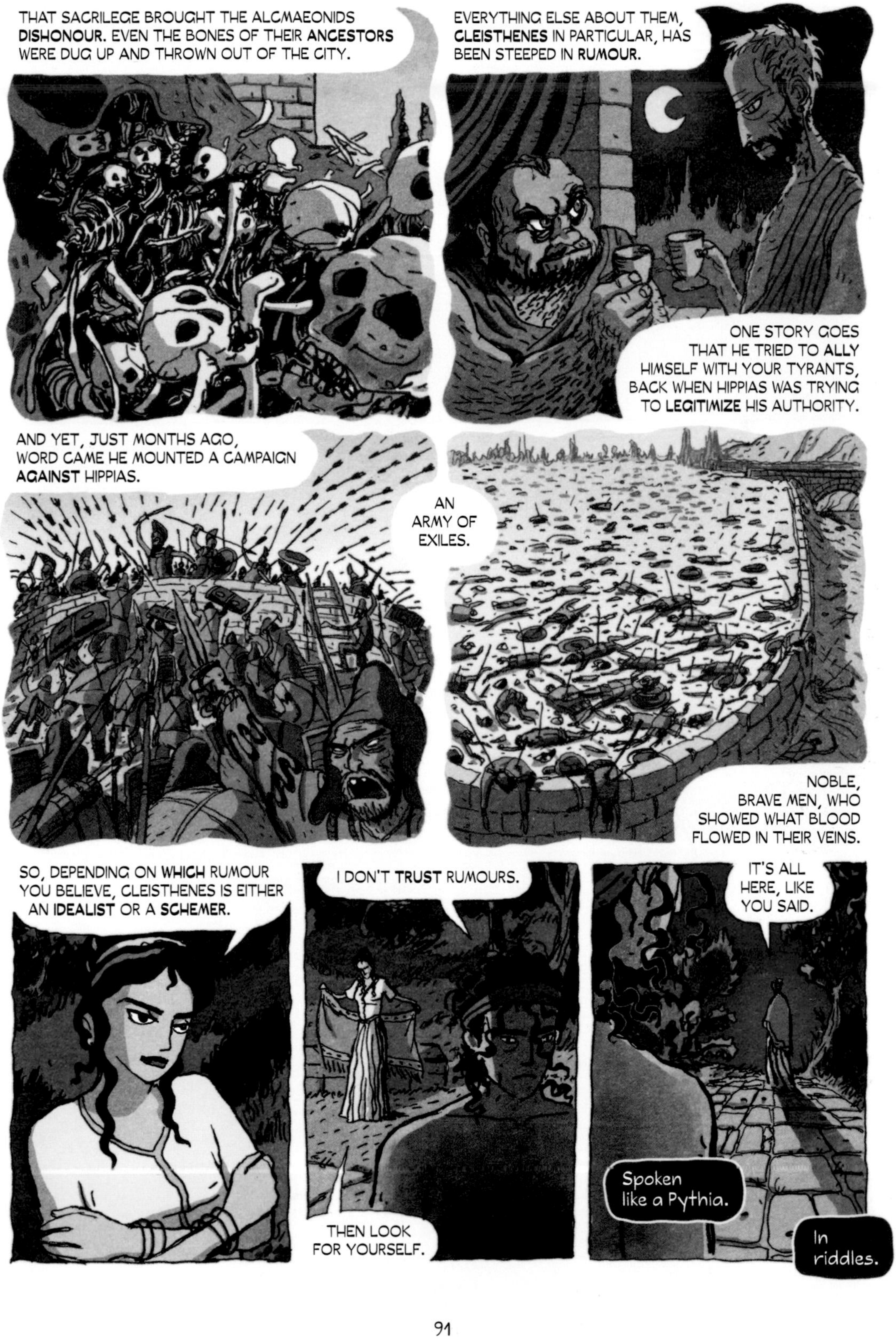
THAT SACRILEGE BROUGHT THE ALCMAEONIDS DISHONOUR. EVEN THE BONES OF THEIR ANCESTORS WERE DUG UP AND THROWN OUT OF THE CITY.
EVERYTHING ELSE ABOUT THEM, CLEISTHENES IN PARTICULAR, HAS BEEN STEEPED IN RUMOUR.
ONE STORY GOES THAT HE TRIED TO ALLY HIMSELF WITH YOUR TYRANTS, BACK WHEN HIPPIAS WAS TRYING TO LEGITIMIZE HIS AUTHORITY.
AND YET, JUST MONTHS AGO, WORD CAME HE MOUNTED A CAMPAIGN AGAINST HIPPIAS.
AN ARMY OF EXILES.
NOBLE, BRAVE MEN, WHO SHOWED WHAT BLOOD FLOWED IN THEIR VEINS.
SO, DEPENDING ON WHICH RUMOUR YOU BELIEVE, CLEISTHENES IS EITHER AN IDEALIST OR A SCHEMER.
I DON'T TRUST RUMOURS.
THEN LOOK FOR YOURSELF.
IT'S ALL HERE, LIKE YOU SAID.
Spoken like a Pythia.
In riddles.

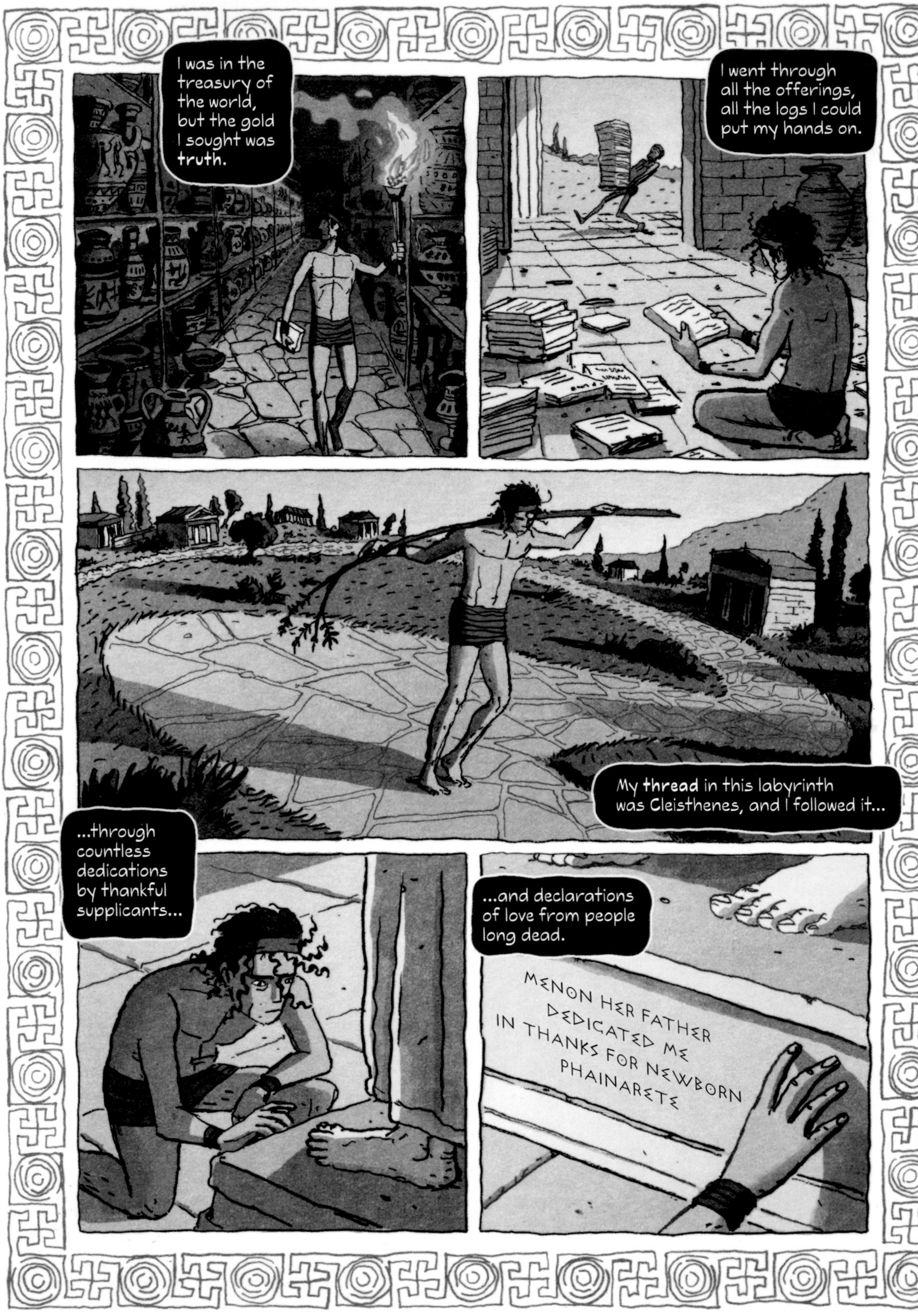

I was in the treasury of the world, but the gold I sought was **truth.**
I went through all the offerings, all the logs I could put my hands on.
My **thread** in this labyrinth was Cleisthenes, and I followed it...
...through countless dedications by thankful supplicants...
...and declarations of love from people long dead.
MENON HER FATHER DEDICATED ME IN THANKS FOR NEWBORN PHAINARETE

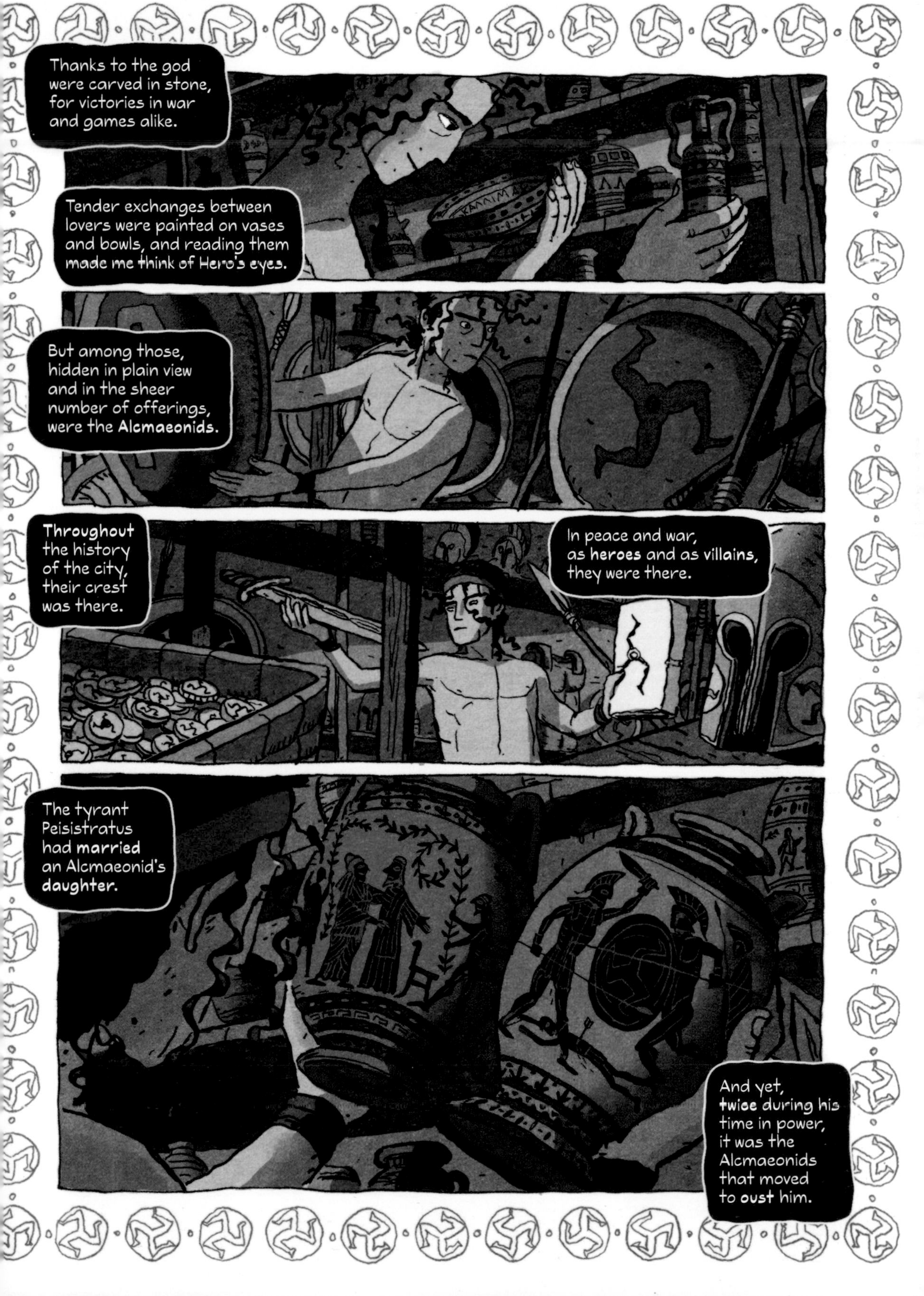

Thanks to the god were carved in stone, for victories in war and games alike.
Tender exchanges between lovers were painted on vases and bowls, and reading them made me think of Hero's eyes.
But among those, hidden in plain view and in the sheer number of offerings, were the **Alcmaeonids**.
Throughout the history of the city, their crest was there.
In peace and war, as **heroes** and as **villains**, they were there.
The tyrant Peisistratus had **married** an Alcmaeonid's **daughter**.
And yet, **twice** during his time in power, it was the Alcmaeonids that moved to **oust** him.

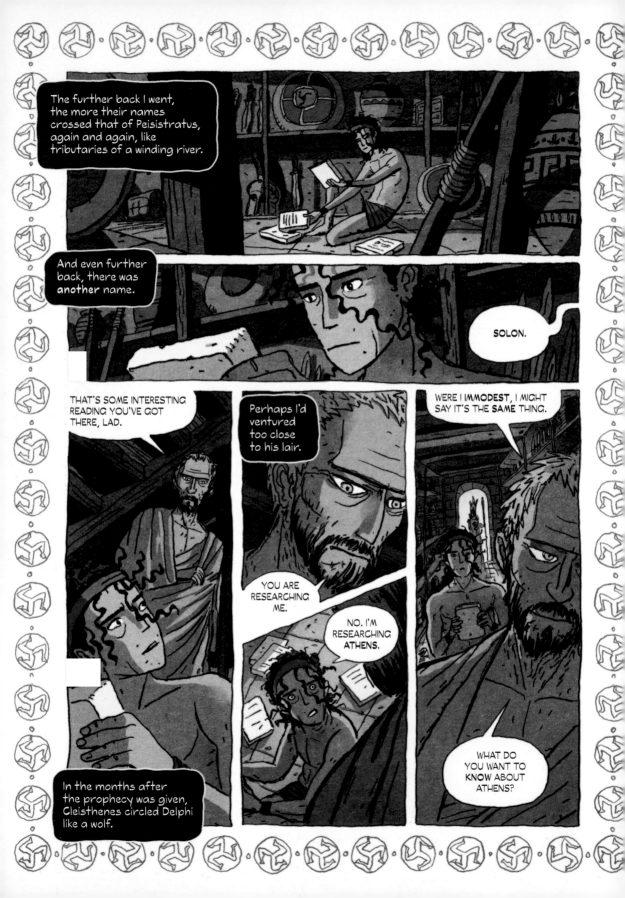

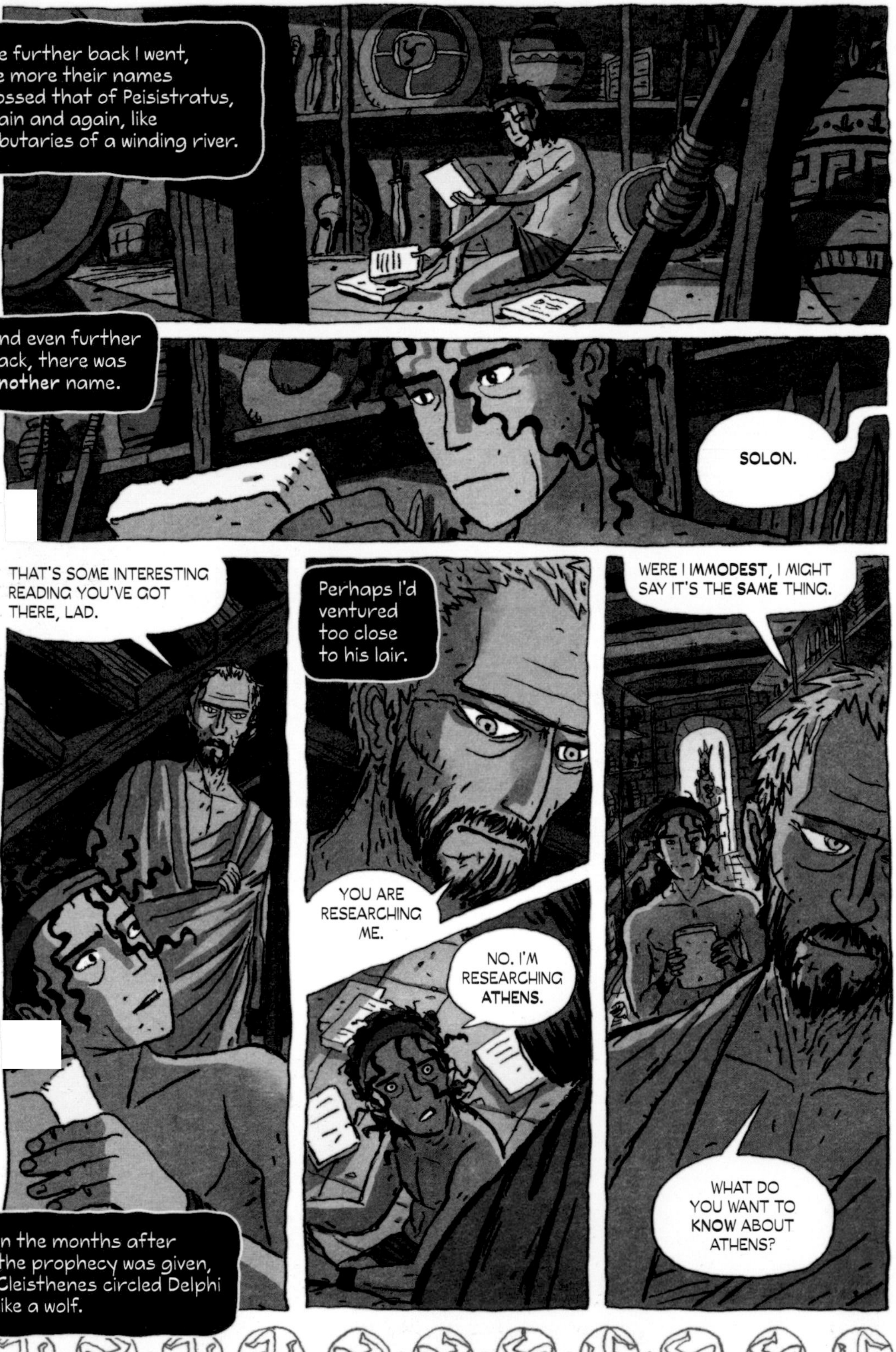
The further back I went, the more their names crossed that of Peisistratus, again and again, like tributaries of a winding river.
And even further back, there was **another** name.
SOLON.
THAT'S SOME INTERESTING READING YOU'VE GOT THERE, LAD.
In the months after the prophecy was given, Cleisthenes circled Delphi like a wolf.
Perhaps I'd ventured too close to his lair.
YOU ARE RESEARCHING ME.
NO. I'M RESEARCHING **ATHENS.**
WERE I **IMMODEST**, I MIGHT SAY IT'S THE **SAME** THING.
WHAT DO YOU WANT TO **KNOW** ABOUT ATHENS?

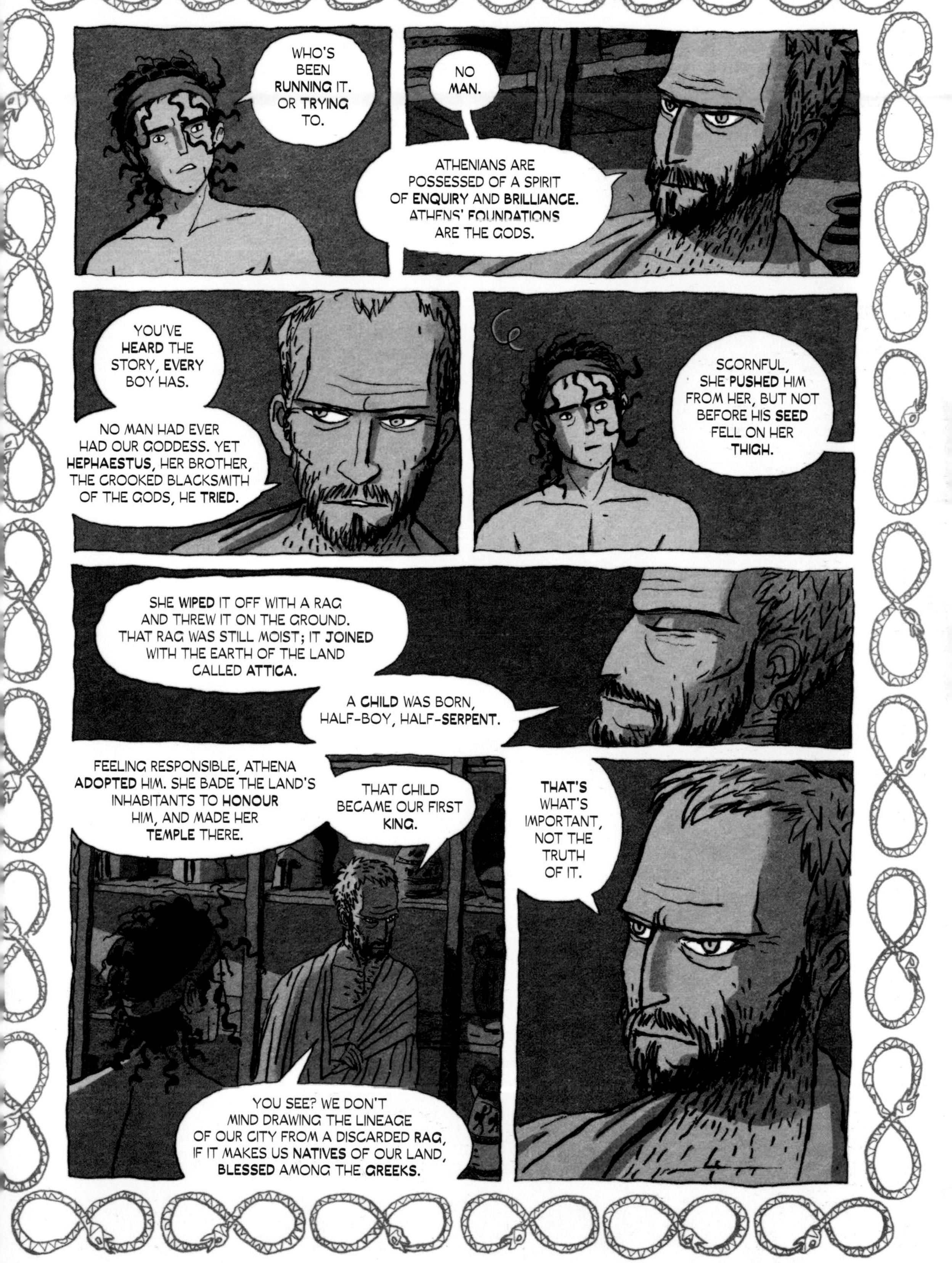
WHO'S BEEN RUNNING IT. OR TRYING TO.
NO MAN.
ATHENIANS ARE POSSESSED OF A SPIRIT OF ENQUIRY AND BRILLIANCE. ATHENS' FOUNDATIONS ARE THE GODS.
YOU'VE HEARD THE STORY, EVERY BOY HAS.
NO MAN HAD EVER HAD OUR GODDESS. YET HEPHAESTUS, HER BROTHER, THE CROOKED BLACKSMITH OF THE GODS, HE TRIED.
SCORNFUL, SHE PUSHED HIM FROM HER, BUT NOT BEFORE HIS SEED FELL ON HER THIGH.
SHE WIPED IT OFF WITH A RAG AND THREW IT ON THE GROUND. THAT RAG WAS STILL MOIST; IT JOINED WITH THE EARTH OF THE LAND CALLED ATTICA.
A CHILD WAS BORN, HALF-BOY, HALF-SERPENT.
FEELING RESPONSIBLE, ATHENA ADOPTED HIM. SHE BADE THE LAND'S INHABITANTS TO HONOUR HIM, AND MADE HER TEMPLE THERE.
THAT CHILD BECAME OUR FIRST KING.
YOU SEE? WE DON'T MIND DRAWING THE LINEAGE OF OUR CITY FROM A DISCARDED RAG, IF IT MAKES US NATIVES OF OUR LAND, BLESSED AMONG THE GREEKS.
THAT'S WHAT'S IMPORTANT, NOT THE TRUTH OF IT.

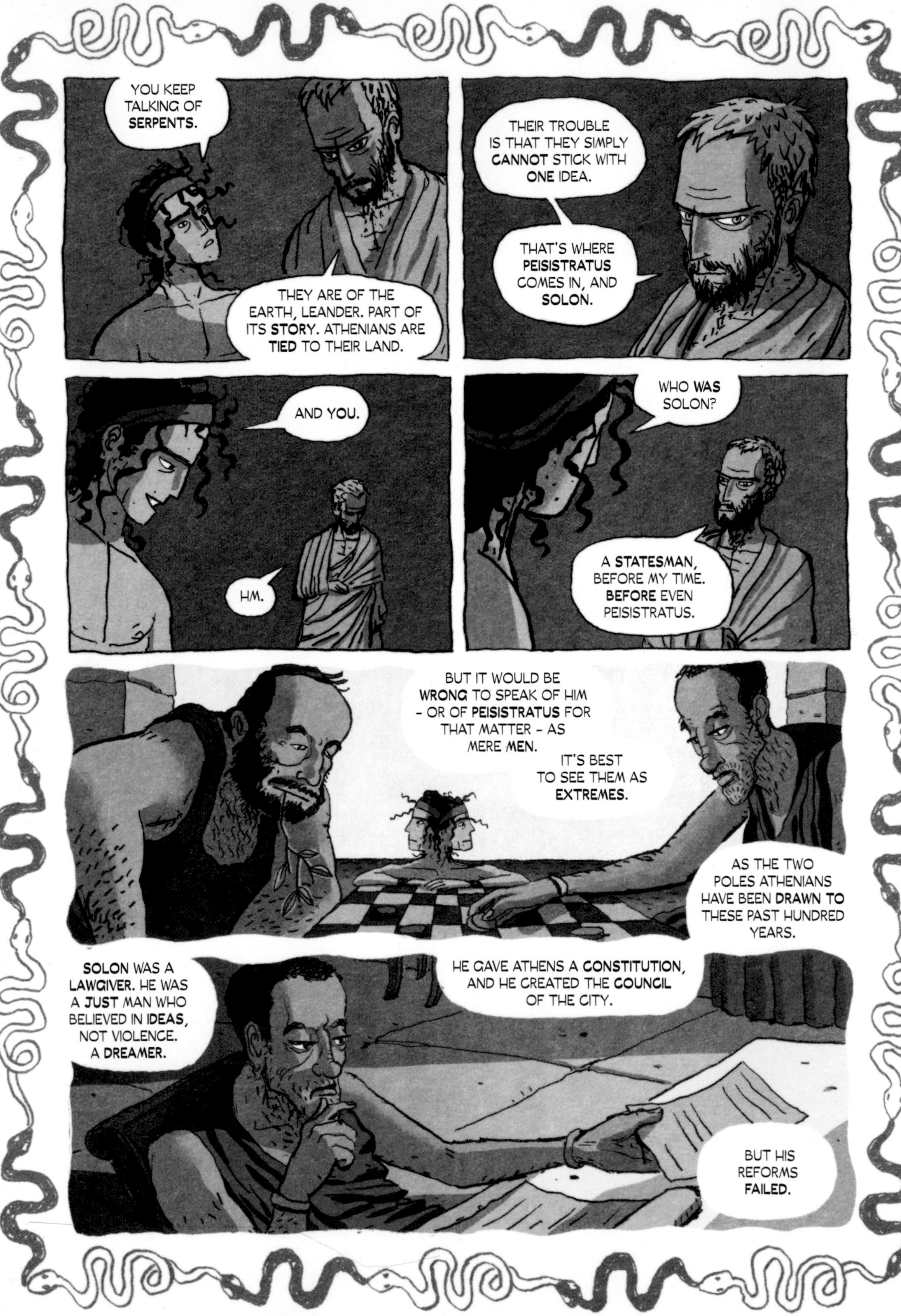

YOU KEEP TALKING OF SERPENTS.
THEY ARE OF THE EARTH, LEANDER. PART OF ITS STORY. ATHENIANS ARE TIED TO THEIR LAND.
THEIR TROUBLE IS THAT THEY SIMPLY CANNOT STICK WITH ONE IDEA.
THAT'S WHERE PEISISTRATUS COMES IN, AND SOLON.
AND YOU.
HM.
WHO WAS SOLON?
A STATESMAN, BEFORE MY TIME. BEFORE EVEN PEISISTRATUS.
BUT IT WOULD BE WRONG TO SPEAK OF HIM - OR OF PEISISTRATUS FOR THAT MATTER - AS MERE MEN.
IT'S BEST TO SEE THEM AS EXTREMES.
AS THE TWO POLES ATHENIANS HAVE BEEN DRAWN TO THESE PAST HUNDRED YEARS.
SOLON WAS A LAWGIVER. HE WAS A JUST MAN WHO BELIEVED IN IDEAS, NOT VIOLENCE. A DREAMER.
HE GAVE ATHENS A CONSTITUTION, AND HE CREATED THE COUNCIL OF THE CITY.
BUT HIS REFORMS FAILED.

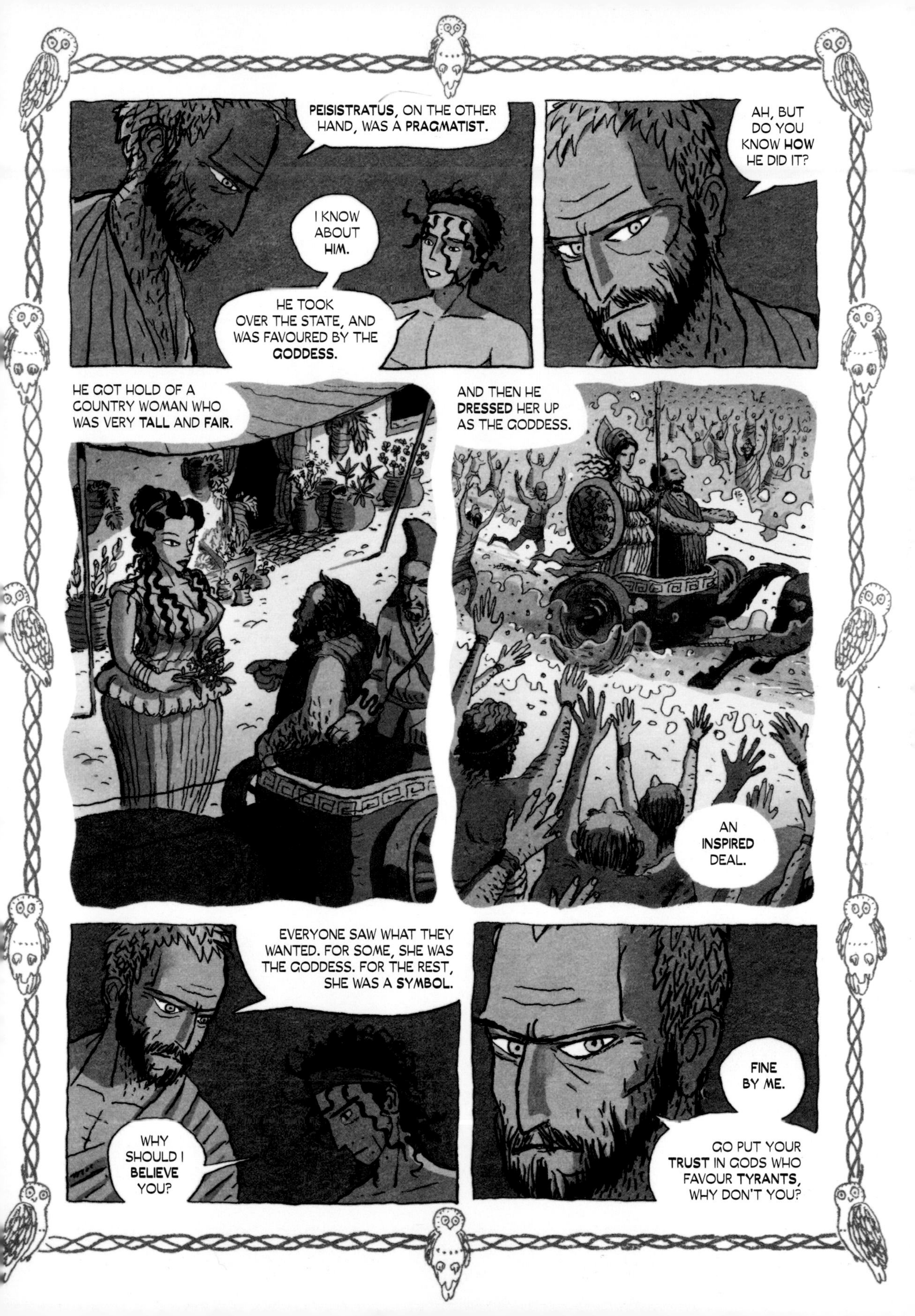
PEISISTRATUS, ON THE OTHER HAND, WAS A PRAGMATIST.
I KNOW ABOUT HIM.
HE TOOK OVER THE STATE, AND WAS FAVOURED BY THE GODDESS.
AH, BUT DO YOU KNOW HOW HE DID IT?
HE GOT HOLD OF A COUNTRY WOMAN WHO WAS VERY TALL AND FAIR.
AND THEN HE DRESSED HER UP AS THE GODDESS.
AN INSPIRED DEAL.
EVERYONE SAW WHAT THEY WANTED. FOR SOME, SHE WAS THE GODDESS. FOR THE REST, SHE WAS A SYMBOL.
WHY SHOULD I BELIEVE YOU?
FINE BY ME.
GO PUT YOUR TRUST IN GODS WHO FAVOUR TYRANTS, WHY DON'T YOU?

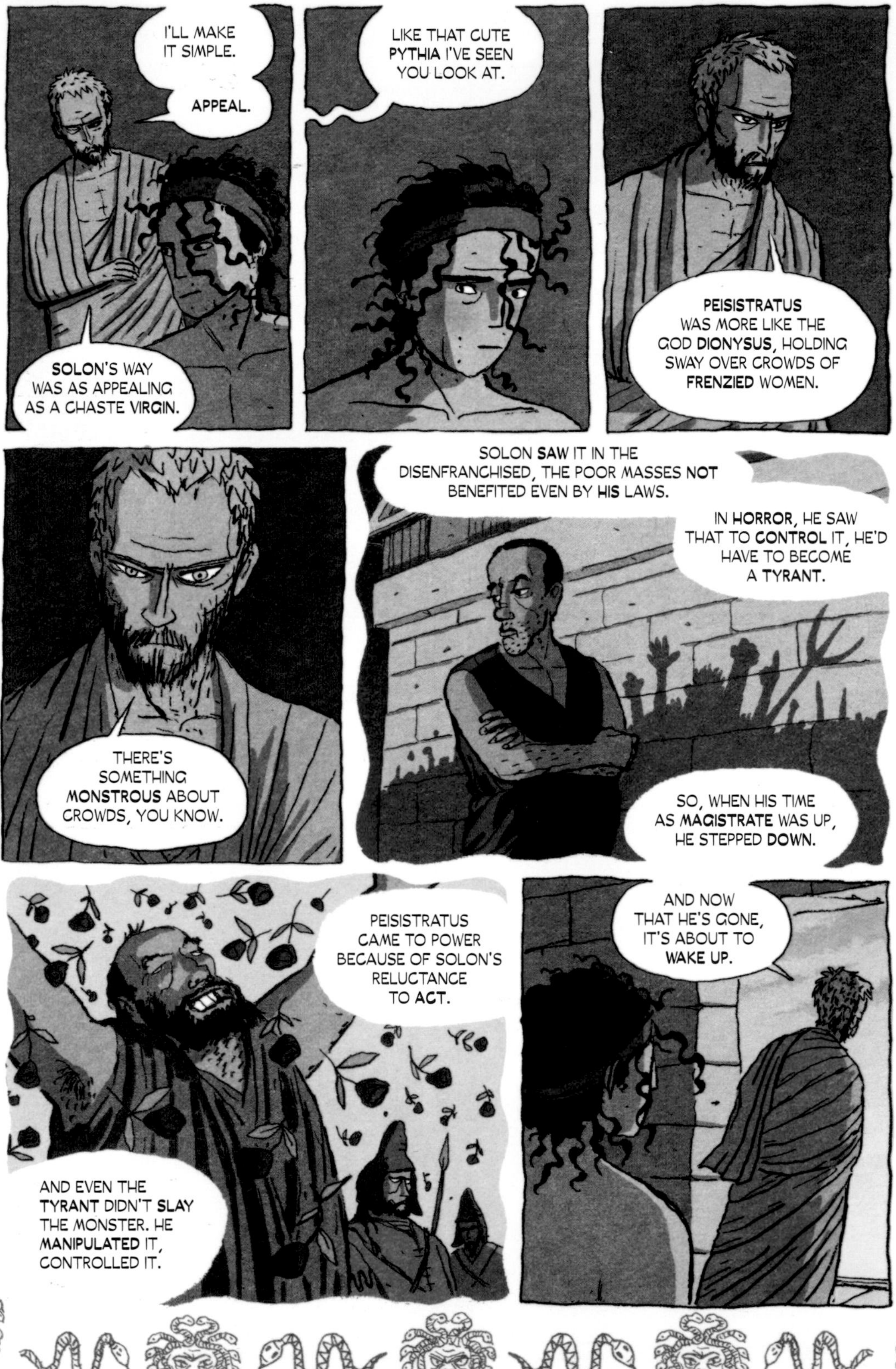
I'LL MAKE IT SIMPLE.
APPEAL.
SOLON'S WAY WAS AS APPEALING AS A CHASTE VIRGIN.
LIKE THAT CUTE PYTHIA I'VE SEEN YOU LOOK AT.
PEISISTRATUS WAS MORE LIKE THE GOD DIONYSUS, HOLDING SWAY OVER CROWDS OF FRENZIED WOMEN.
THERE'S SOMETHING MONSTROUS ABOUT CROWDS, YOU KNOW.
SOLON SAW IT IN THE DISENFRANCHISED, THE POOR MASSES NOT BENEFITED EVEN BY HIS LAWS.
IN HORROR, HE SAW THAT TO CONTROL IT, HE'D HAVE TO BECOME A TYRANT.
SO, WHEN HIS TIME AS MAGISTRATE WAS UP, HE STEPPED DOWN.
PEISISTRATUS CAME TO POWER BECAUSE OF SOLON'S RELUCTANCE TO ACT.
AND EVEN THE TYRANT DIDN'T SLAY THE MONSTER. HE MANIPULATED IT, CONTROLLED IT.
AND NOW THAT HE'S GONE, IT'S ABOUT TO WAKE UP.

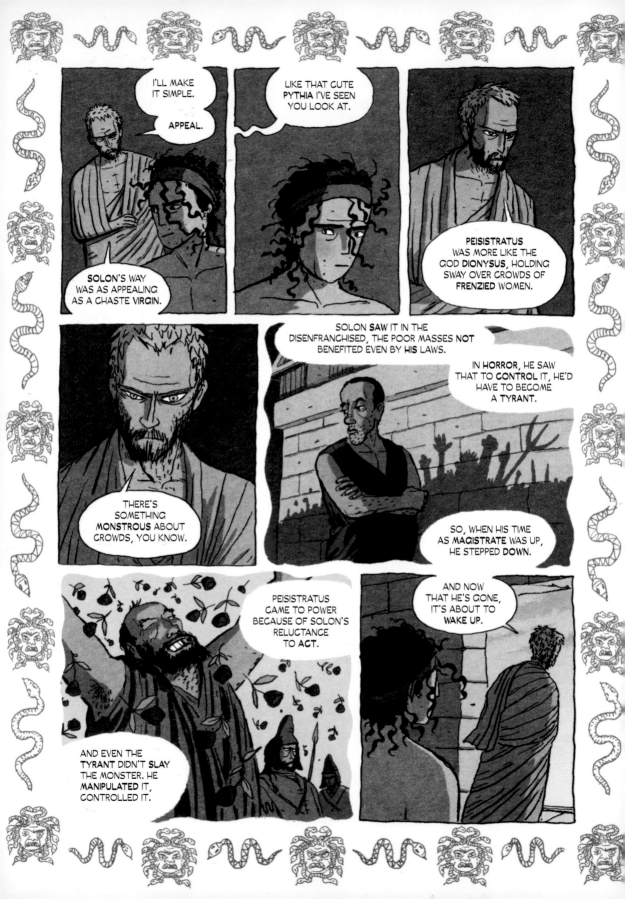

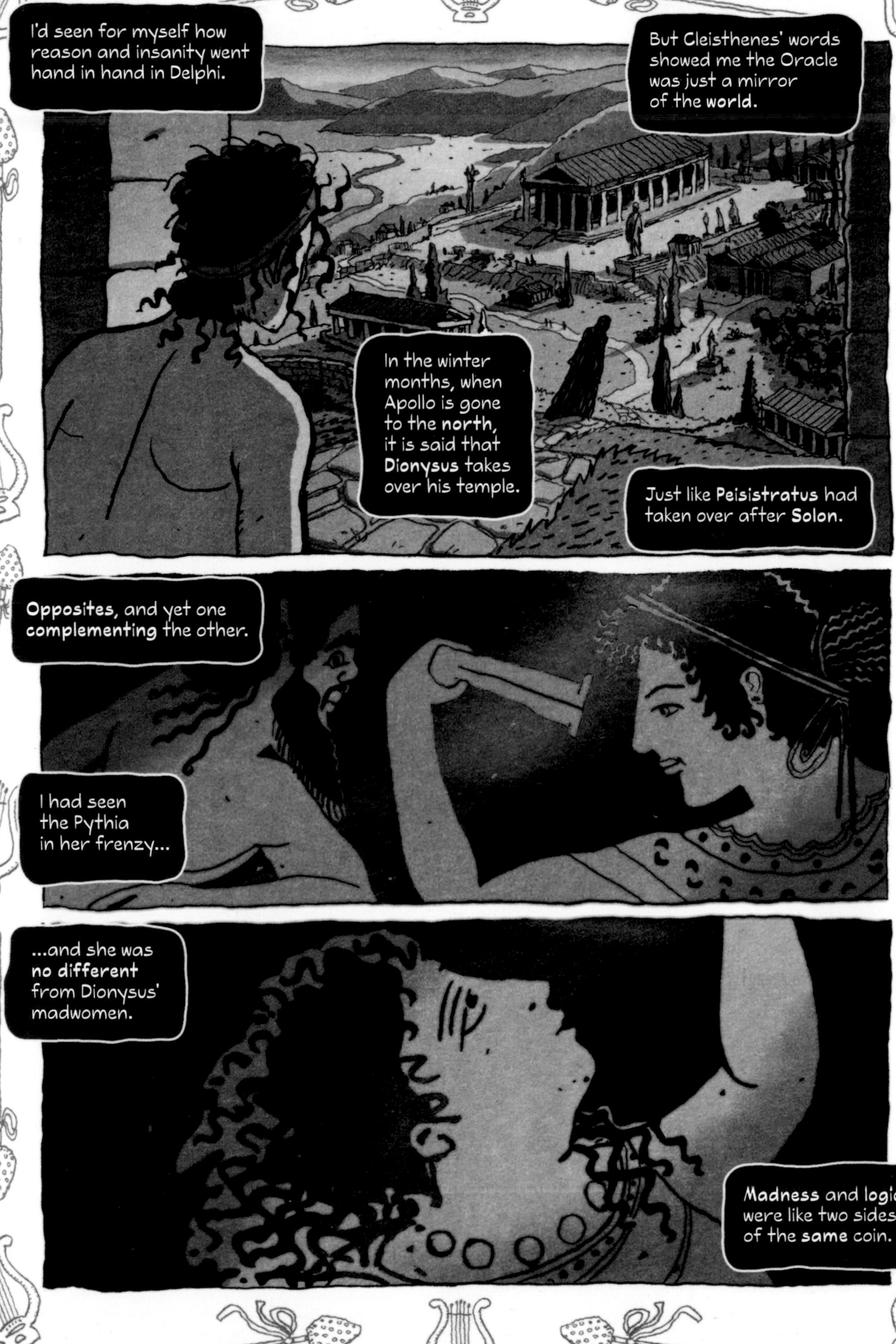
I'd seen for myself how reason and insanity went hand in hand in Delphi.
But Cleisthenes' words showed me the Oracle was just a mirror of the **world.**
In the winter months, when Apollo is gone to the **north,** it is said that **Dionysus** takes over his temple.
Just like **Peisistratus** had taken over after **Solon.**
Opposites, and yet one **complementing** the other.
I had seen the Pythia in her frenzy...
...and she was **no different** from Dionysus' madwomen.
Madness and **logic** were like two sides of the **same** coin.

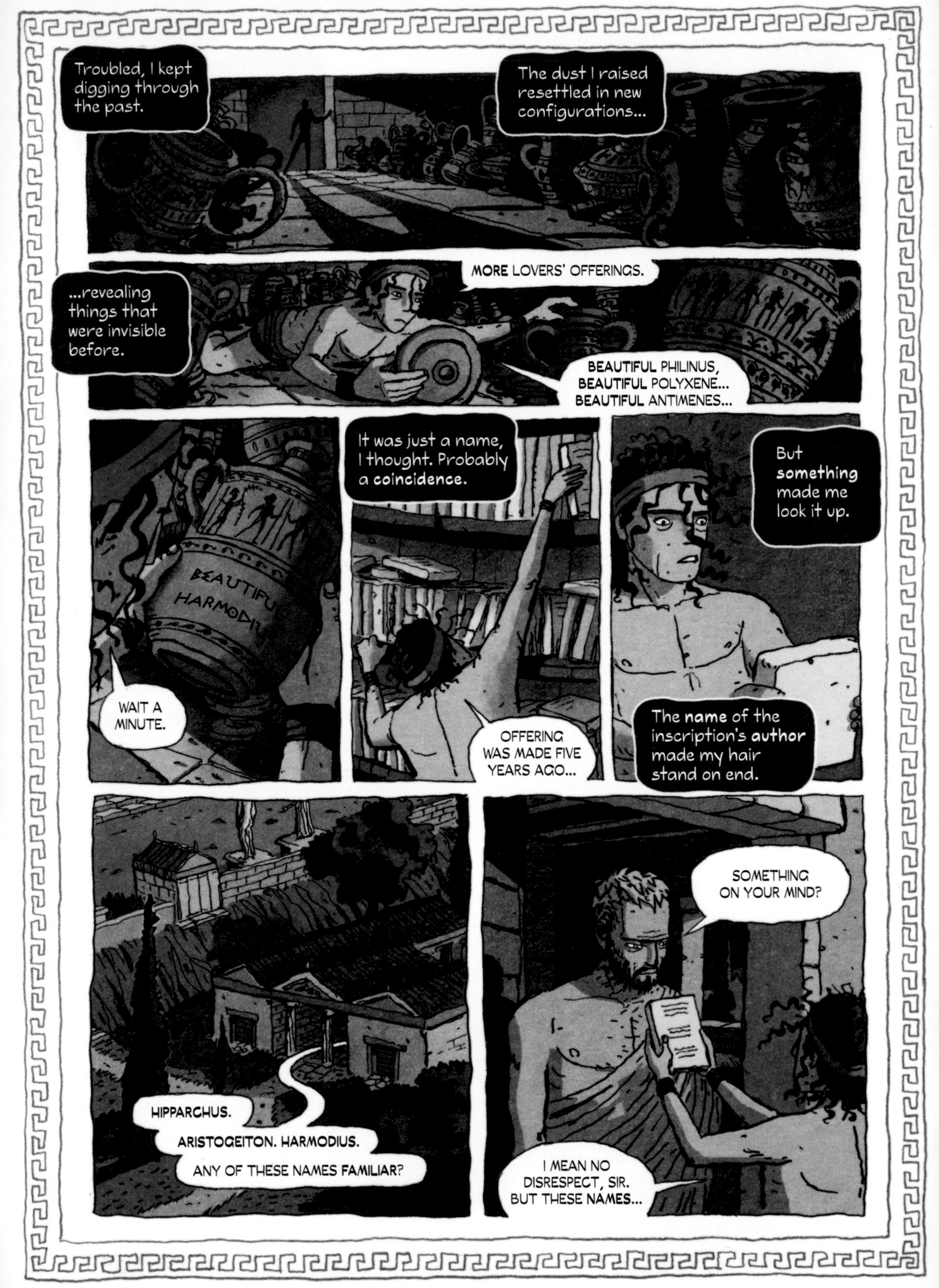
Troubled, I kept digging through the past.
The dust I raised resettled in new configurations...
...revealing things that were invisible before.
MORE LOVERS' OFFERINGS.
BEAUTIFUL PHILINUS, BEAUTIFUL POLYXENE... BEAUTIFUL ANTIMENES...
BEAUTIFU
HARMODIU
WAIT A MINUTE.
It was just a name, I thought. Probably a coincidence.
OFFERING WAS MADE FIVE YEARS AGO...
But something made me look it up.
The name of the inscription's author made my hair stand on end.
HIPPARCHUS.
ARISTOGEITON. HARMODIUS.
ANY OF THESE NAMES FAMILIAR?
SOMETHING ON YOUR MIND?
I MEAN NO DISRESPECT, SIR. BUT THESE NAMES...

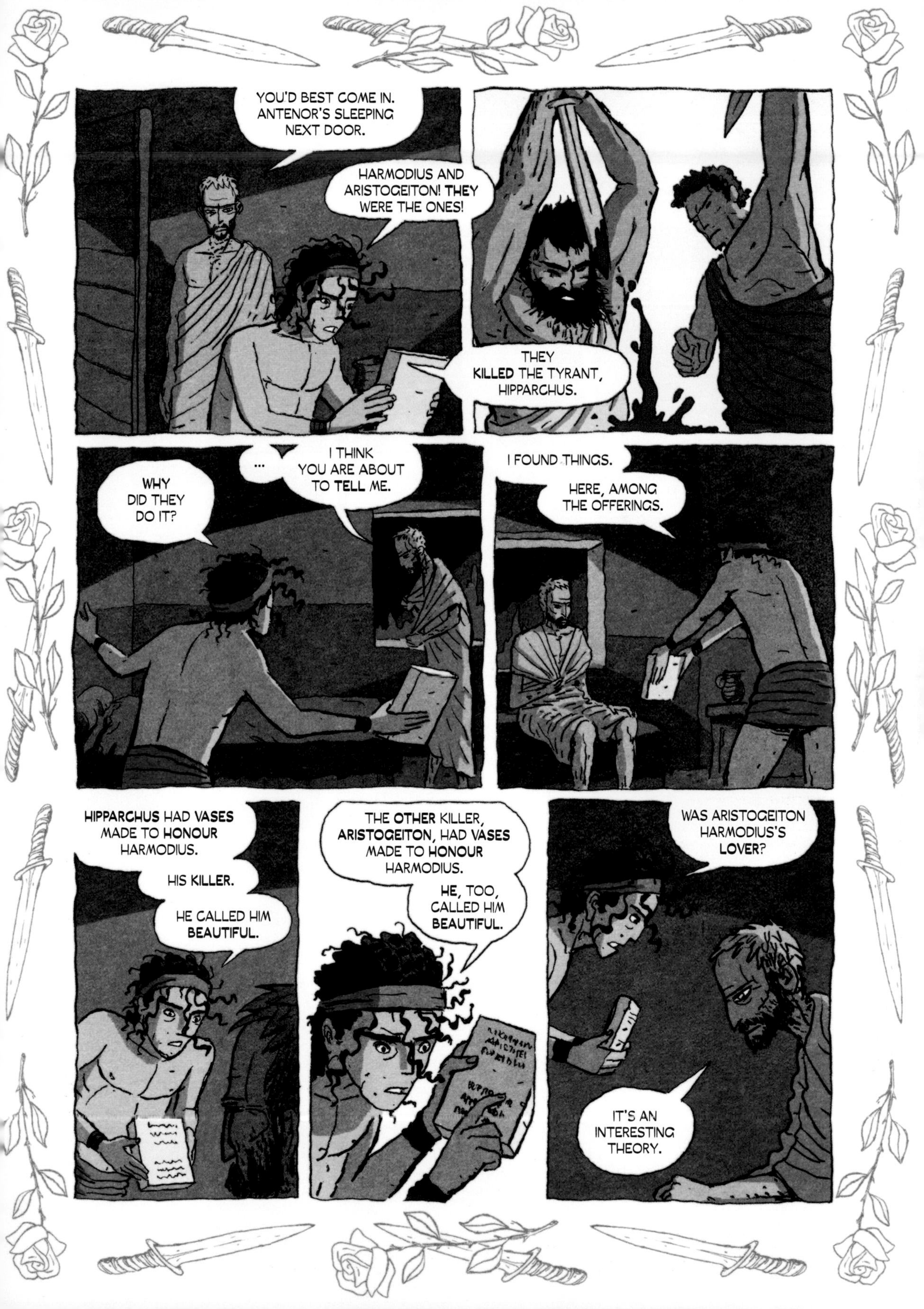
YOU'D BEST COME IN. ANTENOR'S SLEEPING NEXT DOOR.
HARMODIUS AND ARISTOGEITON! THEY WERE THE ONES!
THEY KILLED THE TYRANT, HIPPARCHUS.
WHY DID THEY DO IT?
...
I THINK YOU ARE ABOUT TO TELL ME.
I FOUND THINGS.
HERE, AMONG THE OFFERINGS.
HIPPARCHUS HAD VASES MADE TO HONOUR HARMODIUS.
HIS KILLER.
HE CALLED HIM BEAUTIFUL.
THE OTHER KILLER, ARISTOGEITON, HAD VASES MADE TO HONOUR HARMODIUS.
HE, TOO, CALLED HIM BEAUTIFUL.
WAS ARISTOGEITON HARMODIUS'S LOVER?
IT'S AN INTERESTING THEORY.

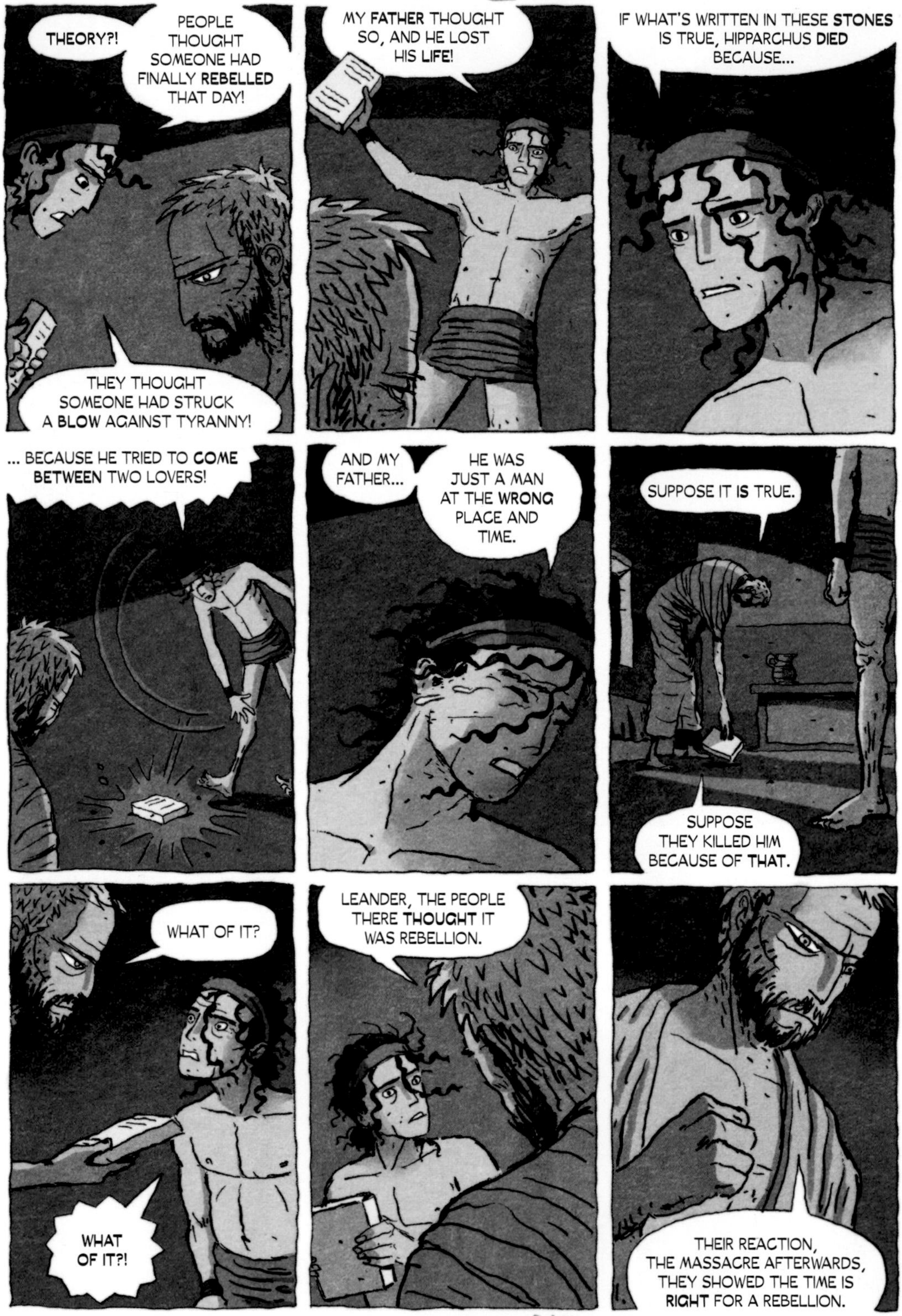
THEORY?!
PEOPLE THOUGHT SOMEONE HAD FINALLY REBELLED THAT DAY!
THEY THOUGHT SOMEONE HAD STRUCK A BLOW AGAINST TYRANNY!
MY FATHER THOUGHT SO, AND HE LOST HIS LIFE!
IF WHAT'S WRITTEN IN THESE STONES IS TRUE, HIPPARCHUS DIED BECAUSE...
... BECAUSE HE TRIED TO COME BETWEEN TWO LOVERS!
AND MY FATHER...
HE WAS JUST A MAN AT THE WRONG PLACE AND TIME.
SUPPOSE IT IS TRUE.
SUPPOSE THEY KILLED HIM BECAUSE OF THAT.
WHAT OF IT?
WHAT OF IT?!
LEANDER, THE PEOPLE THERE THOUGHT IT WAS REBELLION.
THEIR REACTION, THE MASSACRE AFTERWARDS, THEY SHOWED THE TIME IS RIGHT FOR A REBELLION.

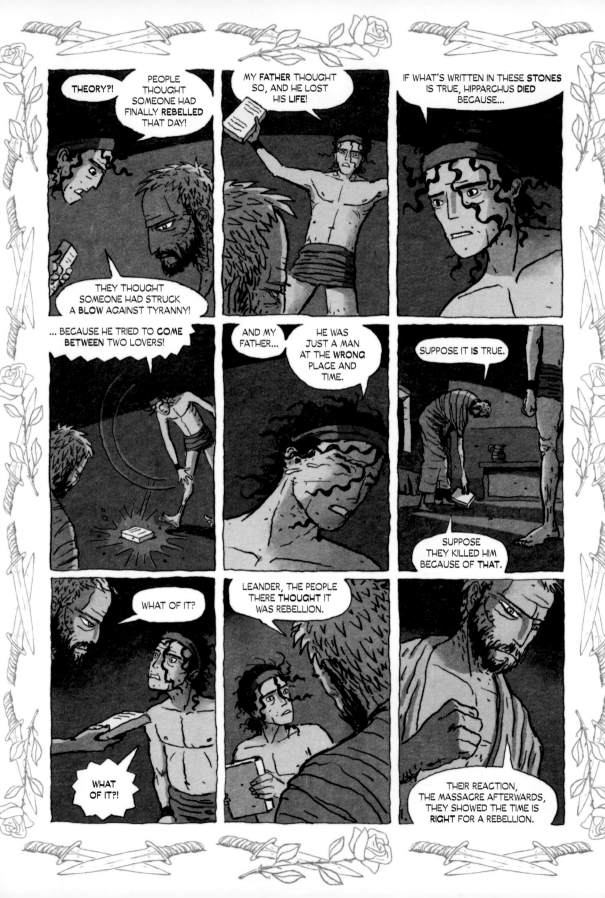

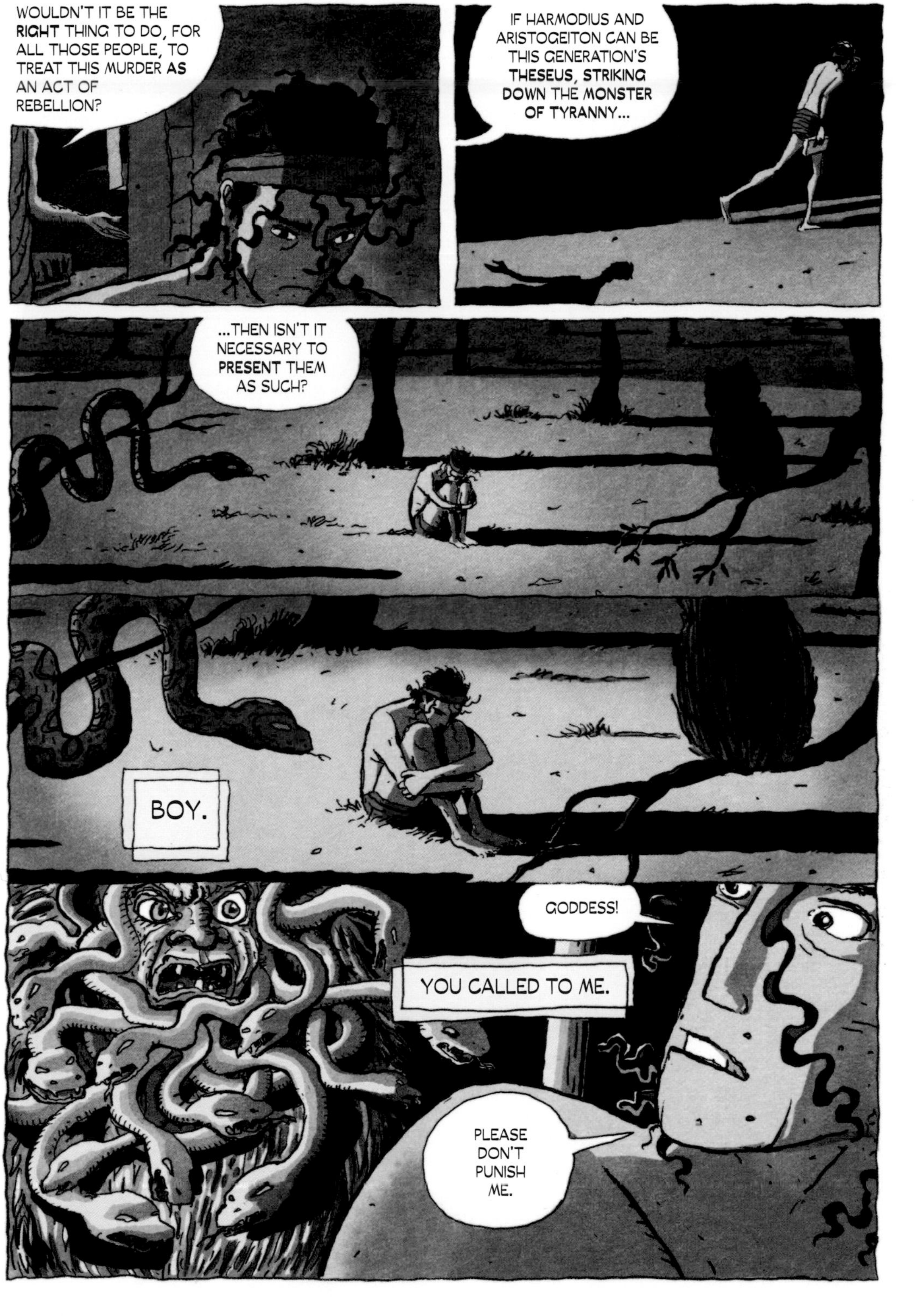
WOULDN'T IT BE THE RIGHT THING TO DO, FOR ALL THOSE PEOPLE, TO TREAT THIS MURDER AS AN ACT OF REBELLION?
IF HARMODIUS AND ARISTOGEITON CAN BE THIS GENERATION'S THESEUS, STRIKING DOWN THE MONSTER OF TYRANNY...
...THEN ISN'T IT NECESSARY TO PRESENT THEM AS SUCH?
BOY.
GODDESS!
YOU CALLED TO ME.
PLEASE DON'T PUNISH ME.

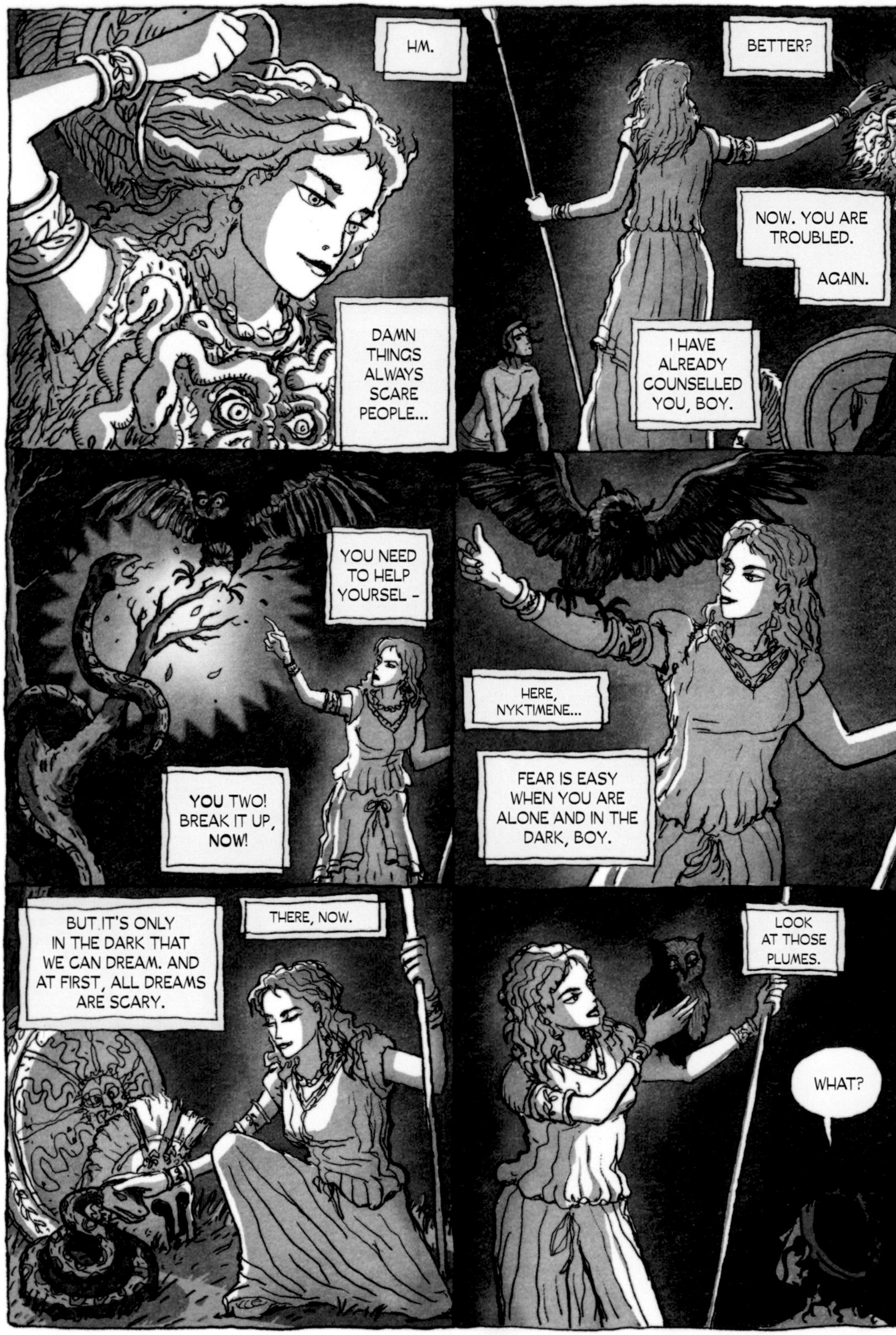
HM.
DAMN THINGS ALWAYS SCARE PEOPLE...
BETTER?
NOW. YOU ARE TROUBLED.
AGAIN.
I HAVE ALREADY COUNSELLED YOU, BOY.
YOU NEED TO HELP YOURSEL –
YOU TWO! BREAK IT UP, NOW!
HERE, NYKTIMENE...
FEAR IS EASY WHEN YOU ARE ALONE AND IN THE DARK, BOY.
BUT IT'S ONLY IN THE DARK THAT WE CAN DREAM. AND AT FIRST, ALL DREAMS ARE SCARY.
THERE, NOW.
LOOK AT THOSE PLUMES.
WHAT?

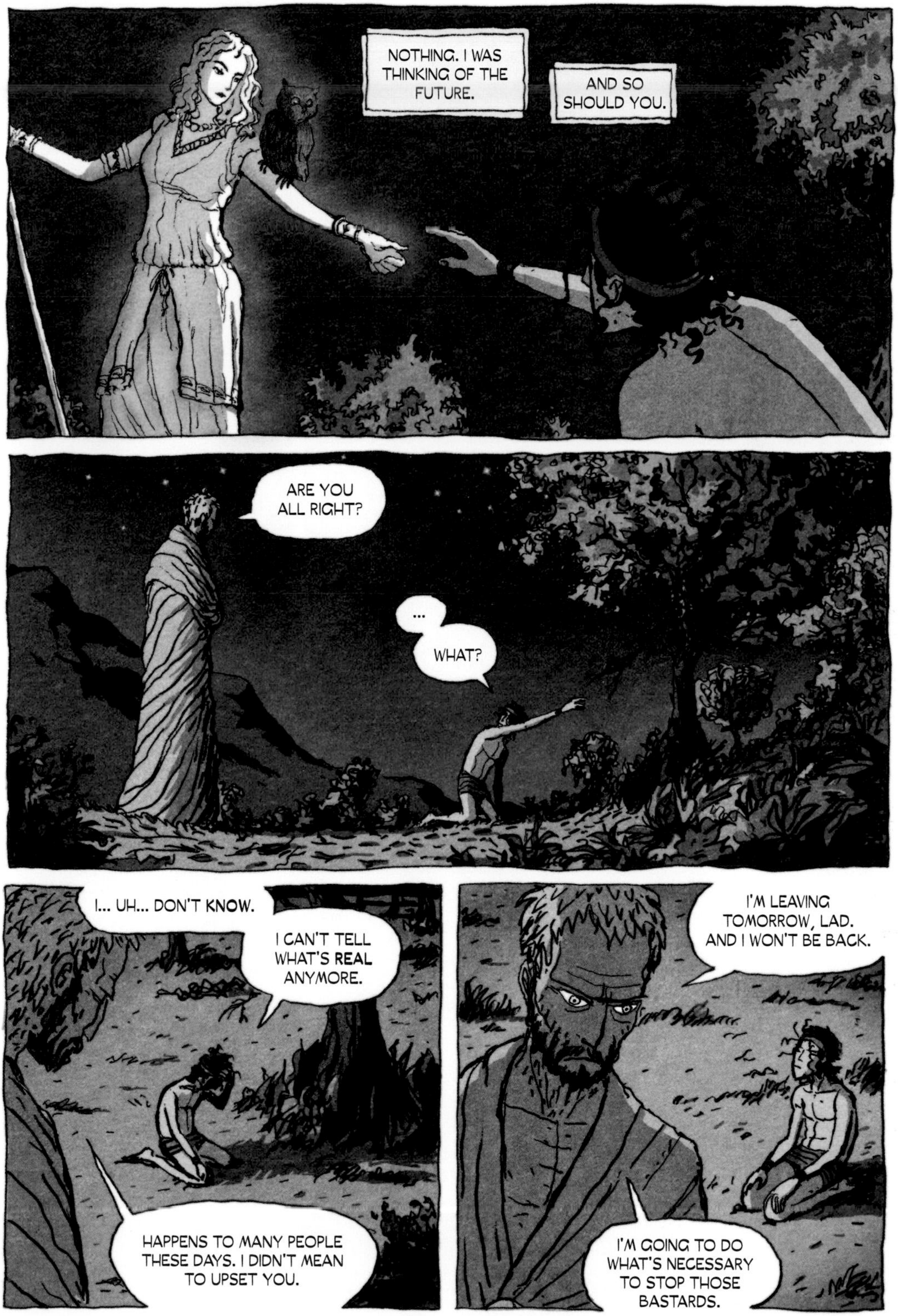
NOTHING. I WAS THINKING OF THE FUTURE.
AND SO SHOULD YOU.
ARE YOU ALL RIGHT?
...
WHAT?
I... UH... DON'T **KNOW**.
I CAN'T TELL WHAT'S **REAL** ANYMORE.
HAPPENS TO MANY PEOPLE THESE DAYS. I DIDN'T MEAN TO UPSET YOU.
I'M LEAVING TOMORROW, LAD. AND I WON'T BE BACK.
I'M GOING TO DO WHAT'S NECESSARY TO STOP THOSE BASTARDS.

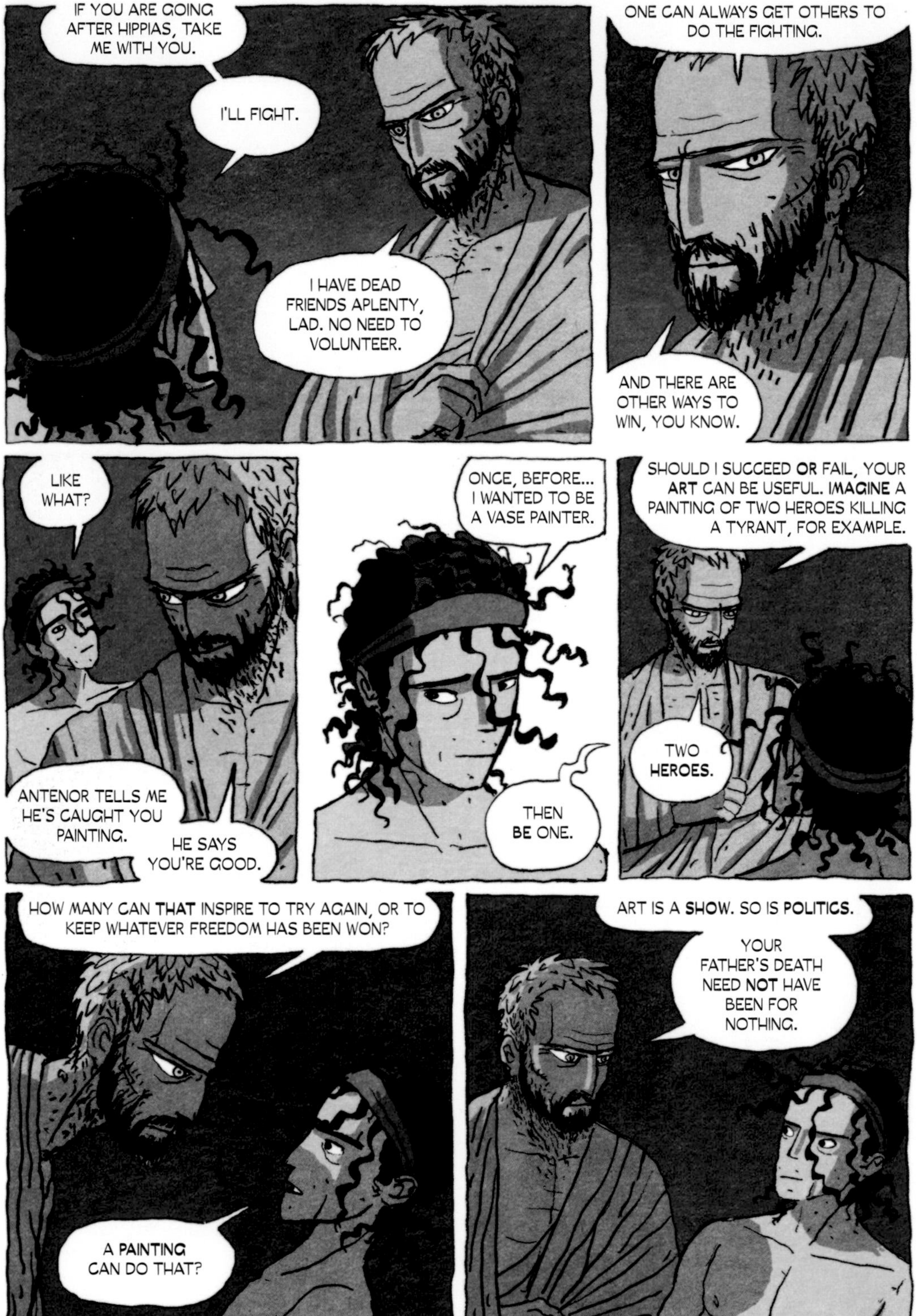
IF YOU ARE GOING AFTER HIPPIAS, TAKE ME WITH YOU.
I'LL FIGHT.
I HAVE DEAD FRIENDS APLENTY, LAD. NO NEED TO VOLUNTEER.
ONE CAN ALWAYS GET OTHERS TO DO THE FIGHTING.
AND THERE ARE OTHER WAYS TO WIN, YOU KNOW.
LIKE WHAT?
ANTENOR TELLS ME HE'S CAUGHT YOU PAINTING.
HE SAYS YOU'RE GOOD.
ONCE, BEFORE... I WANTED TO BE A VASE PAINTER.
THEN **BE** ONE.
SHOULD I SUCCEED **OR** FAIL, YOUR **ART** CAN BE USEFUL. **IMAGINE** A PAINTING OF TWO HEROES KILLING A TYRANT, FOR EXAMPLE.
TWO **HEROES.**
HOW MANY CAN **THAT** INSPIRE TO TRY AGAIN, OR TO KEEP WHATEVER FREEDOM HAS BEEN WON?
A **PAINTING** CAN DO THAT?
ART IS A **SHOW.** SO IS **POLITICS.**
YOUR FATHER'S DEATH NEED **NOT** HAVE BEEN FOR NOTHING.

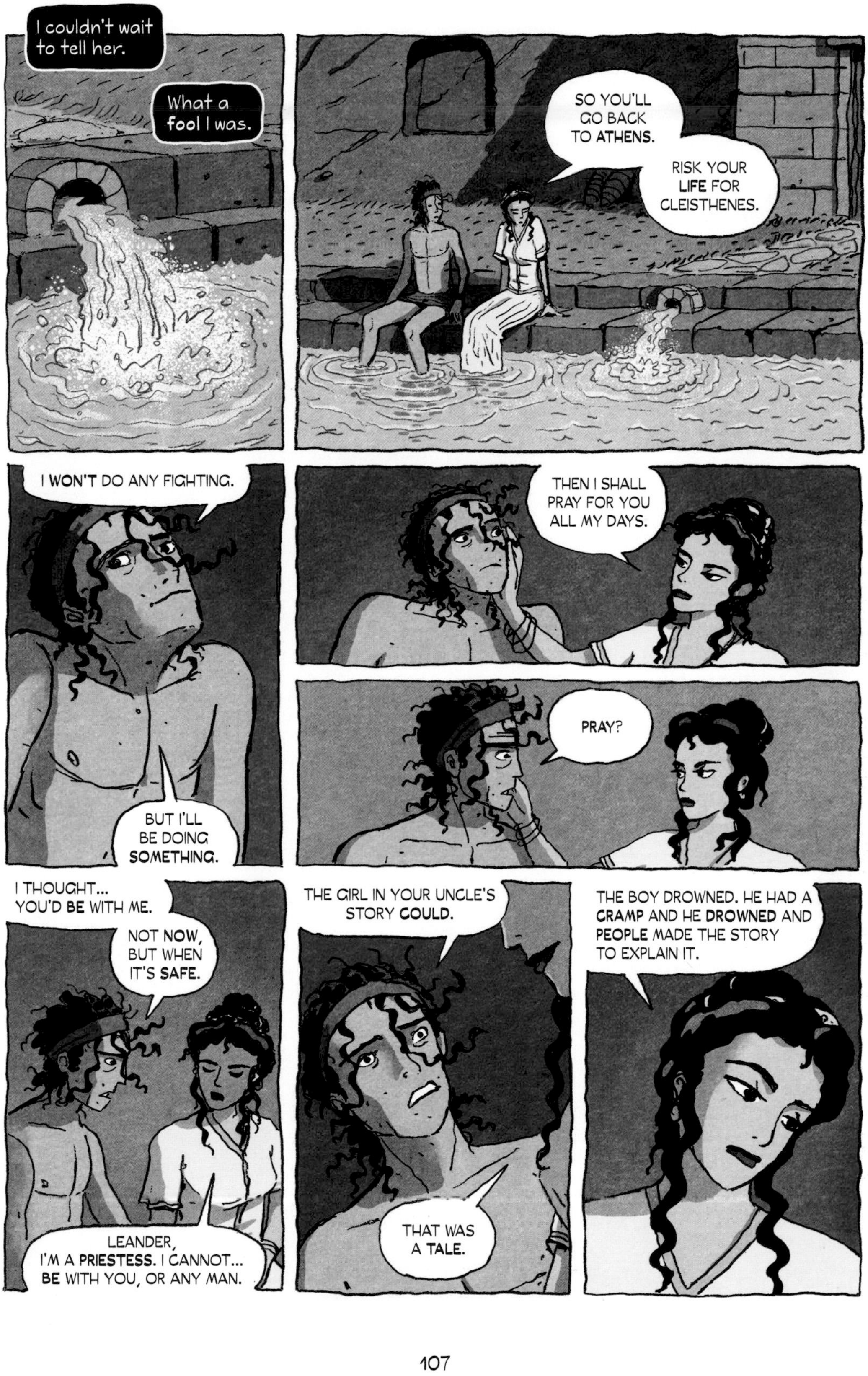

I couldn't wait to tell her.
What a **fool** I was.
SO YOU'LL GO BACK TO **ATHENS**.
RISK YOUR **LIFE** FOR CLEISTHENES.
I **WON'T** DO ANY FIGHTING.
BUT I'LL BE DOING **SOMETHING**.
THEN I SHALL PRAY FOR YOU ALL MY DAYS.
PRAY?
I THOUGHT... YOU'D **BE** WITH ME.
NOT **NOW**, BUT WHEN IT'S **SAFE**.
LEANDER, I'M A **PRIESTESS**. I CANNOT... **BE** WITH YOU, OR ANY MAN.
THE GIRL IN YOUR UNCLE'S STORY **COULD**.
THAT WAS A **TALE**.
THE BOY DROWNED. HE HAD A **CRAMP** AND HE **DROWNED** AND **PEOPLE** MADE THE STORY TO EXPLAIN IT.

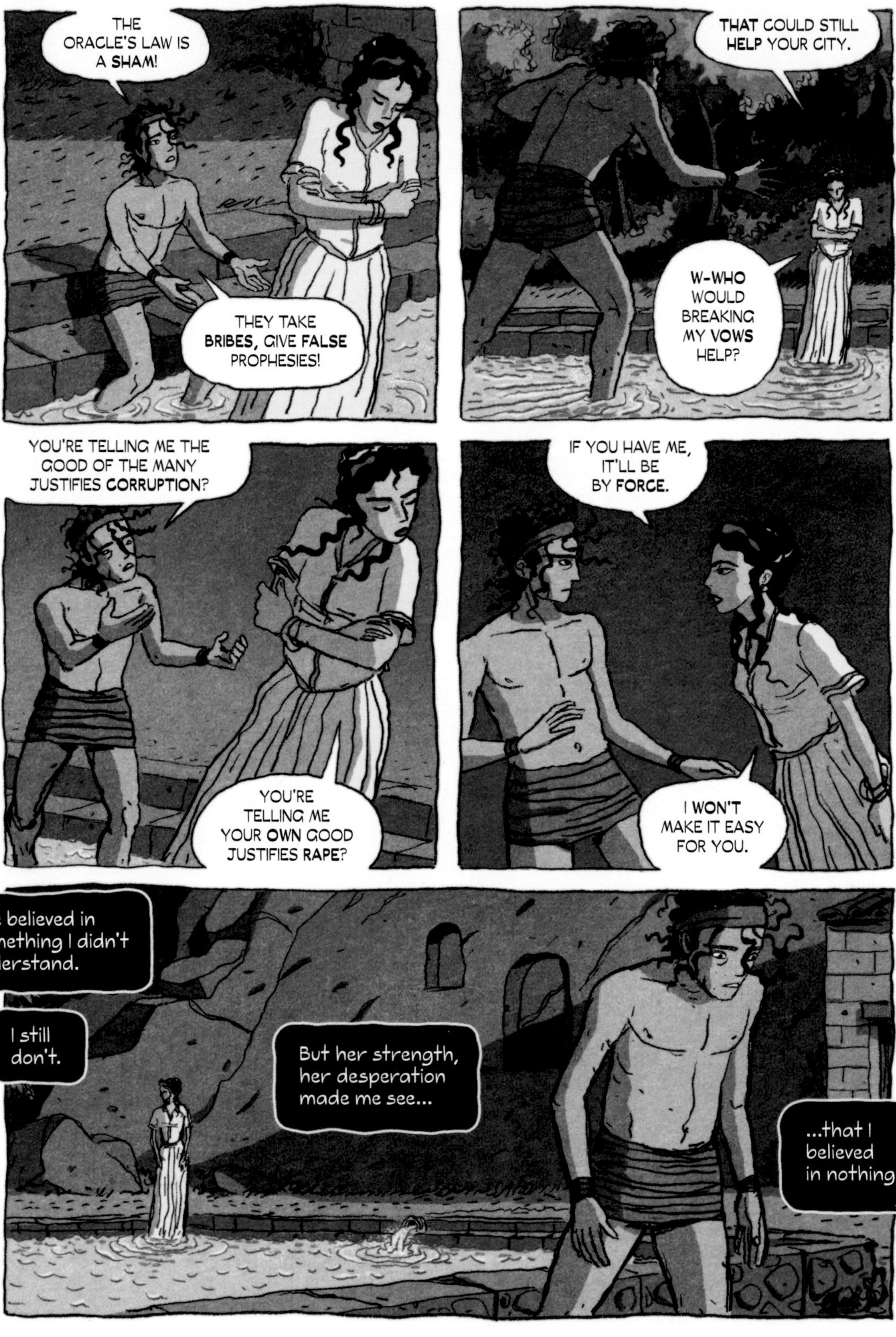
THE ORACLE'S LAW IS A **SHAM**!
THEY TAKE **BRIBES**, GIVE **FALSE** PROPHESIES!
THAT COULD STILL **HELP** YOUR CITY.
W-WHO WOULD BREAKING MY **VOWS** HELP?
YOU'RE TELLING ME THE GOOD OF THE MANY JUSTIFIES **CORRUPTION**?
YOU'RE TELLING ME YOUR **OWN** GOOD JUSTIFIES **RAPE**?
IF YOU HAVE ME, IT'LL BE BY **FORCE**.
I **WON'T** MAKE IT EASY FOR YOU.
She believed in something I didn't understand.
I still don't.
But her strength, her desperation made me see...
...that I believed in nothing.

REMEMBRANCE
FOR SALE

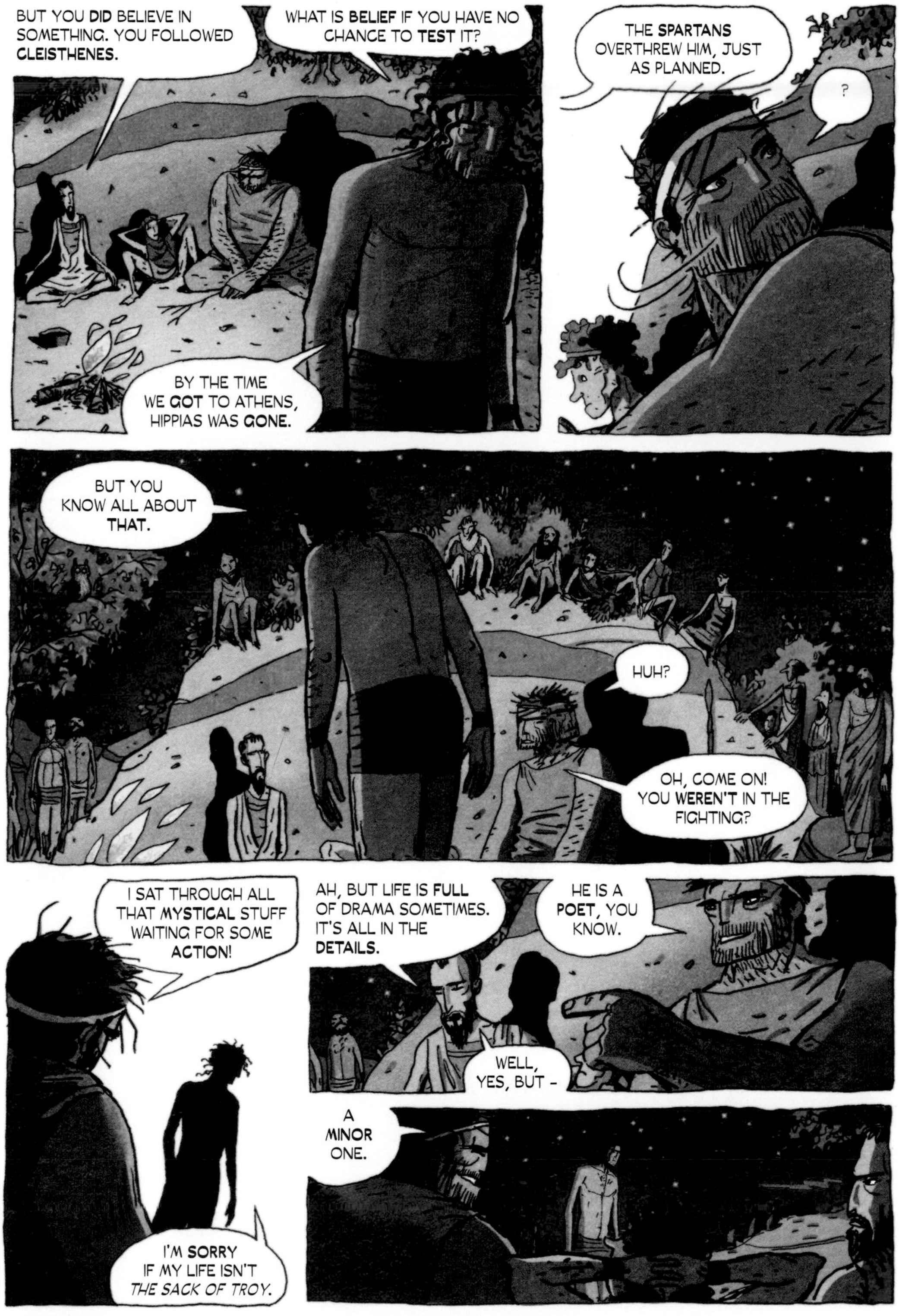
BUT YOU **DID** BELIEVE IN SOMETHING. YOU FOLLOWED **CLEISTHENES.**
WHAT IS **BELIEF** IF YOU HAVE NO CHANCE TO **TEST** IT?
BY THE TIME WE **GOT** TO ATHENS, HIPPIAS WAS **GONE.**
THE **SPARTANS** OVERTHREW HIM, JUST AS PLANNED.
?
BUT YOU KNOW ALL ABOUT **THAT.**
HUH?
OH, COME ON! YOU **WEREN'T** IN THE FIGHTING?
I SAT THROUGH ALL THAT **MYSTICAL** STUFF WAITING FOR SOME **ACTION**!
I'M **SORRY** IF MY LIFE ISN'T *THE SACK OF TROY.*
AH, BUT LIFE IS **FULL** OF DRAMA SOMETIMES. IT'S ALL IN THE **DETAILS.**
HE IS A **POET**, YOU KNOW.
WELL, YES, BUT -
A **MINOR** ONE.

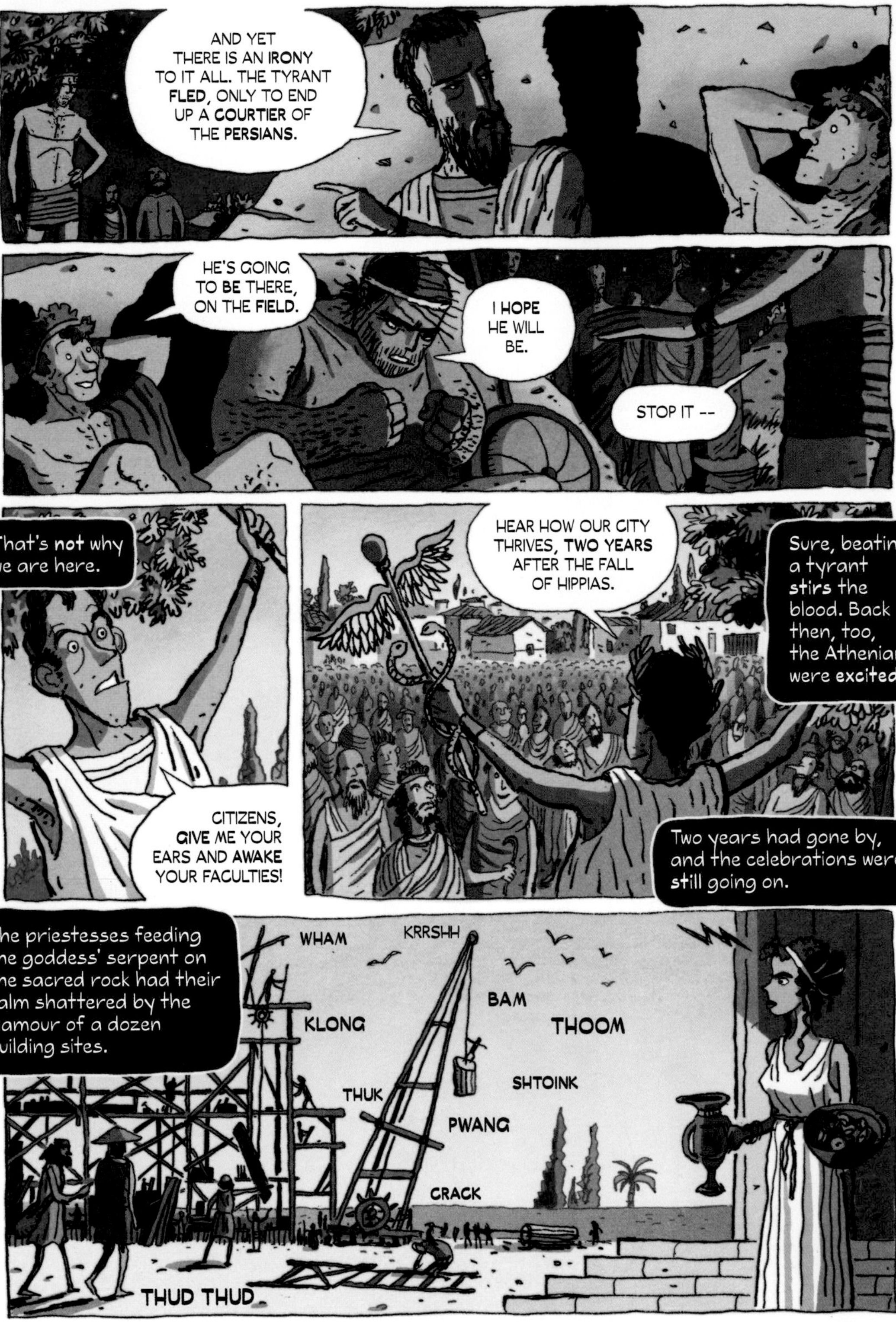
AND YET THERE IS AN IRONY TO IT ALL. THE TYRANT FLED, ONLY TO END UP A COURTIER OF THE PERSIANS.
HE'S GOING TO BE THERE, ON THE FIELD.
I HOPE HE WILL BE.
STOP IT --
That's not why we are here.
CITIZENS, GIVE ME YOUR EARS AND AWAKE YOUR FACULTIES!
HEAR HOW OUR CITY THRIVES, TWO YEARS AFTER THE FALL OF HIPPIAS.
Sure, beating a tyrant stirs the blood. Back then, too, the Athenians were excited.
Two years had gone by, and the celebrations were still going on.
The priestesses feeding the goddess' serpent on the sacred rock had their calm shattered by the clamour of a dozen building sites.
WHAM
KRRSHH
BAM
KLONG
THOOM
SHTOINK
THUK
PWANG
CRACK
THUD THUD

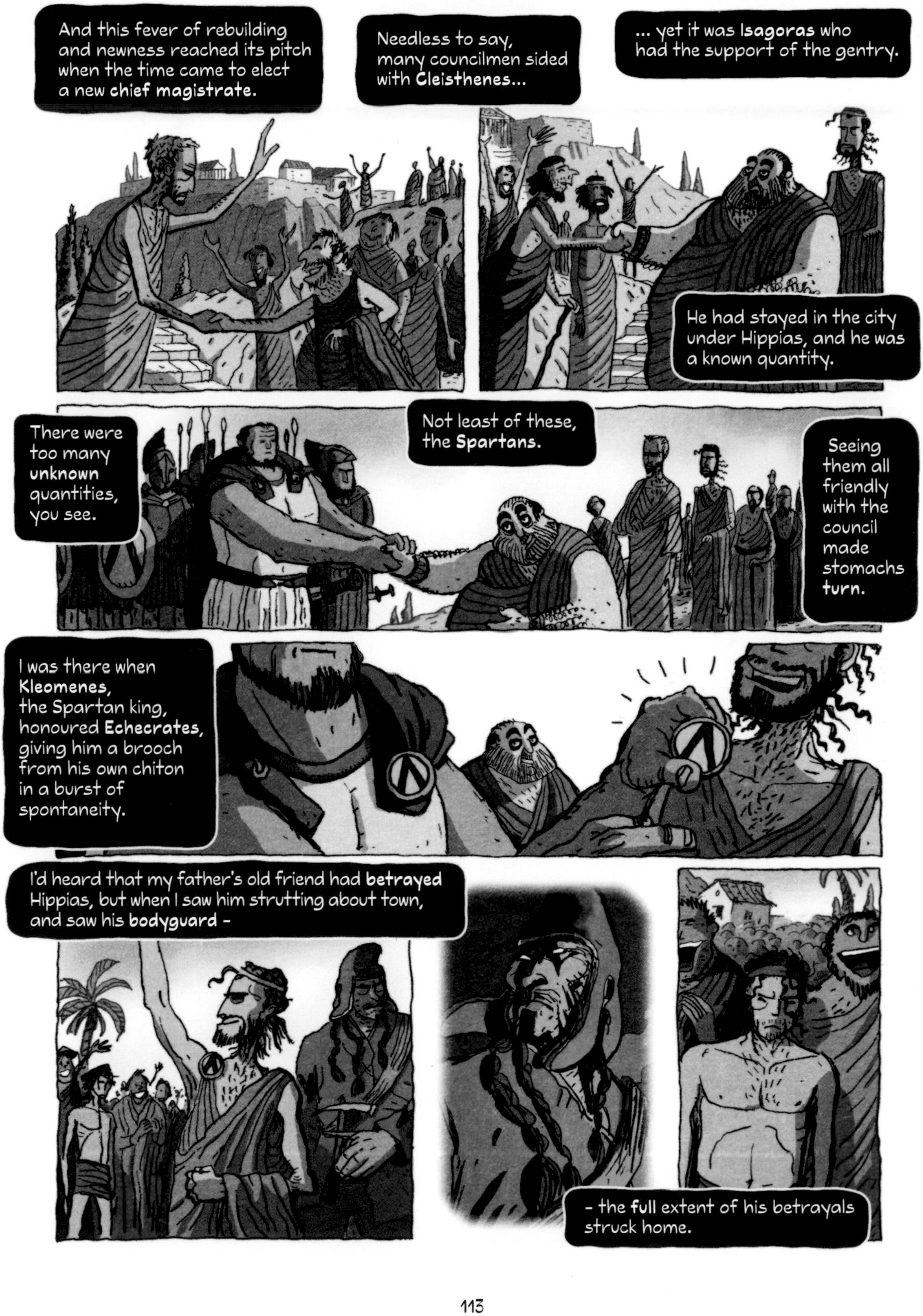
And this fever of rebuilding and newness reached its pitch when the time came to elect a new **chief magistrate**.
Needless to say, many councilmen sided with **Cleisthenes**...
... yet it was **Isagoras** who had the support of the gentry.
He had stayed in the city under Hippias, and he was a known quantity.
There were too many **unknown** quantities, you see.
Not least of these, the **Spartans**.
Seeing them all friendly with the council made stomachs **turn**.
I was there when **Kleomenes**, the Spartan king, honoured **Echecrates**, giving him a brooch from his own chiton in a burst of spontaneity.
I'd heard that my father's old friend had **betrayed** Hippias, but when I saw him strutting about town, and saw his **bodyguard** -
- the **full** extent of his betrayals struck home.

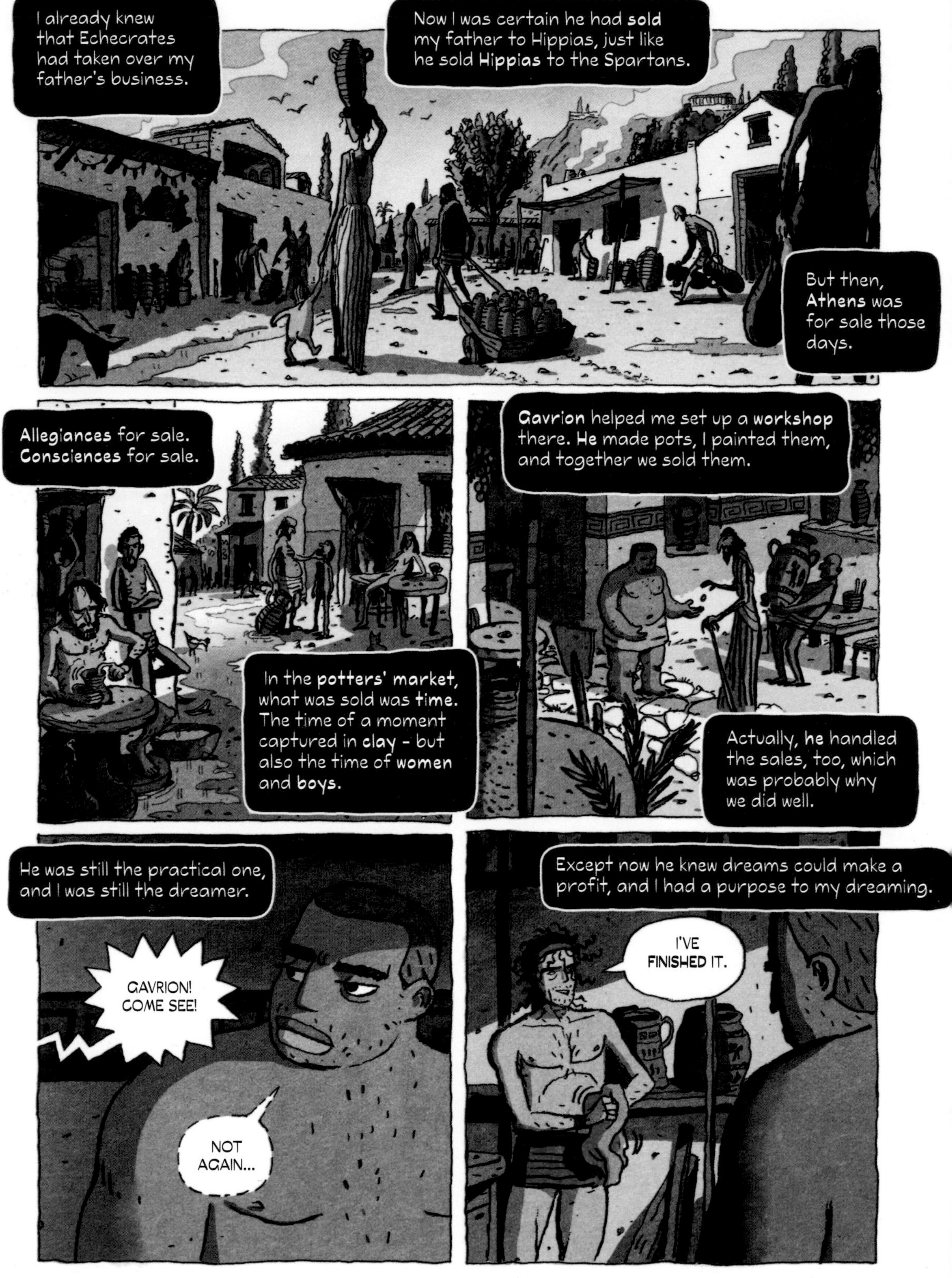
I already knew that Echecrates had taken over my father's business.
Now I was certain he had **sold** my father to Hippias, just like he sold **Hippias** to the Spartans.
But then, **Athens** was for sale those days.
Allegiances for sale. **Consciences** for sale.
In the **potters' market**, what was sold was **time**. The time of a moment captured in **clay** - but also the time of **women** and **boys**.
Gavrion helped me set up a **workshop** there. **He** made pots, I painted them, and together we sold them.
Actually, **he** handled the sales, too, which was probably why we did well.
He was still the practical one, and I was still the dreamer.
GAVRION! COME SEE!
NOT AGAIN...
Except now he knew dreams could make a profit, and I had a purpose to my dreaming.
I'VE **FINISHED** IT.

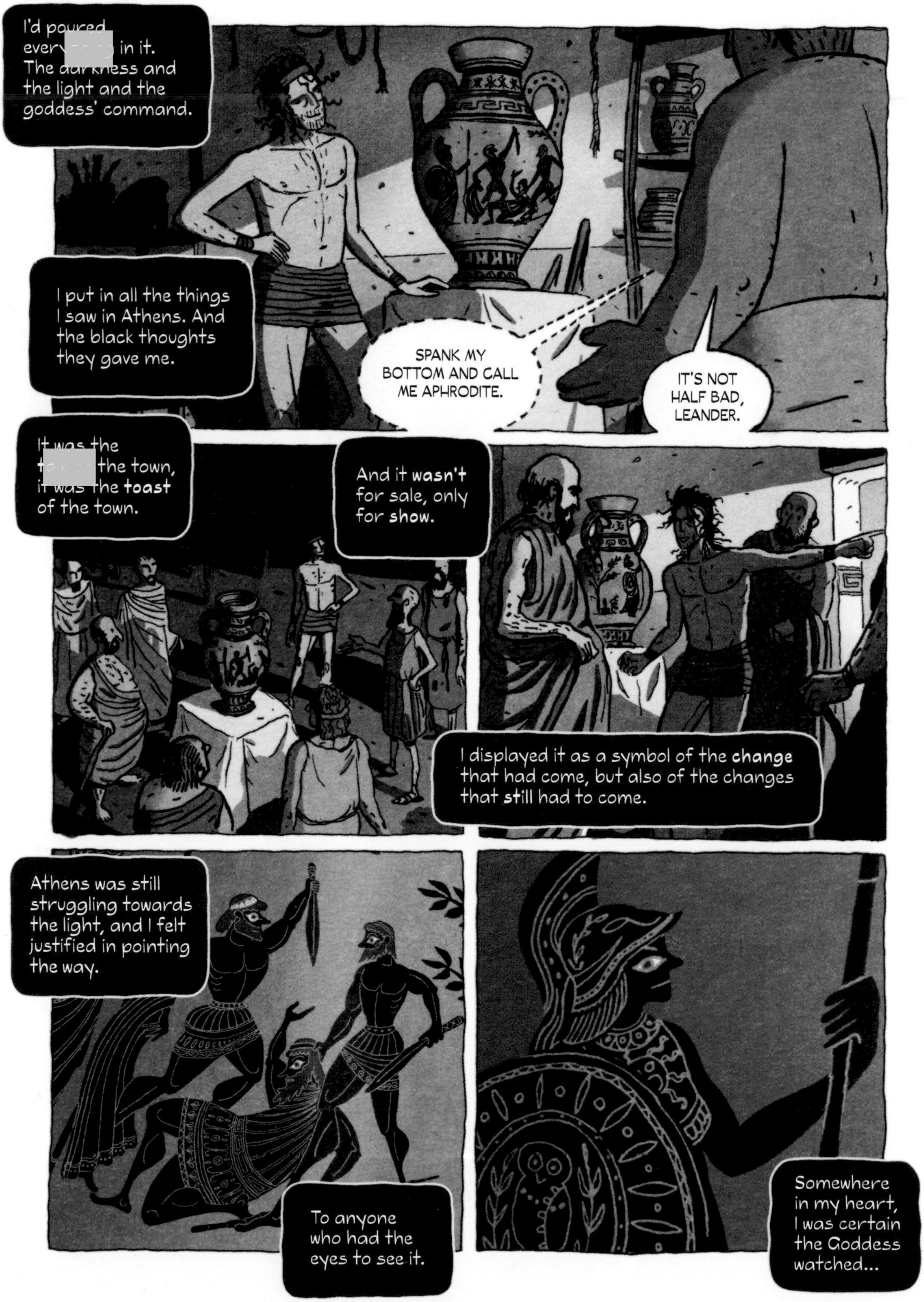
I'd poured everything in it. The darkness and the light and the goddess' command.
I put in all the things I saw in Athens. And the black thoughts they gave me.
SPANK MY BOTTOM AND CALL ME APHRODITE.
IT'S NOT HALF BAD, LEANDER.
It was the talk of the town, it was the **toast** of the town.
And it **wasn't** for sale, only for **show**.
I displayed it as a symbol of the **change** that had come, but also of the changes that **still** had to come.
Athens was still struggling towards the light, and I felt justified in pointing the way.
To anyone who had the eyes to see it.
Somewhere in my heart, I was certain the Goddess watched...

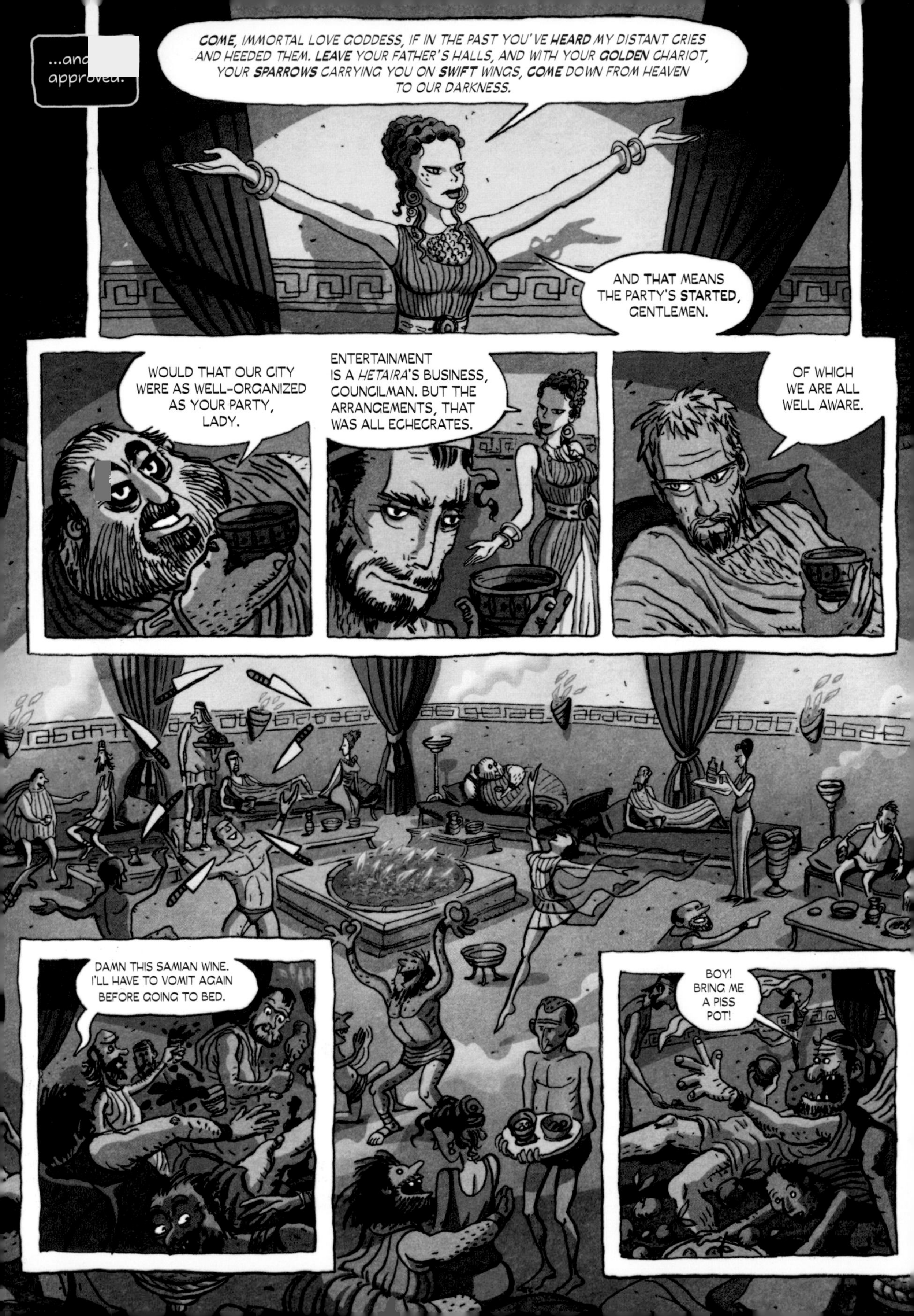

...and approved.
COME, IMMORTAL LOVE GODDESS, IF IN THE PAST YOU'VE HEARD MY DISTANT CRIES AND HEEDED THEM. LEAVE YOUR FATHER'S HALLS, AND WITH YOUR GOLDEN CHARIOT, YOUR SPARROWS CARRYING YOU ON SWIFT WINGS, COME DOWN FROM HEAVEN TO OUR DARKNESS.
AND THAT MEANS THE PARTY'S STARTED, GENTLEMEN.
WOULD THAT OUR CITY WERE AS WELL-ORGANIZED AS YOUR PARTY, LADY.
ENTERTAINMENT IS A HETAIRA'S BUSINESS, COUNCILMAN. BUT THE ARRANGEMENTS, THAT WAS ALL ECHECRATES.
OF WHICH WE ARE ALL WELL AWARE.
DAMN THIS SAMIAN WINE. I'LL HAVE TO VOMIT AGAIN BEFORE GOING TO BED.
BOY! BRING ME A PISS POT!

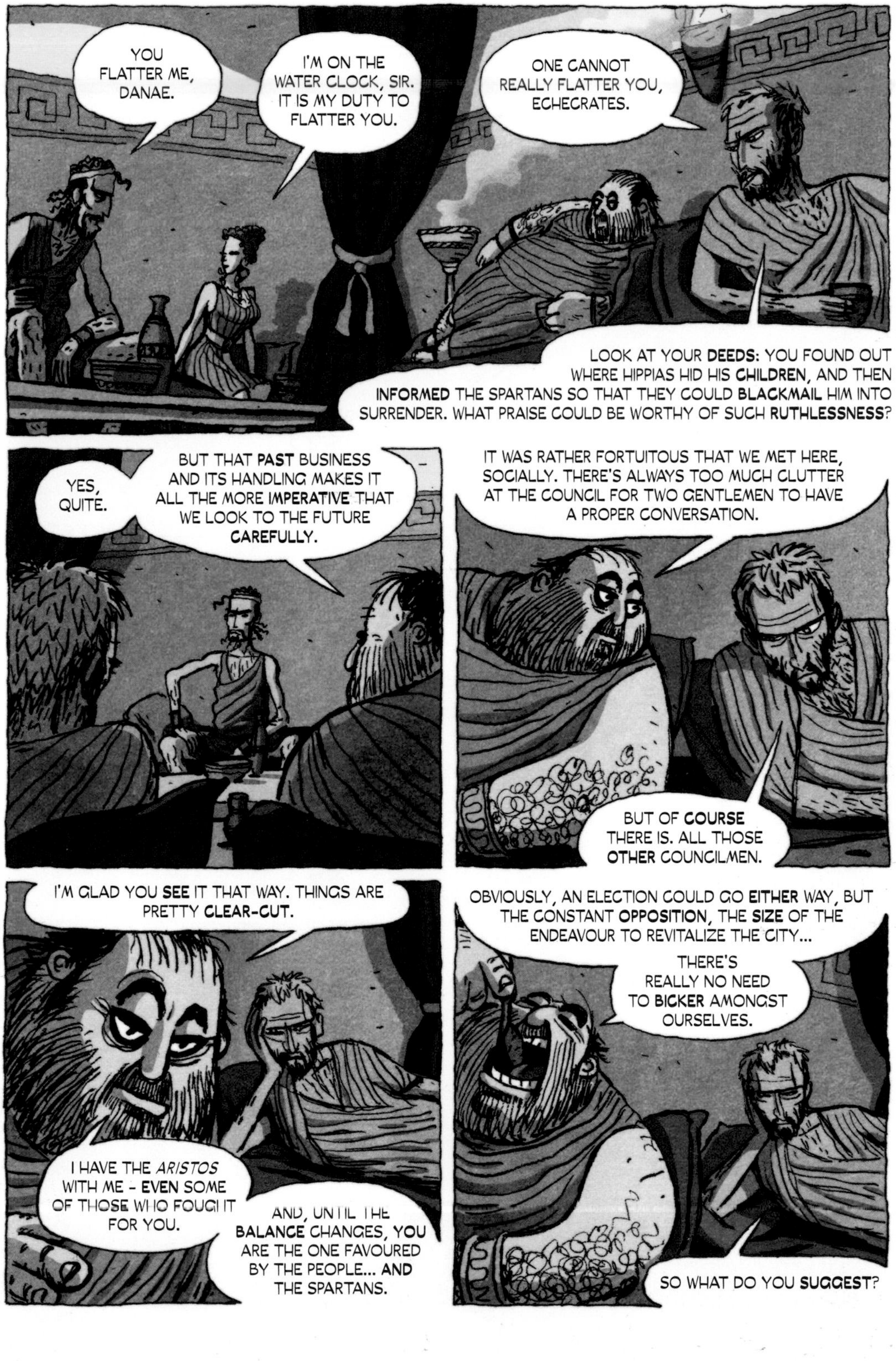
YOU FLATTER ME, DANAE.
I'M ON THE WATER CLOCK, SIR. IT IS MY DUTY TO FLATTER YOU.
ONE CANNOT REALLY FLATTER YOU, ECHECRATES.
LOOK AT YOUR DEEDS: YOU FOUND OUT WHERE HIPPIAS HID HIS CHILDREN, AND THEN INFORMED THE SPARTANS SO THAT THEY COULD BLACKMAIL HIM INTO SURRENDER. WHAT PRAISE COULD BE WORTHY OF SUCH RUTHLESSNESS?
YES, QUITE.
BUT THAT PAST BUSINESS AND ITS HANDLING MAKES IT ALL THE MORE IMPERATIVE THAT WE LOOK TO THE FUTURE CAREFULLY.
IT WAS RATHER FORTUITOUS THAT WE MET HERE, SOCIALLY. THERE'S ALWAYS TOO MUCH CLUTTER AT THE COUNCIL FOR TWO GENTLEMEN TO HAVE A PROPER CONVERSATION.
BUT OF COURSE THERE IS. ALL THOSE OTHER COUNCILMEN.
I'M GLAD YOU SEE IT THAT WAY. THINGS ARE PRETTY CLEAR-CUT.
I HAVE THE ARISTOS WITH ME - EVEN SOME OF THOSE WHO FOUGHT FOR YOU.
AND, UNTIL THE BALANCE CHANGES, YOU ARE THE ONE FAVOURED BY THE PEOPLE... AND THE SPARTANS.
OBVIOUSLY, AN ELECTION COULD GO EITHER WAY, BUT THE CONSTANT OPPOSITION, THE SIZE OF THE ENDEAVOUR TO REVITALIZE THE CITY...
THERE'S REALLY NO NEED TO BICKER AMONGST OURSELVES.
SO WHAT DO YOU SUGGEST?

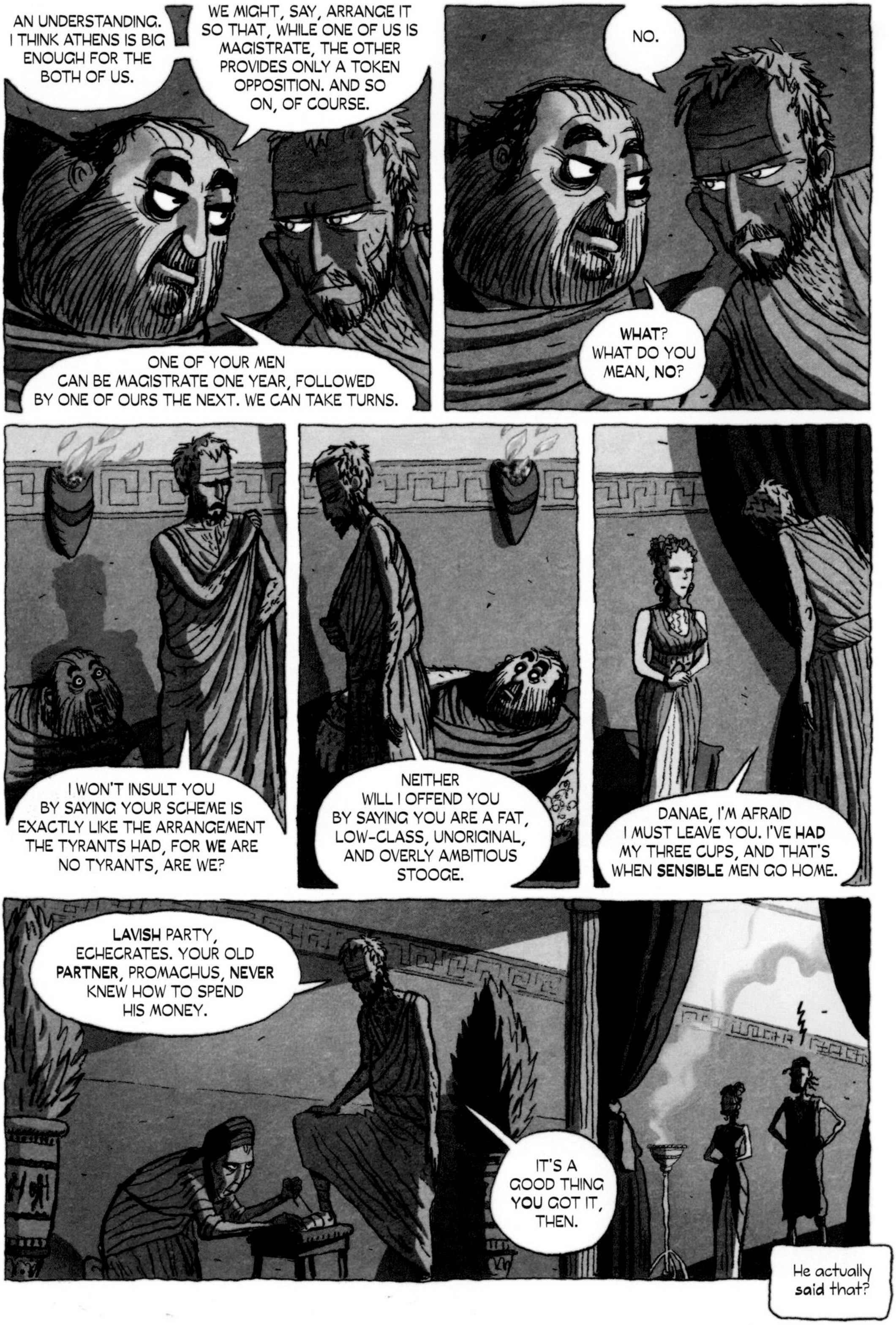
AN UNDERSTANDING. I THINK ATHENS IS BIG ENOUGH FOR THE BOTH OF US.
WE MIGHT, SAY, ARRANGE IT SO THAT, WHILE ONE OF US IS MAGISTRATE, THE OTHER PROVIDES ONLY A TOKEN OPPOSITION. AND SO ON, OF COURSE.
ONE OF YOUR MEN CAN BE MAGISTRATE ONE YEAR, FOLLOWED BY ONE OF OURS THE NEXT. WE CAN TAKE TURNS.
NO.
WHAT? WHAT DO YOU MEAN, **NO**?
I WON'T INSULT YOU BY SAYING YOUR SCHEME IS EXACTLY LIKE THE ARRANGEMENT THE TYRANTS HAD, FOR **WE** ARE NO TYRANTS, ARE WE?
NEITHER WILL I OFFEND YOU BY SAYING YOU ARE A FAT, LOW-CLASS, UNORIGINAL, AND OVERLY AMBITIOUS STOOGE.
DANAE, I'M AFRAID I MUST LEAVE YOU. I'VE **HAD** MY THREE CUPS, AND THAT'S WHEN **SENSIBLE** MEN GO HOME.
LAVISH PARTY, ECHECRATES. YOUR OLD **PARTNER**, PROMACHUS, **NEVER** KNEW HOW TO SPEND HIS MONEY.
IT'S A GOOD THING **YOU** GOT IT, THEN.
He actually **said** that?

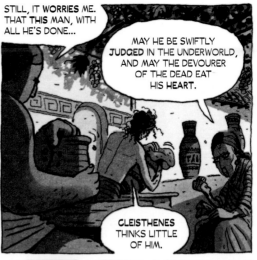

I HEARD HIM WITH MY OWN EARS.
HA! IF ONLY I COULD SEE ECHECRATES' FACE!
SERVES HIM RIGHT, THAT TWO-FACED CUR.
STILL, IT WORRIES ME. THAT THIS MAN, WITH ALL HE'S DONE...
MAY HE BE SWIFTLY JUDGED IN THE UNDERWORLD, AND MAY THE DEVOURER OF THE DEAD EAT HIS HEART.
CLEISTHENES THINKS LITTLE OF HIM.
BUT WHAT DOES ISAGORAS THINK OF HIM?
AT LEAST YOU ARE OUT OF ECHECRATES' HOUSE, OLD MOTHER.
HE GAVE ME TO THE *HETAIRA*, LAST NIGHT. I THINK HE WANTS TO BE HER LOVER.
I'LL GET MONEY, BUY YOU BACK.
THE MAN STOLE YOUR FATHER'S FORTUNE, LITTLE VOICE, NOT JUST ME.
YOU LOOK AFTER YOURSELVES, AND OLD NEFERT WILL COME SEE YOU EVERY TIME SHE'S OUT SHOPPING. THESE ARE THORNY TIMES, AND THE WORST IS YET TO COME.
As the city became increasingly gripped by election fever, Nefert's words were nothing but prophetic.
CLEISTHENES WEAVES LIES
VOTE OUR MAGISTRATE
WIDE-ASSED ISAGORAS
DOWN WITH
The people were split down the middle; tempers flared, and fights broke out...

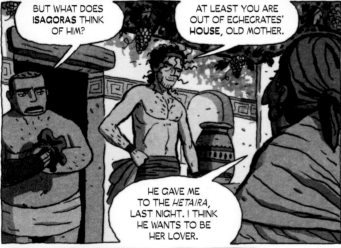

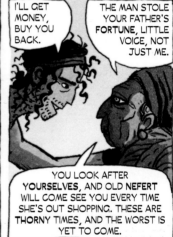

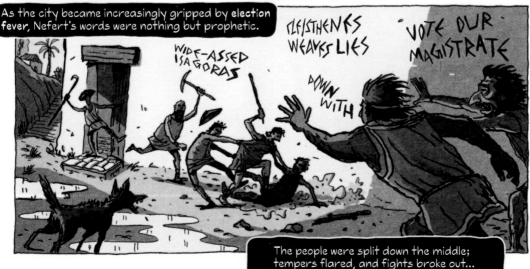

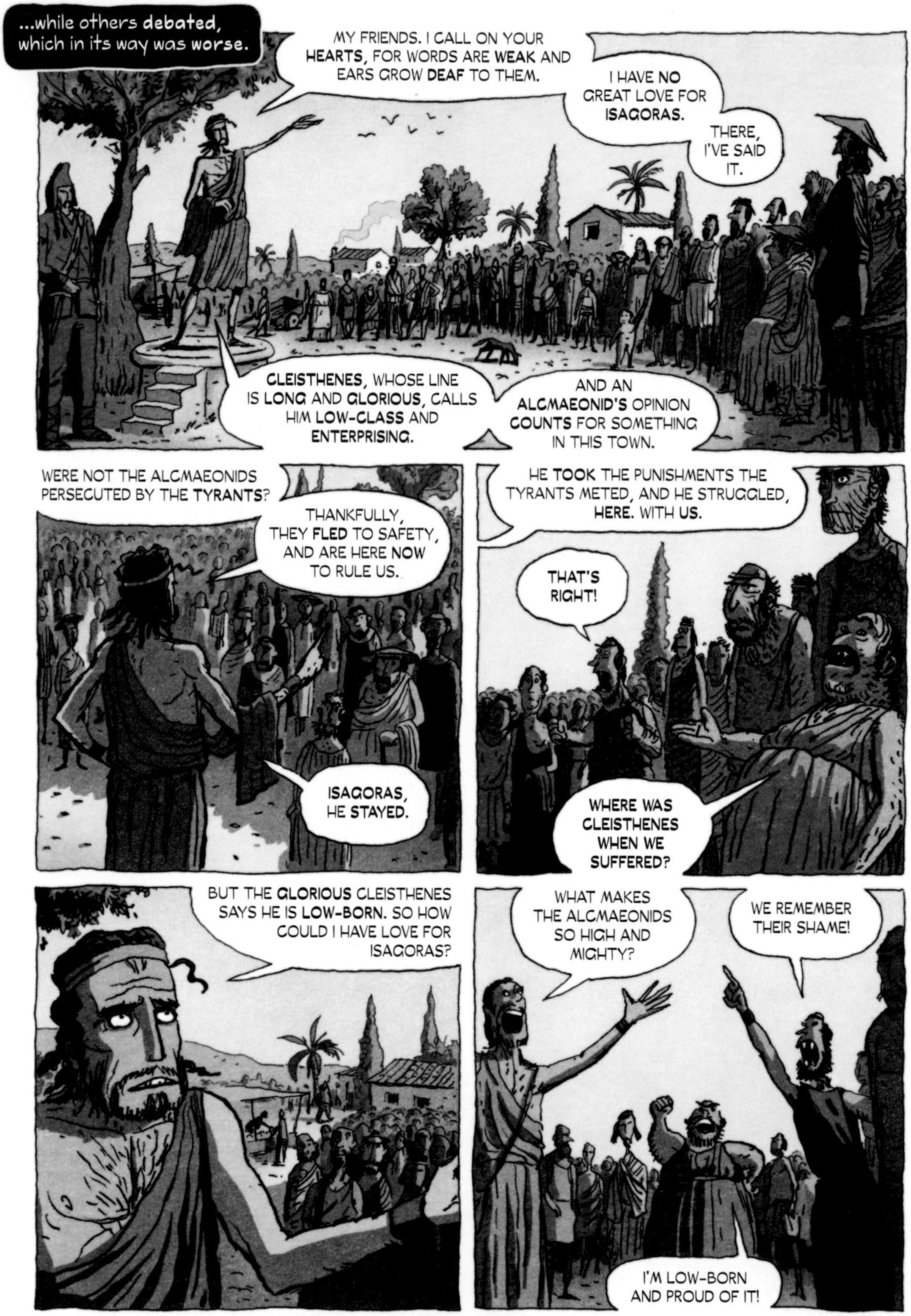
...while others debated, which in its way was worse.
MY FRIENDS. I CALL ON YOUR HEARTS, FOR WORDS ARE WEAK AND EARS GROW DEAF TO THEM.
I HAVE NO GREAT LOVE FOR ISAGORAS.
THERE, I'VE SAID IT.
CLEISTHENES, WHOSE LINE IS LONG AND GLORIOUS, CALLS HIM LOW-CLASS AND ENTERPRISING.
AND AN ALCMAEONID'S OPINION COUNTS FOR SOMETHING IN THIS TOWN.
WERE NOT THE ALCMAEONIDS PERSECUTED BY THE TYRANTS?
THANKFULLY, THEY FLED TO SAFETY, AND ARE HERE NOW TO RULE US.
ISAGORAS, HE STAYED.
HE TOOK THE PUNISHMENTS THE TYRANTS METED, AND HE STRUGGLED, HERE. WITH US.
THAT'S RIGHT!
WHERE WAS CLEISTHENES WHEN WE SUFFERED?
BUT THE GLORIOUS CLEISTHENES SAYS HE IS LOW-BORN. SO HOW COULD I HAVE LOVE FOR ISAGORAS?
WHAT MAKES THE ALCMAEONIDS SO HIGH AND MIGHTY?
WE REMEMBER THEIR SHAME!
I'M LOW-BORN AND PROUD OF IT!

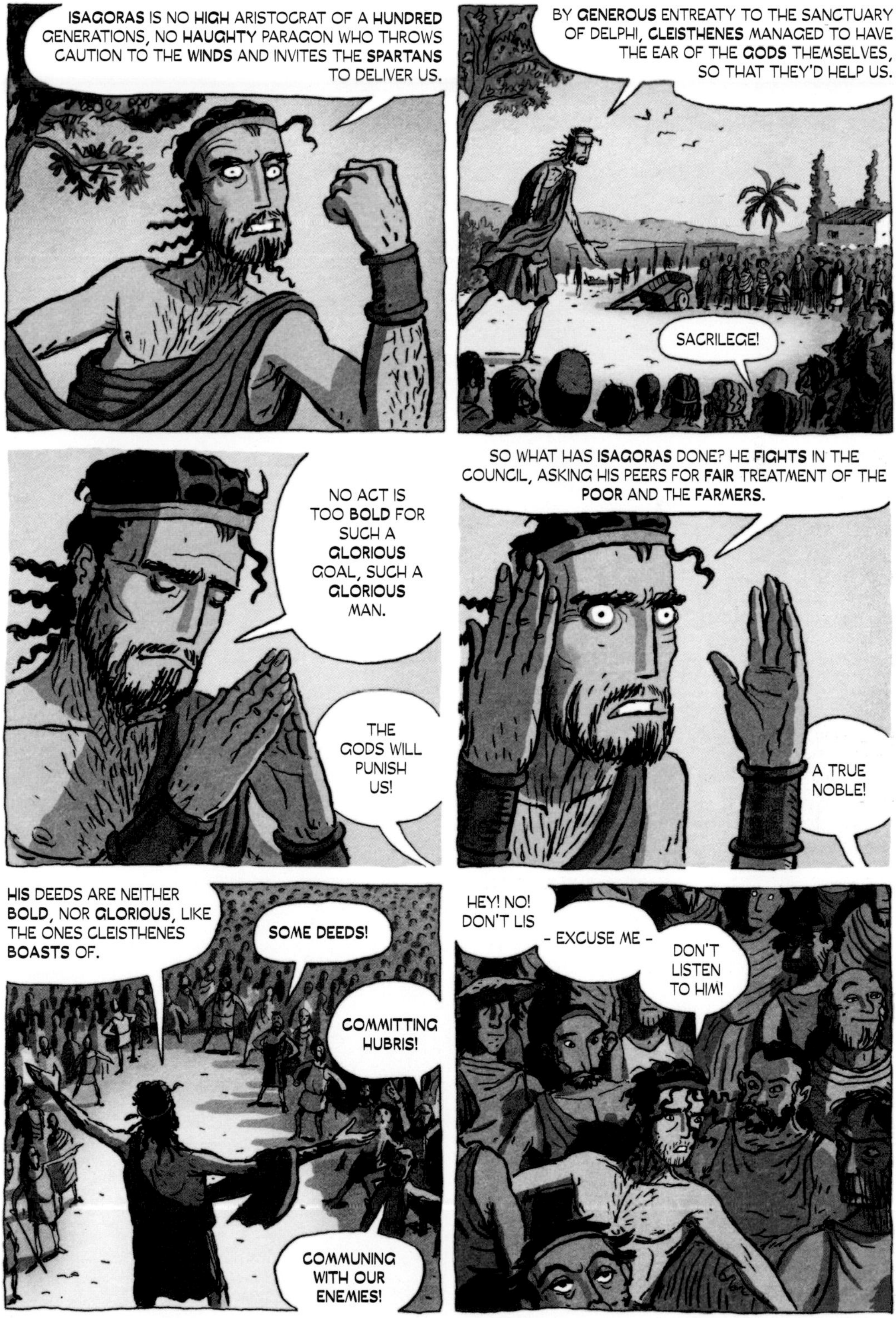
ISAGORAS IS NO HIGH ARISTOCRAT OF A HUNDRED GENERATIONS, NO HAUGHTY PARAGON WHO THROWS CAUTION TO THE WINDS AND INVITES THE SPARTANS TO DELIVER US.
BY GENEROUS ENTREATY TO THE SANCTUARY OF DELPHI, CLEISTHENES MANAGED TO HAVE THE EAR OF THE GODS THEMSELVES, SO THAT THEY'D HELP US.
SACRILEGE!
NO ACT IS TOO BOLD FOR SUCH A GLORIOUS GOAL, SUCH A GLORIOUS MAN.
THE GODS WILL PUNISH US!
SO WHAT HAS ISAGORAS DONE? HE FIGHTS IN THE COUNCIL, ASKING HIS PEERS FOR FAIR TREATMENT OF THE POOR AND THE FARMERS.
A TRUE NOBLE!
HIS DEEDS ARE NEITHER BOLD, NOR GLORIOUS, LIKE THE ONES CLEISTHENES BOASTS OF.
SOME DEEDS!
COMMITTING HUBRIS!
COMMUNING WITH OUR ENEMIES!
HEY! NO! DON'T LIS
- EXCUSE ME -
DON'T LISTEN TO HIM!

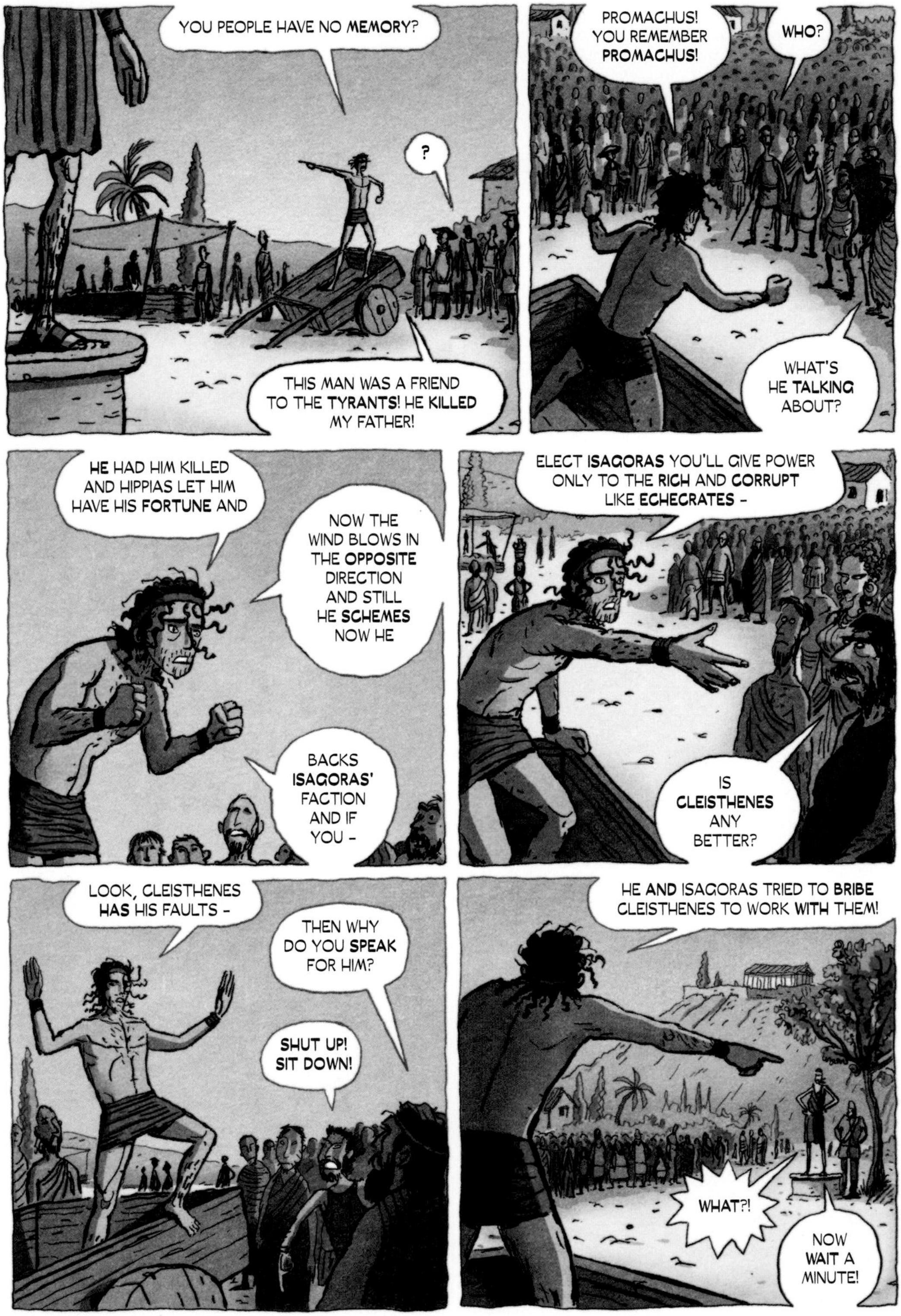
YOU PEOPLE HAVE NO MEMORY?
?
THIS MAN WAS A FRIEND TO THE TYRANTS! HE KILLED MY FATHER!
PROMACHUS! YOU REMEMBER PROMACHUS!
WHO?
WHAT'S HE TALKING ABOUT?
HE HAD HIM KILLED AND HIPPIAS LET HIM HAVE HIS FORTUNE AND
NOW THE WIND BLOWS IN THE OPPOSITE DIRECTION AND STILL HE SCHEMES NOW HE
BACKS ISAGORAS' FACTION AND IF YOU –
ELECT ISAGORAS YOU'LL GIVE POWER ONLY TO THE RICH AND CORRUPT LIKE ECHECRATES –
IS CLEISTHENES ANY BETTER?
LOOK, CLEISTHENES HAS HIS FAULTS –
THEN WHY DO YOU SPEAK FOR HIM?
SHUT UP! SIT DOWN!
HE AND ISAGORAS TRIED TO BRIBE CLEISTHENES TO WORK WITH THEM!
WHAT?!
NOW WAIT A MINUTE!

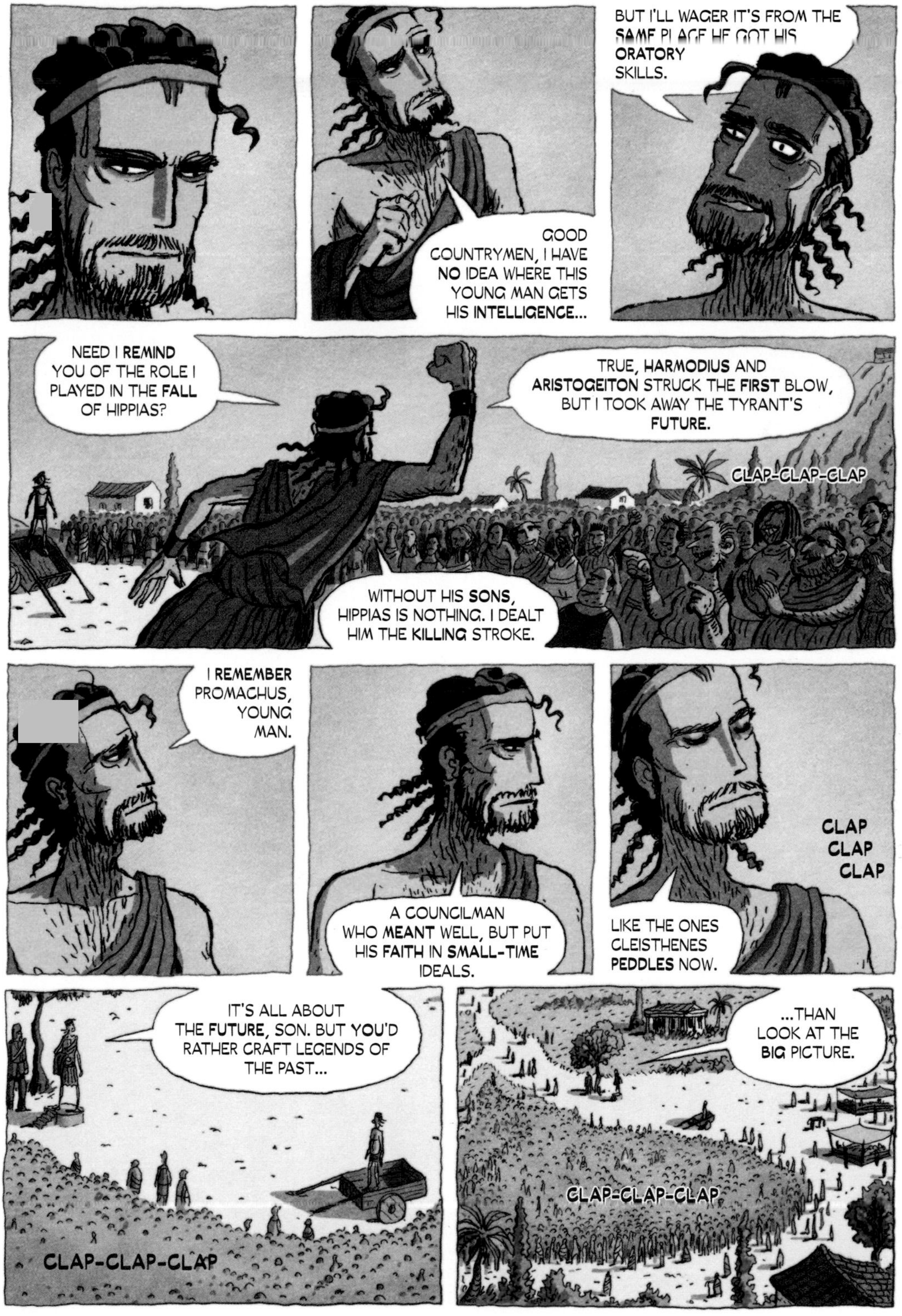
GOOD COUNTRYMEN, I HAVE NO IDEA WHERE THIS YOUNG MAN GETS HIS INTELLIGENCE...
BUT I'LL WAGER IT'S FROM THE SAME PLACE HE GOT HIS ORATORY SKILLS.
NEED I REMIND YOU OF THE ROLE I PLAYED IN THE FALL OF HIPPIAS?
TRUE, HARMODIUS AND ARISTOGEITON STRUCK THE FIRST BLOW, BUT I TOOK AWAY THE TYRANT'S FUTURE.
CLAP-CLAP-CLAP
WITHOUT HIS SONS, HIPPIAS IS NOTHING. I DEALT HIM THE KILLING STROKE.
I REMEMBER PROMACHUS, YOUNG MAN.
A COUNCILMAN WHO MEANT WELL, BUT PUT HIS FAITH IN SMALL-TIME IDEALS.
CLAP
CLAP
CLAP
LIKE THE ONES CLEISTHENES PEDDLES NOW.
IT'S ALL ABOUT THE FUTURE, SON. BUT YOU'D RATHER CRAFT LEGENDS OF THE PAST...
CLAP-CLAP-CLAP
...THAN LOOK AT THE BIG PICTURE.
CLAP-CLAP-CLAP

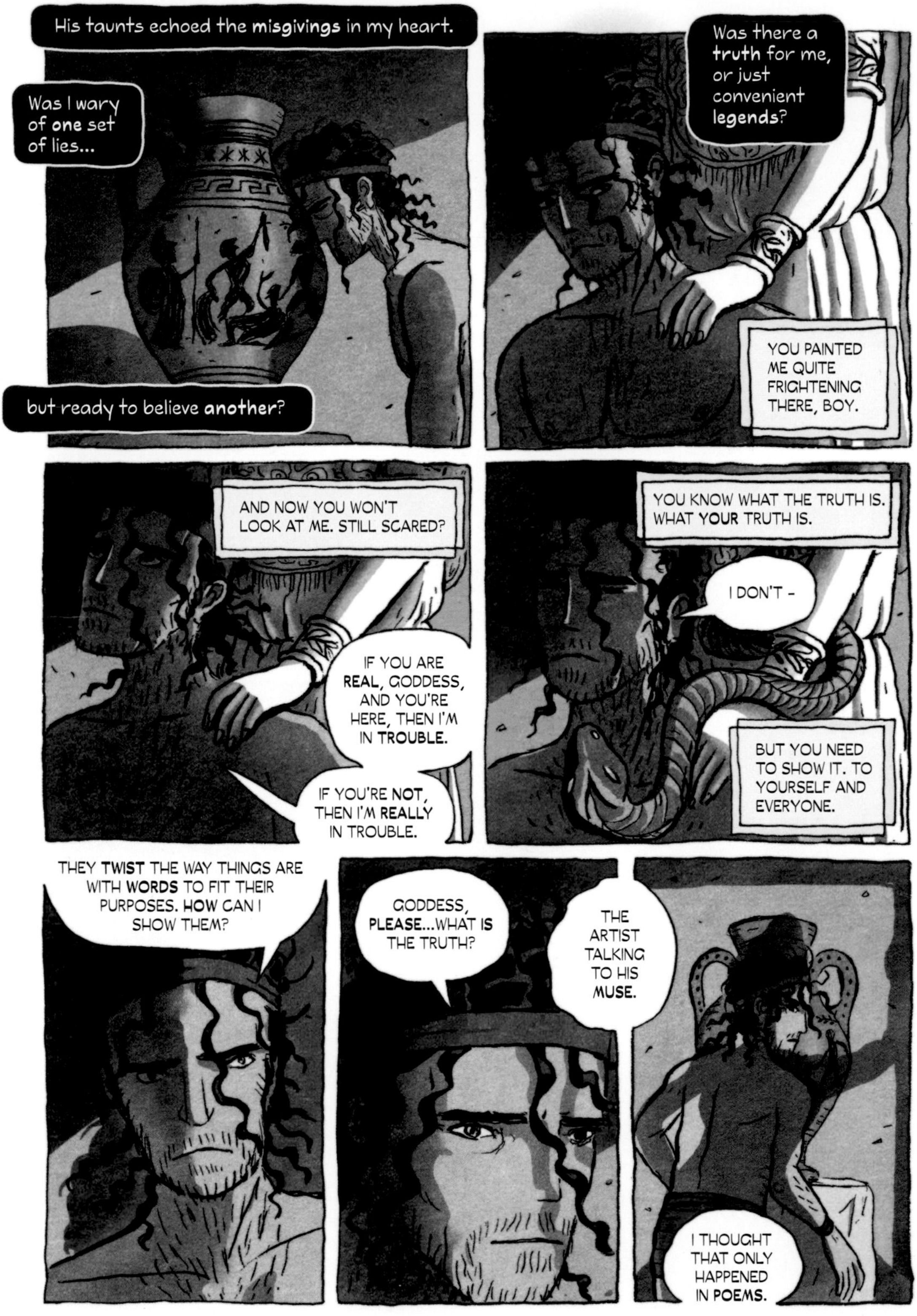
His taunts echoed the **misgivings** in my heart.
Was I wary of **one** set of lies...
but ready to believe **another**?
Was there a **truth** for me, or just convenient **legends**?
YOU PAINTED ME QUITE FRIGHTENING THERE, BOY.
AND NOW YOU WON'T LOOK AT ME. STILL SCARED?
IF YOU ARE **REAL**, GODDESS, AND YOU'RE HERE, THEN I'M IN **TROUBLE**.
IF YOU'RE **NOT**, THEN I'M **REALLY** IN TROUBLE.
YOU KNOW WHAT THE TRUTH IS. WHAT **YOUR** TRUTH IS.
I DON'T -
BUT YOU NEED TO SHOW IT. TO YOURSELF AND EVERYONE.
THEY **TWIST** THE WAY THINGS ARE WITH **WORDS** TO FIT THEIR PURPOSES. **HOW CAN I** SHOW THEM?
GODDESS, **PLEASE**...WHAT **IS** THE TRUTH?
THE ARTIST TALKING TO HIS **MUSE**.
I THOUGHT THAT ONLY HAPPENED IN **POEMS**.

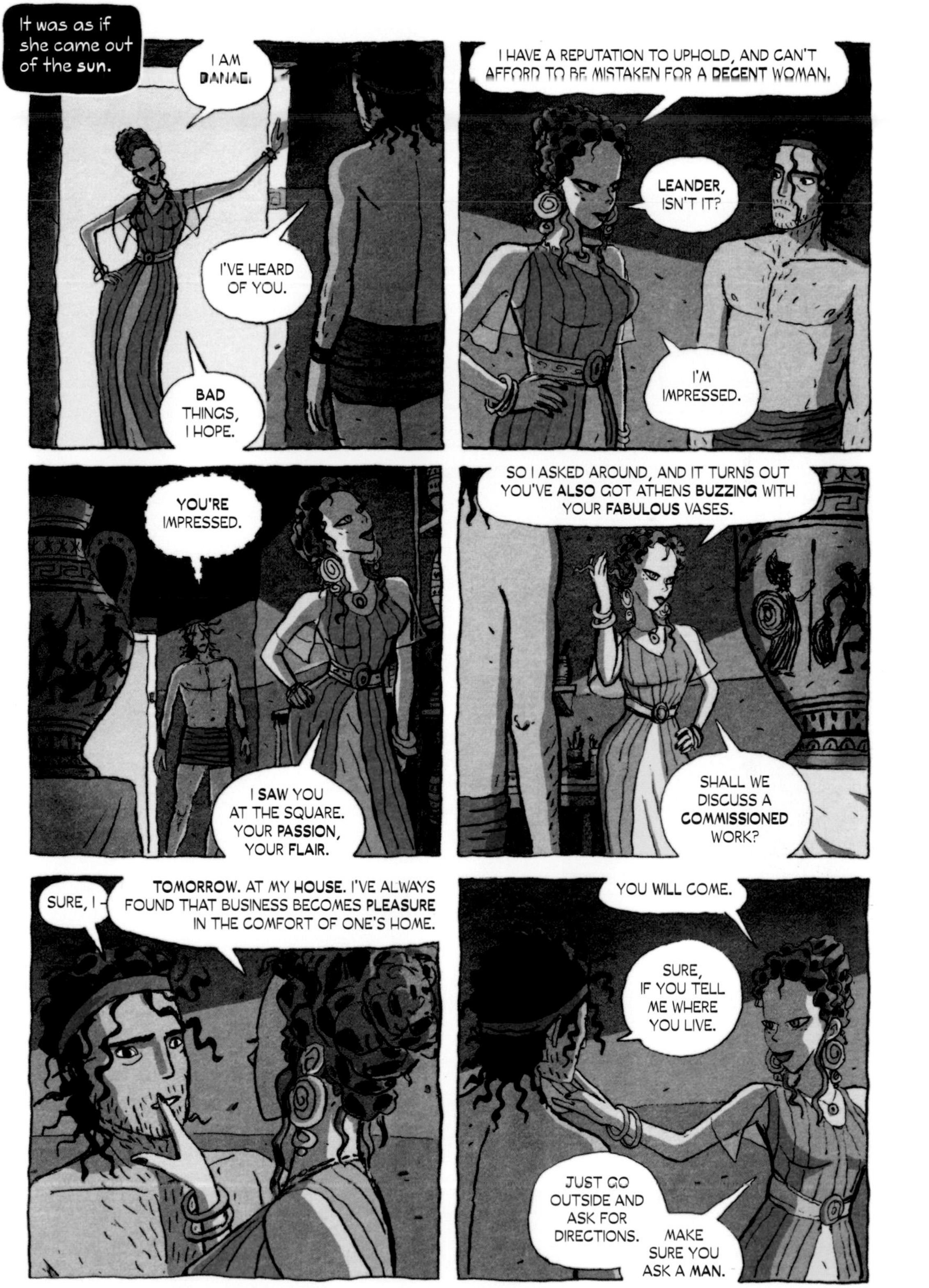
It was as if she came out of the sun.
I AM DANAE.
I'VE HEARD OF YOU.
BAD THINGS, I HOPE.
I HAVE A REPUTATION TO UPHOLD, AND CAN'T AFFORD TO BE MISTAKEN FOR A DECENT WOMAN.
LEANDER, ISN'T IT?
I'M IMPRESSED.
YOU'RE IMPRESSED.
I SAW YOU AT THE SQUARE. YOUR PASSION, YOUR FLAIR.
SO I ASKED AROUND, AND IT TURNS OUT YOU'VE ALSO GOT ATHENS BUZZING WITH YOUR FABULOUS VASES.
SHALL WE DISCUSS A COMMISSIONED WORK?
SURE, I –
TOMORROW. AT MY HOUSE. I'VE ALWAYS FOUND THAT BUSINESS BECOMES PLEASURE IN THE COMFORT OF ONE'S HOME.
YOU WILL COME.
SURE, IF YOU TELL ME WHERE YOU LIVE.
JUST GO OUTSIDE AND ASK FOR DIRECTIONS.
MAKE SURE YOU ASK A MAN.

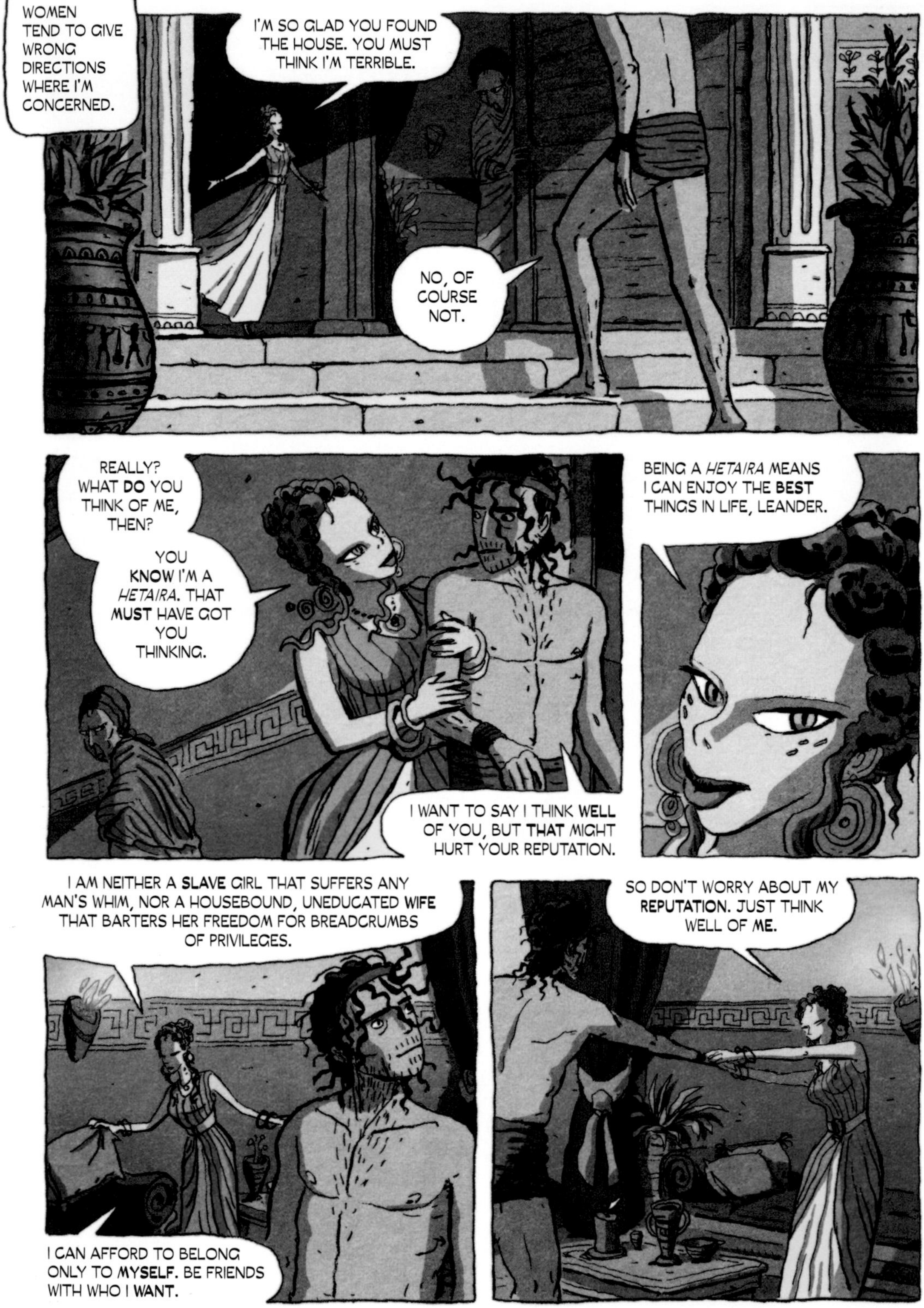
WOMEN TEND TO GIVE WRONG DIRECTIONS WHERE I'M CONCERNED.
I'M SO GLAD YOU FOUND THE HOUSE. YOU MUST THINK I'M TERRIBLE.
NO, OF COURSE NOT.
REALLY? WHAT DO YOU THINK OF ME, THEN?
YOU KNOW I'M A HETAIRA. THAT MUST HAVE GOT YOU THINKING.
I WANT TO SAY I THINK WELL OF YOU, BUT THAT MIGHT HURT YOUR REPUTATION.
BEING A HETAIRA MEANS I CAN ENJOY THE BEST THINGS IN LIFE, LEANDER.
I AM NEITHER A SLAVE GIRL THAT SUFFERS ANY MAN'S WHIM, NOR A HOUSEBOUND, UNEDUCATED WIFE THAT BARTERS HER FREEDOM FOR BREADCRUMBS OF PRIVILEGES.
I CAN AFFORD TO BELONG ONLY TO MYSELF. BE FRIENDS WITH WHO I WANT.
SO DON'T WORRY ABOUT MY REPUTATION. JUST THINK WELL OF ME.

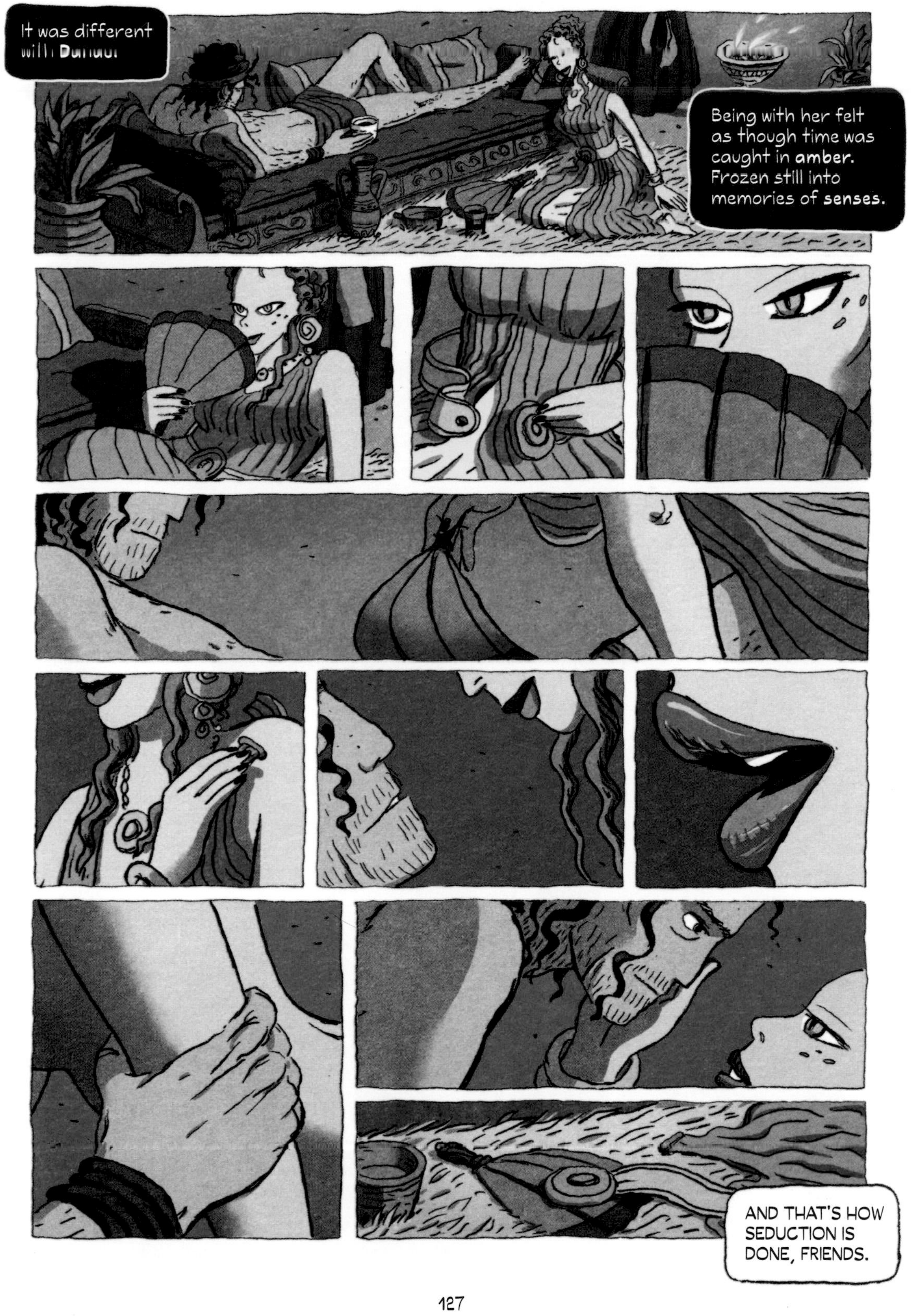
It was different
Being with her felt as though time was caught in **amber**. Frozen still into memories of **senses**.
AND THAT'S HOW SEDUCTION IS DONE, FRIENDS.

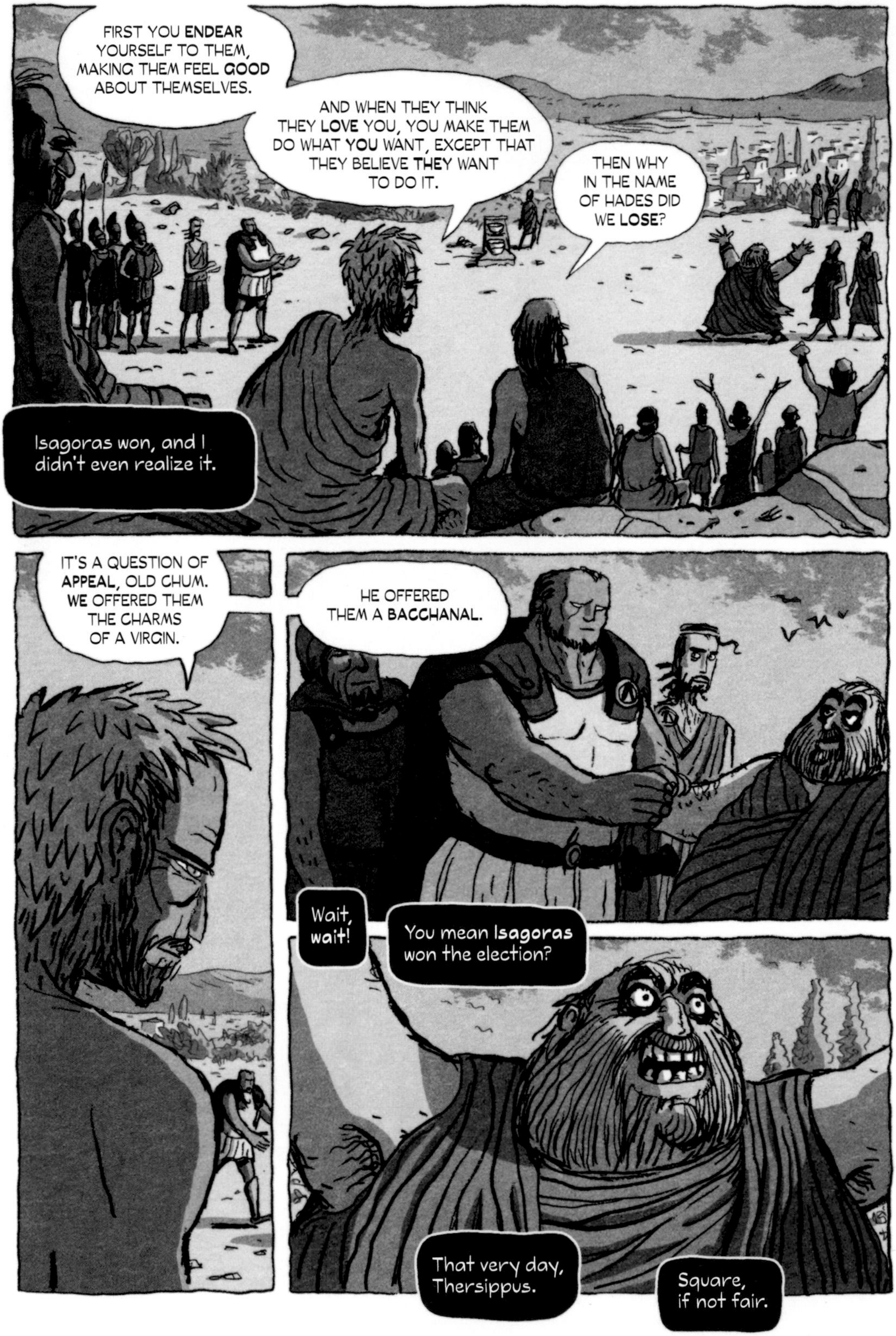

FIRST YOU **ENDEAR** YOURSELF TO THEM, MAKING THEM FEEL **GOOD** ABOUT THEMSELVES.
AND WHEN THEY THINK THEY **LOVE** YOU, YOU MAKE THEM DO WHAT **YOU** WANT, EXCEPT THAT THEY BELIEVE **THEY** WANT TO DO IT.
THEN WHY IN THE NAME OF HADES DID WE **LOSE**?
Isagoras won, and I didn't even realize it.
IT'S A QUESTION OF **APPEAL**, OLD CHUM. **WE** OFFERED THEM THE CHARMS OF A VIRGIN.
HE OFFERED THEM A **BACCHANAL.**
Wait, **wait!**
You mean **Isagoras** won the election?
That very day, Thersippus.
Square, if not fair.

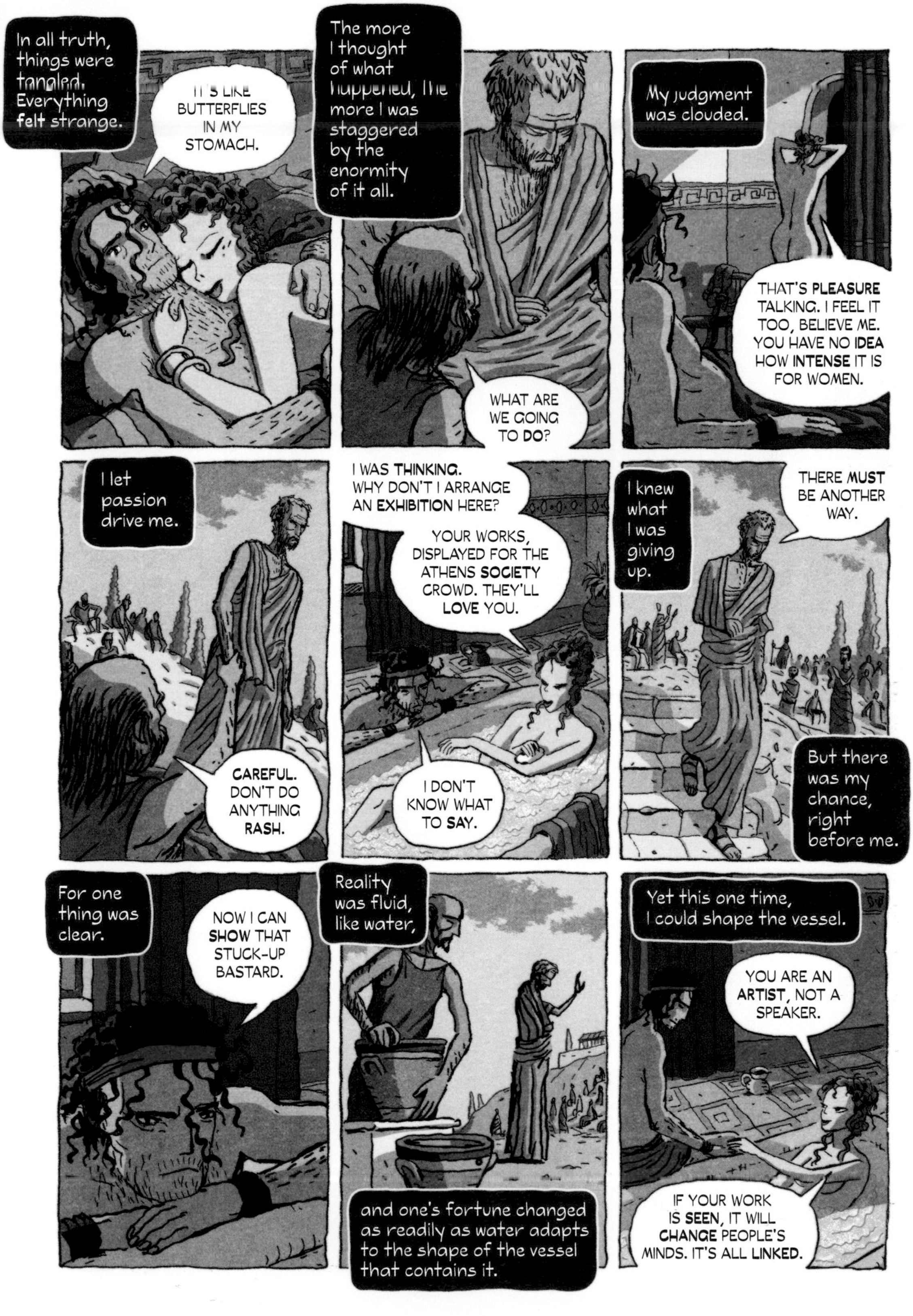

In all truth, things were tangled. Everything felt strange.
IT'S LIKE BUTTERFLIES IN MY STOMACH.
The more I thought of what happened, the more I was staggered by the enormity of it all.
WHAT ARE WE GOING TO DO?
My judgment was clouded.
THAT'S PLEASURE TALKING. I FEEL IT TOO, BELIEVE ME. YOU HAVE NO IDEA HOW INTENSE IT IS FOR WOMEN.
I let passion drive me.
CAREFUL. DON'T DO ANYTHING RASH.
I WAS THINKING. WHY DON'T I ARRANGE AN EXHIBITION HERE?
YOUR WORKS, DISPLAYED FOR THE ATHENS SOCIETY CROWD. THEY'LL LOVE YOU.
I DON'T KNOW WHAT TO SAY.
I knew what I was giving up.
THERE MUST BE ANOTHER WAY.
But there was my chance, right before me.
For one thing was clear.
NOW I CAN SHOW THAT STUCK-UP BASTARD.
Reality was fluid, like water,
and one's fortune changed as readily as water adapts to the shape of the vessel that contains it.
Yet this one time, I could shape the vessel.
YOU ARE AN ARTIST, NOT A SPEAKER.
IF YOUR WORK IS SEEN, IT WILL CHANGE PEOPLE'S MINDS. IT'S ALL LINKED.

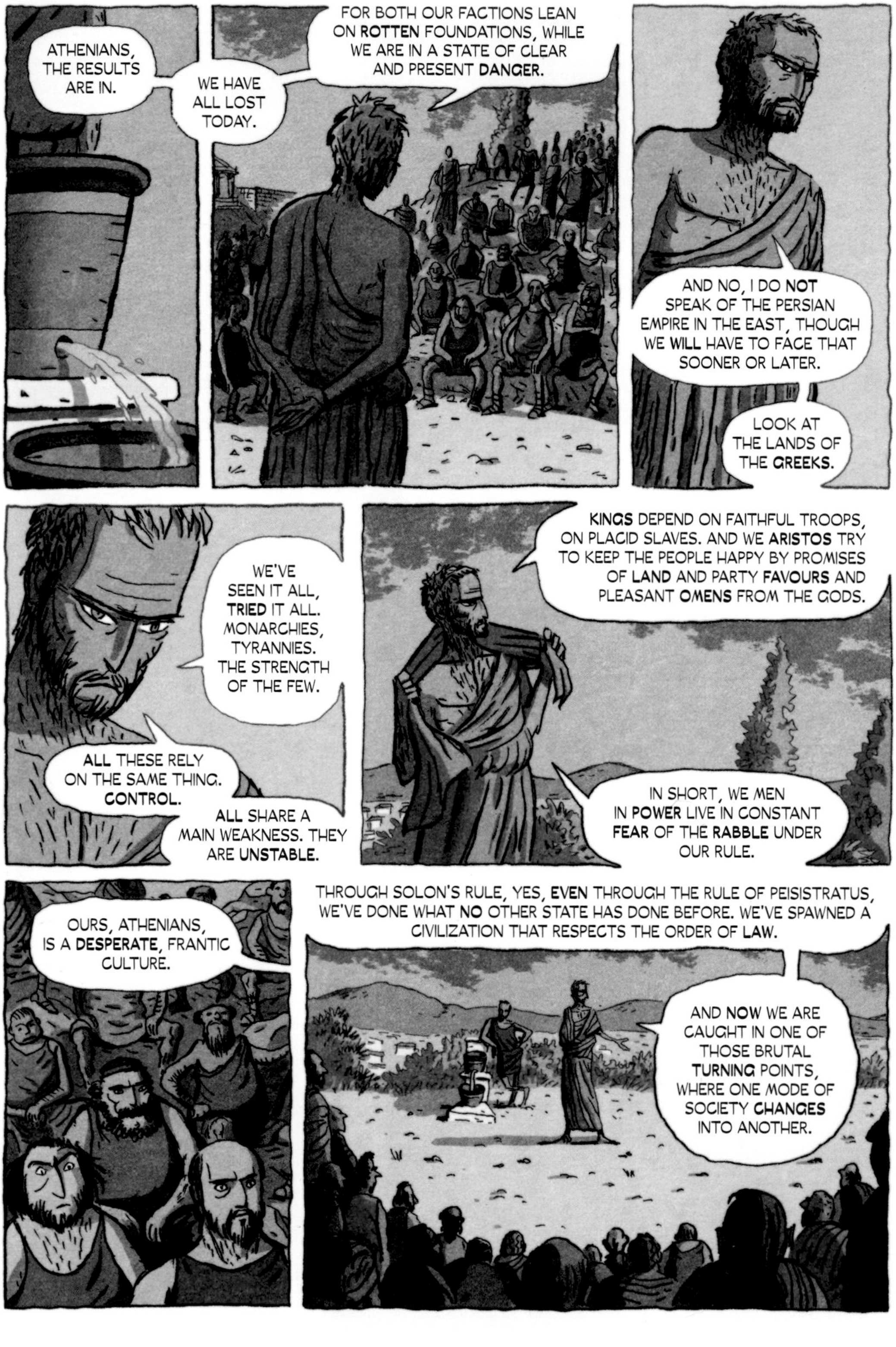

ATHENIANS, THE RESULTS ARE IN.
WE HAVE ALL LOST TODAY.
FOR BOTH OUR FACTIONS LEAN ON **ROTTEN** FOUNDATIONS, WHILE WE ARE IN A STATE OF CLEAR AND PRESENT **DANGER.**
AND NO, I DO **NOT** SPEAK OF THE PERSIAN EMPIRE IN THE EAST, THOUGH WE **WILL** HAVE TO FACE THAT SOONER OR LATER.
LOOK AT THE LANDS OF THE **GREEKS.**
WE'VE SEEN IT ALL, **TRIED** IT ALL. MONARCHIES, TYRANNIES. THE STRENGTH OF THE FEW.
ALL THESE RELY ON THE SAME THING. **CONTROL.**
ALL SHARE A MAIN WEAKNESS. THEY ARE **UNSTABLE.**
KINGS DEPEND ON FAITHFUL TROOPS, ON PLACID SLAVES. AND WE **ARISTOS** TRY TO KEEP THE PEOPLE HAPPY BY PROMISES OF **LAND** AND PARTY **FAVOURS** AND PLEASANT **OMENS** FROM THE GODS.
IN SHORT, WE MEN IN **POWER** LIVE IN CONSTANT **FEAR** OF THE **RABBLE** UNDER OUR RULE.
OURS, ATHENIANS, IS A **DESPERATE**, FRANTIC CULTURE.
THROUGH SOLON'S RULE, YES, **EVEN** THROUGH THE RULE OF PEISISTRATUS, WE'VE DONE WHAT **NO** OTHER STATE HAS DONE BEFORE. WE'VE SPAWNED A CIVILIZATION THAT RESPECTS THE ORDER OF **LAW.**
AND **NOW** WE ARE CAUGHT IN ONE OF THOSE BRUTAL **TURNING** POINTS, WHERE ONE MODE OF SOCIETY **CHANGES** INTO ANOTHER.

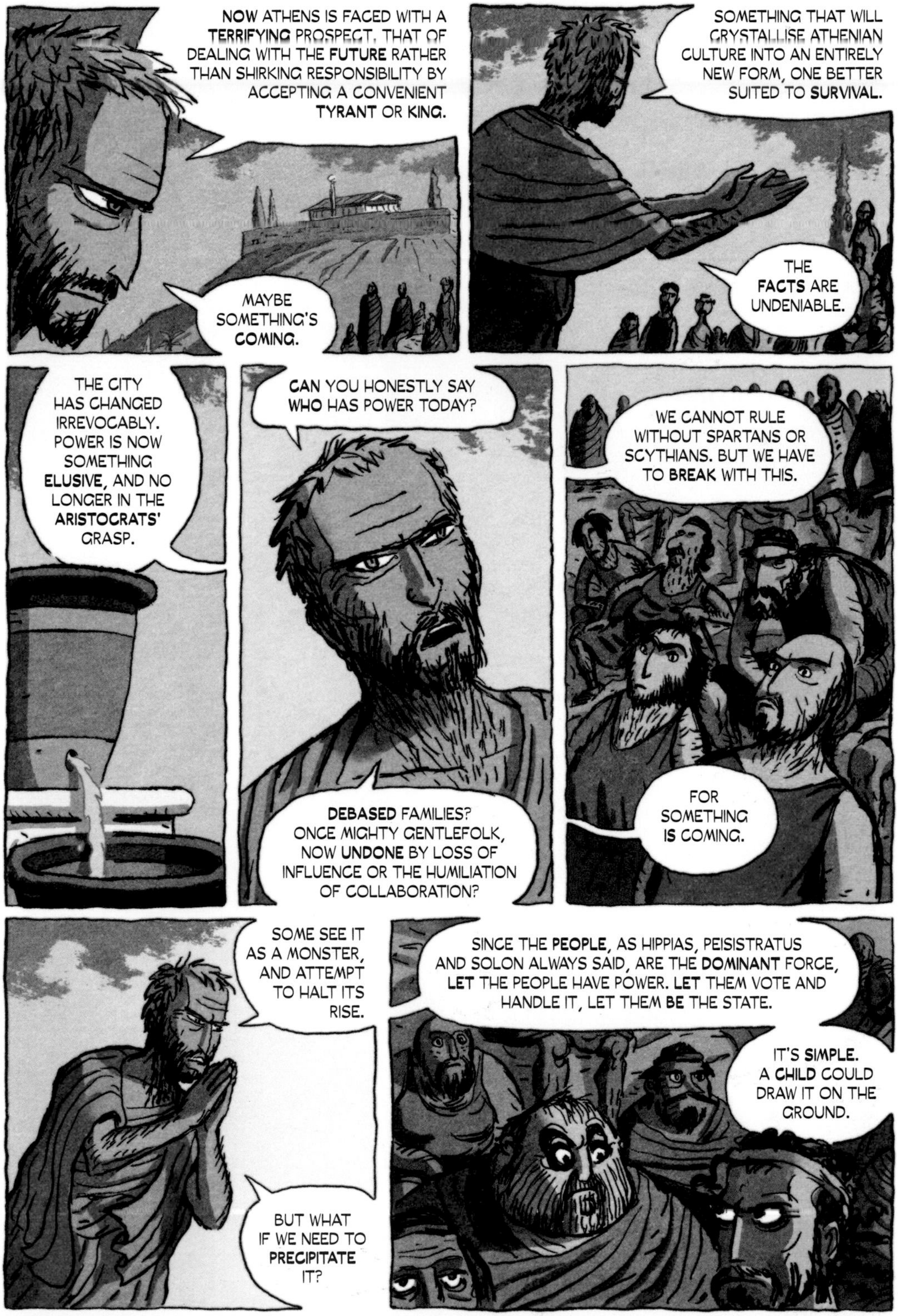
NOW ATHENS IS FACED WITH A TERRIFYING PROSPECT, THAT OF DEALING WITH THE FUTURE RATHER THAN SHIRKING RESPONSIBILITY BY ACCEPTING A CONVENIENT TYRANT OR KING.
MAYBE SOMETHING'S COMING.
SOMETHING THAT WILL CRYSTALLISE ATHENIAN CULTURE INTO AN ENTIRELY NEW FORM, ONE BETTER SUITED TO SURVIVAL.
THE FACTS ARE UNDENIABLE.
THE CITY HAS CHANGED IRREVOCABLY. POWER IS NOW SOMETHING ELUSIVE, AND NO LONGER IN THE ARISTOCRATS' GRASP.
CAN YOU HONESTLY SAY WHO HAS POWER TODAY?
DEBASED FAMILIES? ONCE MIGHTY GENTLEFOLK, NOW UNDONE BY LOSS OF INFLUENCE OR THE HUMILIATION OF COLLABORATION?
WE CANNOT RULE WITHOUT SPARTANS OR SCYTHIANS. BUT WE HAVE TO BREAK WITH THIS.
FOR SOMETHING IS COMING.
SOME SEE IT AS A MONSTER, AND ATTEMPT TO HALT ITS RISE.
BUT WHAT IF WE NEED TO PRECIPITATE IT?
SINCE THE PEOPLE, AS HIPPIAS, PEISISTRATUS AND SOLON ALWAYS SAID, ARE THE DOMINANT FORCE, LET THE PEOPLE HAVE POWER. LET THEM VOTE AND HANDLE IT, LET THEM BE THE STATE.
IT'S SIMPLE. A CHILD COULD DRAW IT ON THE GROUND.

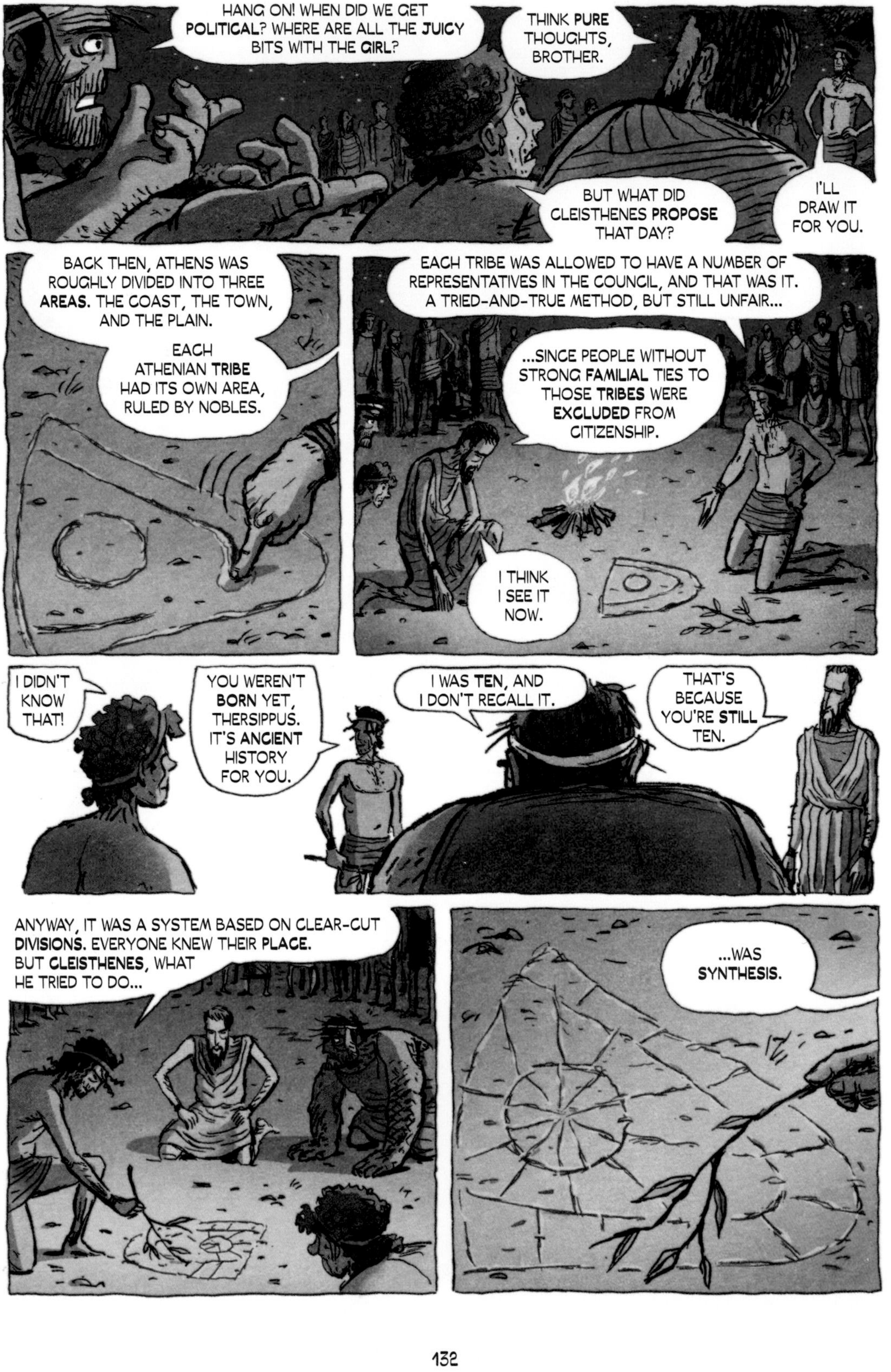
HANG ON! WHEN DID WE GET POLITICAL? WHERE ARE ALL THE JUICY BITS WITH THE GIRL?
THINK PURE THOUGHTS, BROTHER.
BUT WHAT DID CLEISTHENES PROPOSE THAT DAY?
I'LL DRAW IT FOR YOU.
BACK THEN, ATHENS WAS ROUGHLY DIVIDED INTO THREE AREAS. THE COAST, THE TOWN, AND THE PLAIN.
EACH ATHENIAN TRIBE HAD ITS OWN AREA, RULED BY NOBLES.
EACH TRIBE WAS ALLOWED TO HAVE A NUMBER OF REPRESENTATIVES IN THE COUNCIL, AND THAT WAS IT. A TRIED-AND-TRUE METHOD, BUT STILL UNFAIR...
...SINCE PEOPLE WITHOUT STRONG FAMILIAL TIES TO THOSE TRIBES WERE EXCLUDED FROM CITIZENSHIP.
I THINK I SEE IT NOW.
I DIDN'T KNOW THAT!
YOU WEREN'T BORN YET, THERSIPPUS. IT'S ANCIENT HISTORY FOR YOU.
I WAS TEN, AND I DON'T RECALL IT.
THAT'S BECAUSE YOU'RE STILL TEN.
ANYWAY, IT WAS A SYSTEM BASED ON CLEAR-CUT DIVISIONS. EVERYONE KNEW THEIR PLACE. BUT CLEISTHENES, WHAT HE TRIED TO DO...
...WAS SYNTHESIS.

HOW IS **THIS** SYNTHESIS? YOU **CUT UP** EACH AREA IN, WHAT, FOUR, FIVE...

TEN SEGMENTS. THIRTY, ALL IN ALL.

BEAR WITH ME.

CLEISTHENES SUGGESTED THAT WE **DO AWAY** WITH THE OLD TRIBAL SYSTEM.

HE PROPOSED **TEN** NEW TRIBES.

TEN? BUT THERE'S **THIRTY** SEGMENTS HERE.

EXACTLY. **EACH** NEW TRIBE WOULD BE COMPOSED BY THE INHABITANTS OF **THREE** SEGMENTS. **ONE** FROM THE PLAIN, **ONE** FROM THE TOWN, AND **ONE** FROM THE COAST.

I **STILL** DON'T GET IT.

DON'T YOU **SEE?** EACH NEW TRIBE WOULD BE COMPOSED BY PEOPLE FROM **ALL THREE** AREAS. IT'D NO LONGER –

HERE, GIVE ME ONE CLOVE OF **GARLIC** EACH, I'LL EXPLAIN.

GREAT, NOW HE'S **LOOTING** OUR BREAKFAST.

SHUT UP, CYNEGEIRUS.

SUPPOSE EACH ONE OF YOU IS AN INHABITANT OF ONE OF THE THREE MAIN AREAS.

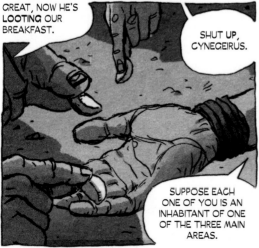

WITH YOUR CLOVES, I'M MAKING **ONE** BULB. ONE NEW **TRIBE.** BUT THE **THREE** PARTS THAT **MAKE UP** THE WHOLE...

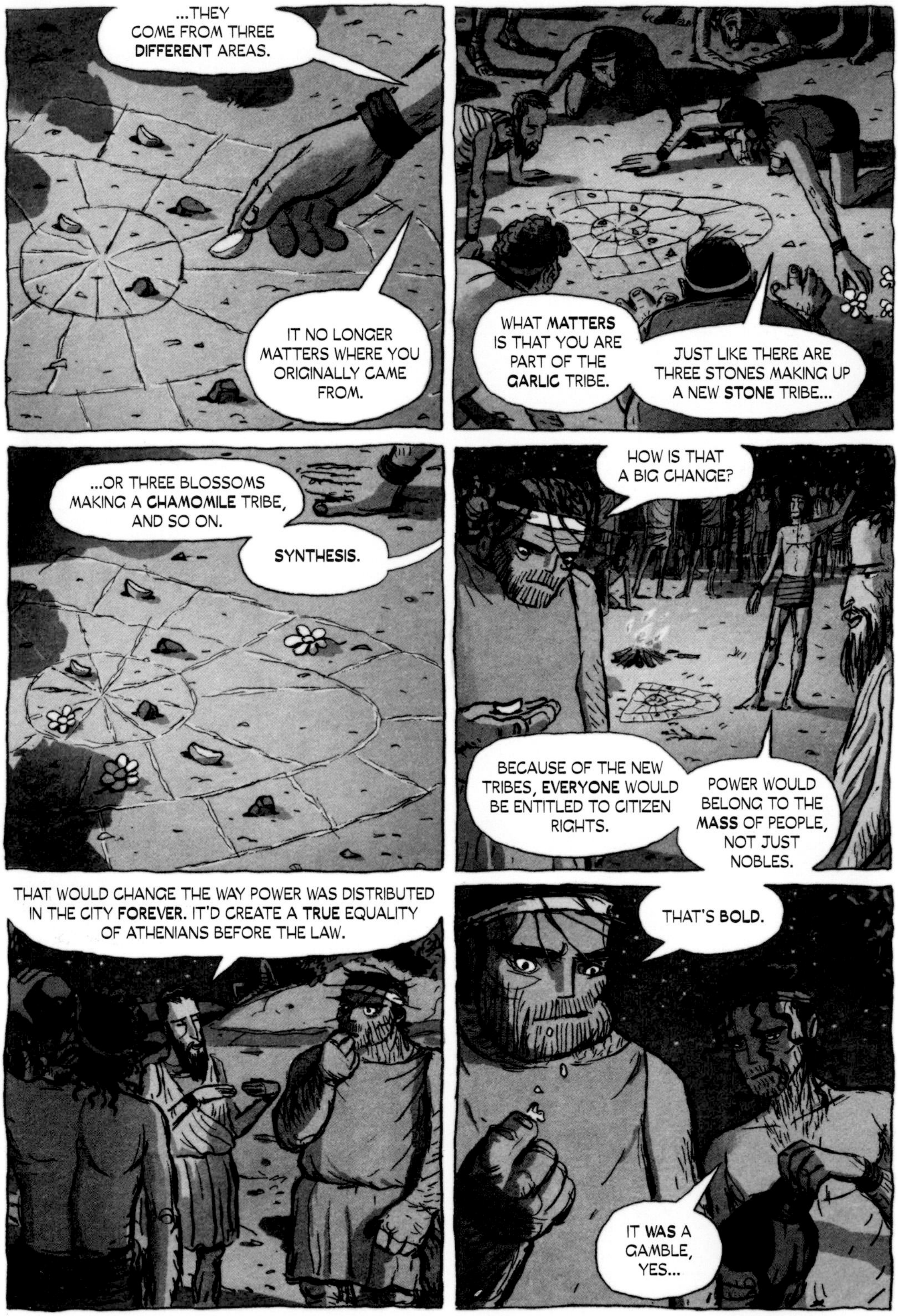
...THEY COME FROM THREE DIFFERENT AREAS.
IT NO LONGER MATTERS WHERE YOU ORIGINALLY CAME FROM.
WHAT MATTERS IS THAT YOU ARE PART OF THE GARLIC TRIBE.
JUST LIKE THERE ARE THREE STONES MAKING UP A NEW STONE TRIBE...
...OR THREE BLOSSOMS MAKING A CHAMOMILE TRIBE, AND SO ON.
SYNTHESIS.
HOW IS THAT A BIG CHANGE?
BECAUSE OF THE NEW TRIBES, EVERYONE WOULD BE ENTITLED TO CITIZEN RIGHTS.
POWER WOULD BELONG TO THE MASS OF PEOPLE, NOT JUST NOBLES.
THAT WOULD CHANGE THE WAY POWER WAS DISTRIBUTED IN THE CITY FOREVER. IT'D CREATE A TRUE EQUALITY OF ATHENIANS BEFORE THE LAW.
THAT'S BOLD.
IT WAS A GAMBLE, YES...

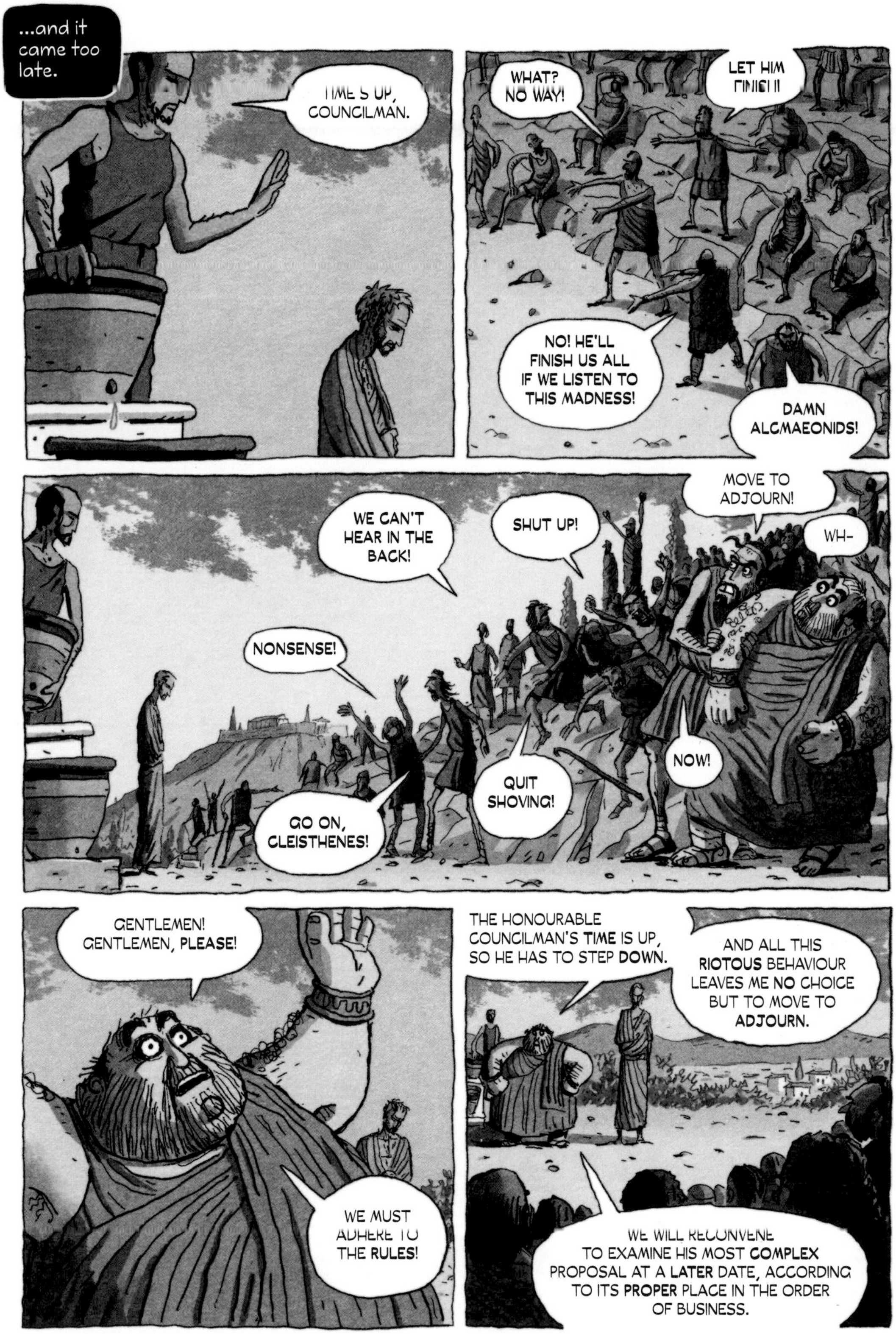

...and it came too late.
TIME'S UP, COUNCILMAN.
WHAT? NO WAY!
LET HIM FINISH!
NO! HE'LL FINISH US ALL IF WE LISTEN TO THIS MADNESS!
DAMN ALCMAEONIDS!
WE CAN'T HEAR IN THE BACK!
SHUT UP!
MOVE TO ADJOURN!
WH-
NONSENSE!
QUIT SHOVING!
NOW!
GO ON, CLEISTHENES!
GENTLEMEN! GENTLEMEN, PLEASE!
WE MUST ADHERE TO THE RULES!
THE HONOURABLE COUNCILMAN'S TIME IS UP, SO HE HAS TO STEP DOWN.
AND ALL THIS RIOTOUS BEHAVIOUR LEAVES ME NO CHOICE BUT TO MOVE TO ADJOURN.
WE WILL RECONVENE TO EXAMINE HIS MOST COMPLEX PROPOSAL AT A LATER DATE, ACCORDING TO ITS PROPER PLACE IN THE ORDER OF BUSINESS.

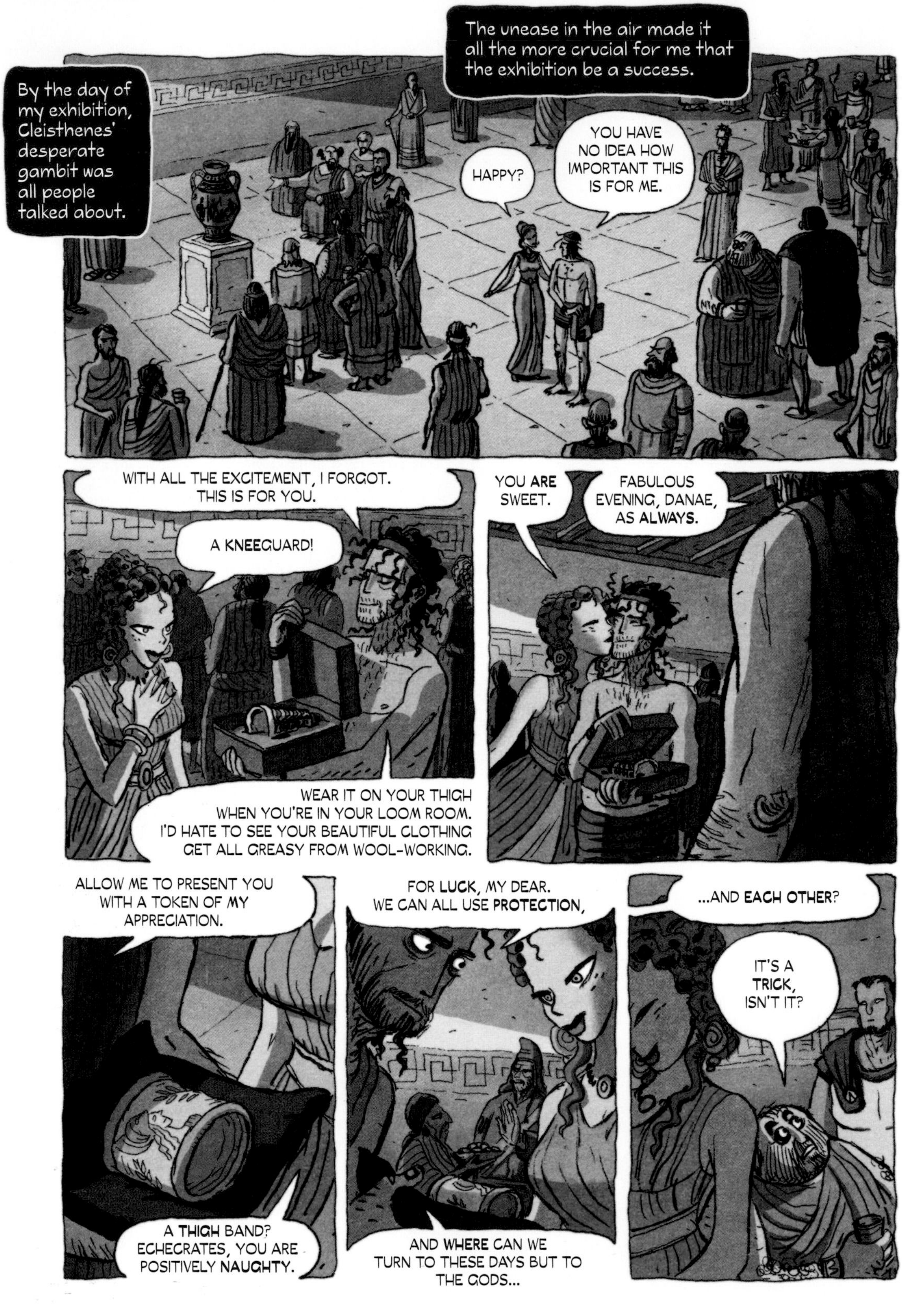
By the day of my exhibition, Cleisthenes' desperate gambit was all people talked about.
The unease in the air made it all the more crucial for me that the exhibition be a success.
HAPPY?
YOU HAVE NO IDEA HOW IMPORTANT THIS IS FOR ME.
WITH ALL THE EXCITEMENT, I FORGOT. THIS IS FOR YOU.
A KNEEGUARD!
WEAR IT ON YOUR THIGH WHEN YOU'RE IN YOUR LOOM ROOM. I'D HATE TO SEE YOUR BEAUTIFUL CLOTHING GET ALL GREASY FROM WOOL-WORKING.
YOU ARE SWEET.
FABULOUS EVENING, DANAE, AS ALWAYS.
ALLOW ME TO PRESENT YOU WITH A TOKEN OF MY APPRECIATION.
A THIGH BAND? ECHECRATES, YOU ARE POSITIVELY NAUGHTY.
FOR LUCK, MY DEAR. WE CAN ALL USE PROTECTION,
AND WHERE CAN WE TURN TO THESE DAYS BUT TO THE GODS...
...AND EACH OTHER?
IT'S A TRICK, ISN'T IT?

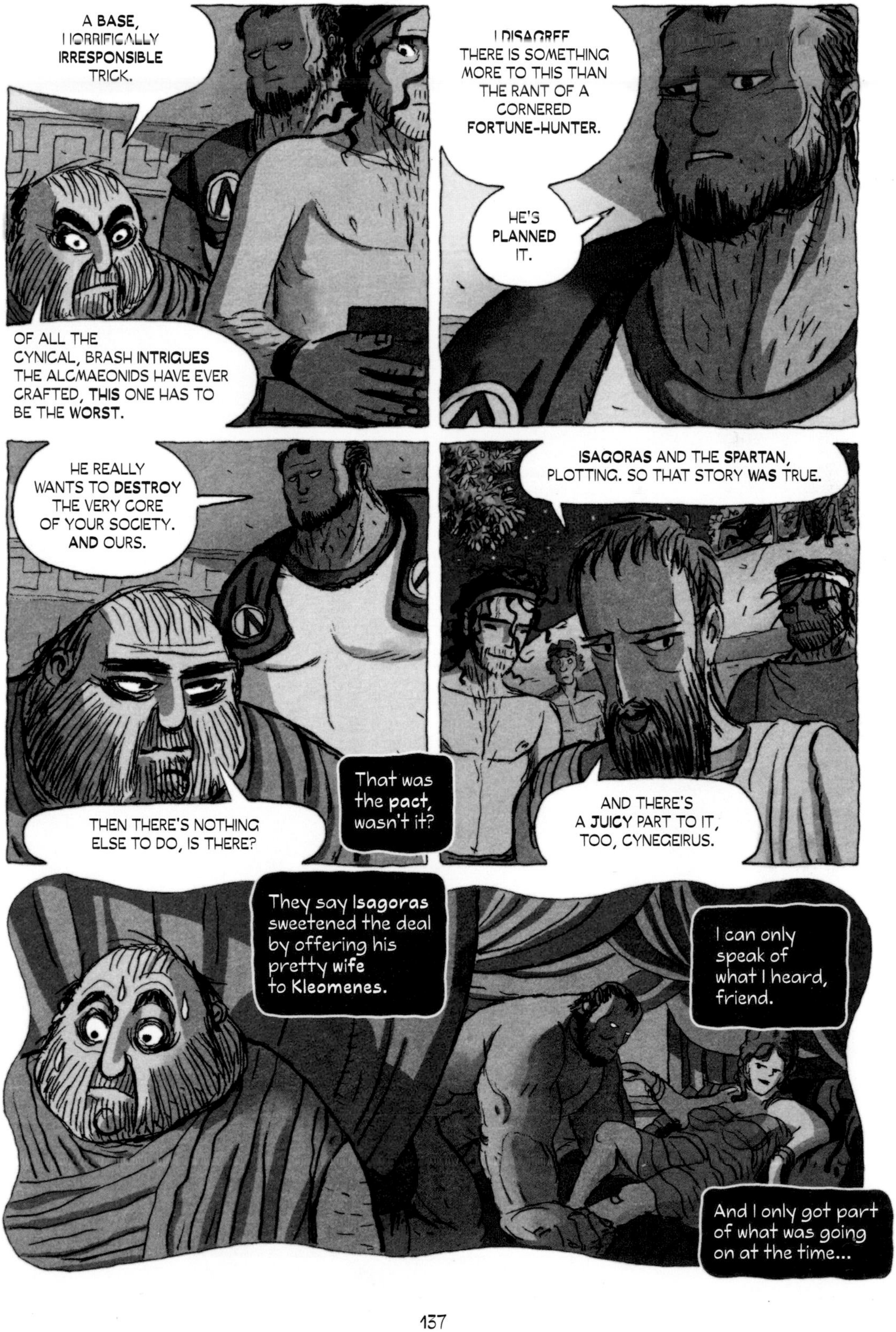

A BASE, HORRIFICALLY IRRESPONSIBLE TRICK.
OF ALL THE CYNICAL, BRASH INTRIGUES THE ALCMAEONIDS HAVE EVER CRAFTED, THIS ONE HAS TO BE THE WORST.
I DISAGREE. THERE IS SOMETHING MORE TO THIS THAN THE RANT OF A CORNERED FORTUNE-HUNTER.
HE'S PLANNED IT.
HE REALLY WANTS TO DESTROY THE VERY CORE OF YOUR SOCIETY. AND OURS.
THEN THERE'S NOTHING ELSE TO DO, IS THERE?
That was the pact, wasn't it?
ISAGORAS AND THE SPARTAN, PLOTTING. SO THAT STORY WAS TRUE.
AND THERE'S A JUICY PART TO IT, TOO, CYNEGEIRUS.
They say Isagoras sweetened the deal by offering his pretty wife to Kleomenes.
I can only speak of what I heard, friend.
And I only got part of what was going on at the time...

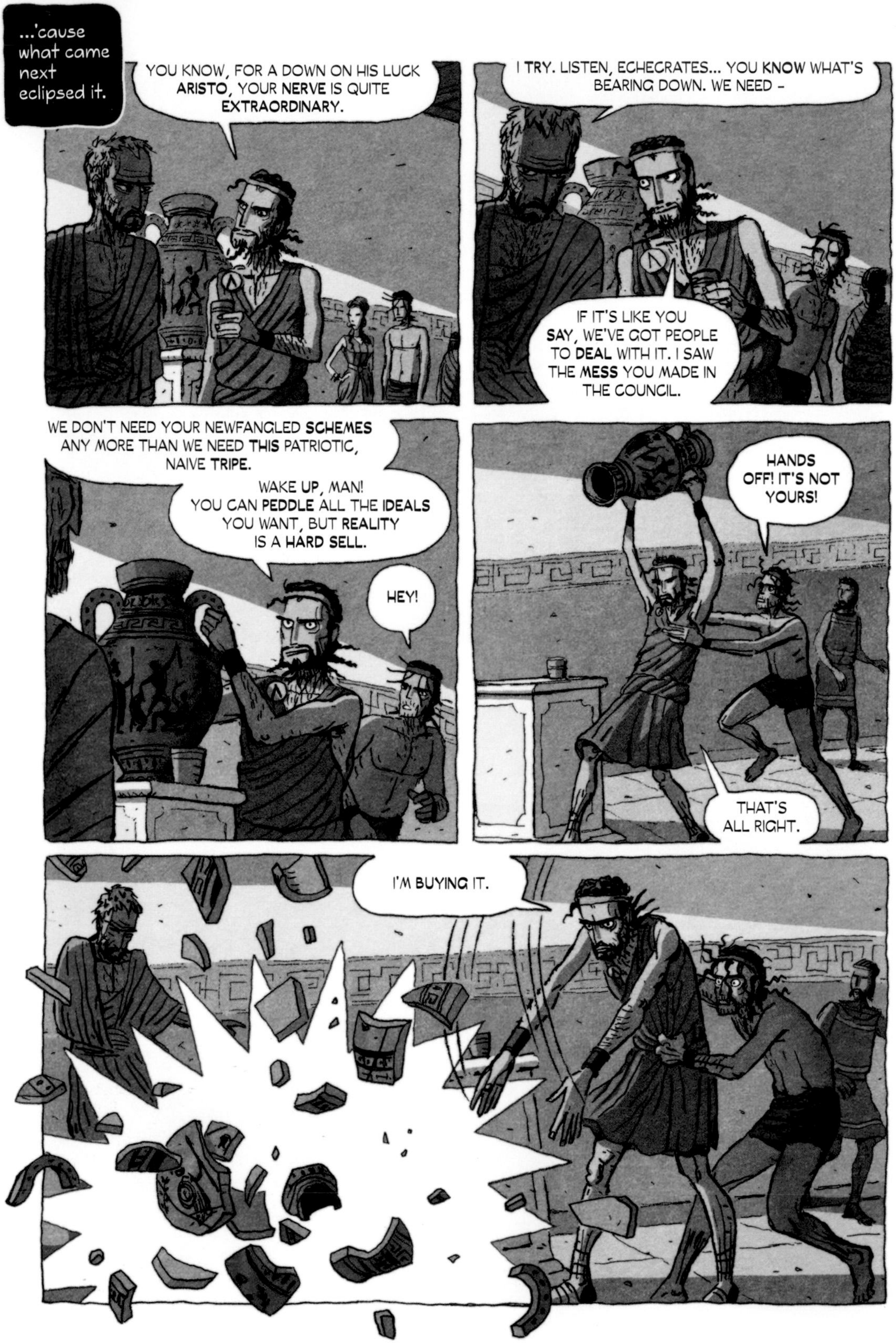
...'cause what came next eclipsed it.
YOU KNOW, FOR A DOWN ON HIS LUCK ARISTO, YOUR NERVE IS QUITE EXTRAORDINARY.
I TRY. LISTEN, ECHECRATES... YOU KNOW WHAT'S BEARING DOWN. WE NEED –
IF IT'S LIKE YOU SAY, WE'VE GOT PEOPLE TO DEAL WITH IT. I SAW THE MESS YOU MADE IN THE COUNCIL.
WE DON'T NEED YOUR NEWFANGLED SCHEMES ANY MORE THAN WE NEED THIS PATRIOTIC, NAIVE TRIPE.
WAKE UP, MAN! YOU CAN PEDDLE ALL THE IDEALS YOU WANT, BUT REALITY IS A HARD SELL.
HEY!
HANDS OFF! IT'S NOT YOURS!
THAT'S ALL RIGHT.
I'M BUYING IT.

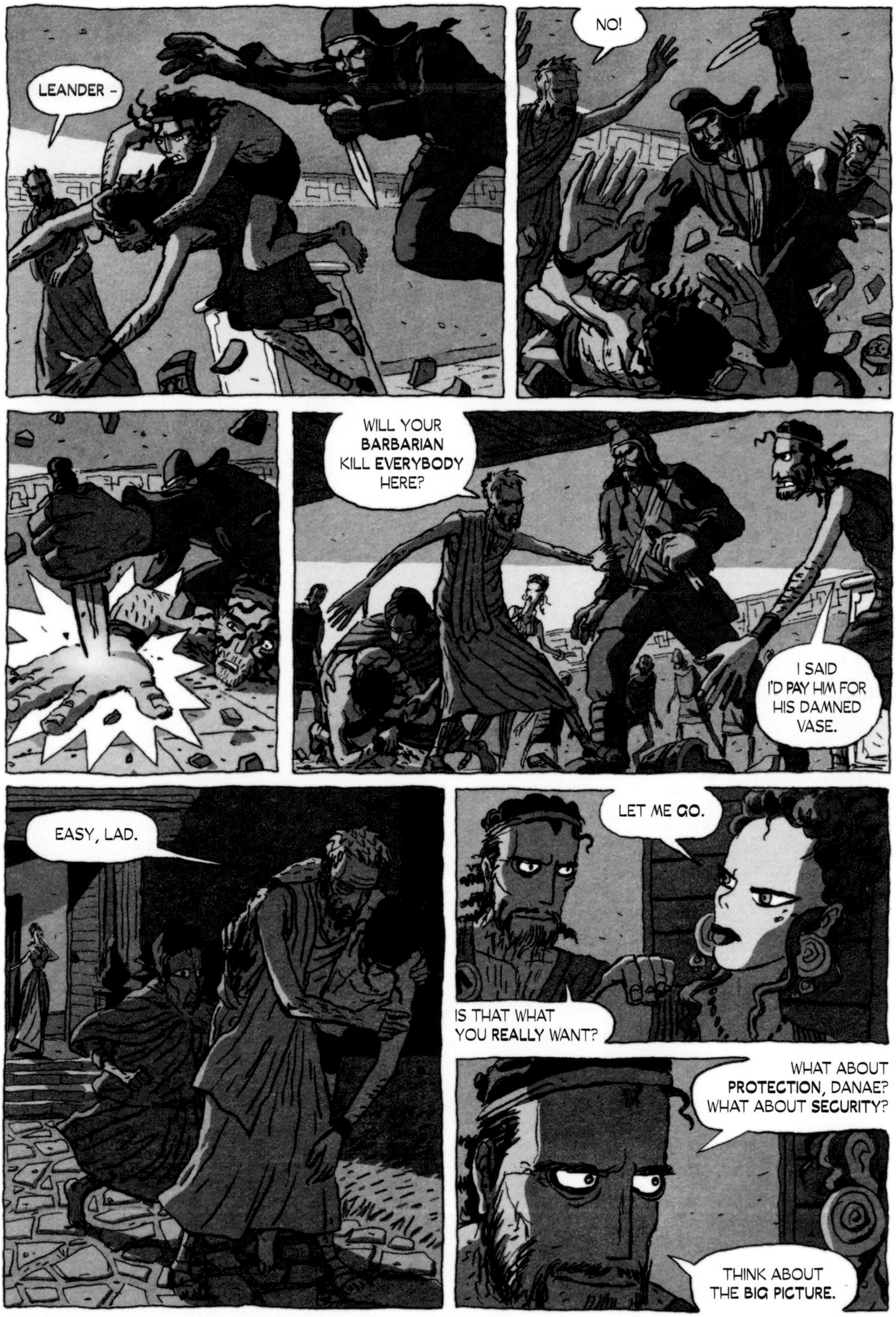
LEANDER -
NO!
WILL YOUR BARBARIAN KILL EVERYBODY HERE?
I SAID I'D PAY HIM FOR HIS DAMNED VASE.
EASY, LAD.
LET ME GO.
IS THAT WHAT YOU REALLY WANT?
WHAT ABOUT PROTECTION, DANAE? WHAT ABOUT SECURITY?
THINK ABOUT THE BIG PICTURE.

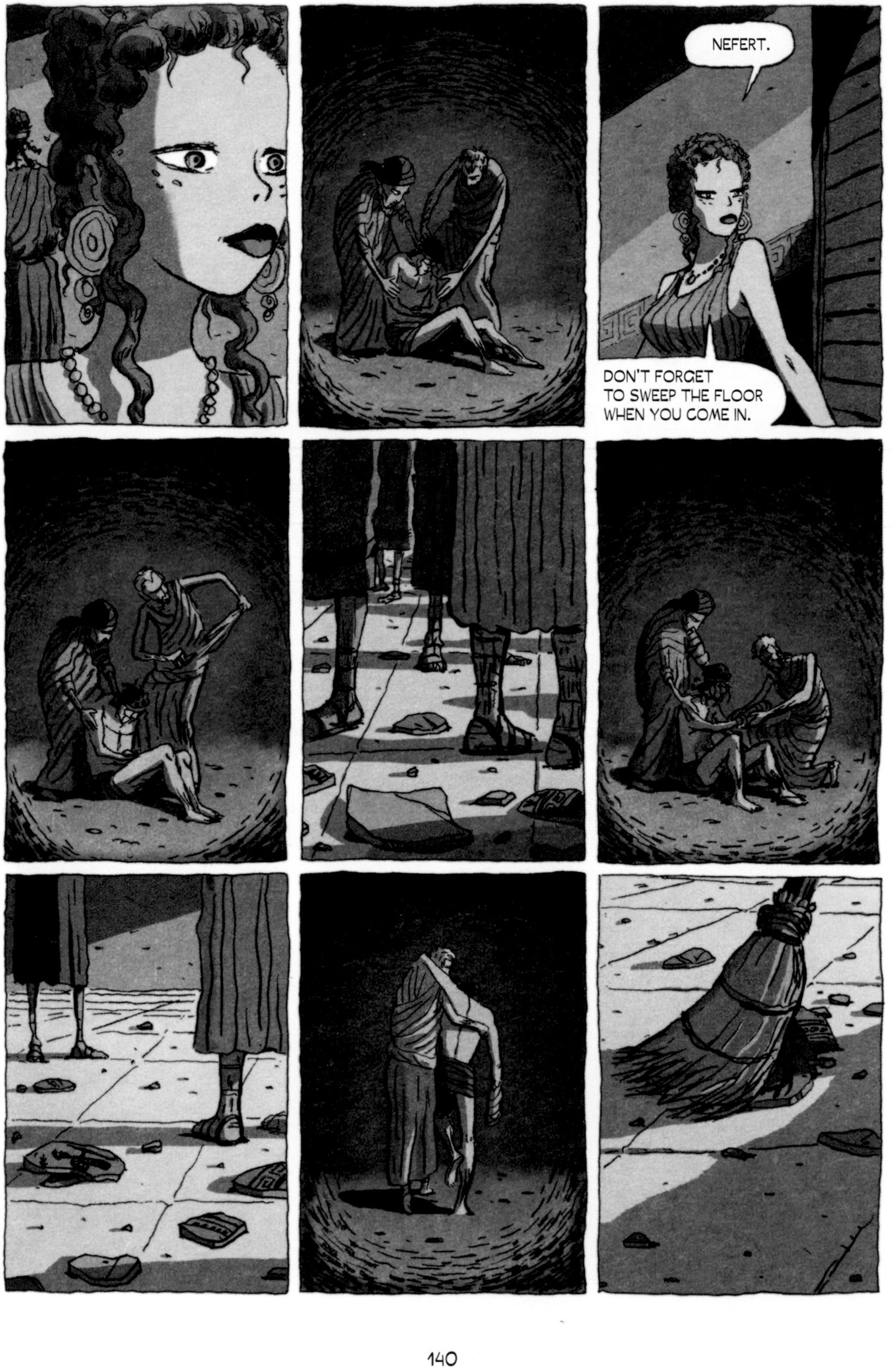
NEFERT.
DON'T FORGET TO SWEEP THE FLOOR WHEN YOU COME IN.

THE GORGON'S
FACE

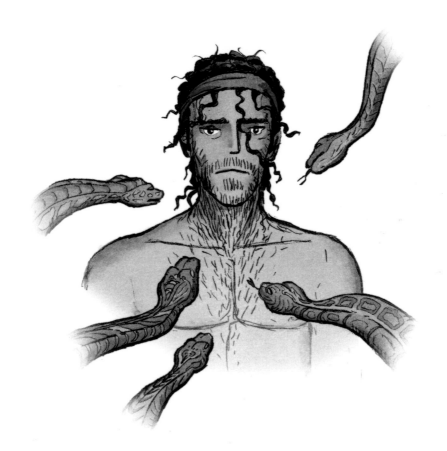

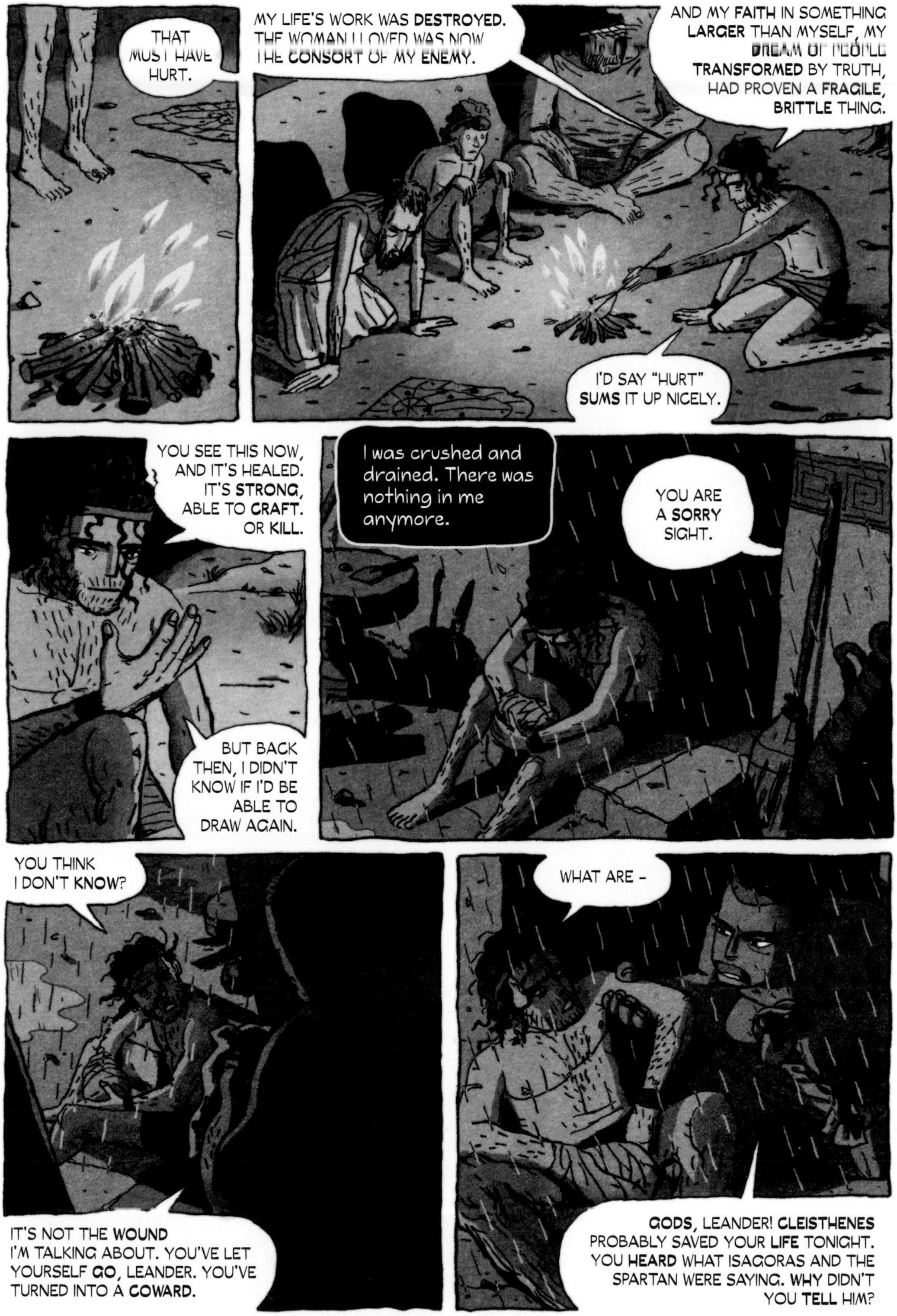
THAT MUST HAVE HURT.
MY LIFE'S WORK WAS DESTROYED. THE WOMAN I LOVED WAS NOW THE CONSORT OF MY ENEMY.
AND MY FAITH IN SOMETHING LARGER THAN MYSELF, MY DREAM OF PEOPLE TRANSFORMED BY TRUTH, HAD PROVEN A FRAGILE, BRITTLE THING.
I'D SAY "HURT" SUMS IT UP NICELY.
YOU SEE THIS NOW, AND IT'S HEALED. IT'S STRONG, ABLE TO CRAFT. OR KILL.
BUT BACK THEN, I DIDN'T KNOW IF I'D BE ABLE TO DRAW AGAIN.
I was crushed and drained. There was nothing in me anymore.
YOU ARE A SORRY SIGHT.
YOU THINK I DON'T KNOW?
IT'S NOT THE WOUND I'M TALKING ABOUT. YOU'VE LET YOURSELF GO, LEANDER. YOU'VE TURNED INTO A COWARD.
WHAT ARE –
GODS, LEANDER! CLEISTHENES PROBABLY SAVED YOUR LIFE TONIGHT. YOU HEARD WHAT ISAGORAS AND THE SPARTAN WERE SAYING. WHY DIDN'T YOU TELL HIM?

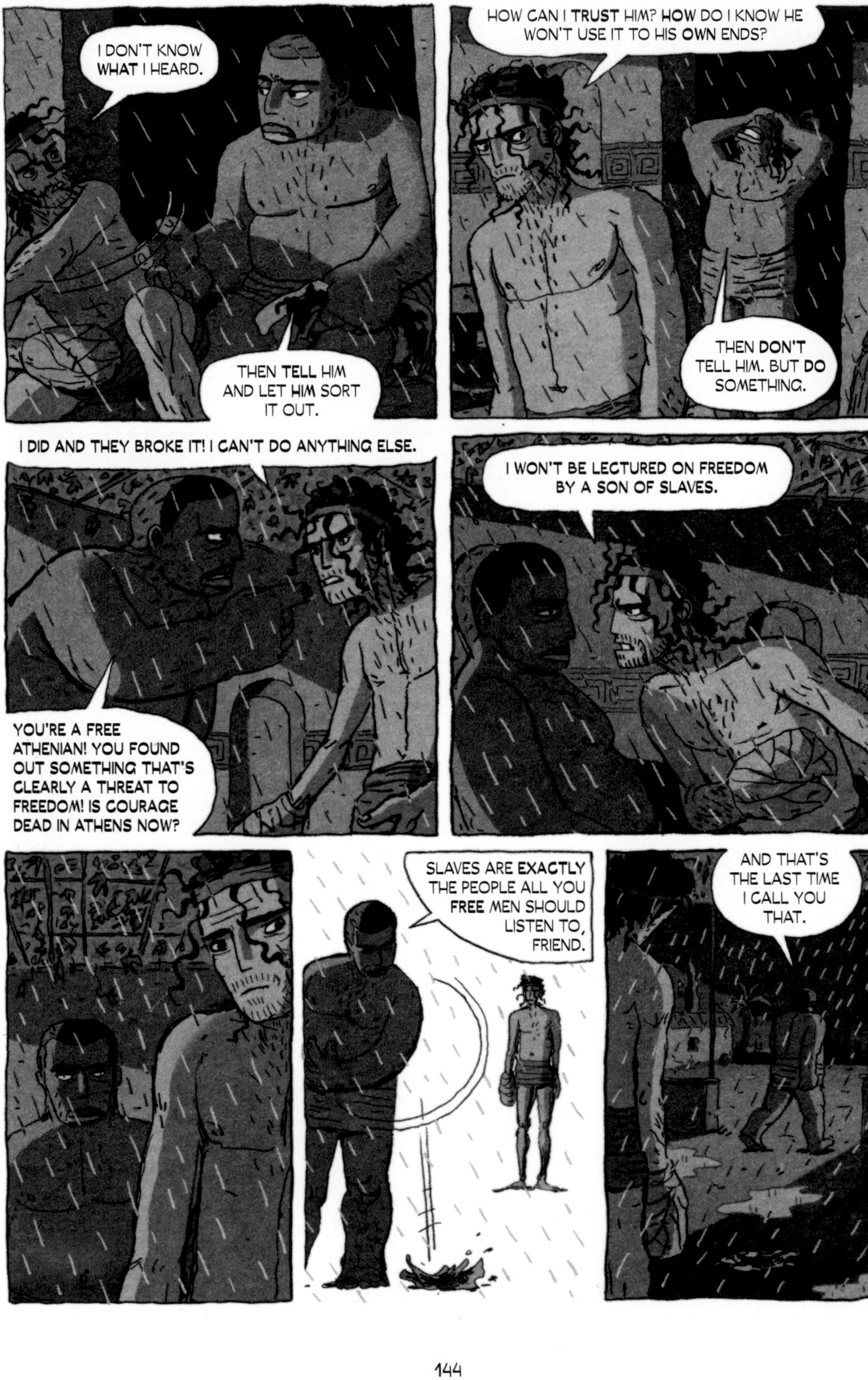
I DON'T KNOW WHAT I HEARD.
THEN TELL HIM AND LET HIM SORT IT OUT.
HOW CAN I TRUST HIM? HOW DO I KNOW HE WON'T USE IT TO HIS OWN ENDS?
THEN DON'T TELL HIM. BUT DO SOMETHING.
I DID AND THEY BROKE IT! I CAN'T DO ANYTHING ELSE.
YOU'RE A FREE ATHENIAN! YOU FOUND OUT SOMETHING THAT'S CLEARLY A THREAT TO FREEDOM! IS COURAGE DEAD IN ATHENS NOW?
I WON'T BE LECTURED ON FREEDOM BY A SON OF SLAVES.
SLAVES ARE EXACTLY THE PEOPLE ALL YOU FREE MEN SHOULD LISTEN TO, FRIEND.
AND THAT'S THE LAST TIME I CALL YOU THAT.

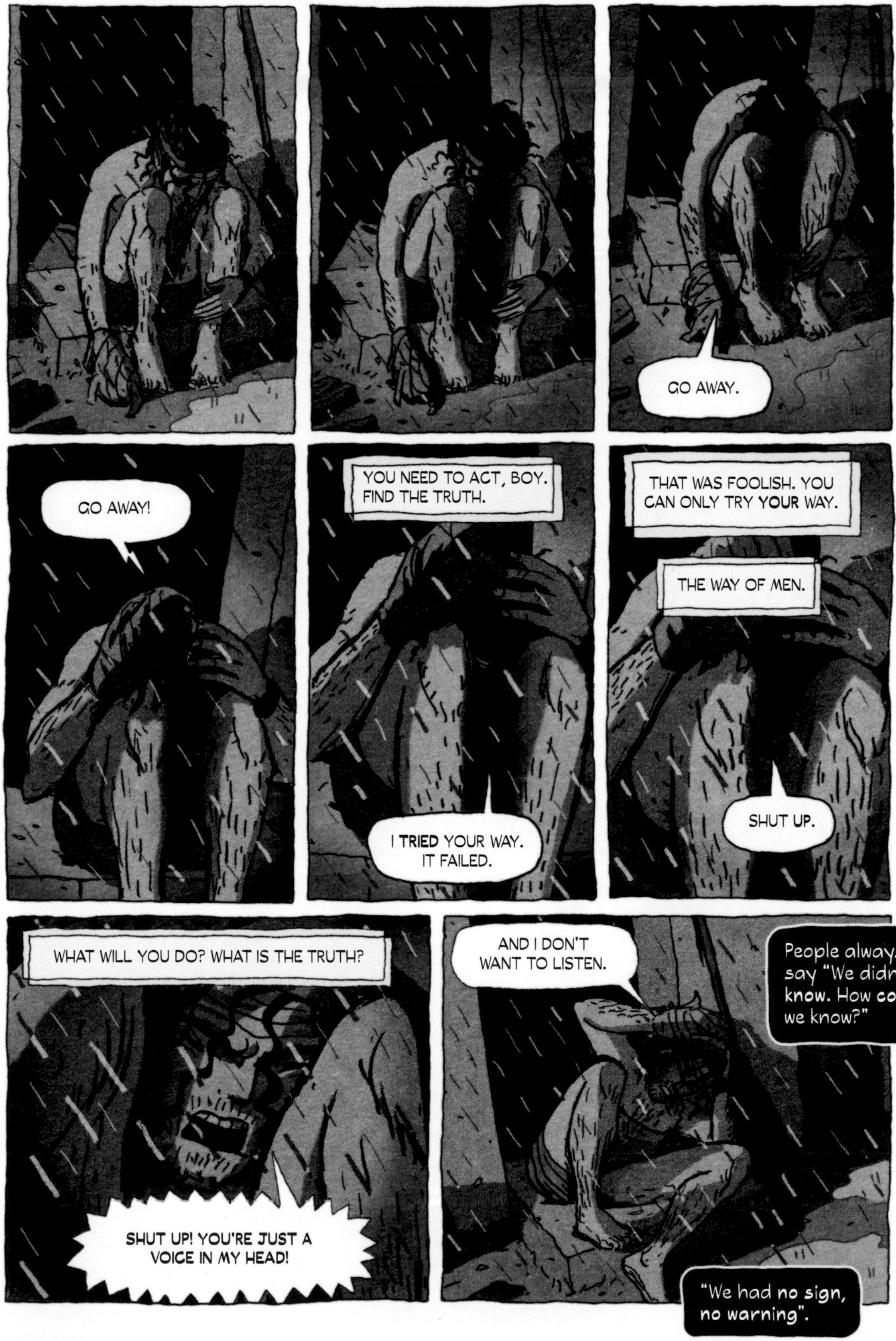
GO AWAY.
GO AWAY!
YOU NEED TO ACT, BOY. FIND THE TRUTH.
I TRIED YOUR WAY. IT FAILED.
THAT WAS FOOLISH. YOU CAN ONLY TRY YOUR WAY.
THE WAY OF MEN.
SHUT UP.
WHAT WILL YOU DO? WHAT IS THE TRUTH?
SHUT UP! YOU'RE JUST A VOICE IN MY HEAD!
AND I DON'T WANT TO LISTEN.
People always say "We didn't know. How could we know?"
"We had no sign, no warning".

The truth is, there are **always** signs and warnings.

But we can live with them.

TODAY, CITIZENS, A **MOTION** WAS SUBMITTED TO THE COUNCIL.

A DIRE **POLLUTION** INFESTS OUR LAND, AND WE HAVE BEEN **TOO** LONG IN **CLEANSING** IT.

WE HAVE ENTERED A **NEW** ERA, AND THIS NEW ERA REQUIRES NEW **RESPONSIBILITIES.**

THE COUNCIL'S RESPONSIBILITY IS TO **PROTECT** CITIZENS, AND **THAT STARTS** WITH THE **SECURITY** OF OUR CITY.

HOW CAN OUR CITY MOVE **FORWARD** TO ITS FUTURE **GLORY,** WHILE THERE ARE STILL MEMBERS OF A **CURSED** FAMILY LIVING AMONG US?

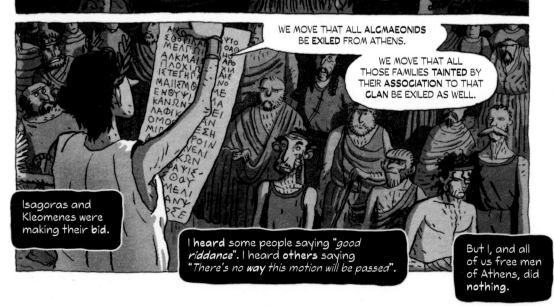

WE MOVE THAT ALL **ALCMAEONIDS** BE **EXILED** FROM ATHENS.

WE MOVE THAT ALL THOSE FAMILIES **TAINTED** BY THEIR **ASSOCIATION** TO THAT **CLAN** BE EXILED AS WELL.

Isagoras and Kleomenes were making their **bid.**

I **heard** some people saying "*good riddance*". I heard **others** saying "*There's no way this motion will be passed*".

But I, and all of us free men of Athens, did **nothing.**

146

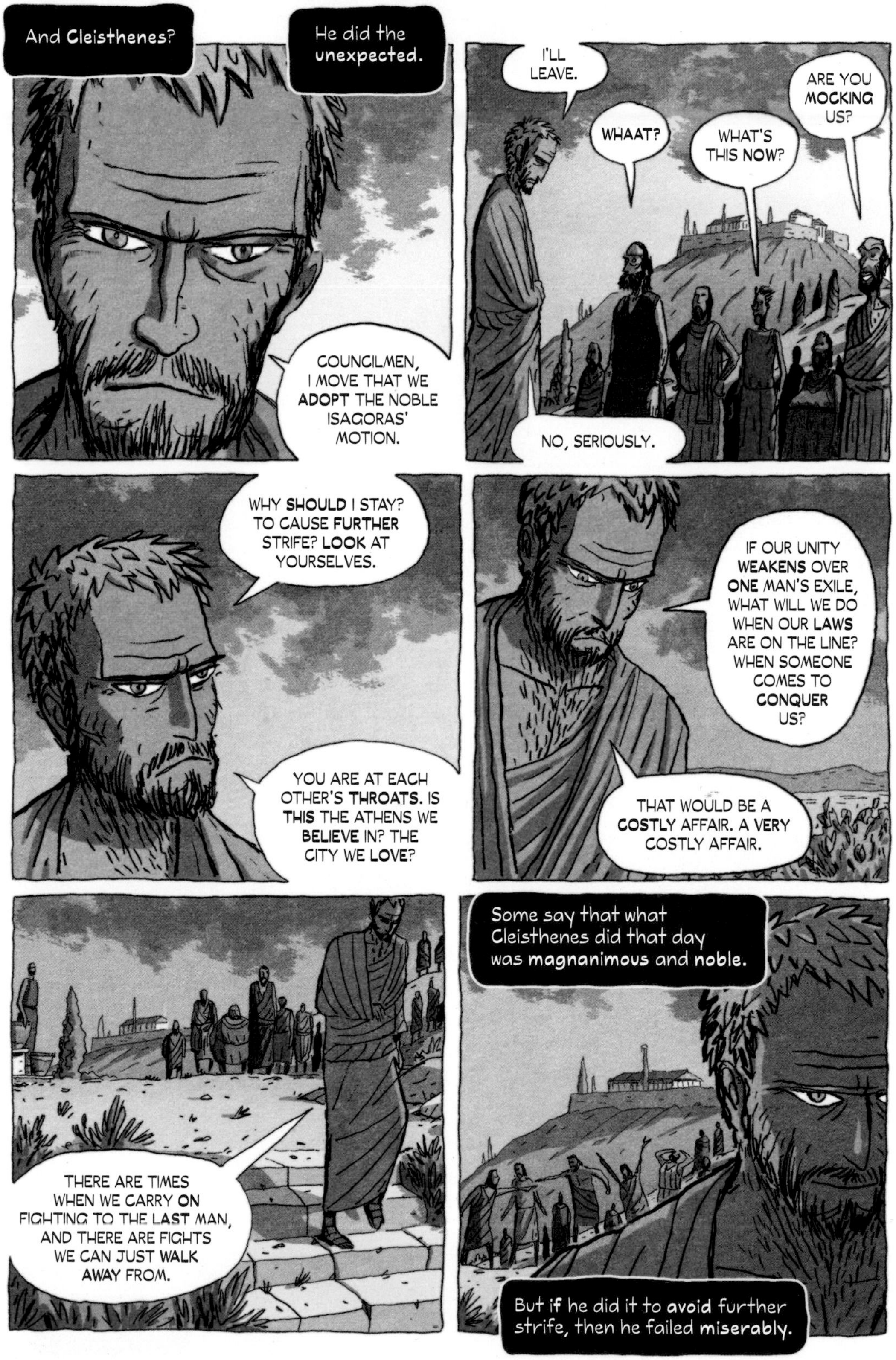

And Cleisthenes?
He did the unexpected.
COUNCILMEN, I MOVE THAT WE ADOPT THE NOBLE ISAGORAS' MOTION.
I'LL LEAVE.
WHAAT?
WHAT'S THIS NOW?
ARE YOU MOCKING US?
NO, SERIOUSLY.
WHY SHOULD I STAY? TO CAUSE FURTHER STRIFE? LOOK AT YOURSELVES.
YOU ARE AT EACH OTHER'S THROATS. IS THIS THE ATHENS WE BELIEVE IN? THE CITY WE LOVE?
IF OUR UNITY WEAKENS OVER ONE MAN'S EXILE, WHAT WILL WE DO WHEN OUR LAWS ARE ON THE LINE? WHEN SOMEONE COMES TO CONQUER US?
THAT WOULD BE A COSTLY AFFAIR. A VERY COSTLY AFFAIR.
THERE ARE TIMES WHEN WE CARRY ON FIGHTING TO THE LAST MAN, AND THERE ARE FIGHTS WE CAN JUST WALK AWAY FROM.
Some say that what Cleisthenes did that day was magnanimous and noble.
But if he did it to avoid further strife, then he failed miserably.

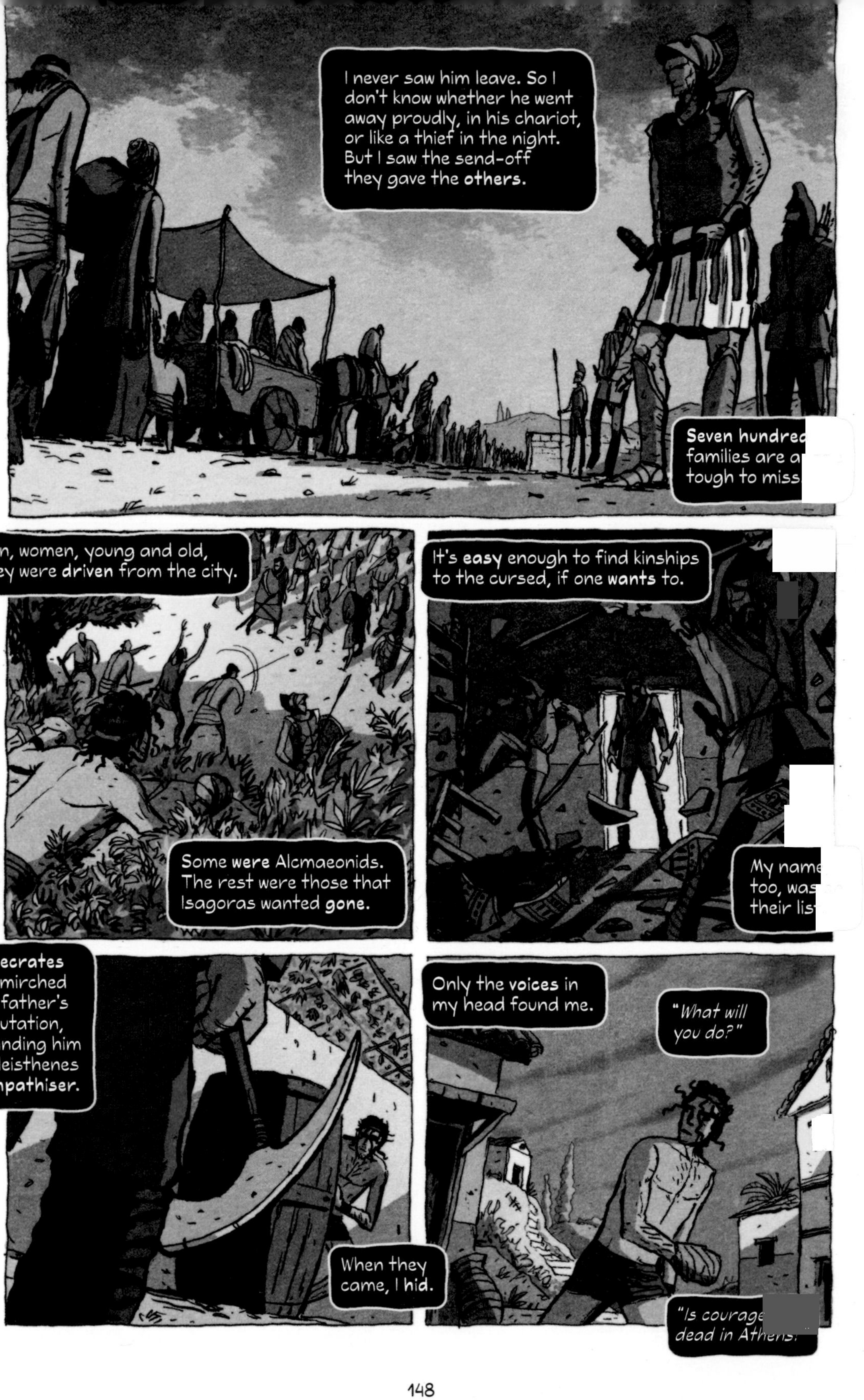
I never saw him leave. So I don't know whether he went away proudly, in his chariot, or like a thief in the night. But I saw the send-off they gave the **others**.
Seven hundre
families are a
tough to miss
Men, women, young and old, they were **driven** from the city.
Some **were** Alcmaeonids. The rest were those that Isagoras wanted **gone**.
It's **easy** enough to find kinships to the cursed, if one **wants** to.
My name
too, was
their lis
Echecrates besmirched my father's reputation, branding him a Cleisthenes **sympathiser**.
When they came, I **hid**.
Only the **voices** in my head found me.
"What will you do?"
"Is courage
dead in Athens

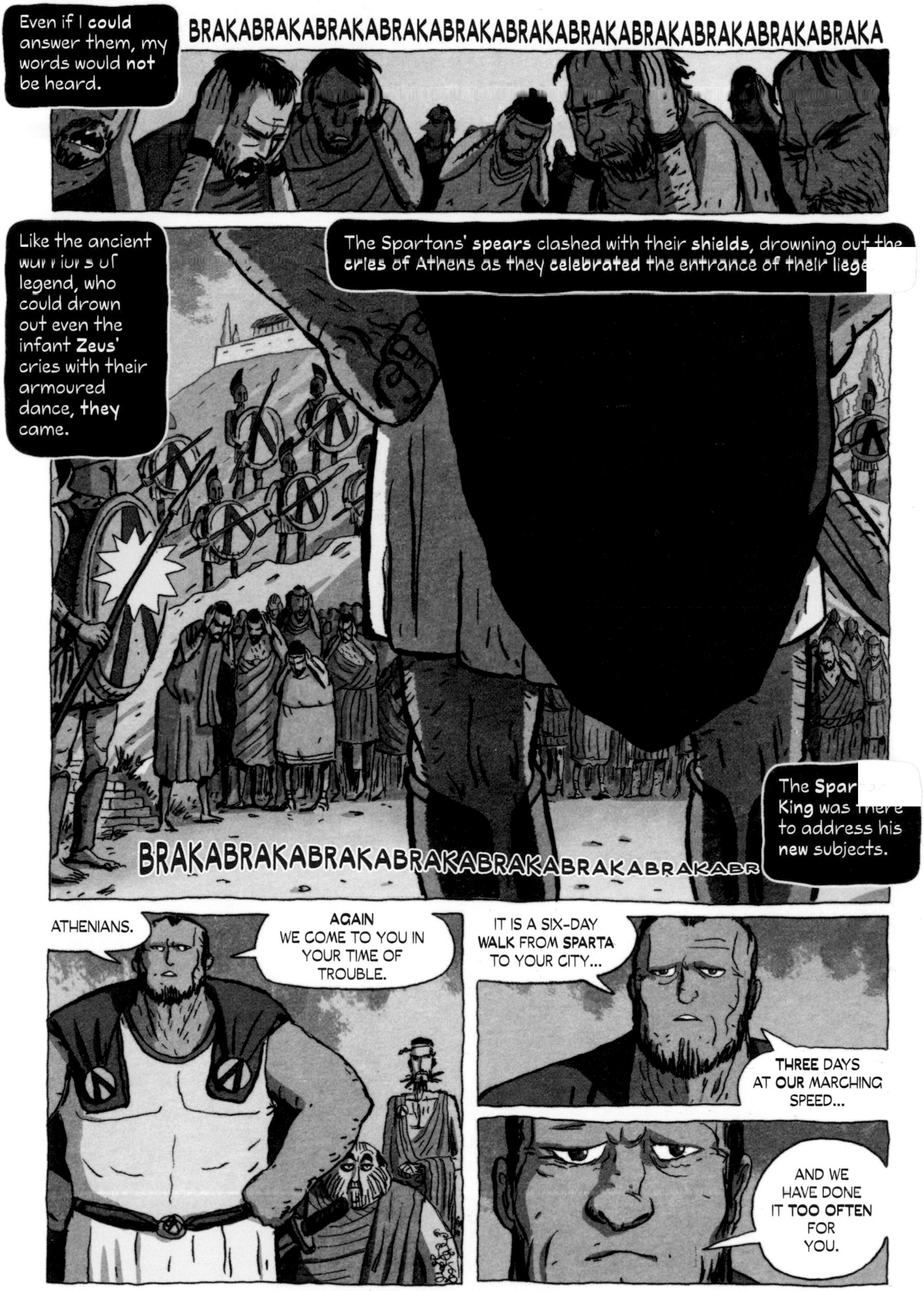

Even if I could answer them, my words would not be heard.
BRAKABRAKABRAKABRAKABRAKABRAKABRAKABRAKABRAKABRAKABRAKA
Like the ancient warriors of legend, who could drown out even the infant Zeus' cries with their armoured dance, they came.
The Spartans' spears clashed with their shields, drowning out the cries of Athens as they celebrated the entrance of their liege
BRAKABRAKABRAKABRAKABRAKABRAKABRAKABR
The Spar King was there to address his new subjects.
ATHENIANS.
AGAIN WE COME TO YOU IN YOUR TIME OF TROUBLE.
IT IS A SIX-DAY WALK FROM SPARTA TO YOUR CITY...
THREE DAYS AT OUR MARCHING SPEED...
AND WE HAVE DONE IT TOO OFTEN FOR YOU.

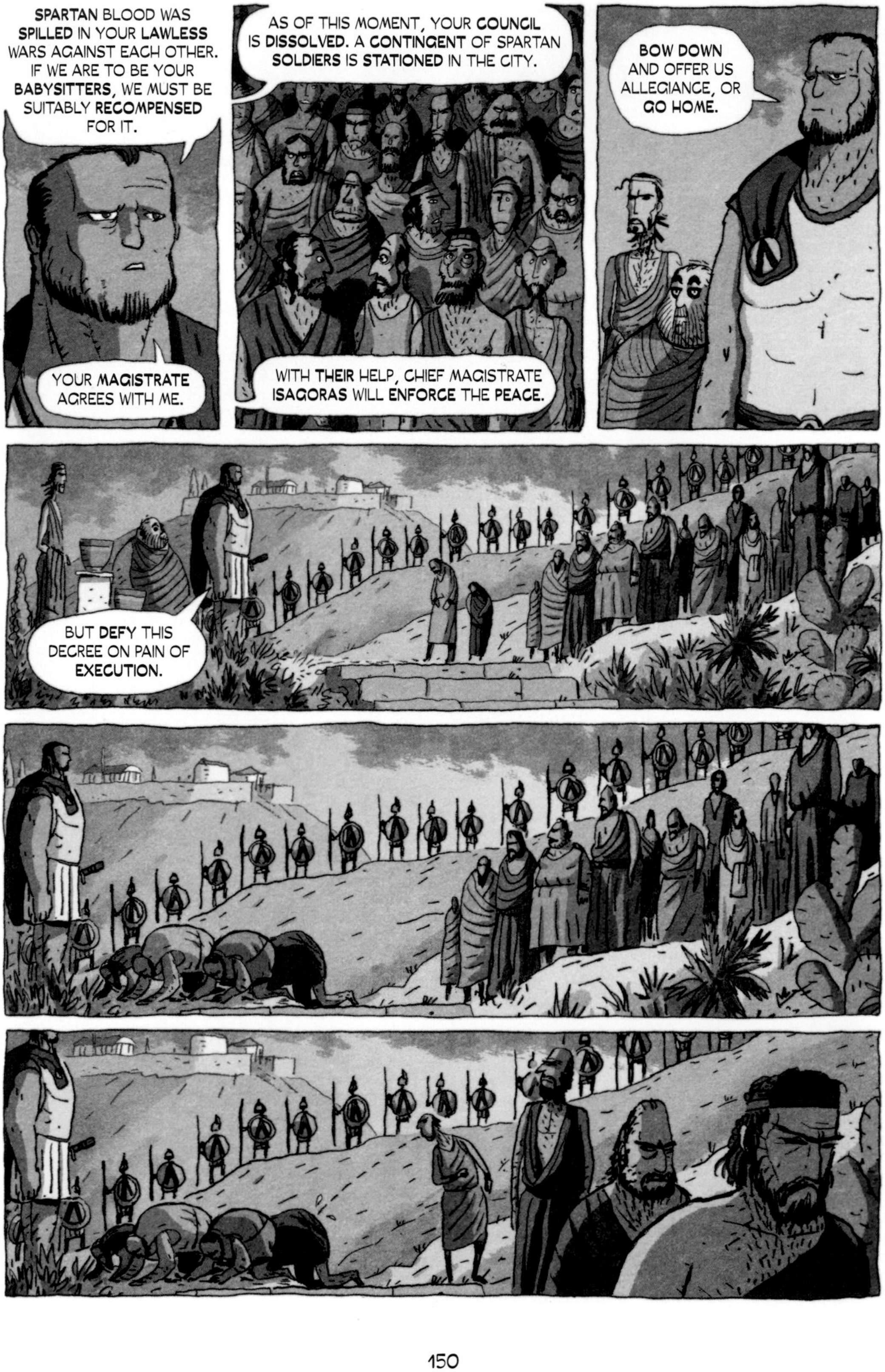
SPARTAN BLOOD WAS SPILLED IN YOUR LAWLESS WARS AGAINST EACH OTHER. IF WE ARE TO BE YOUR BABYSITTERS, WE MUST BE SUITABLY RECOMPENSED FOR IT.
YOUR MAGISTRATE AGREES WITH ME.
AS OF THIS MOMENT, YOUR COUNCIL IS DISSOLVED. A CONTINGENT OF SPARTAN SOLDIERS IS STATIONED IN THE CITY.
WITH THEIR HELP, CHIEF MAGISTRATE ISAGORAS WILL ENFORCE THE PEACE.
BOW DOWN AND OFFER US ALLEGIANCE, OR GO HOME.
BUT DEFY THIS DECREE ON PAIN OF EXECUTION.

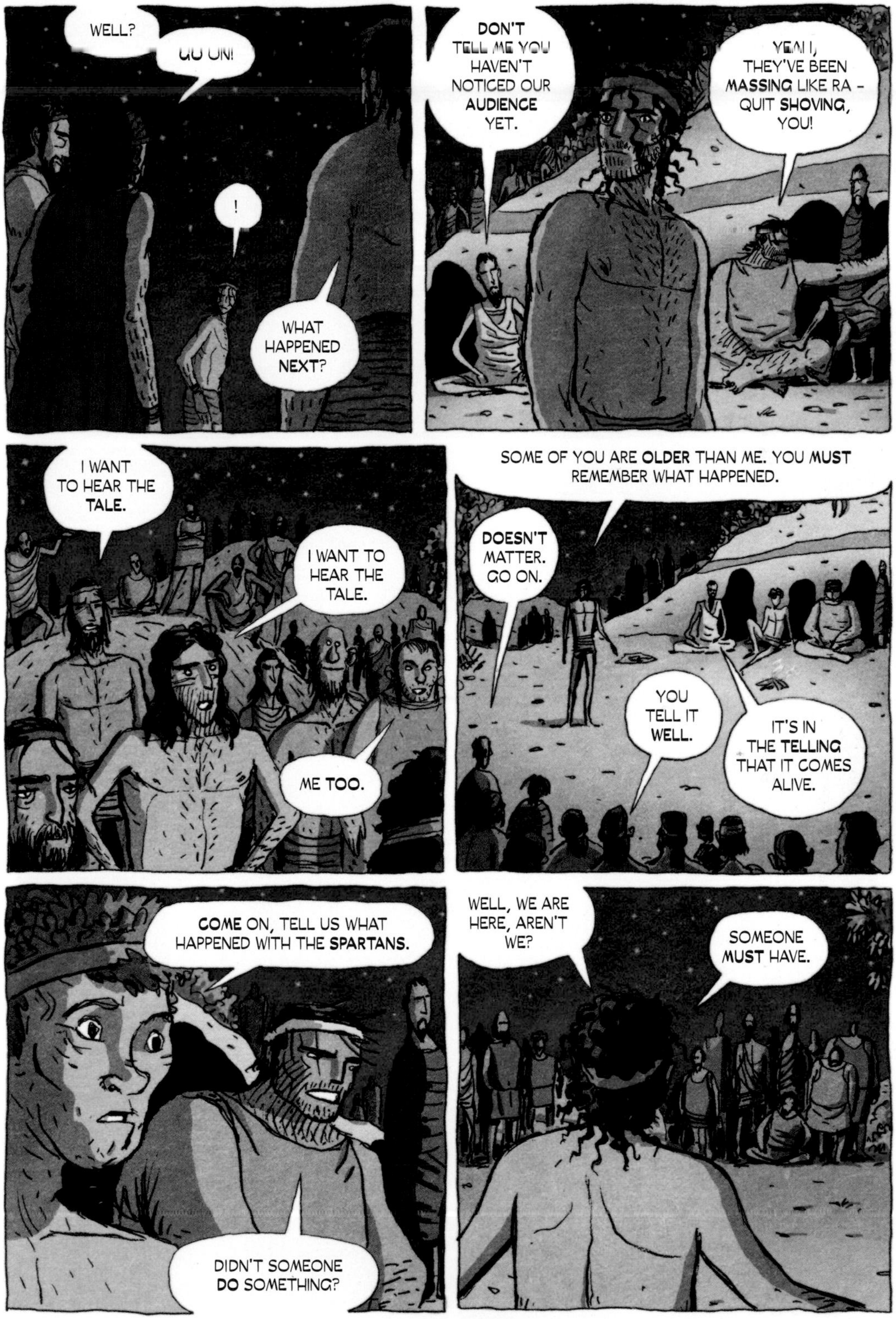
WELL?
GO ON!
!
WHAT HAPPENED NEXT?
DON'T TELL ME YOU HAVEN'T NOTICED OUR AUDIENCE YET.
YEAH, THEY'VE BEEN MASSING LIKE RA - QUIT SHOVING, YOU!
I WANT TO HEAR THE TALE.
I WANT TO HEAR THE TALE.
ME TOO.
SOME OF YOU ARE OLDER THAN ME. YOU MUST REMEMBER WHAT HAPPENED.
DOESN'T MATTER. GO ON.
YOU TELL IT WELL.
IT'S IN THE TELLING THAT IT COMES ALIVE.
COME ON, TELL US WHAT HAPPENED WITH THE SPARTANS.
DIDN'T SOMEONE DO SOMETHING?
WELL, WE ARE HERE, AREN'T WE?
SOMEONE MUST HAVE.

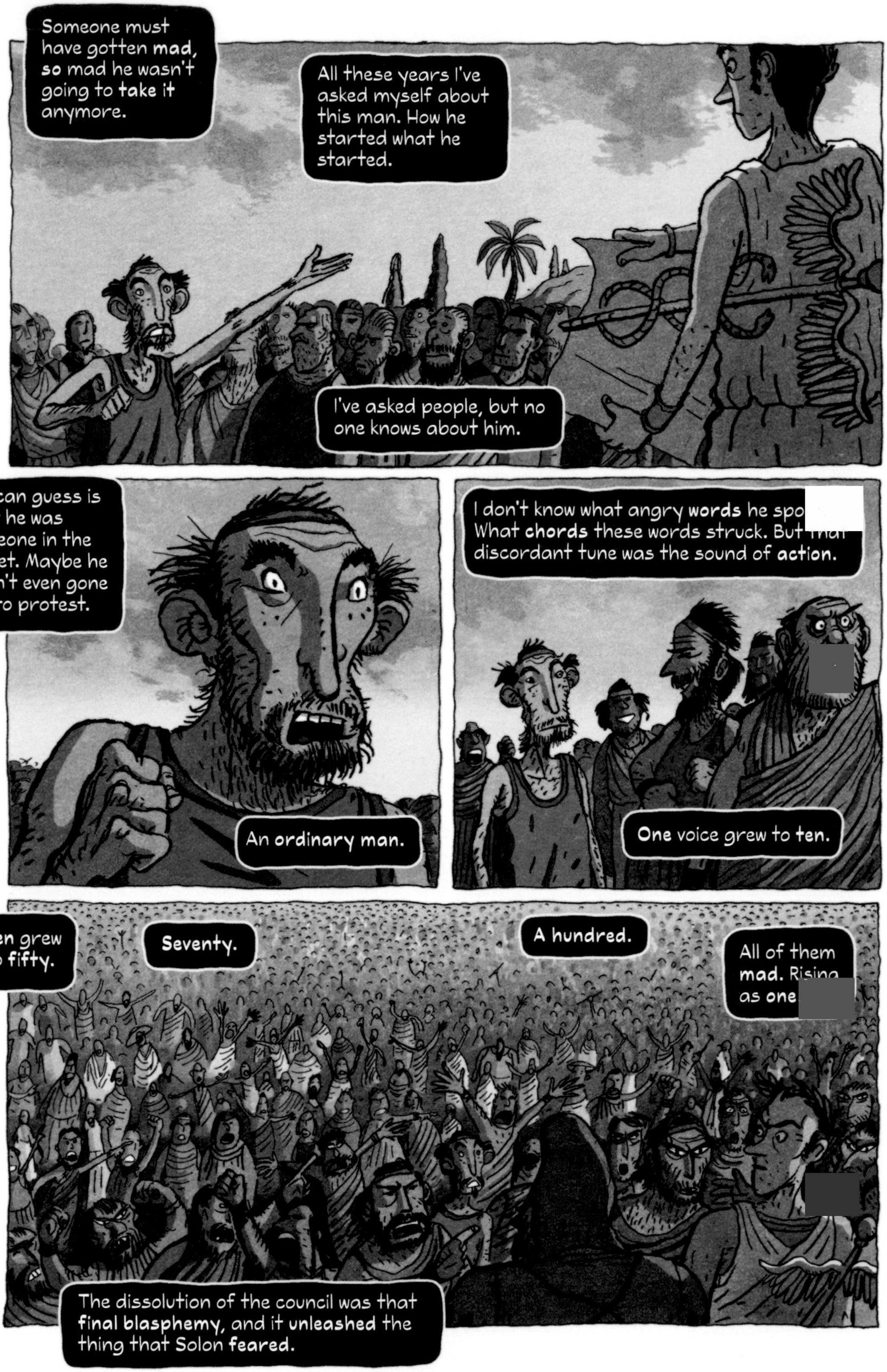
Someone must have gotten mad, so mad he wasn't going to take it anymore.
All these years I've asked myself about this man. How he started what he started.
I've asked people, but no one knows about him.
All I can guess is that he was someone in the street. Maybe he hadn't even gone out to protest.
An ordinary man.
I don't know what angry words he spo
What chords these words struck. But
discordant tune was the sound of action.
One voice grew to ten.
Ten grew to fifty.
Seventy.
A hundred.
All of them mad. Rising as one
The dissolution of the council was that final blasphemy, and it unleashed the thing that Solon feared.

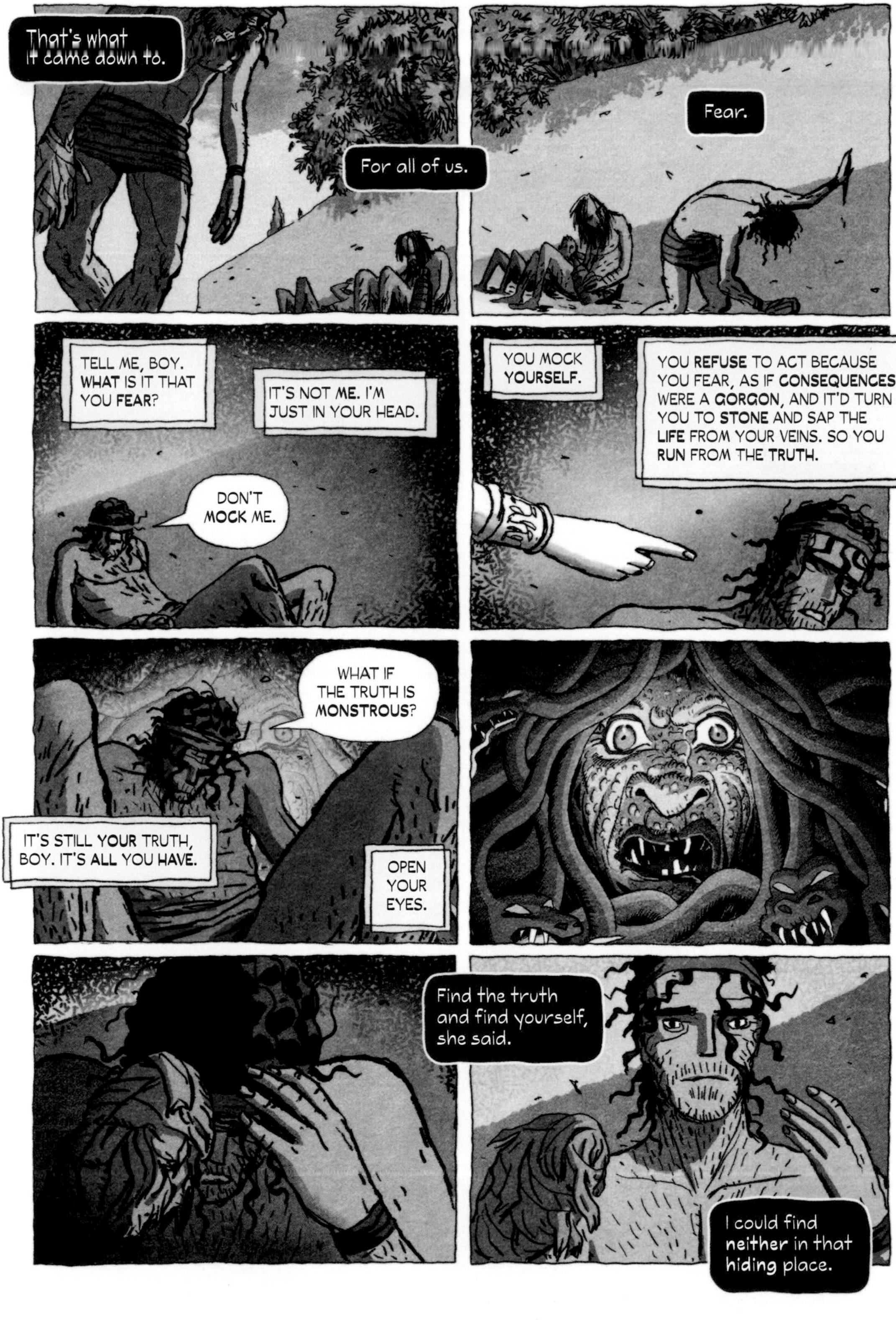
That's what it came down to.
For all of us.
Fear.
TELL ME, BOY. WHAT IS IT THAT YOU FEAR?
IT'S NOT ME. I'M JUST IN YOUR HEAD.
DON'T MOCK ME.
YOU MOCK YOURSELF.
YOU REFUSE TO ACT BECAUSE YOU FEAR, AS IF CONSEQUENCES WERE A GORGON, AND IT'D TURN YOU TO STONE AND SAP THE LIFE FROM YOUR VEINS. SO YOU RUN FROM THE TRUTH.
WHAT IF THE TRUTH IS MONSTROUS?
IT'S STILL YOUR TRUTH, BOY. IT'S ALL YOU HAVE.
OPEN YOUR EYES.
Find the truth and find yourself, she said.
I could find neither in that hiding place.

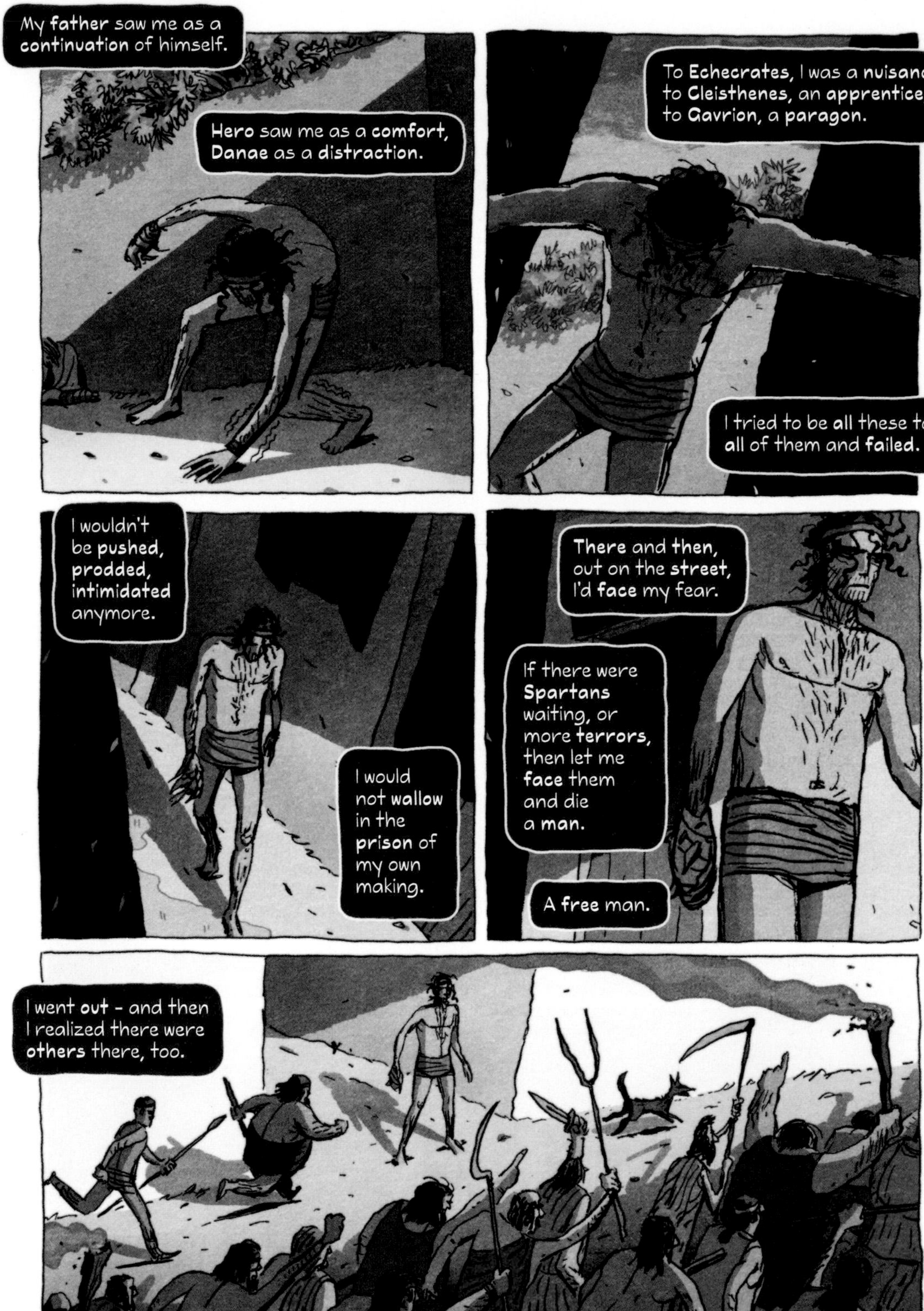
My father saw me as a continuation of himself.
Hero saw me as a comfort, Danae as a distraction.
To Echecrates, I was a nuisance, to Cleisthenes, an apprentice, to Gavrion, a paragon.
I tried to be all these to all of them and failed.
I wouldn't be pushed, prodded, intimidated anymore.
I would not wallow in the prison of my own making.
There and then, out on the street, I'd face my fear.
If there were Spartans waiting, or more terrors, then let me face them and die a man.
A free man.
I went out - and then I realized there were others there, too.

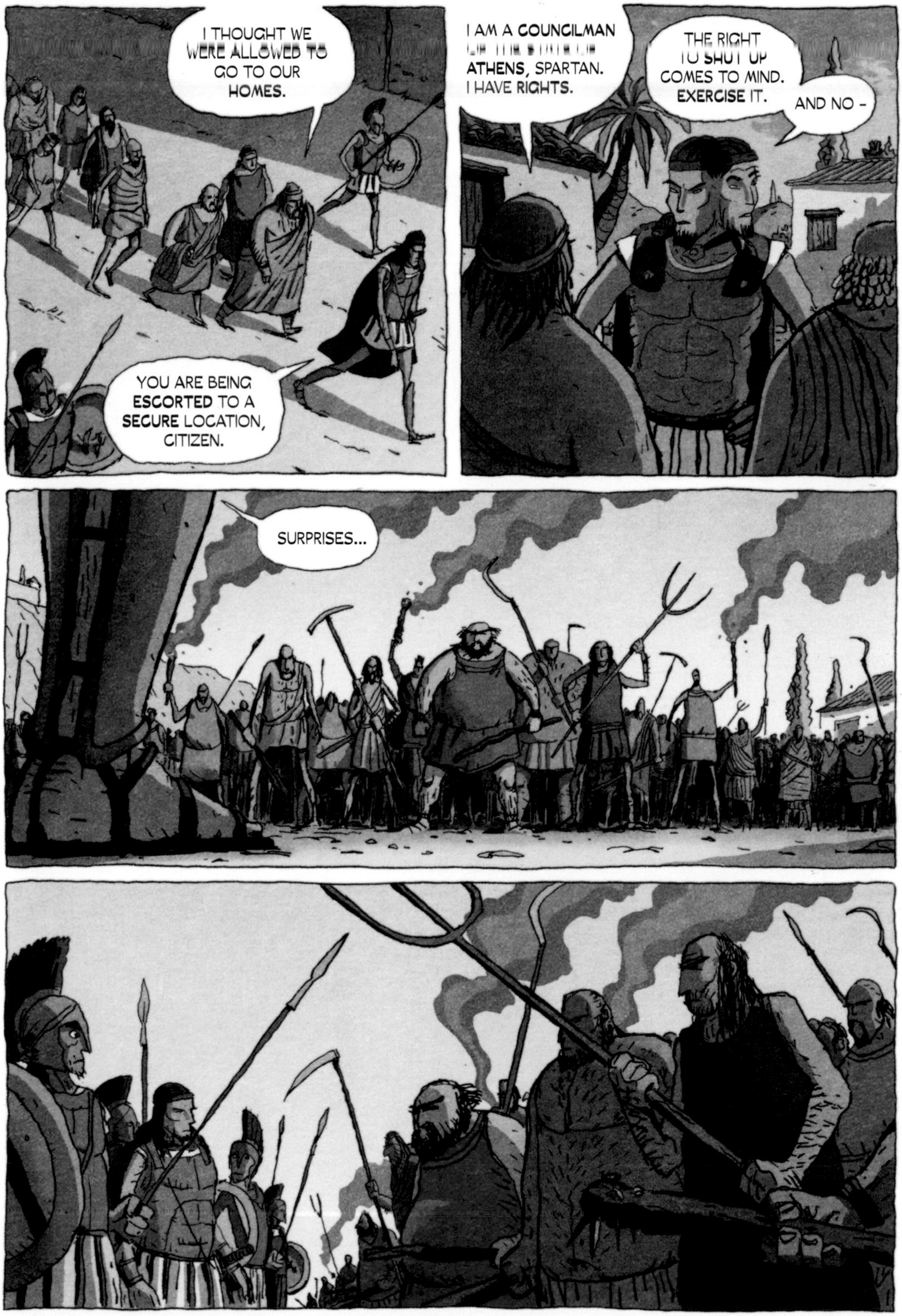
I THOUGHT WE WERE ALLOWED TO GO TO OUR HOMES.
YOU ARE BEING ESCORTED TO A SECURE LOCATION, CITIZEN.
I AM A COUNCILMAN
ATHENS, SPARTAN. I HAVE RIGHTS.
THE RIGHT TO SHUT UP COMES TO MIND. EXERCISE IT.
AND NO -
SURPRISES...

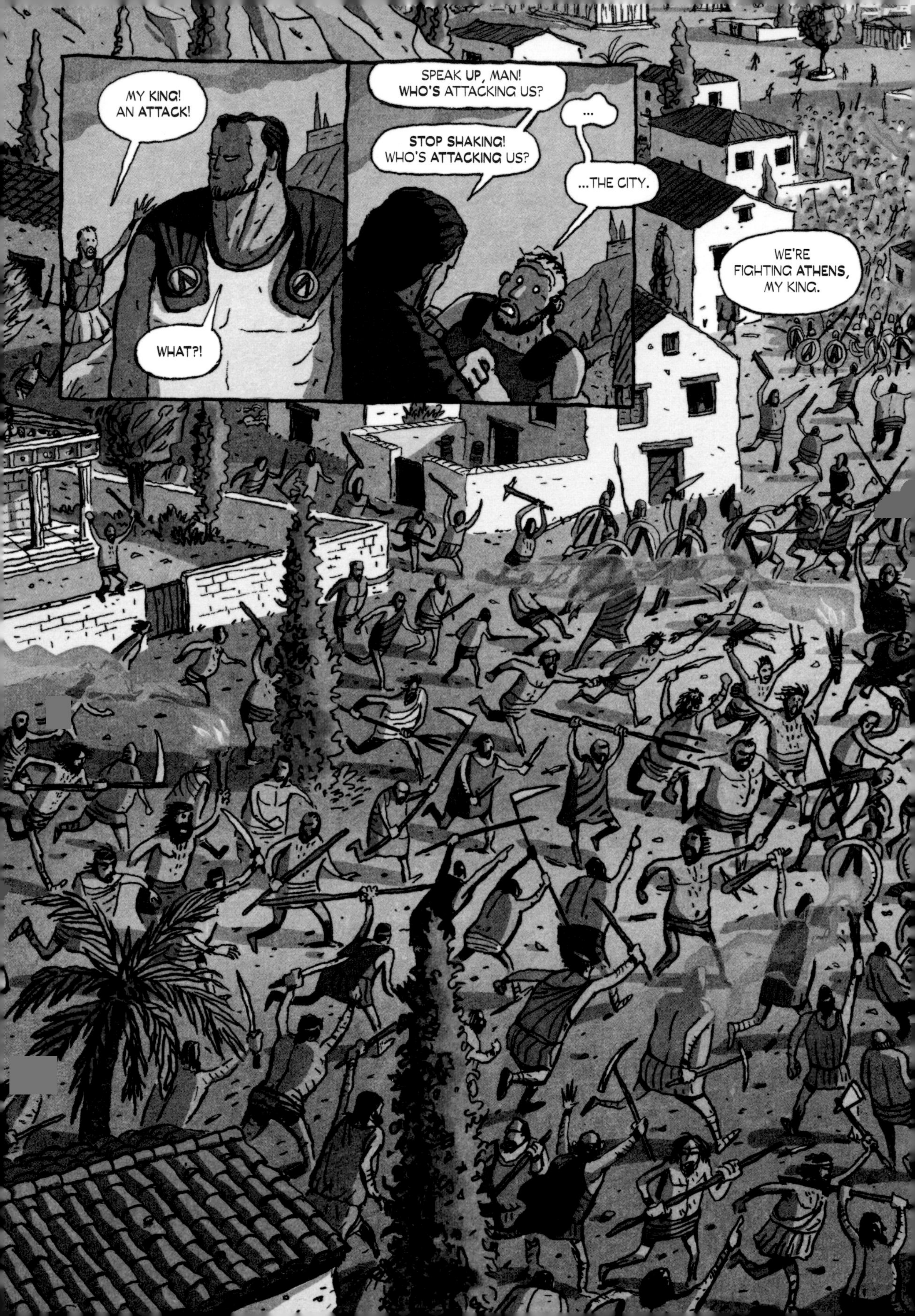
MY KING! AN ATTACK!
WHAT?!
SPEAK UP, MAN! WHO'S ATTACKING US?
STOP SHAKING! WHO'S ATTACKING US?
...
...THE CITY.
WE'RE FIGHTING ATHENS, MY KING.

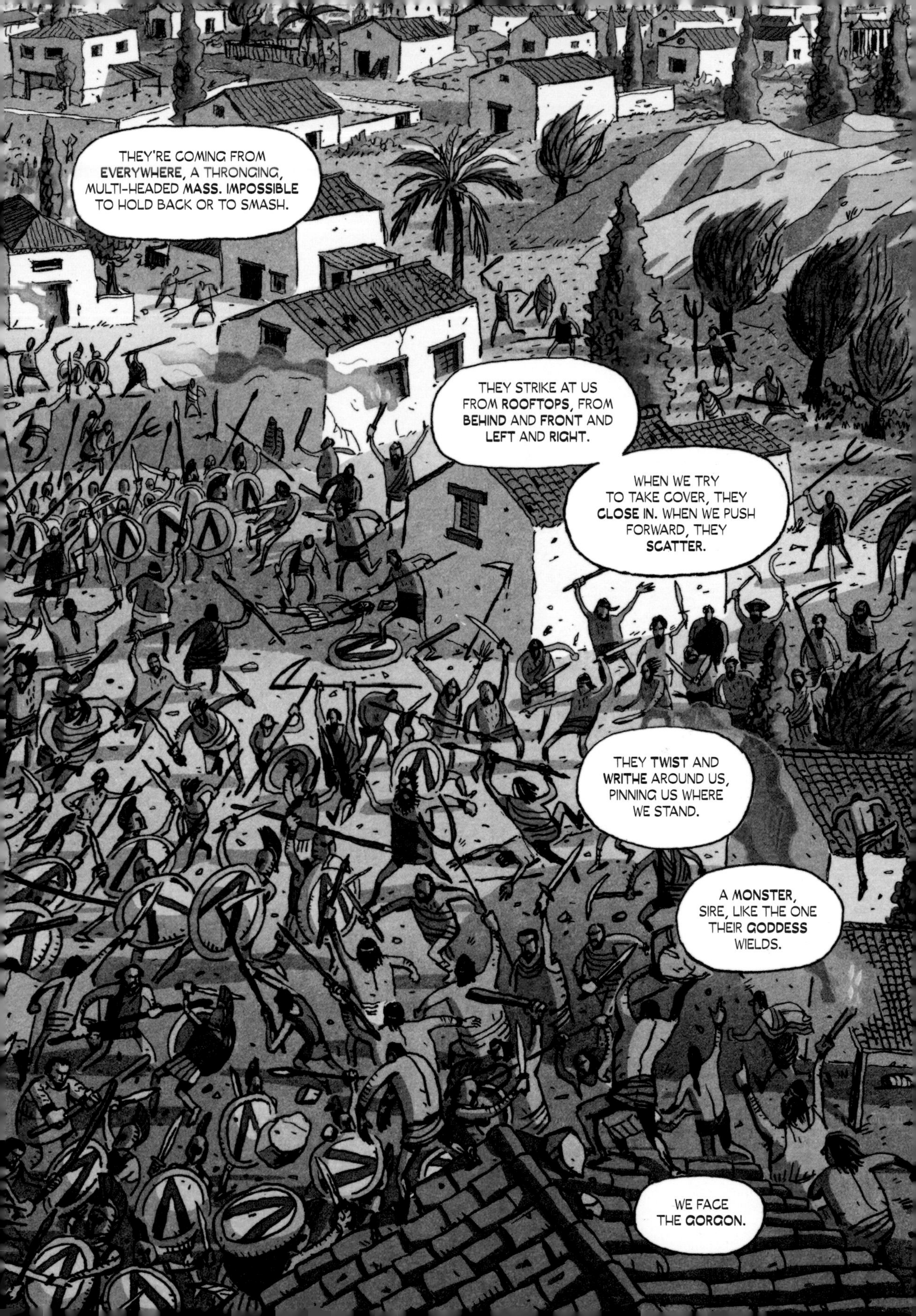
THEY'RE COMING FROM EVERYWHERE, A THRONGING, MULTI-HEADED MASS. IMPOSSIBLE TO HOLD BACK OR TO SMASH.
THEY STRIKE AT US FROM ROOFTOPS, FROM BEHIND AND FRONT AND LEFT AND RIGHT.
WHEN WE TRY TO TAKE COVER, THEY CLOSE IN. WHEN WE PUSH FORWARD, THEY SCATTER.
THEY TWIST AND WRITHE AROUND US, PINNING US WHERE WE STAND.
A MONSTER, SIRE, LIKE THE ONE THEIR GODDESS WIELDS.
WE FACE THE GORGON.

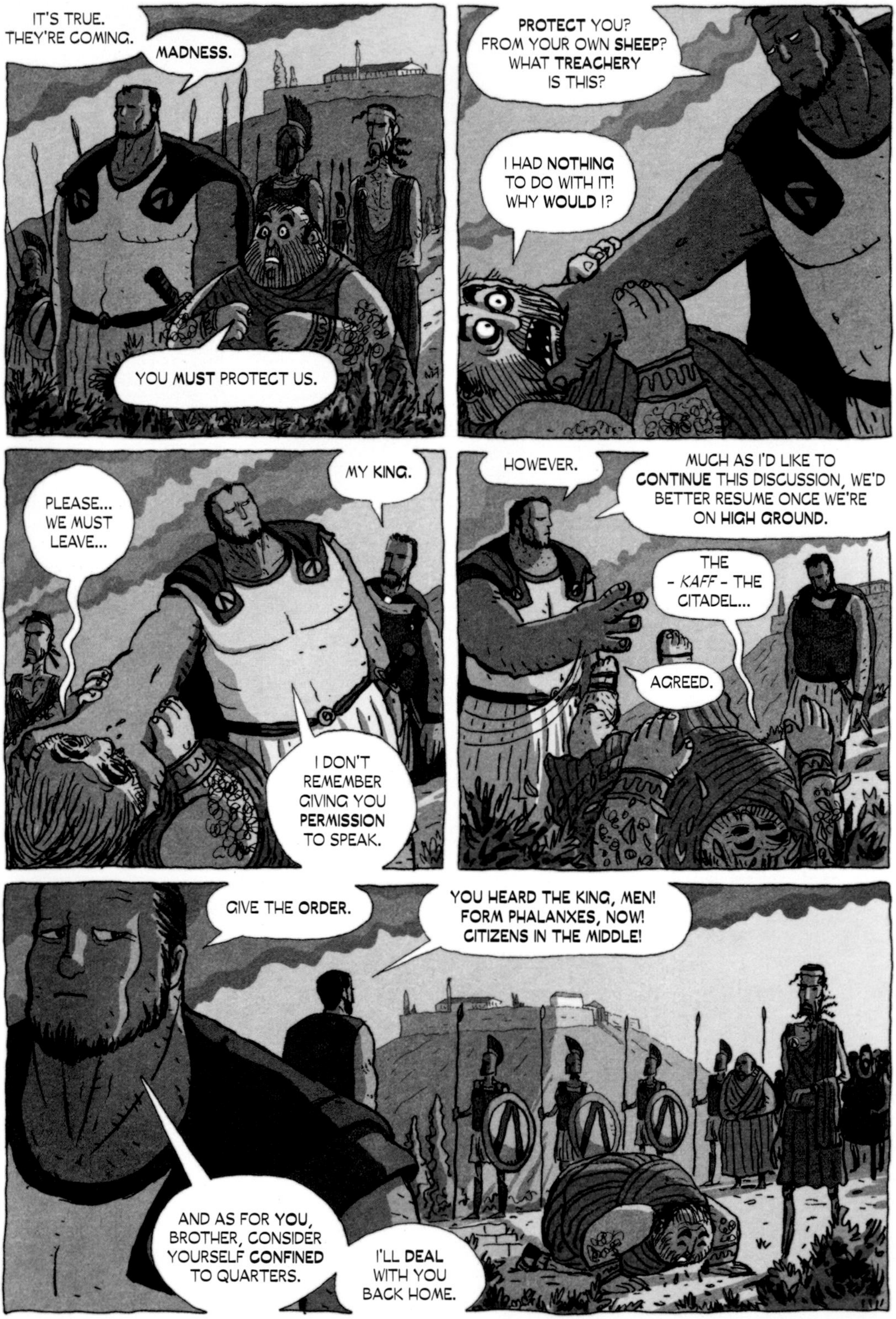
IT'S TRUE. THEY'RE COMING.
MADNESS.
YOU **MUST** PROTECT US.
PROTECT YOU? FROM YOUR OWN **SHEEP**? WHAT **TREACHERY** IS THIS?
I HAD **NOTHING** TO DO WITH IT! WHY **WOULD** I?
PLEASE... WE MUST LEAVE...
MY **KING**.
I DON'T REMEMBER GIVING YOU **PERMISSION** TO SPEAK.
HOWEVER.
MUCH AS I'D LIKE TO **CONTINUE** THIS DISCUSSION, WE'D BETTER RESUME ONCE WE'RE ON **HIGH GROUND**.
THE - *KAFF* - THE CITADEL...
AGREED.
GIVE THE **ORDER**.
YOU HEARD THE KING, MEN! FORM PHALANXES, NOW! CITIZENS IN THE MIDDLE!
AND AS FOR **YOU**, BROTHER, CONSIDER YOURSELF **CONFINED** TO QUARTERS.
I'LL **DEAL** WITH YOU BACK HOME.

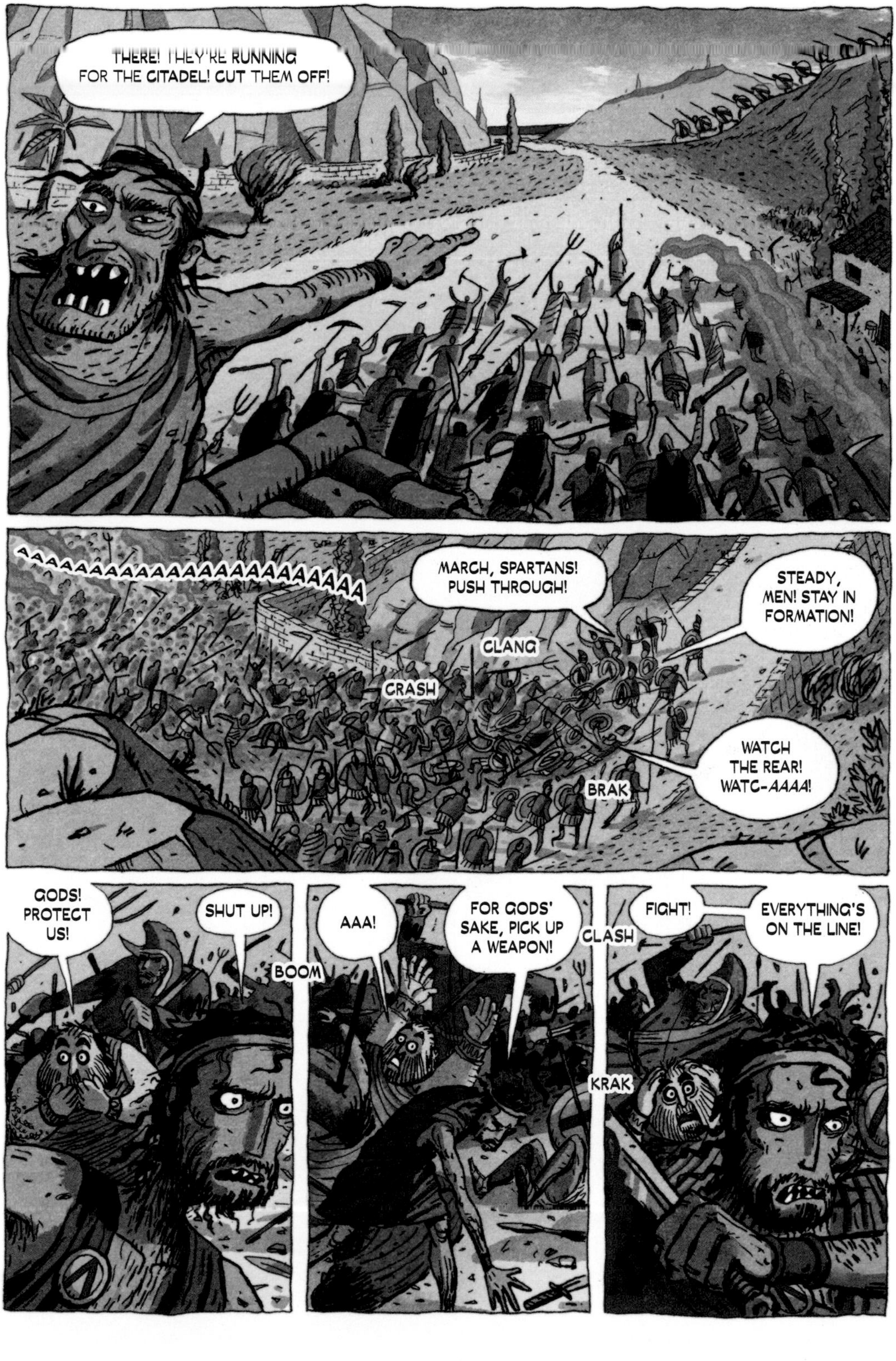
THERE! THEY'RE RUNNING FOR THE CITADEL! CUT THEM OFF!
AAAAAAAAAAAAAAAAAAAAAAAAA
MARCH, SPARTANS! PUSH THROUGH!
STEADY, MEN! STAY IN FORMATION!
CLANG
CRASH
WATCH THE REAR! WATC-AAAA!
BRAK
GODS! PROTECT US!
SHUT UP!
BOOM
AAA!
FOR GODS' SAKE, PICK UP A WEAPON!
CLASH
FIGHT!
EVERYTHING'S ON THE LINE!
KRAK

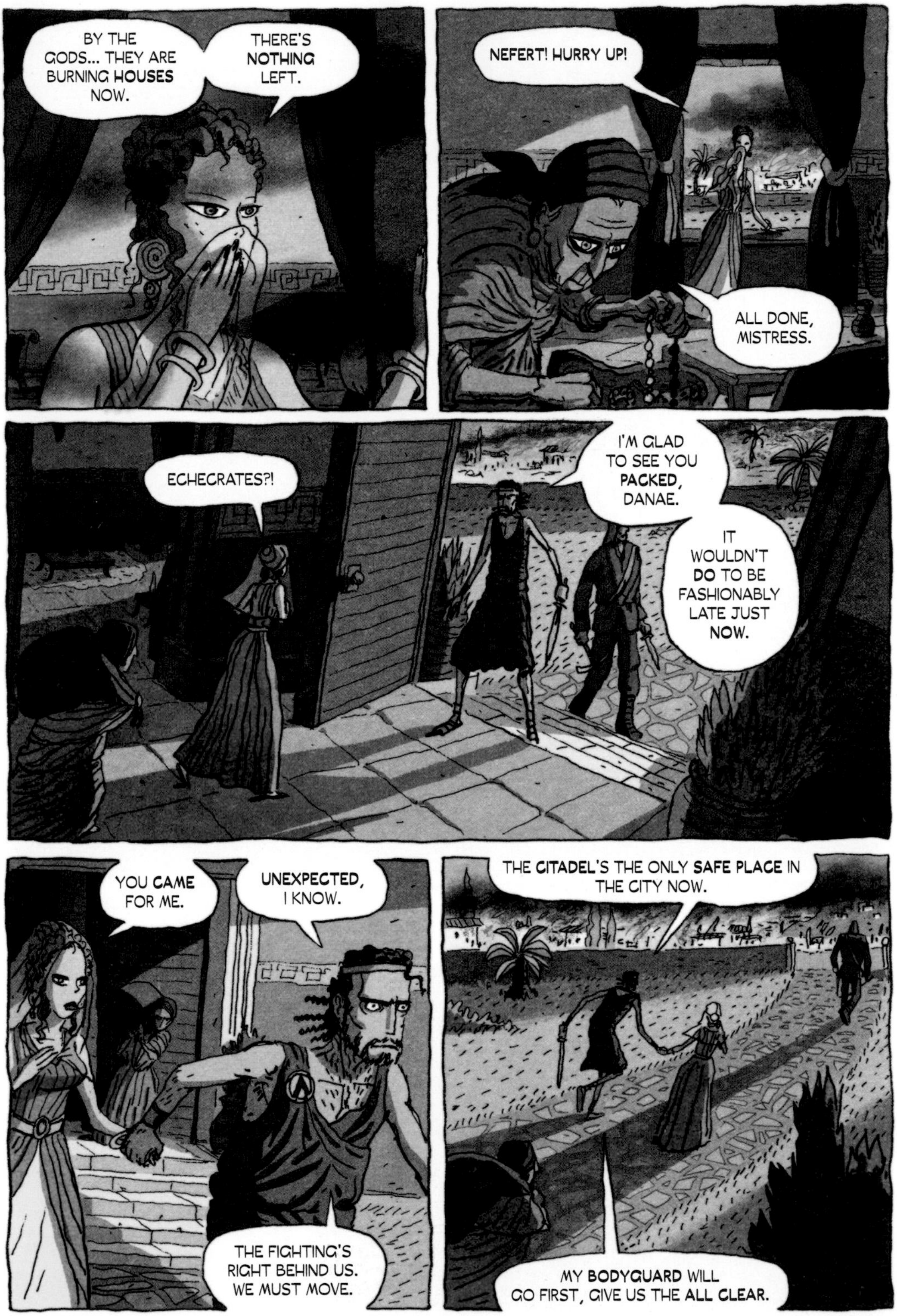
BY THE GODS... THEY ARE BURNING HOUSES NOW.
THERE'S NOTHING LEFT.
NEFERT! HURRY UP!
ALL DONE, MISTRESS.
ECHECRATES?!
I'M GLAD TO SEE YOU PACKED, DANAE.
IT WOULDN'T DO TO BE FASHIONABLY LATE JUST NOW.
YOU CAME FOR ME.
UNEXPECTED, I KNOW.
THE FIGHTING'S RIGHT BEHIND US. WE MUST MOVE.
THE CITADEL'S THE ONLY SAFE PLACE IN THE CITY NOW.
MY BODYGUARD WILL GO FIRST, GIVE US THE ALL CLEAR.

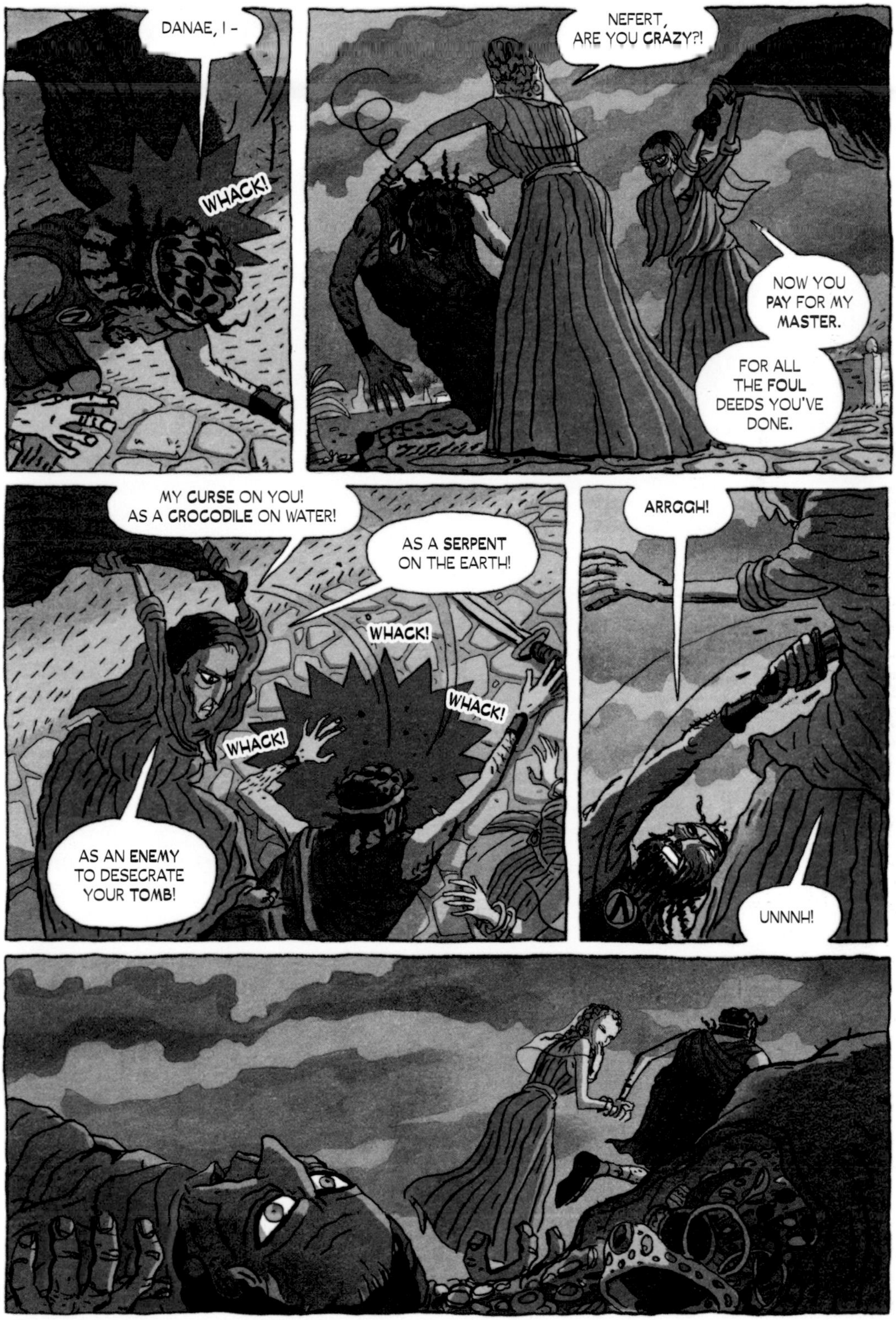
DANAE, I -
WHACK!
NEFERT, ARE YOU CRAZY?!
NOW YOU PAY FOR MY MASTER.
FOR ALL THE FOUL DEEDS YOU'VE DONE.
MY CURSE ON YOU! AS A CROCODILE ON WATER!
AS A SERPENT ON THE EARTH!
WHACK!
WHACK!
WHACK!
AS AN ENEMY TO DESECRATE YOUR TOMB!
ARRGGH!
UNNNH!

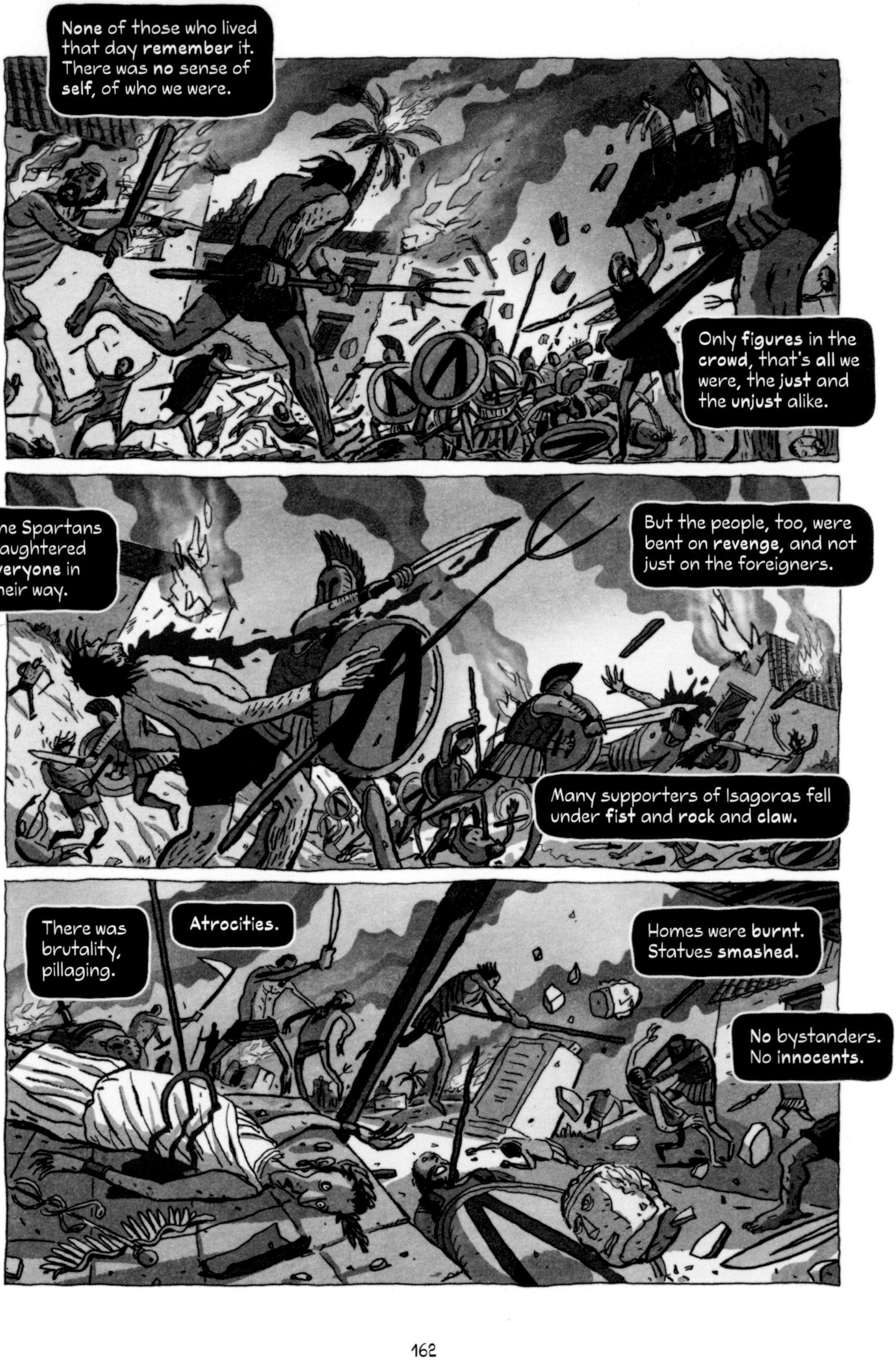
None of those who lived that day remember it. There was no sense of self, of who we were.
Only figures in the crowd, that's all we were, the just and the unjust alike.
The Spartans slaughtered everyone in their way.
But the people, too, were bent on revenge, and not just on the foreigners.
Many supporters of Isagoras fell under fist and rock and claw.
There was brutality, pillaging.
Atrocities.
Homes were burnt. Statues smashed.
No bystanders. No innocents.

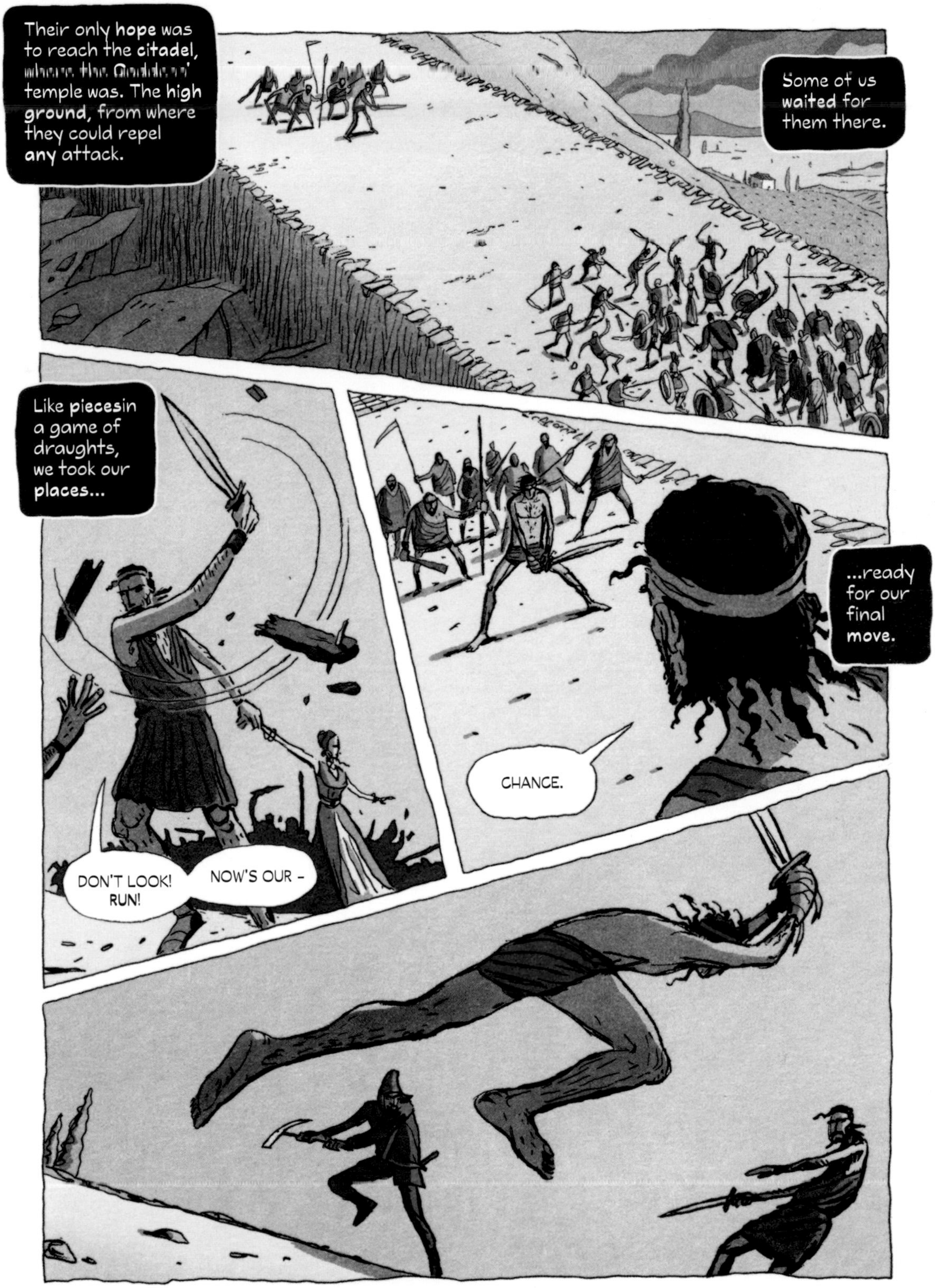
Their only hope was to reach the citadel, where the Goddess' temple was. The high ground, from where they could repel any attack.
Some of us waited for them there.
Like piecesin a game of draughts, we took our places...
...ready for our final move.
DON'T LOOK! RUN!
NOW'S OUR –
CHANCE.

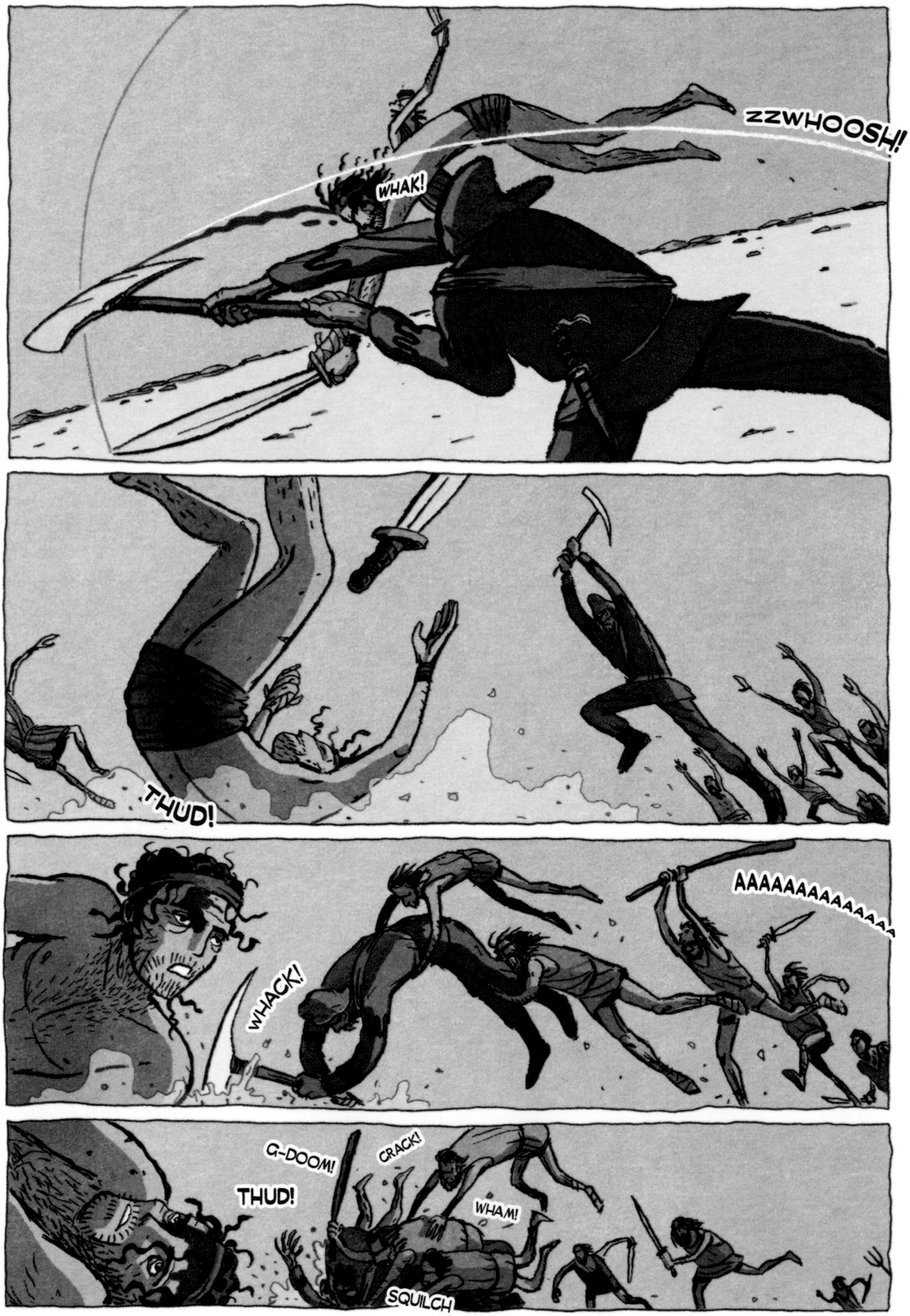
ZZWHOOSH!
WHAK!
THUD!
AAAAAAAAAAAAAA
WHACK!
G-DOOM!
CRACK!
THUD!
WHAM!
SQUILCH

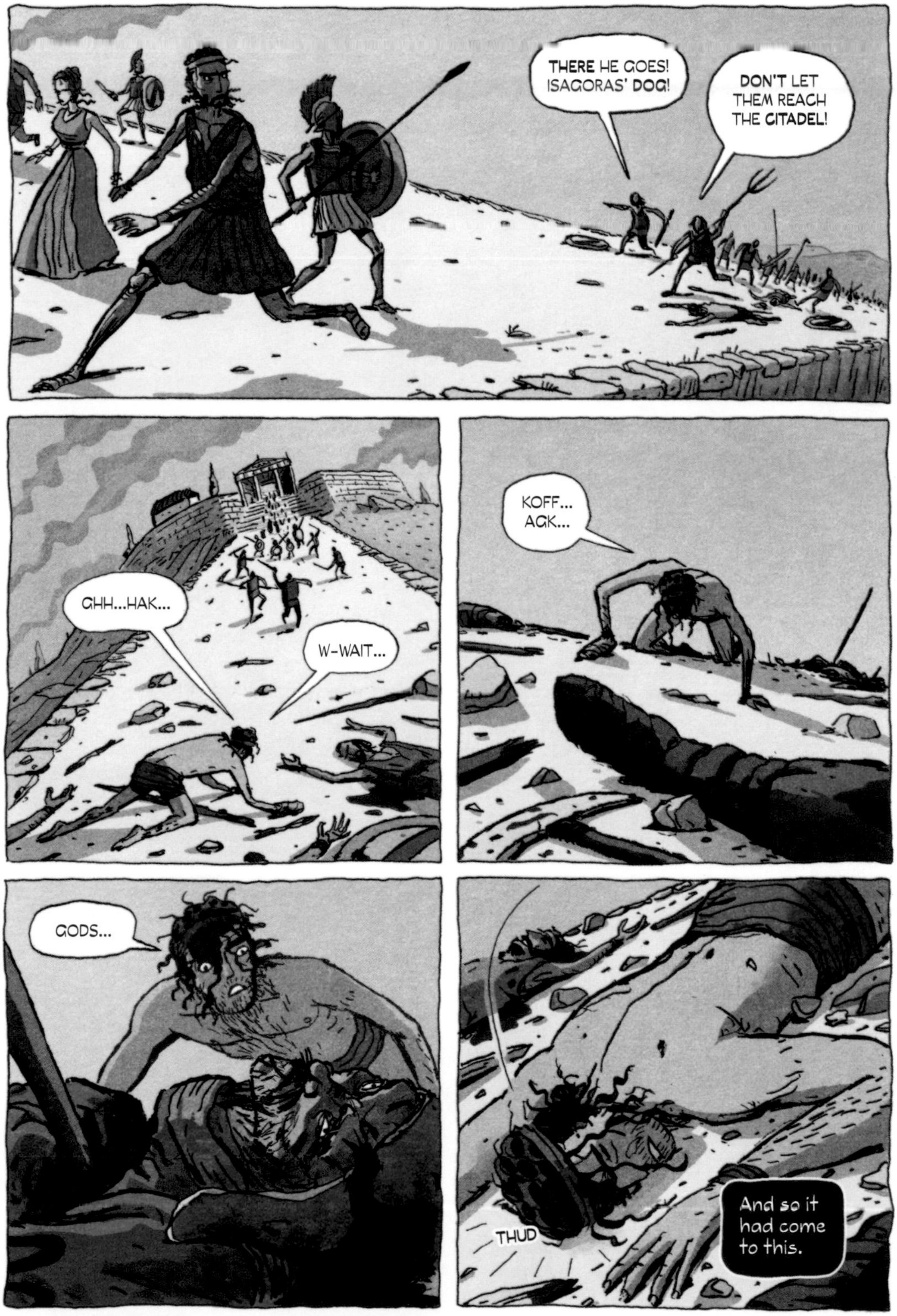
THERE HE GOES! ISAGORAS' DOG!
DON'T LET THEM REACH THE CITADEL!
GHH...HAK...
W-WAIT...
KOFF... AGK...
GODS...
THUD
And so it had come to this.

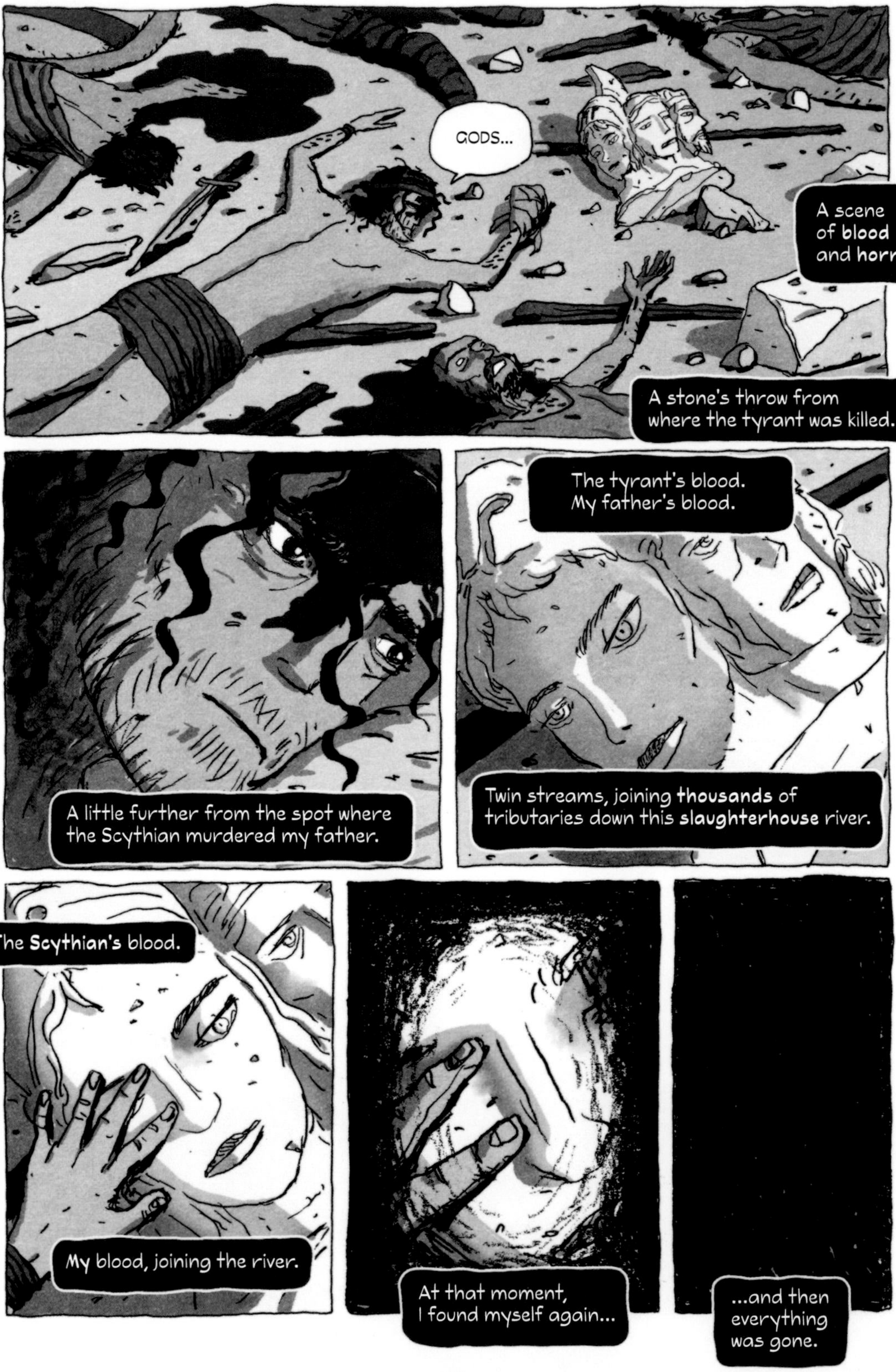
GODS...
A scene of blood and horror.
A stone's throw from where the tyrant was killed.
A little further from the spot where the Scythian murdered my father.
The tyrant's blood. My father's blood.
Twin streams, joining thousands of tributaries down this slaughterhouse river.
The Scythian's blood.
My blood, joining the river.
At that moment, I found myself again...
...and then everything was gone.

BLOOD AND WINE

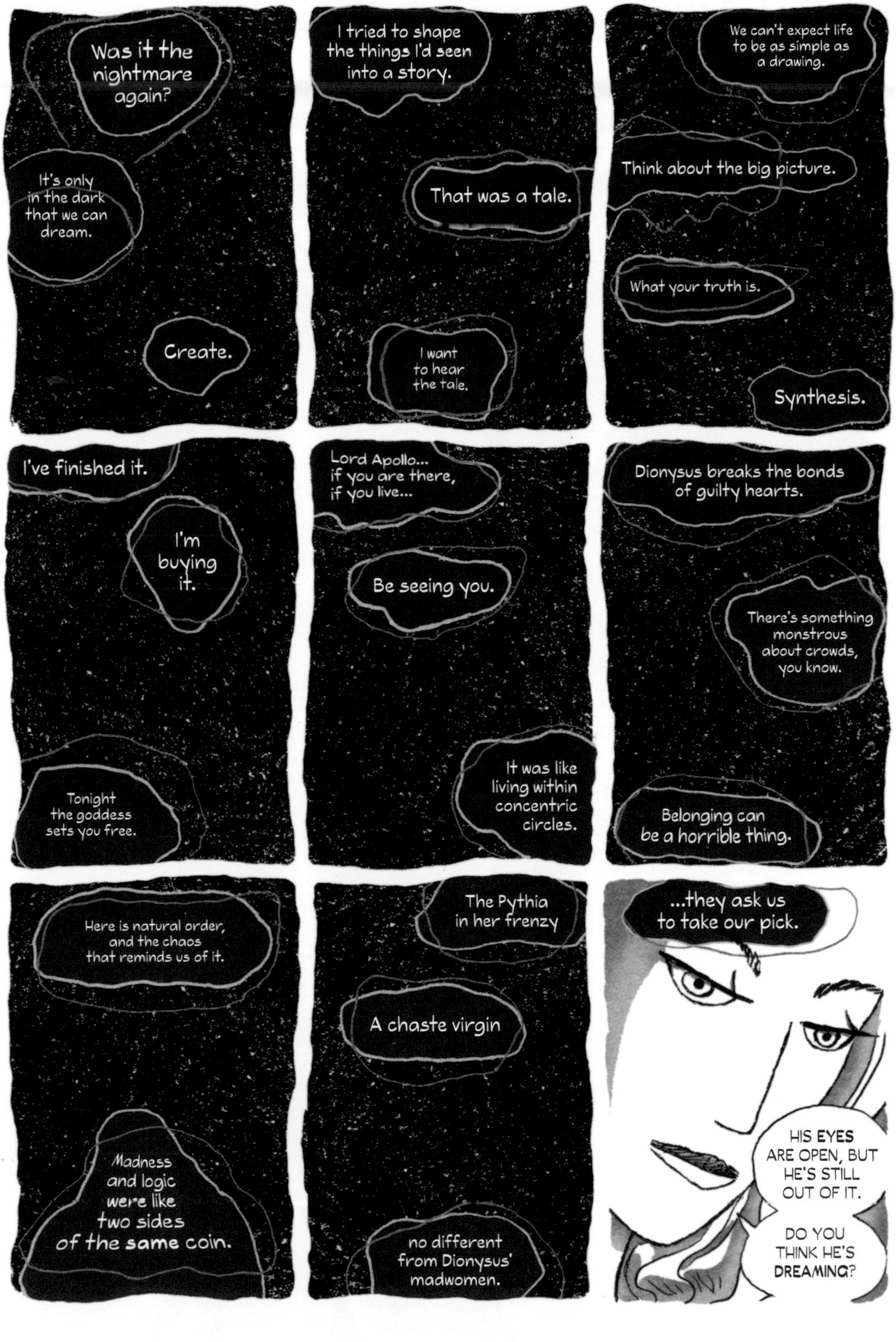

Was it the nightmare again?
It's only in the dark that we can dream.
Create.
I tried to shape the things I'd seen into a story.
That was a tale.
I want to hear the tale.
We can't expect life to be as simple as a drawing.
Think about the big picture.
What your truth is.
Synthesis.
I've finished it.
I'm buying it.
Tonight the goddess sets you free.
Lord Apollo... if you are there, if you live...
Be seeing you.
It was like living within concentric circles.
Dionysus breaks the bonds of guilty hearts.
There's something monstrous about crowds, you know.
Belonging can be a horrible thing.
Here is natural order, and the chaos that reminds us of it.
Madness and logic were like two sides of the same coin.
The Pythia in her frenzy
A chaste virgin
no different from Dionysus' madwomen.
...they ask us to take our pick.
HIS EYES ARE OPEN, BUT HE'S STILL OUT OF IT.
DO YOU THINK HE'S DREAMING?

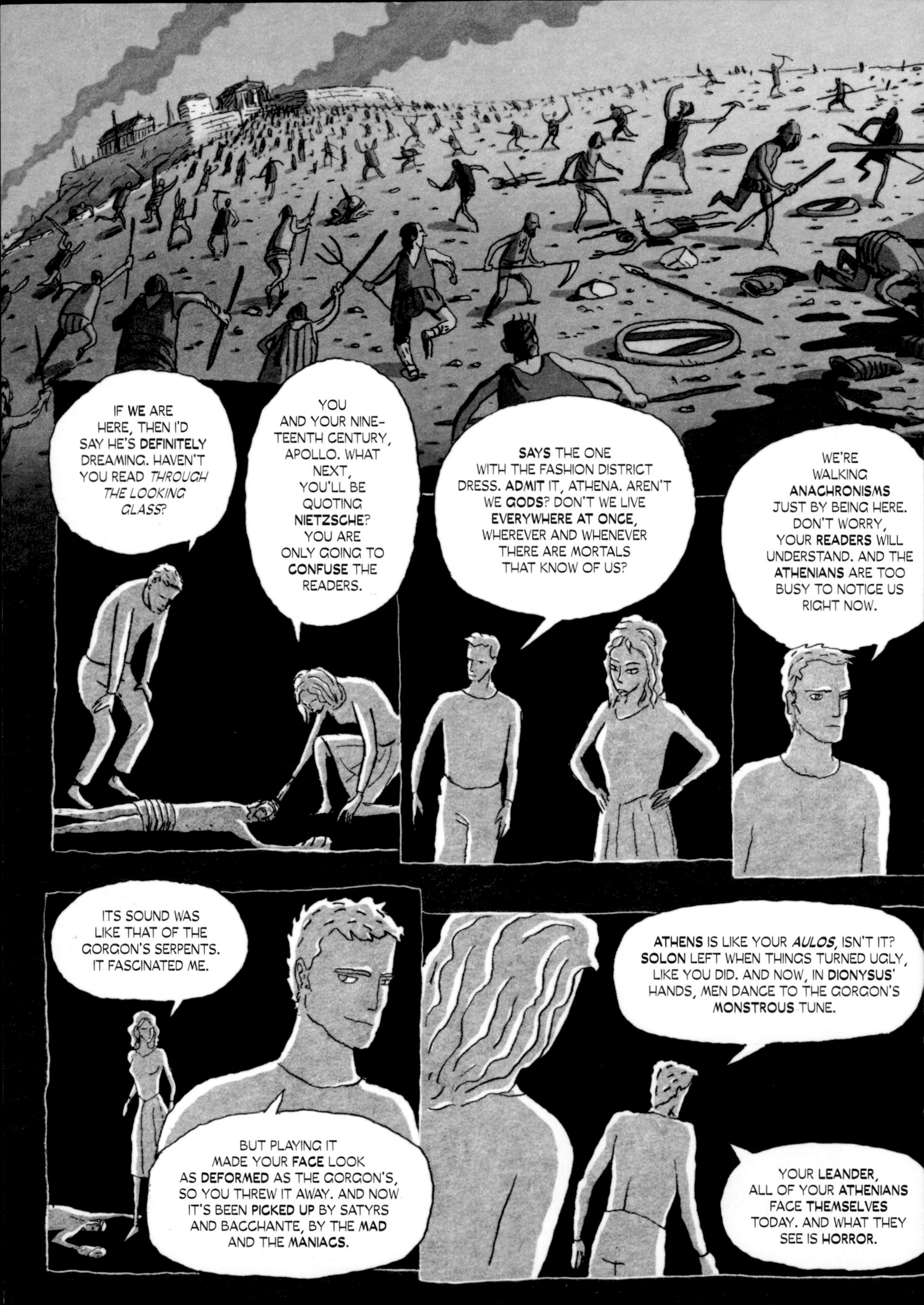
IF WE ARE HERE, THEN I'D SAY HE'S DEFINITELY DREAMING. HAVEN'T YOU READ *THROUGH THE LOOKING GLASS*?
YOU AND YOUR NINETEENTH CENTURY, APOLLO. WHAT NEXT, YOU'LL BE QUOTING NIETZSCHE? YOU ARE ONLY GOING TO CONFUSE THE READERS.
SAYS THE ONE WITH THE FASHION DISTRICT DRESS. ADMIT IT, ATHENA. AREN'T WE GODS? DON'T WE LIVE EVERYWHERE AT ONCE, WHEREVER AND WHENEVER THERE ARE MORTALS THAT KNOW OF US?
WE'RE WALKING ANACHRONISMS JUST BY BEING HERE. DON'T WORRY, YOUR READERS WILL UNDERSTAND. AND THE ATHENIANS ARE TOO BUSY TO NOTICE US RIGHT NOW.
ITS SOUND WAS LIKE THAT OF THE GORGON'S SERPENTS. IT FASCINATED ME.
BUT PLAYING IT MADE YOUR FACE LOOK AS DEFORMED AS THE GORGON'S, SO YOU THREW IT AWAY. AND NOW IT'S BEEN PICKED UP BY SATYRS AND BACCHANTE, BY THE MAD AND THE MANIACS.
ATHENS IS LIKE YOUR *AULOS*, ISN'T IT? SOLON LEFT WHEN THINGS TURNED UGLY, LIKE YOU DID. AND NOW, IN DIONYSUS' HANDS, MEN DANCE TO THE GORGON'S MONSTROUS TUNE.
YOUR LEANDER, ALL OF YOUR ATHENIANS FACE THEMSELVES TODAY. AND WHAT THEY SEE IS HORROR.

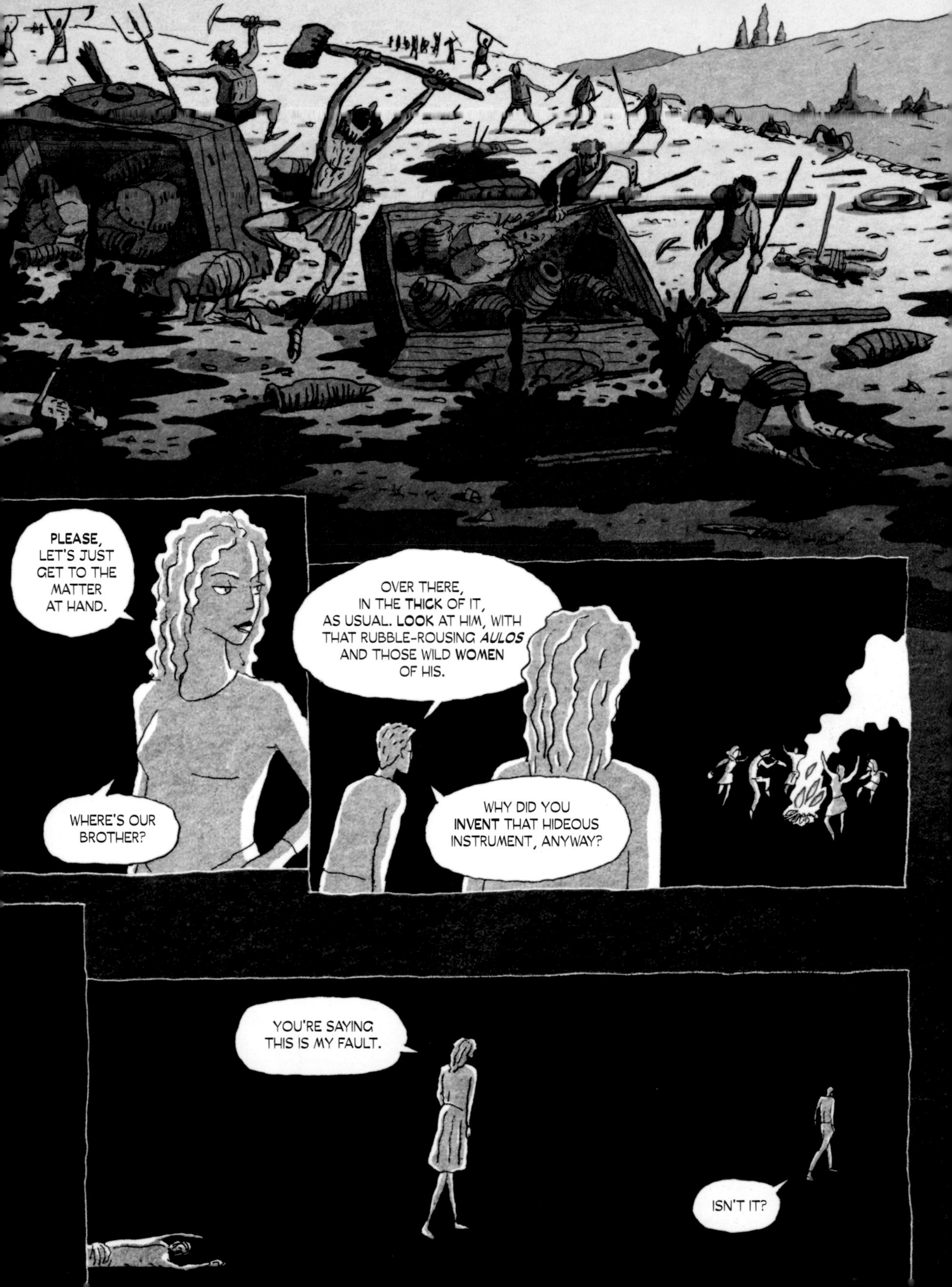
PLEASE, LET'S JUST GET TO THE MATTER AT HAND.
WHERE'S OUR BROTHER?
OVER THERE, IN THE THICK OF IT, AS USUAL. LOOK AT HIM, WITH THAT RUBBLE-ROUSING AULOS AND THOSE WILD WOMEN OF HIS.
WHY DID YOU INVENT THAT HIDEOUS INSTRUMENT, ANYWAY?
YOU'RE SAYING THIS IS MY FAULT.
ISN'T IT?

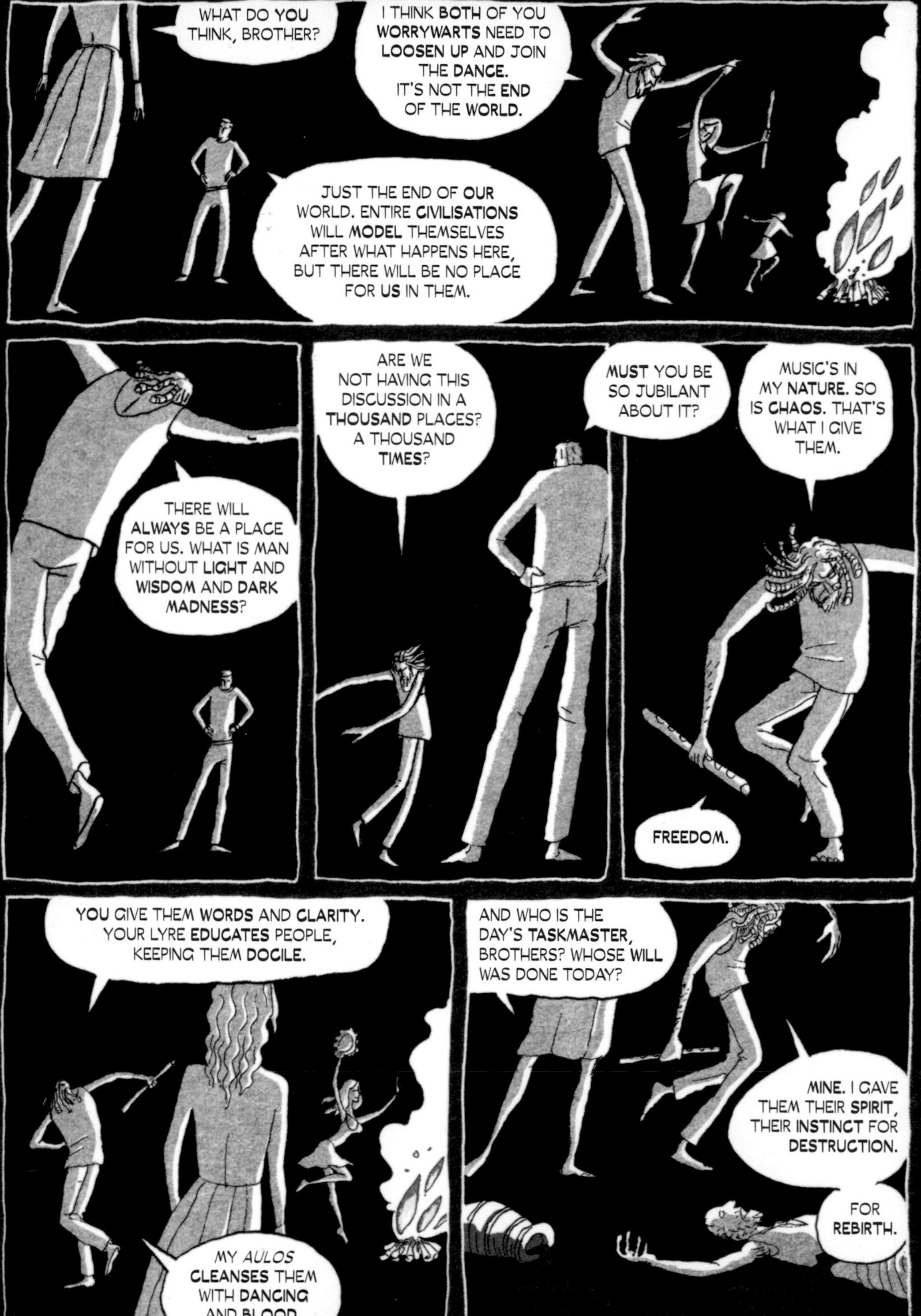
WHAT DO YOU THINK, BROTHER?
I THINK BOTH OF YOU WORRYWARTS NEED TO LOOSEN UP AND JOIN THE DANCE. IT'S NOT THE END OF THE WORLD.
JUST THE END OF OUR WORLD. ENTIRE CIVILISATIONS WILL MODEL THEMSELVES AFTER WHAT HAPPENS HERE, BUT THERE WILL BE NO PLACE FOR US IN THEM.
THERE WILL ALWAYS BE A PLACE FOR US. WHAT IS MAN WITHOUT LIGHT AND WISDOM AND DARK MADNESS?
ARE WE NOT HAVING THIS DISCUSSION IN A THOUSAND PLACES? A THOUSAND TIMES?
MUST YOU BE SO JUBILANT ABOUT IT?
MUSIC'S IN MY NATURE. SO IS CHAOS. THAT'S WHAT I GIVE THEM.
FREEDOM.
YOU GIVE THEM WORDS AND CLARITY. YOUR LYRE EDUCATES PEOPLE, KEEPING THEM DOCILE.
MY AULOS CLEANSES THEM WITH DANCING AND BLOOD.
AND WHO IS THE DAY'S TASKMASTER, BROTHERS? WHOSE WILL WAS DONE TODAY?
MINE. I GAVE THEM THEIR SPIRIT, THEIR INSTINCT FOR DESTRUCTION.
FOR REBIRTH.

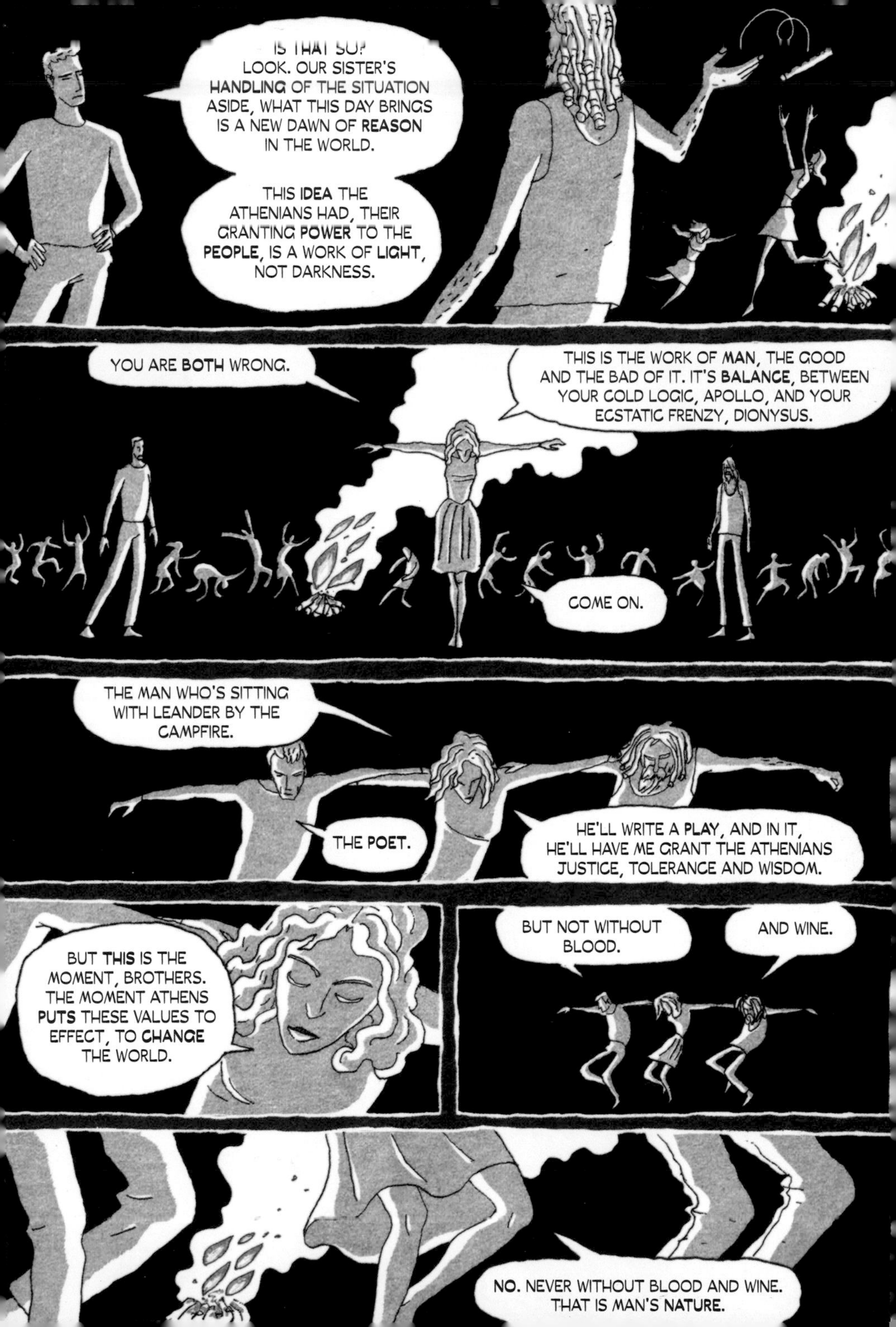

IS THAT SO? LOOK. OUR SISTER'S HANDLING OF THE SITUATION ASIDE, WHAT THIS DAY BRINGS IS A NEW DAWN OF REASON IN THE WORLD.
THIS IDEA THE ATHENIANS HAD, THEIR GRANTING POWER TO THE PEOPLE, IS A WORK OF LIGHT, NOT DARKNESS.
YOU ARE BOTH WRONG.
THIS IS THE WORK OF MAN, THE GOOD AND THE BAD OF IT. IT'S BALANCE, BETWEEN YOUR COLD LOGIC, APOLLO, AND YOUR ECSTATIC FRENZY, DIONYSUS.
COME ON.
THE MAN WHO'S SITTING WITH LEANDER BY THE CAMPFIRE.
THE POET.
HE'LL WRITE A PLAY, AND IN IT, HE'LL HAVE ME GRANT THE ATHENIANS JUSTICE, TOLERANCE AND WISDOM.
BUT THIS IS THE MOMENT, BROTHERS. THE MOMENT ATHENS PUTS THESE VALUES TO EFFECT, TO CHANGE THE WORLD.
BUT NOT WITHOUT BLOOD.
AND WINE.
NO. NEVER WITHOUT BLOOD AND WINE. THAT IS MAN'S NATURE.

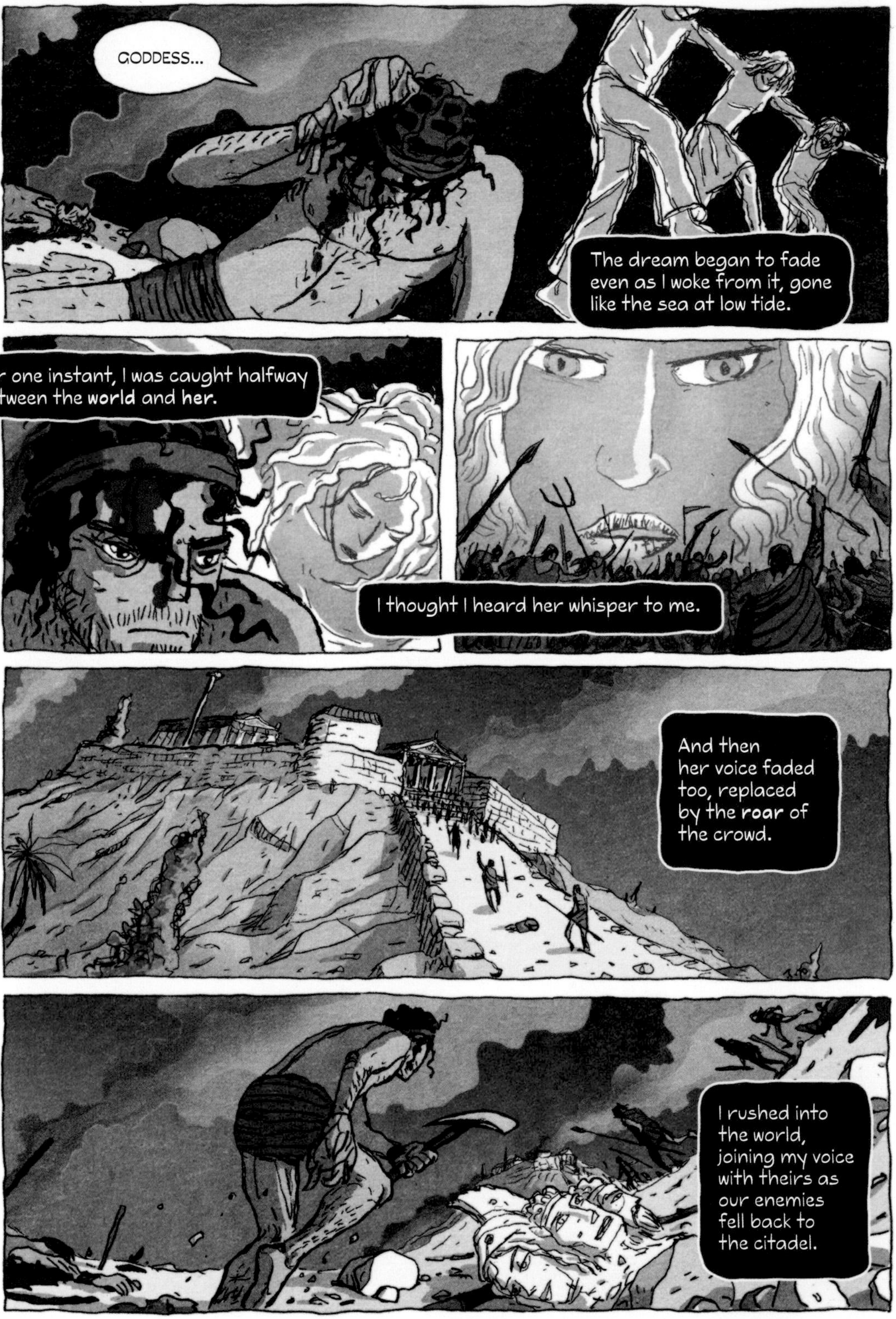
GODDESS...
The dream began to fade even as I woke from it, gone like the sea at low tide.
For one instant, I was caught halfway between the **world** and **her**.
I thought I heard her whisper to me.
And then her voice faded too, replaced by the **roar** of the crowd.
I rushed into the world, joining my voice with theirs as our enemies fell back to the citadel.

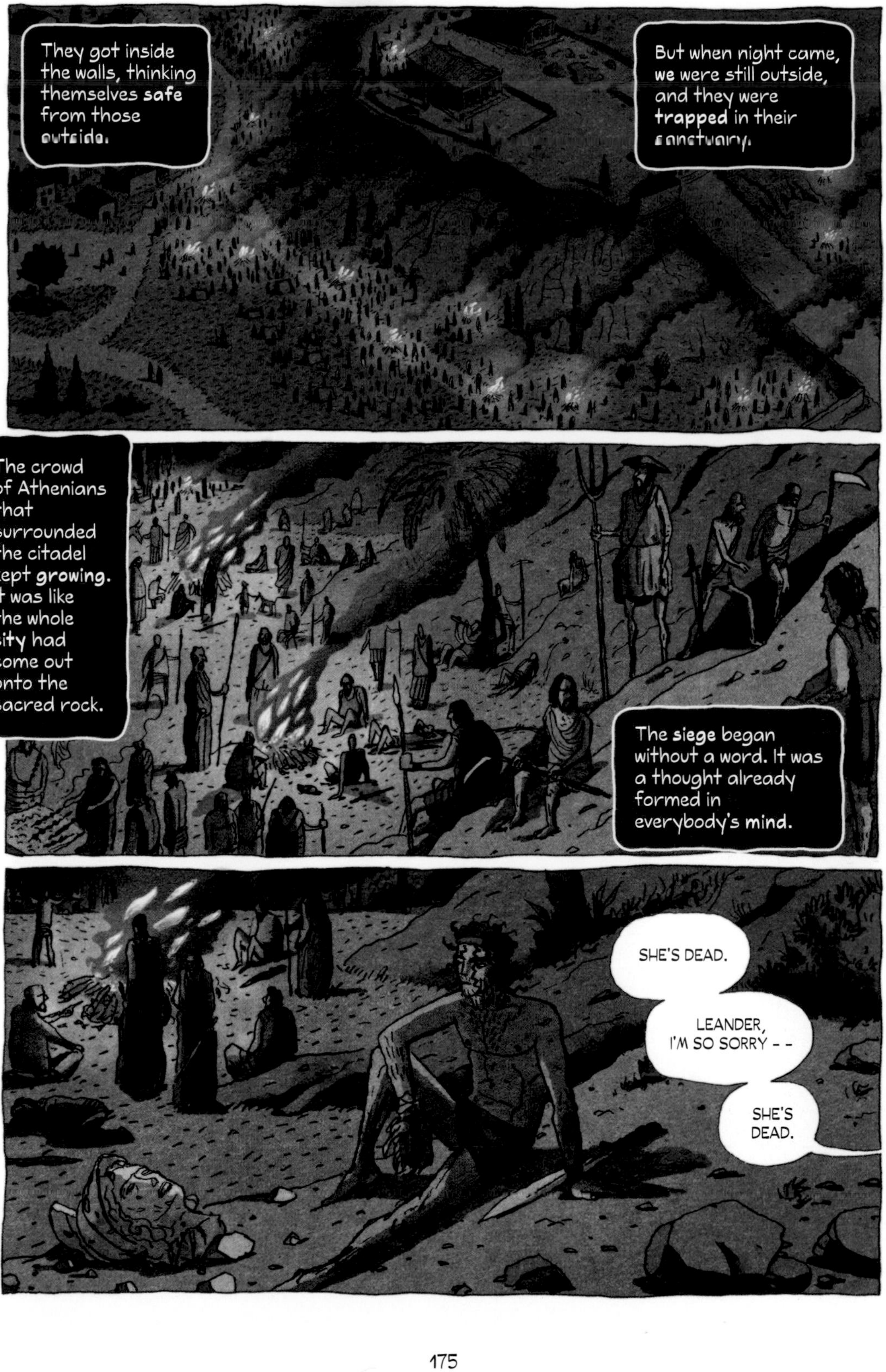

They got inside the walls, thinking themselves **safe** from those **outside.**
But when night came, **we** were still outside, and they were **trapped** in their **sanctuary.**
The crowd of Athenians that surrounded the citadel kept **growing.** It was like the whole **city** had come out onto the sacred rock.
The **siege** began without a word. It was a thought already formed in everybody's **mind.**
SHE'S DEAD.
LEANDER, I'M SO SORRY - -
SHE'S DEAD.

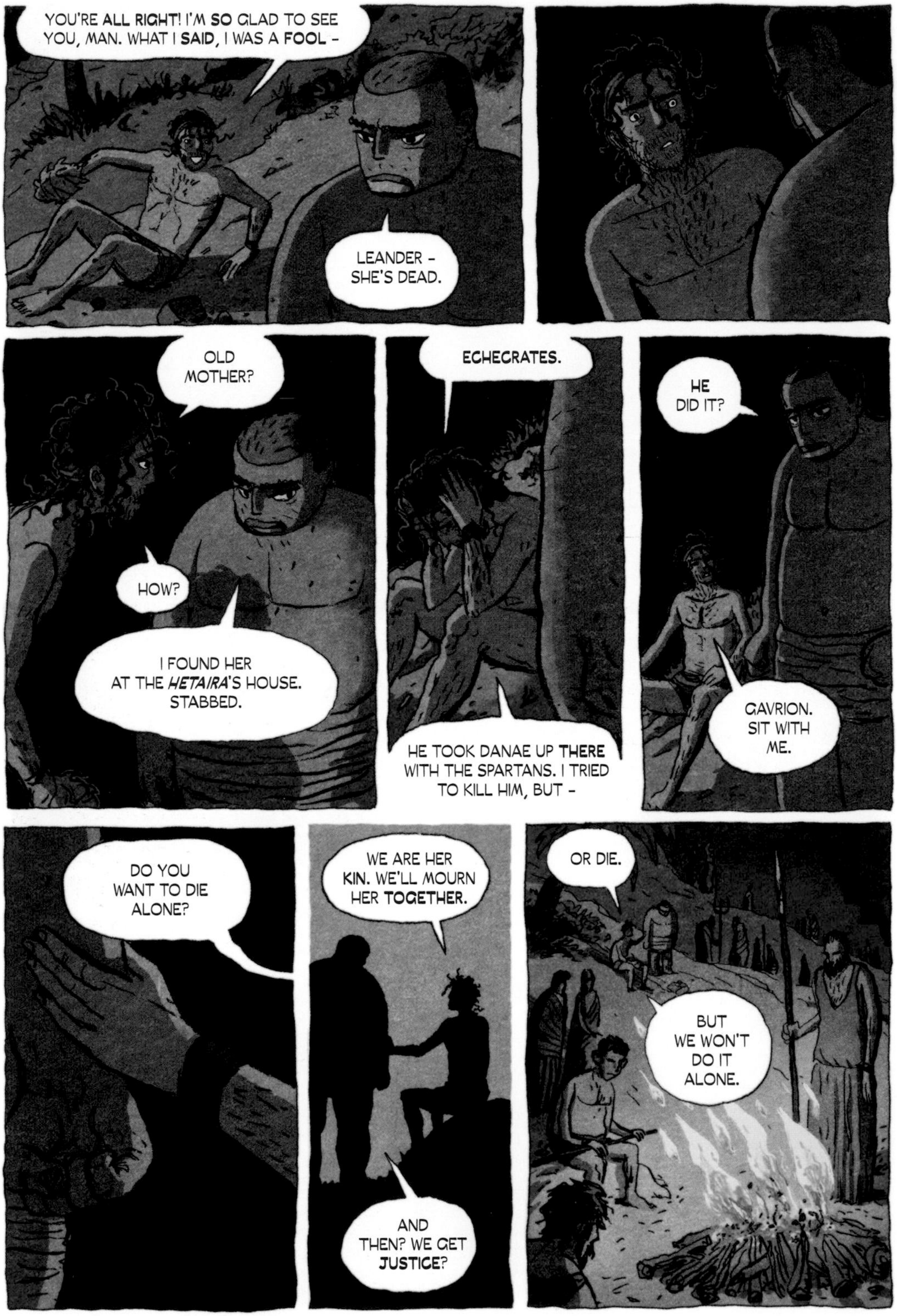
YOU'RE **ALL RIGHT**! I'M **SO** GLAD TO SEE YOU, MAN. WHAT I **SAID**, I WAS A **FOOL** –
LEANDER – SHE'S DEAD.
OLD MOTHER?
HOW?
I FOUND HER AT THE ***HETAIRA***'S HOUSE. STABBED.
ECHECRATES.
HE TOOK DANAE UP **THERE** WITH THE SPARTANS. I TRIED TO KILL HIM, BUT –
HE DID IT?
GAVRION. SIT WITH ME.
DO YOU WANT TO DIE ALONE?
WE ARE HER **KIN**. WE'LL MOURN HER **TOGETHER**.
AND THEN? WE GET **JUSTICE**?
OR DIE.
BUT WE WON'T DO IT ALONE.

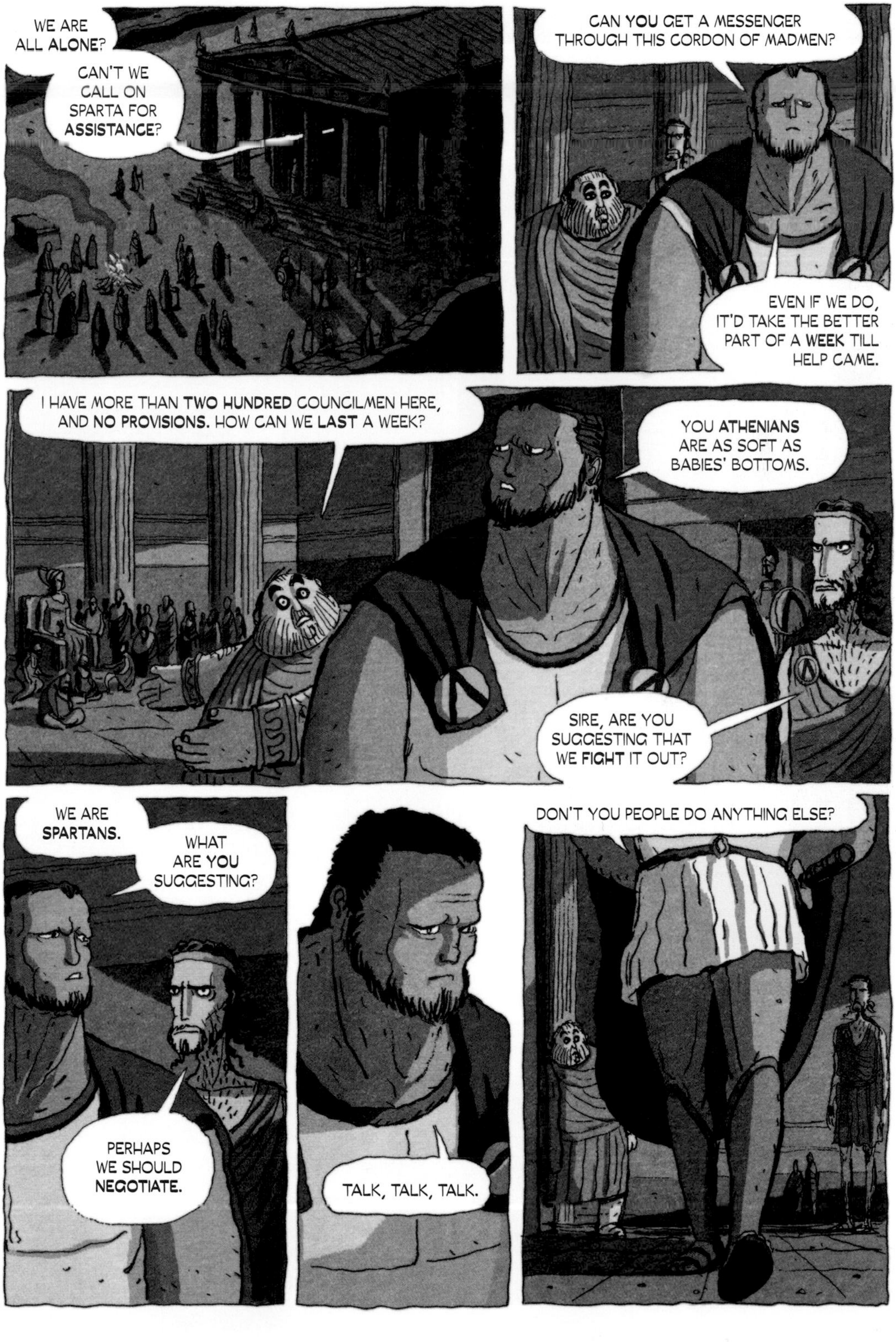
WE ARE ALL ALONE?
CAN'T WE CALL ON SPARTA FOR ASSISTANCE?
CAN YOU GET A MESSENGER THROUGH THIS CORDON OF MADMEN?
EVEN IF WE DO, IT'D TAKE THE BETTER PART OF A WEEK TILL HELP CAME.
I HAVE MORE THAN TWO HUNDRED COUNCILMEN HERE, AND NO PROVISIONS. HOW CAN WE LAST A WEEK?
YOU ATHENIANS ARE AS SOFT AS BABIES' BOTTOMS.
SIRE, ARE YOU SUGGESTING THAT WE FIGHT IT OUT?
WE ARE SPARTANS.
WHAT ARE YOU SUGGESTING?
PERHAPS WE SHOULD NEGOTIATE.
TALK, TALK, TALK.
DON'T YOU PEOPLE DO ANYTHING ELSE?

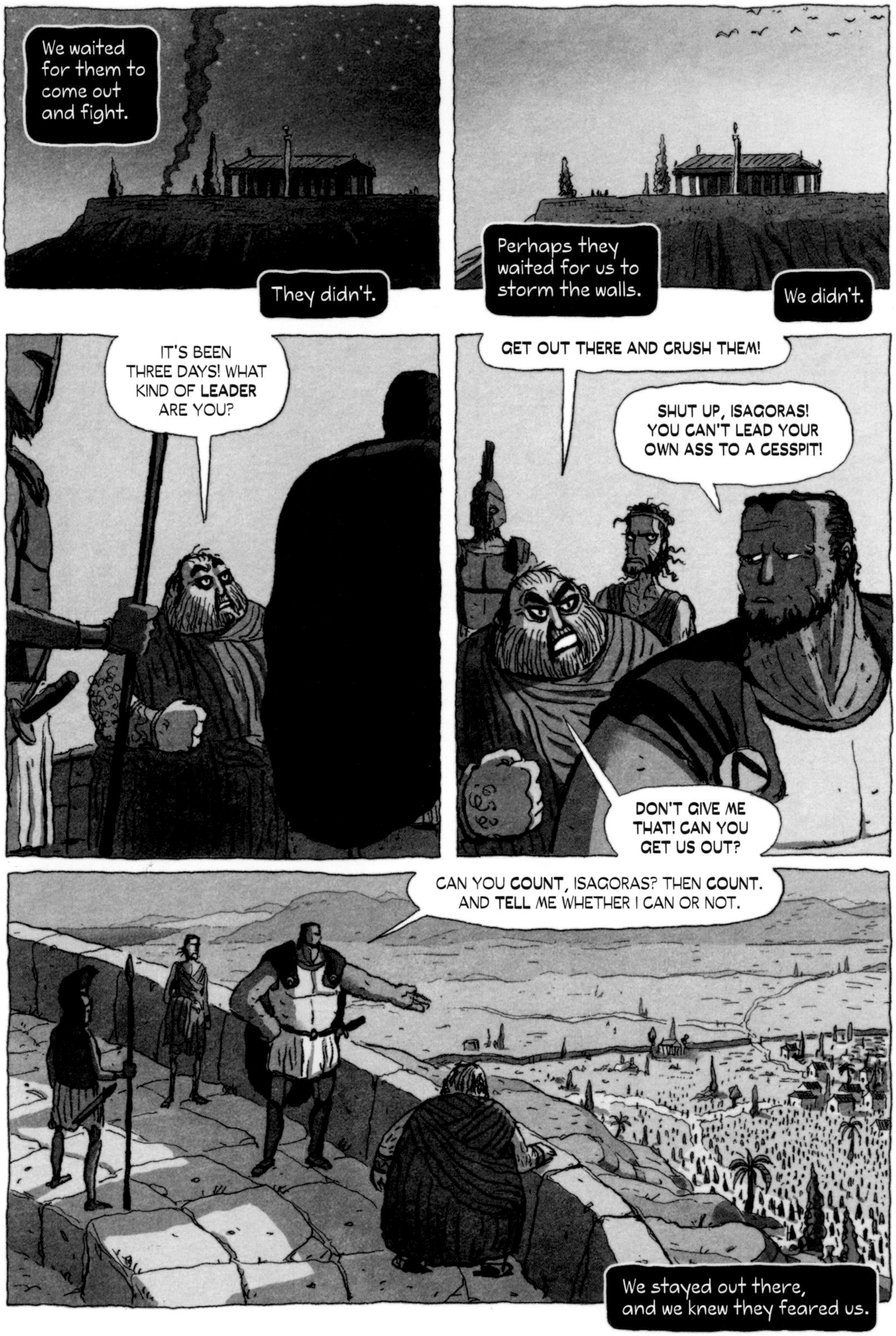
We waited for them to come out and fight.
They didn't.
Perhaps they waited for us to storm the walls.
We didn't.
IT'S BEEN THREE DAYS! WHAT KIND OF LEADER ARE YOU?
GET OUT THERE AND CRUSH THEM!
SHUT UP, ISAGORAS! YOU CAN'T LEAD YOUR OWN ASS TO A CESSPIT!
DON'T GIVE ME THAT! CAN YOU GET US OUT?
CAN YOU COUNT, ISAGORAS? THEN COUNT. AND TELL ME WHETHER I CAN OR NOT.
We stayed out there, and we knew they feared us.

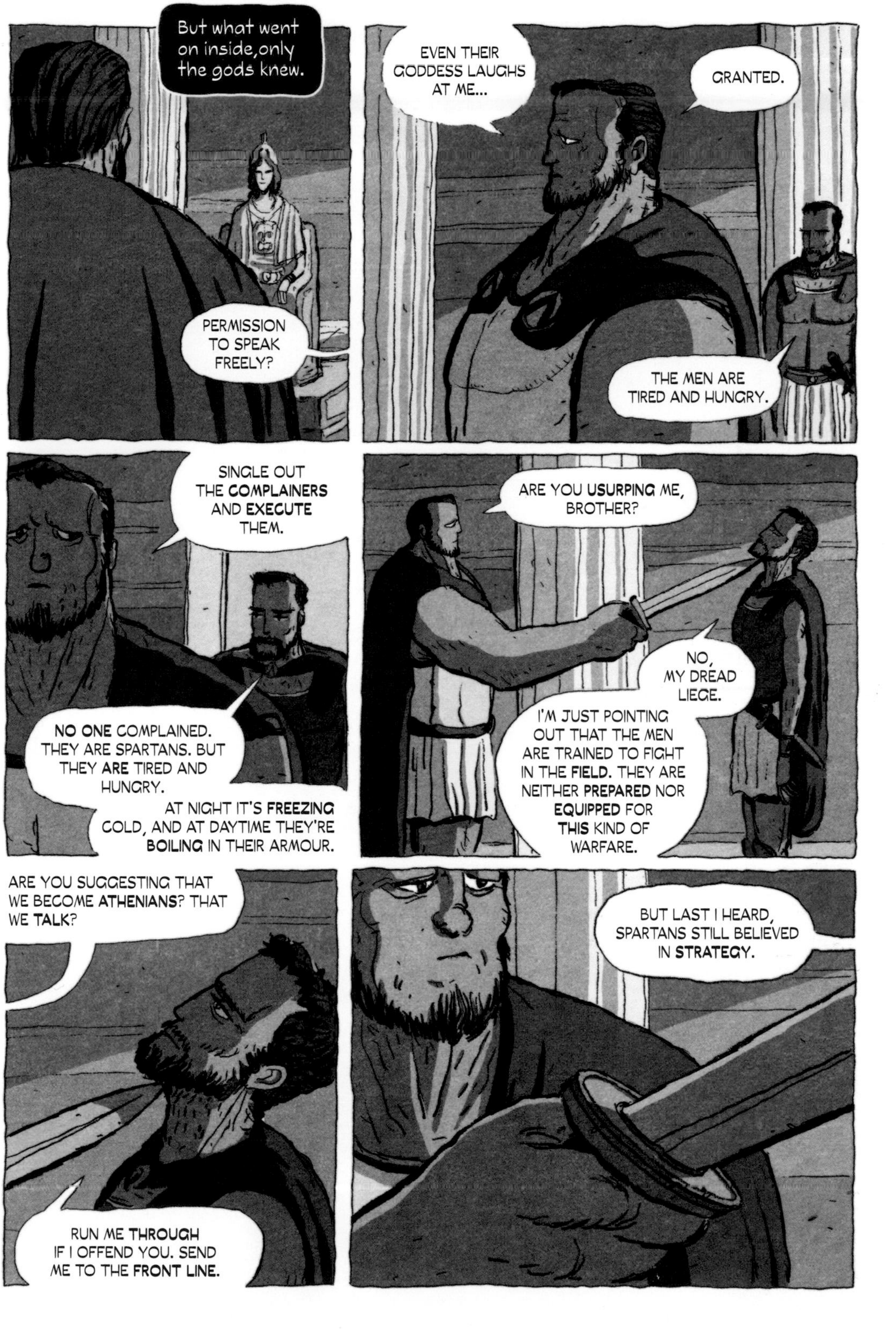
But what went on inside, only the gods knew.
PERMISSION TO SPEAK FREELY?
EVEN THEIR GODDESS LAUGHS AT ME...
GRANTED.
THE MEN ARE TIRED AND HUNGRY.
SINGLE OUT THE COMPLAINERS AND EXECUTE THEM.
NO ONE COMPLAINED. THEY ARE SPARTANS. BUT THEY ARE TIRED AND HUNGRY.
AT NIGHT IT'S FREEZING COLD, AND AT DAYTIME THEY'RE BOILING IN THEIR ARMOUR.
ARE YOU USURPING ME, BROTHER?
NO, MY DREAD LIEGE.
I'M JUST POINTING OUT THAT THE MEN ARE TRAINED TO FIGHT IN THE FIELD. THEY ARE NEITHER PREPARED NOR EQUIPPED FOR THIS KIND OF WARFARE.
ARE YOU SUGGESTING THAT WE BECOME ATHENIANS? THAT WE TALK?
RUN ME THROUGH IF I OFFEND YOU. SEND ME TO THE FRONT LINE.
BUT LAST I HEARD, SPARTANS STILL BELIEVED IN STRATEGY.

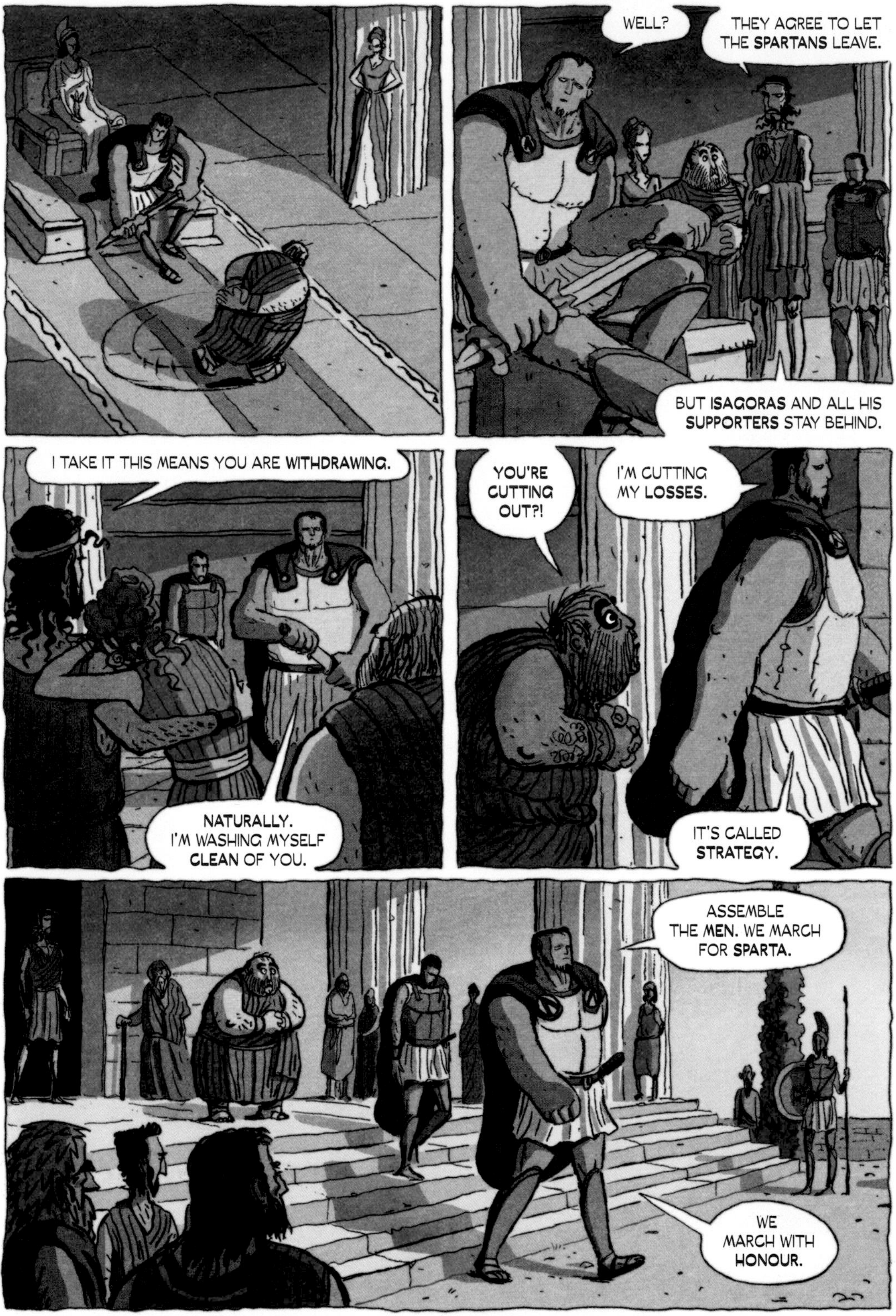
WELL?
THEY AGREE TO LET THE SPARTANS LEAVE.
BUT ISAGORAS AND ALL HIS SUPPORTERS STAY BEHIND.
I TAKE IT THIS MEANS YOU ARE WITHDRAWING.
NATURALLY. I'M WASHING MYSELF CLEAN OF YOU.
YOU'RE CUTTING OUT?!
I'M CUTTING MY LOSSES.
IT'S CALLED STRATEGY.
ASSEMBLE THE MEN. WE MARCH FOR SPARTA.
WE MARCH WITH HONOUR.

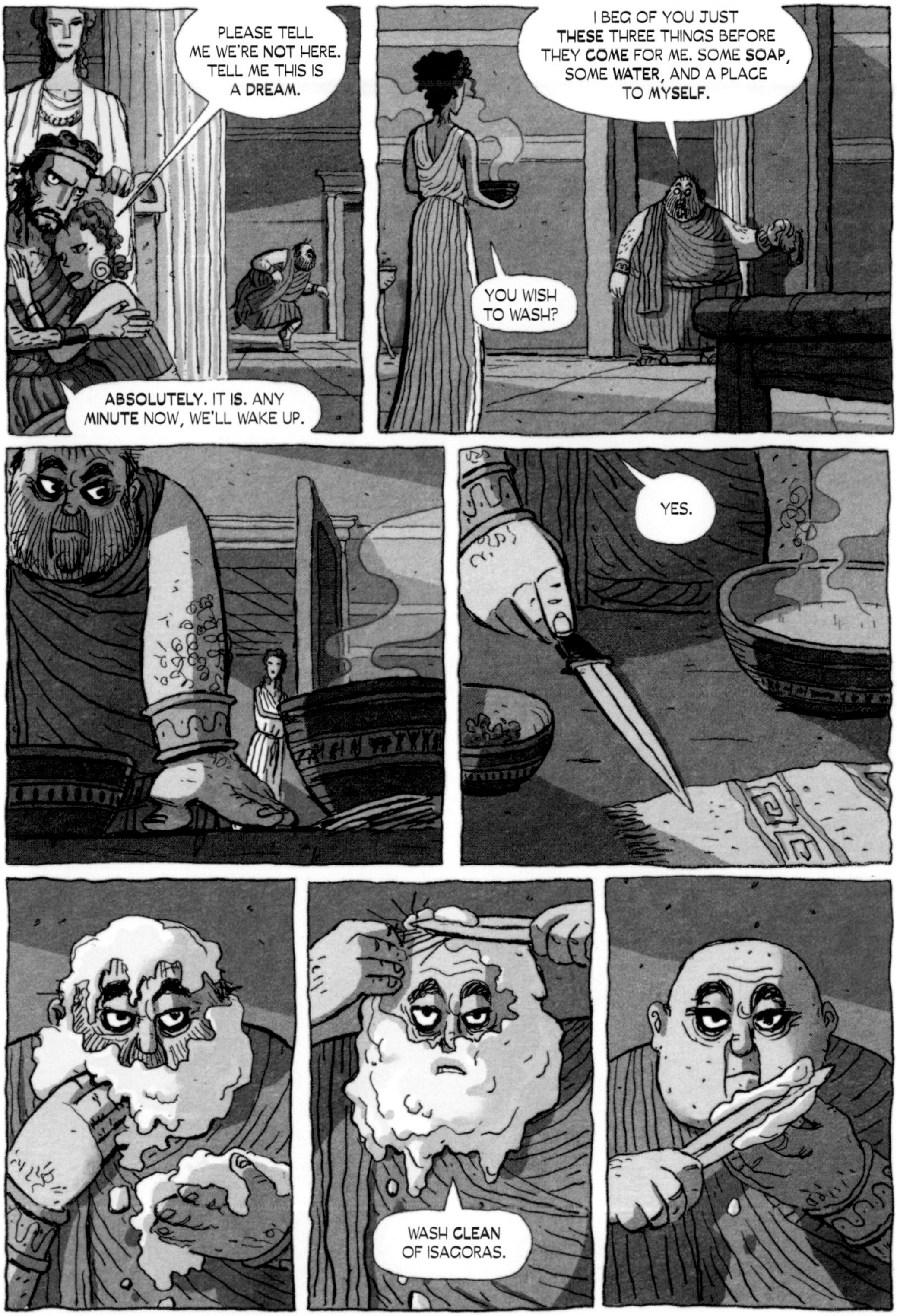
PLEASE TELL ME WE'RE NOT HERE. TELL ME THIS IS A DREAM.
ABSOLUTELY. IT IS. ANY MINUTE NOW, WE'LL WAKE UP.
I BEG OF YOU JUST THESE THREE THINGS BEFORE THEY COME FOR ME. SOME SOAP, SOME WATER, AND A PLACE TO MYSELF.
YOU WISH TO WASH?
YES.
WASH CLEAN OF ISAGORAS.

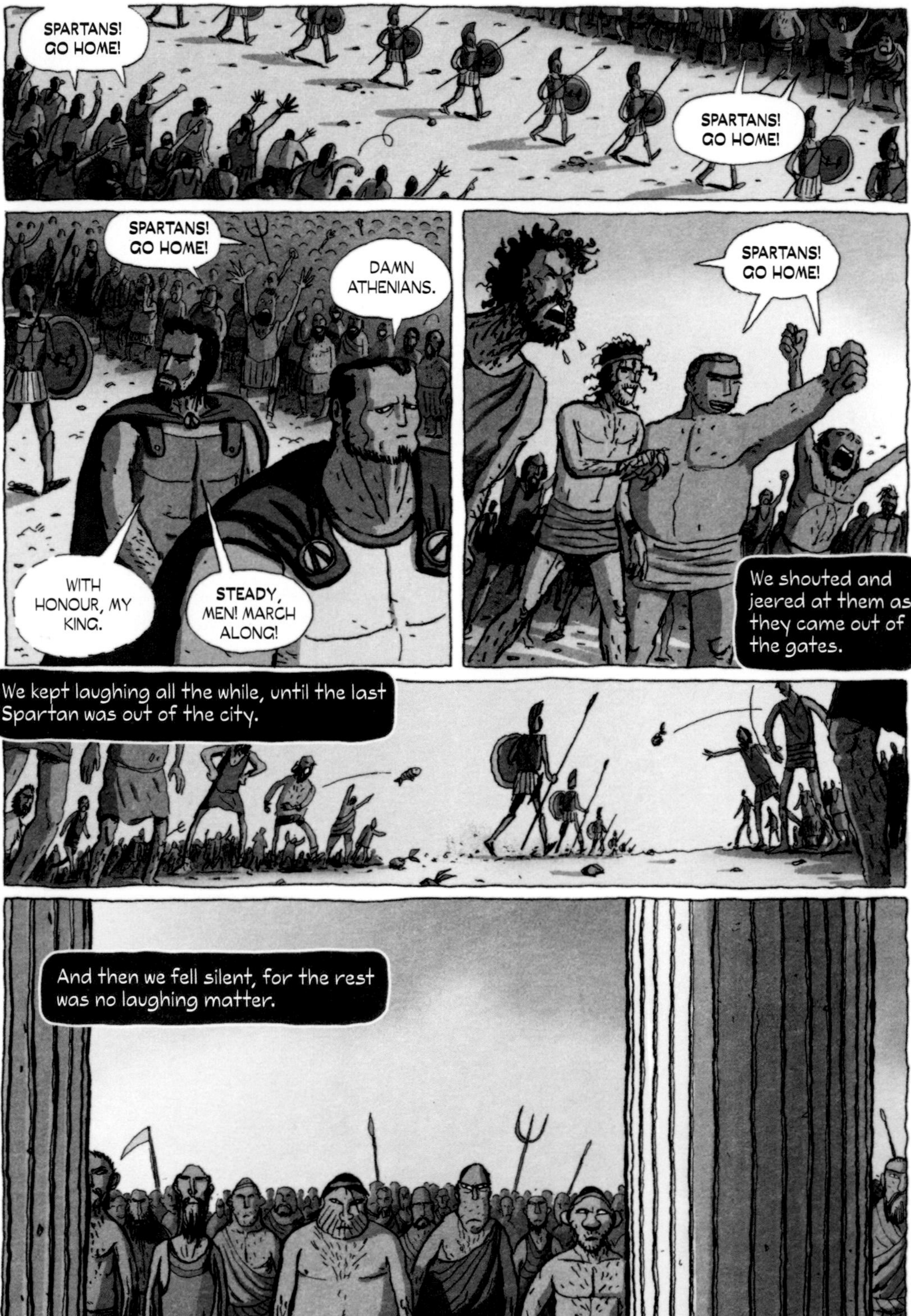
SPARTANS! GO HOME!
SPARTANS! GO HOME!
SPARTANS! GO HOME!
DAMN ATHENIANS.
WITH HONOUR, MY KING.
STEADY, MEN! MARCH ALONG!
SPARTANS! GO HOME!
We shouted and jeered at them as they came out of the gates.
We kept laughing all the while, until the last Spartan was out of the city.
And then we fell silent, for the rest was no laughing matter.

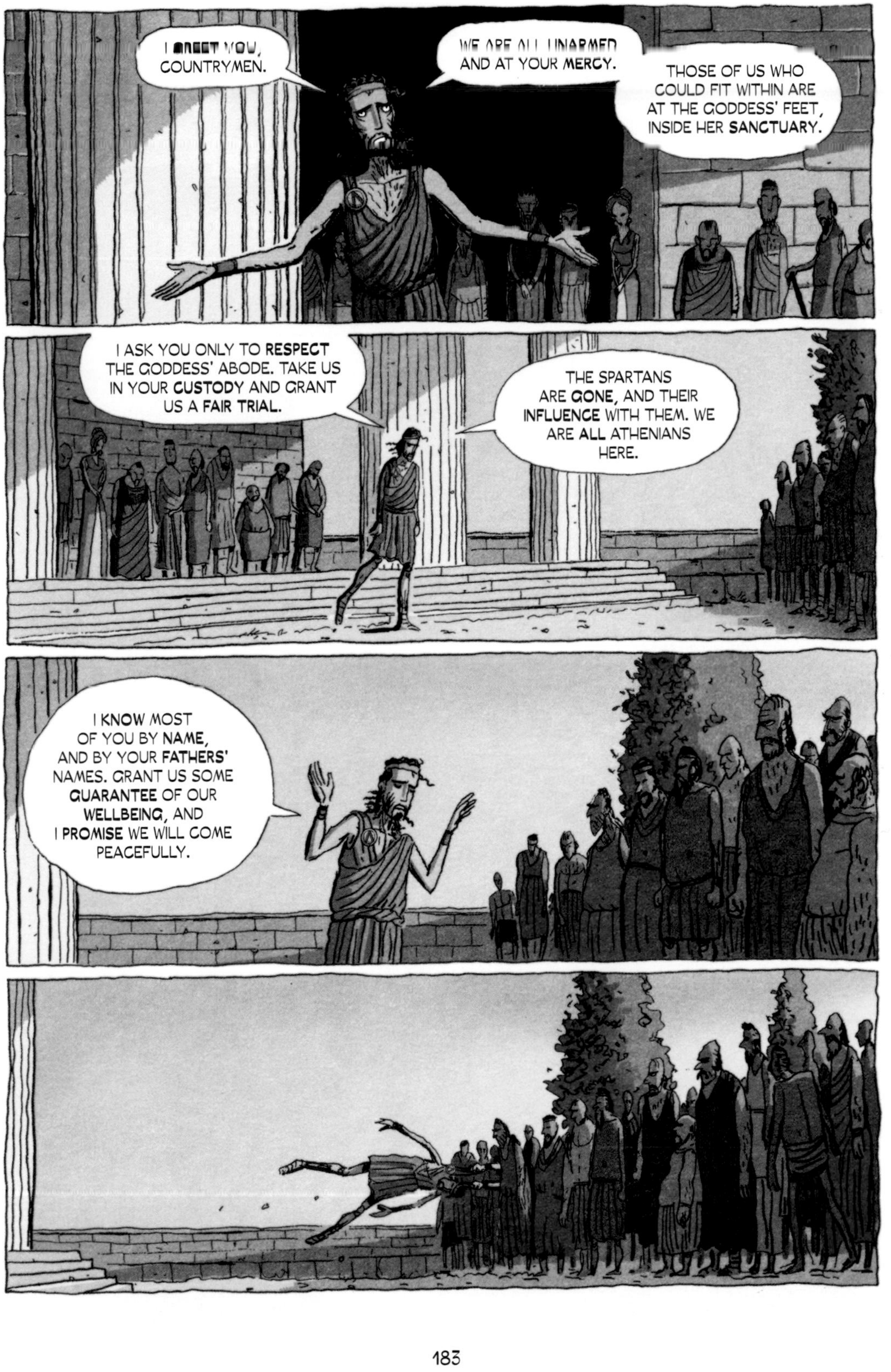
I GREET YOU, COUNTRYMEN.
WE ARE ALL UNARMED AND AT YOUR MERCY.
THOSE OF US WHO COULD FIT WITHIN ARE AT THE GODDESS' FEET, INSIDE HER SANCTUARY.
I ASK YOU ONLY TO RESPECT THE GODDESS' ABODE. TAKE US IN YOUR CUSTODY AND GRANT US A FAIR TRIAL.
THE SPARTANS ARE GONE, AND THEIR INFLUENCE WITH THEM. WE ARE ALL ATHENIANS HERE.
I KNOW MOST OF YOU BY NAME, AND BY YOUR FATHERS' NAMES. GRANT US SOME GUARANTEE OF OUR WELLBEING, AND I PROMISE WE WILL COME PEACEFULLY.

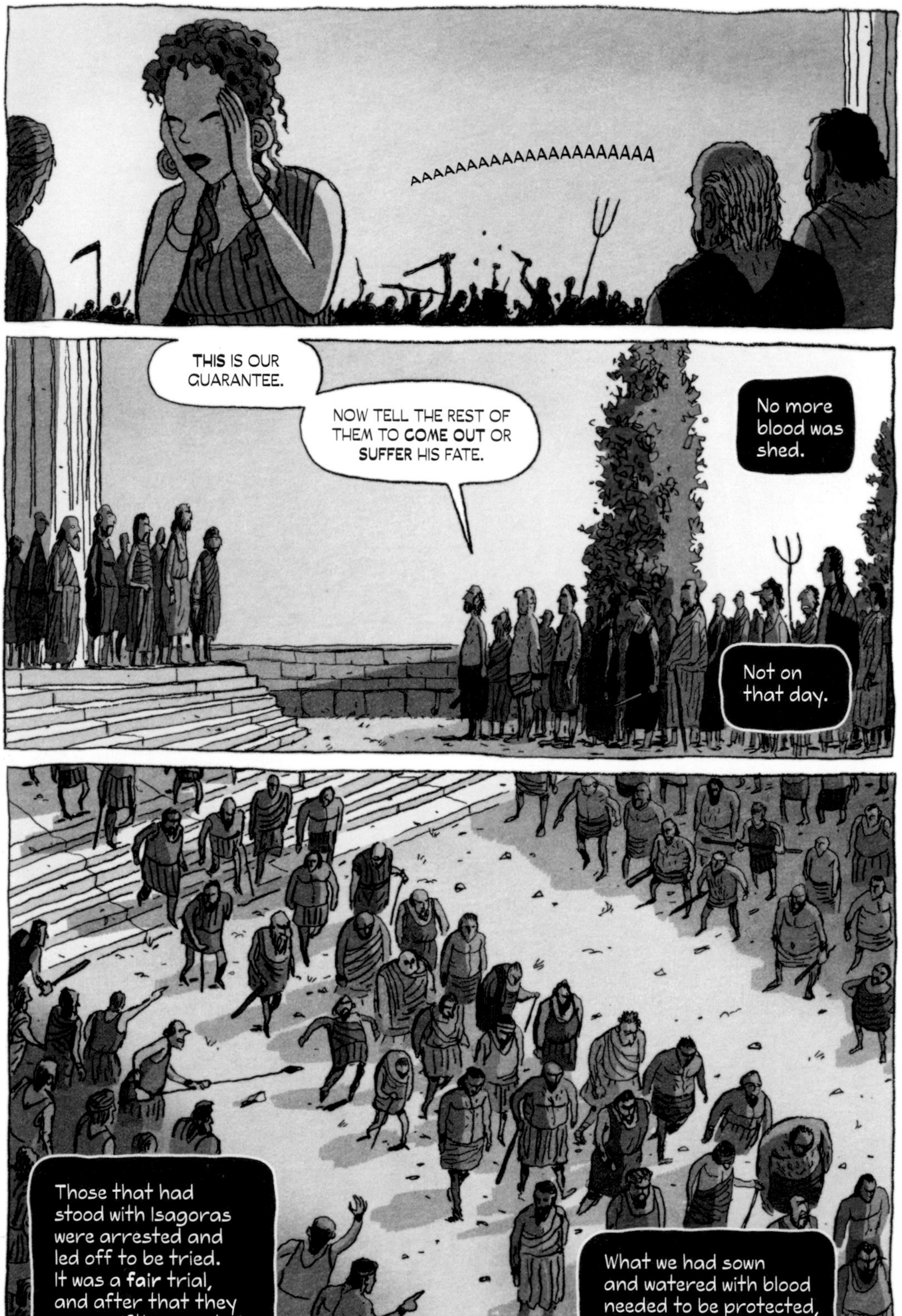
AAAAAAAAAAAAAAAAAAAAAA
THIS IS OUR GUARANTEE.
NOW TELL THE REST OF THEM TO **COME OUT** OR **SUFFER** HIS FATE.
No more blood was shed.
Not on that day.
Those that had stood with Isagoras were arrested and led off to be tried. It was a **fair** trial, and after that they were swiftly **executed**.
What we had sown and watered with blood needed to be protected, after all.

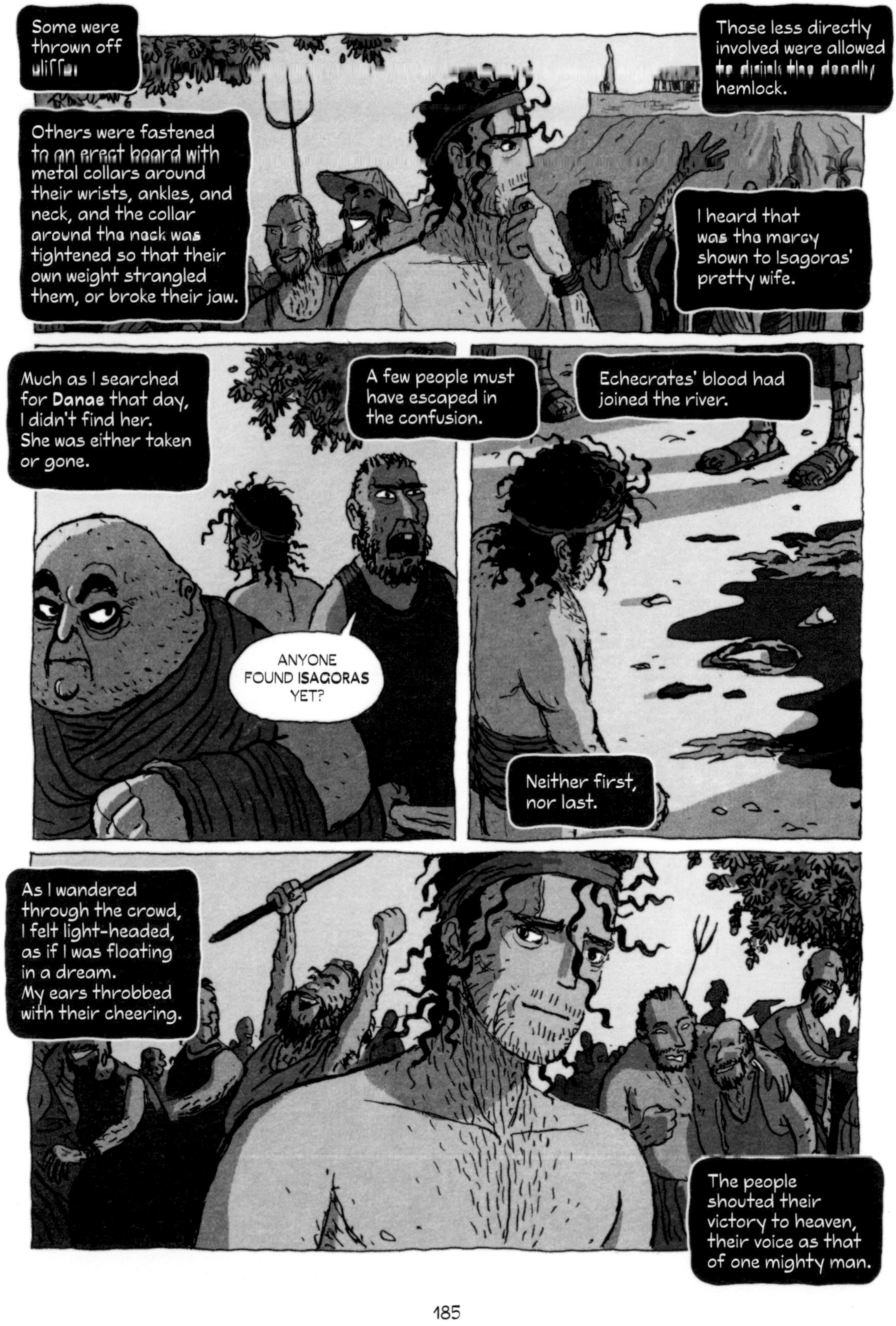
Some were thrown off cliffs.
Others were fastened to an erect board with metal collars around their wrists, ankles, and neck, and the collar around the neck was tightened so that their own weight strangled them, or broke their jaw.
Those less directly involved were allowed to drink the deadly hemlock.
I heard that was the mercy shown to Isagoras' pretty wife.
Much as I searched for Danae that day, I didn't find her. She was either taken or gone.
A few people must have escaped in the confusion.
ANYONE FOUND ISAGORAS YET?
Echecrates' blood had joined the river.
Neither first, nor last.
As I wandered through the crowd, I felt light-headed, as if I was floating in a dream. My ears throbbed with their cheering.
The people shouted their victory to heaven, their voice as that of one mighty man.

GODDESS, I STAND BEFORE YOU NOW, AND I CAN LOOK YOU IN THE EYE.

I KNOW THE TRUTH.

YOU AND THE CITY ARE **ONE**. YOU TURN INTO **US**, AND **WE** TURN INTO YOU.

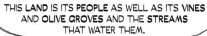

THIS **LAND** IS ITS PEOPLE AS WELL AS ITS VINES AND **OLIVE GROVES** AND THE **STREAMS** THAT WATER THEM.

THE WILD **MARJORAM** AND THE SCENTED **THYME**, THE **DAFFODIL** FIELDS, THE **MARBLE** GLEAMING ON HILLS AND PLAINS AND VALLEYS...

...THEY ARE AS MUCH A PART OF US AS **FLESH** AND **BONE** AND **SINEW**. WE ARE THE **TREES** OF YOUR WOODS, MY GODDESS. THE **CLAY** FROM YOUR SOIL.

WHETHER WE GROW OR WE WITHER IS UP TO OURSELVES. FOR THE **LIGHT** THAT NURTURES OUR ROOTS, THE **FIRE** THAT HARDENS THE CLAY, THEY COME FROM **WITHIN US**, NOT FROM THE GODS OR OUR RULERS.

AND **BLOOD** WATERS THE **GROUND** WHERE WE GROW. **BLOOD** IS THE WATER MIXED WITH OUR **CLAY**.

IT'S PART OF OUR **NATURE**.

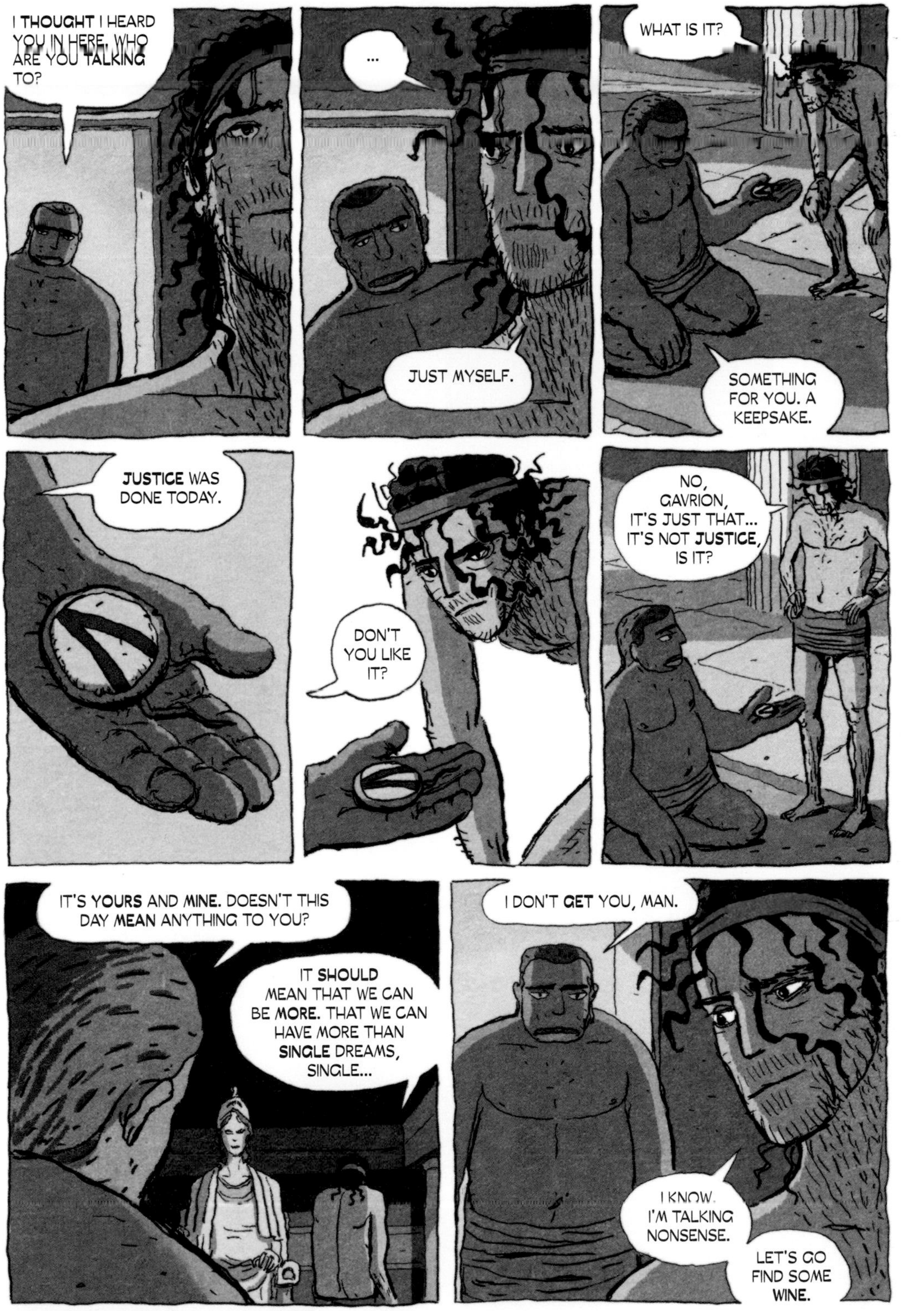
I THOUGHT I HEARD YOU IN HERE. WHO ARE YOU TALKING TO?
...
JUST MYSELF.
WHAT IS IT?
SOMETHING FOR YOU. A KEEPSAKE.
JUSTICE WAS DONE TODAY.
DON'T YOU LIKE IT?
NO, GAVRION, IT'S JUST THAT... IT'S NOT JUSTICE, IS IT?
IT'S YOURS AND MINE. DOESN'T THIS DAY MEAN ANYTHING TO YOU?
IT SHOULD MEAN THAT WE CAN BE MORE. THAT WE CAN HAVE MORE THAN SINGLE DREAMS, SINGLE...
I DON'T GET YOU, MAN.
I KNOW. I'M TALKING NONSENSE.
LET'S GO FIND SOME WINE.

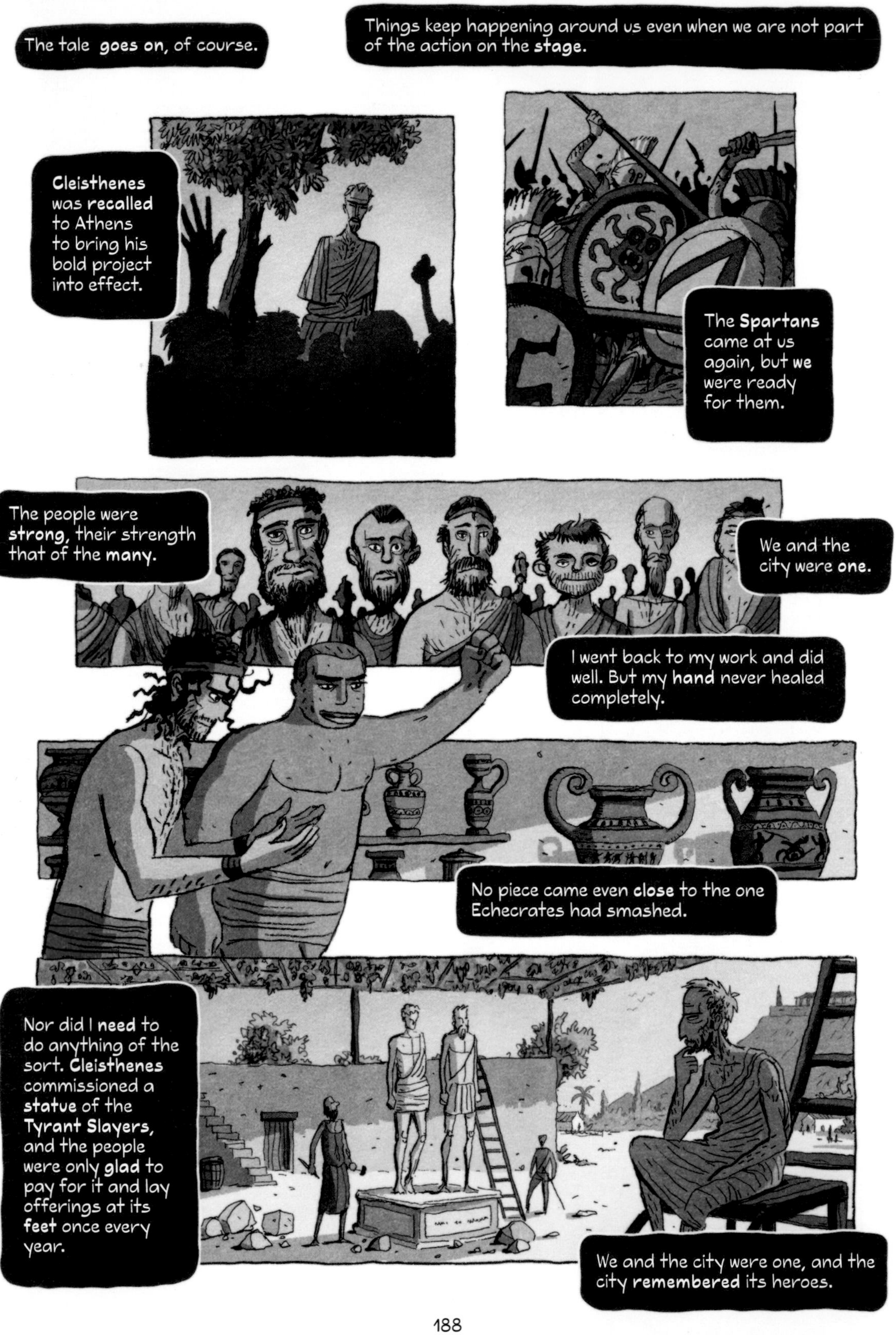
The tale goes on, of course.
Things keep happening around us even when we are not part of the action on the stage.
Cleisthenes was recalled to Athens to bring his bold project into effect.
The Spartans came at us again, but we were ready for them.
The people were strong, their strength that of the many.
We and the city were one.
I went back to my work and did well. But my hand never healed completely.
No piece came even close to the one Echecrates had smashed.
Nor did I need to do anything of the sort. Cleisthenes commissioned a statue of the Tyrant Slayers, and the people were only glad to pay for it and lay offerings at its feet once every year.
We and the city were one, and the city remembered its heroes.

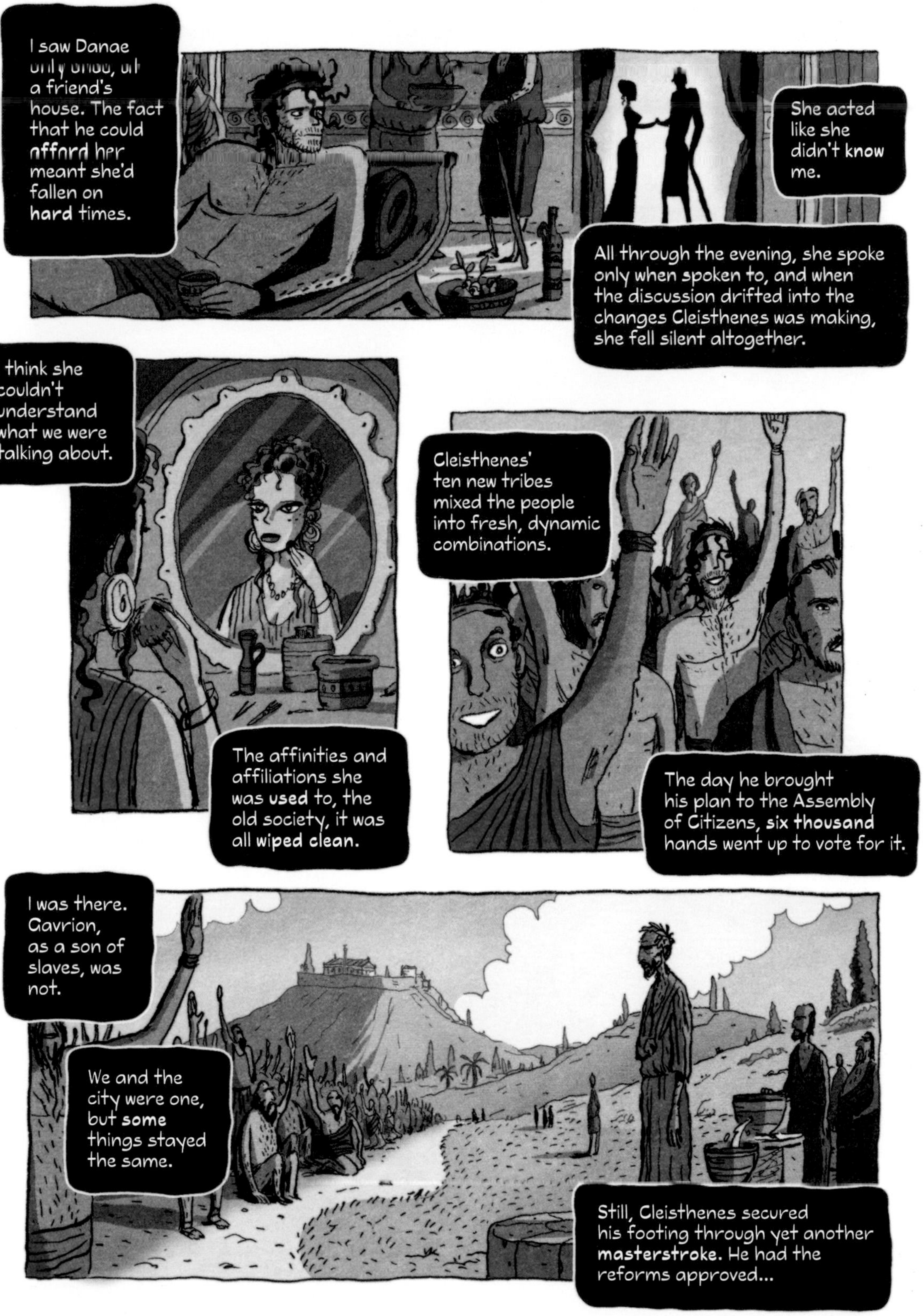
I saw Danae only once, at a friend's house. The fact that he could **afford** her meant she'd fallen on **hard** times.
She acted like she didn't **know** me.
All through the evening, she spoke only when spoken to, and when the discussion drifted into the changes Cleisthenes was making, she fell silent altogether.
I think she couldn't understand what we were talking about.
The affinities and affiliations she was **used** to, the old society, it was all **wiped clean.**
Cleisthenes' ten new tribes mixed the people into fresh, dynamic combinations.
The day he brought his plan to the Assembly of Citizens, **six thousand** hands went up to vote for it.
I was there. Gavrion, as a son of slaves, was not.
We and the city were one, but **some** things stayed the same.
Still, Cleisthenes secured his footing through yet another **masterstroke.** He had the reforms approved...

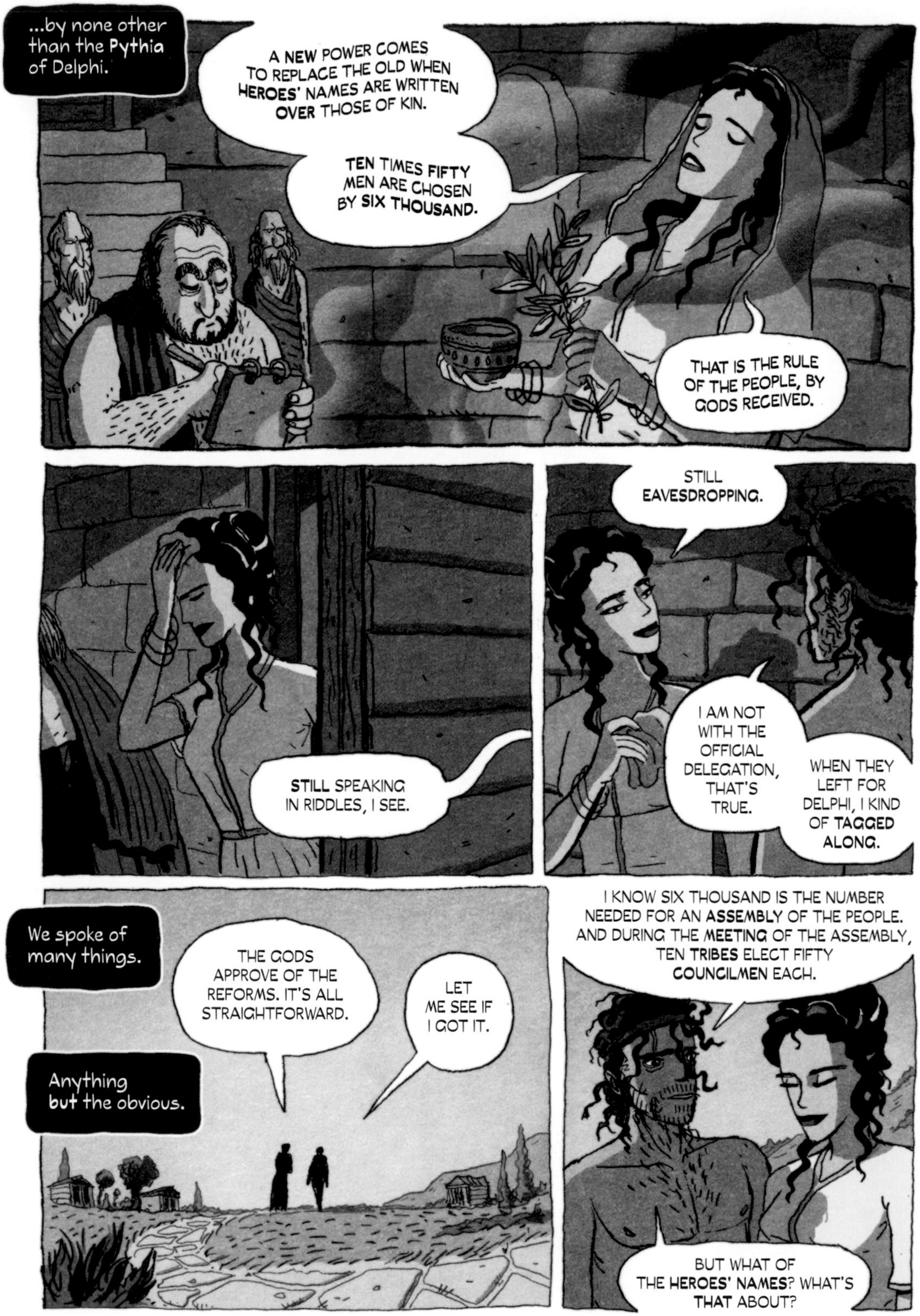

...by none other than the Pythia of Delphi.
A NEW POWER COMES TO REPLACE THE OLD WHEN HEROES' NAMES ARE WRITTEN OVER THOSE OF KIN.
TEN TIMES FIFTY MEN ARE CHOSEN BY SIX THOUSAND.
THAT IS THE RULE OF THE PEOPLE, BY GODS RECEIVED.
STILL SPEAKING IN RIDDLES, I SEE.
STILL EAVESDROPPING.
I AM NOT WITH THE OFFICIAL DELEGATION, THAT'S TRUE.
WHEN THEY LEFT FOR DELPHI, I KIND OF TAGGED ALONG.
We spoke of many things.
THE GODS APPROVE OF THE REFORMS. IT'S ALL STRAIGHTFORWARD.
LET ME SEE IF I GOT IT.
Anything but the obvious.
I KNOW SIX THOUSAND IS THE NUMBER NEEDED FOR AN ASSEMBLY OF THE PEOPLE. AND DURING THE MEETING OF THE ASSEMBLY, TEN TRIBES ELECT FIFTY COUNCILMEN EACH.
BUT WHAT OF THE HEROES' NAMES? WHAT'S THAT ABOUT?

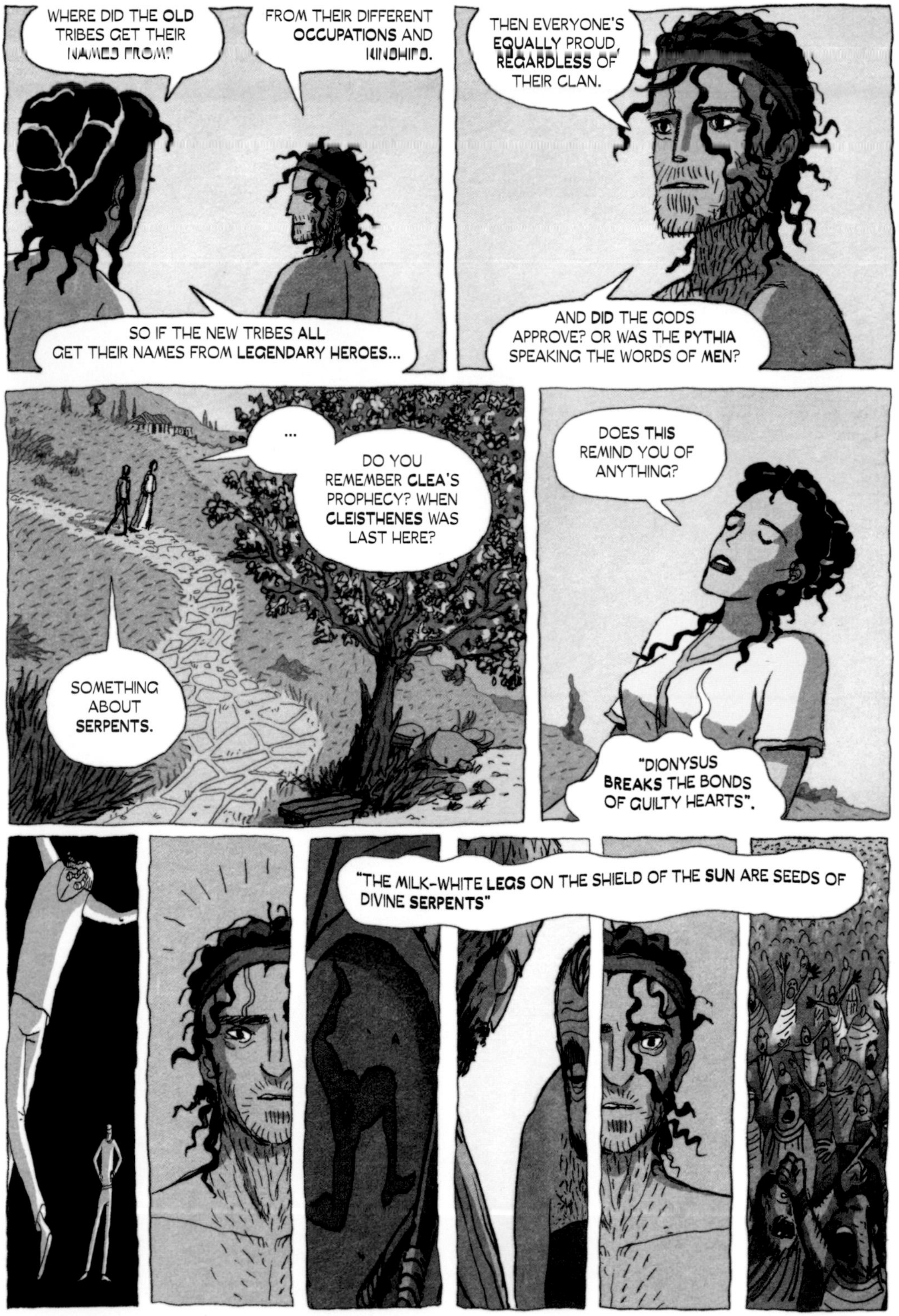

WHERE DID THE OLD TRIBES GET THEIR NAMES FROM?
FROM THEIR DIFFERENT OCCUPATIONS AND KINSHIPS.
SO IF THE NEW TRIBES ALL GET THEIR NAMES FROM LEGENDARY HEROES...
THEN EVERYONE'S EQUALLY PROUD, REGARDLESS OF THEIR CLAN.
AND DID THE GODS APPROVE? OR WAS THE PYTHIA SPEAKING THE WORDS OF MEN?
...
DO YOU REMEMBER CLEA'S PROPHECY? WHEN CLEISTHENES WAS LAST HERE?
SOMETHING ABOUT SERPENTS.
DOES THIS REMIND YOU OF ANYTHING?
"DIONYSUS BREAKS THE BONDS OF GUILTY HEARTS".
"THE MILK-WHITE LEGS ON THE SHIELD OF THE SUN ARE SEEDS OF DIVINE SERPENTS"

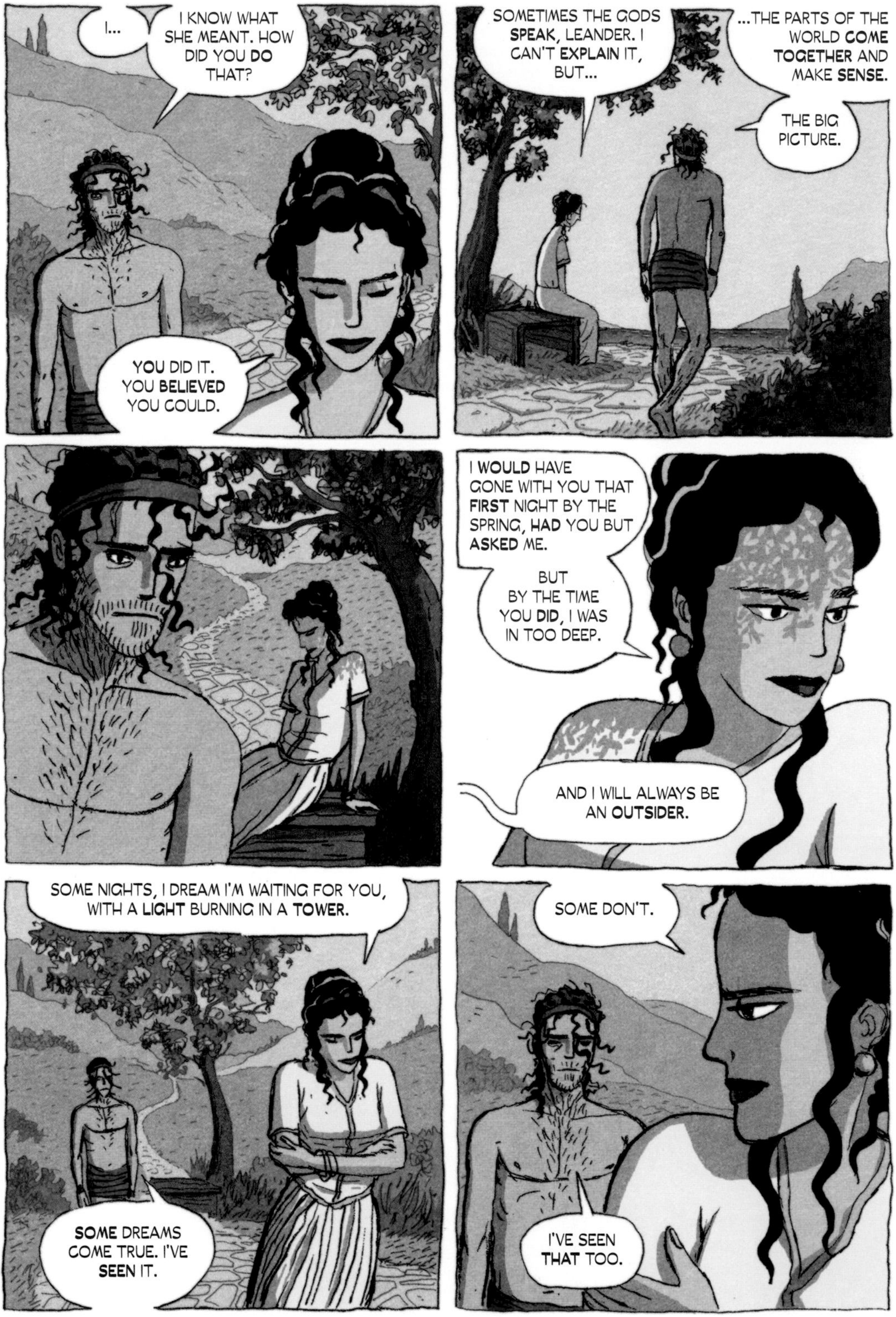
I...
I KNOW WHAT SHE MEANT. HOW DID YOU DO THAT?
YOU DID IT. YOU BELIEVED YOU COULD.
SOMETIMES THE GODS SPEAK, LEANDER. I CAN'T EXPLAIN IT, BUT...
...THE PARTS OF THE WORLD COME TOGETHER AND MAKE SENSE.
THE BIG PICTURE.
I WOULD HAVE GONE WITH YOU THAT FIRST NIGHT BY THE SPRING, HAD YOU BUT ASKED ME.
BUT BY THE TIME YOU DID, I WAS IN TOO DEEP.
AND I WILL ALWAYS BE AN OUTSIDER.
SOME NIGHTS, I DREAM I'M WAITING FOR YOU, WITH A LIGHT BURNING IN A TOWER.
SOME DREAMS COME TRUE. I'VE SEEN IT.
SOME DON'T.
I'VE SEEN THAT TOO.

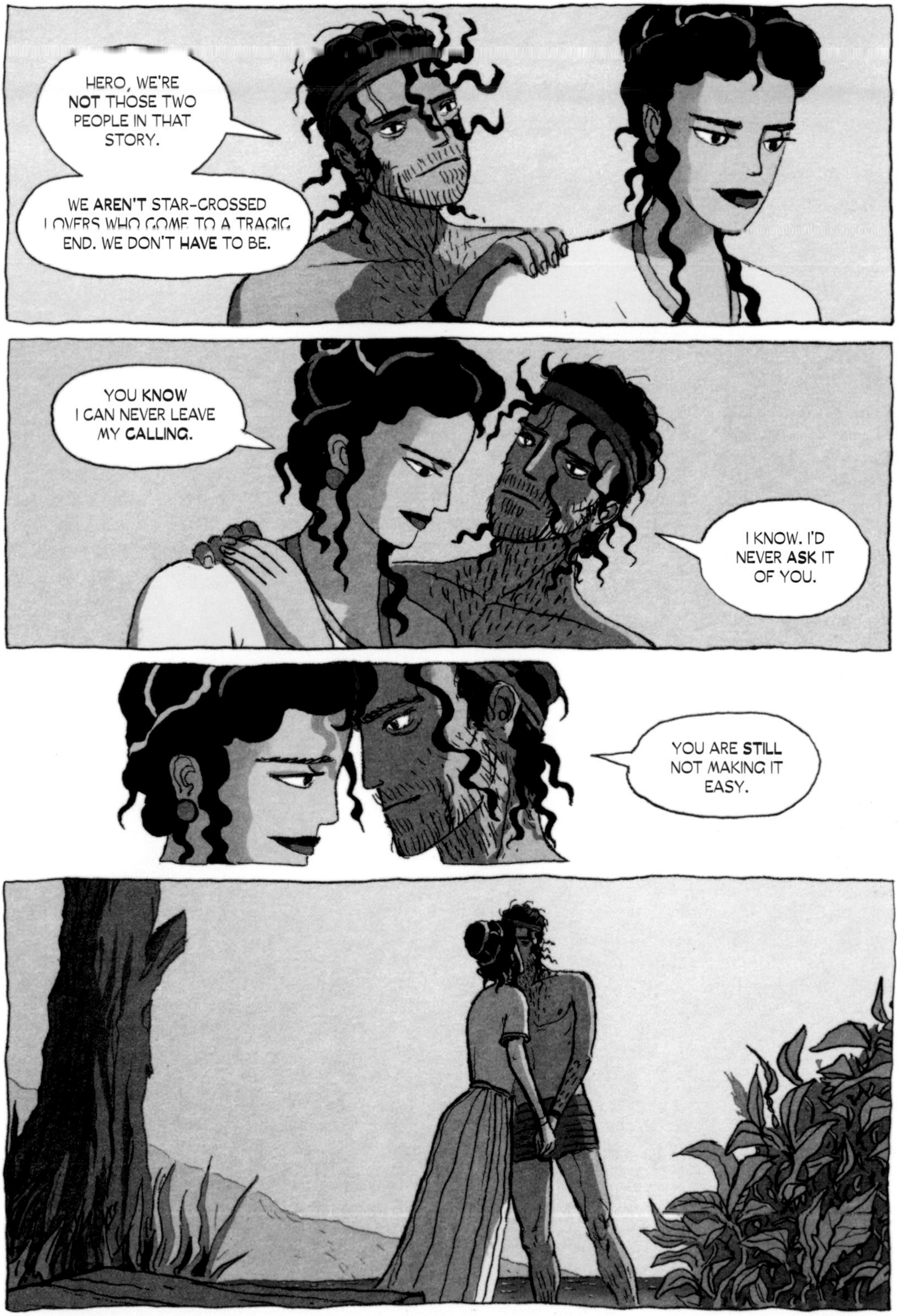
HERO, WE'RE NOT THOSE TWO PEOPLE IN THAT STORY.
WE AREN'T STAR-CROSSED LOVERS WHO COME TO A TRAGIC END. WE DON'T HAVE TO BE.
YOU KNOW I CAN NEVER LEAVE MY CALLING.
I KNOW. I'D NEVER ASK IT OF YOU.
YOU ARE STILL NOT MAKING IT EASY.

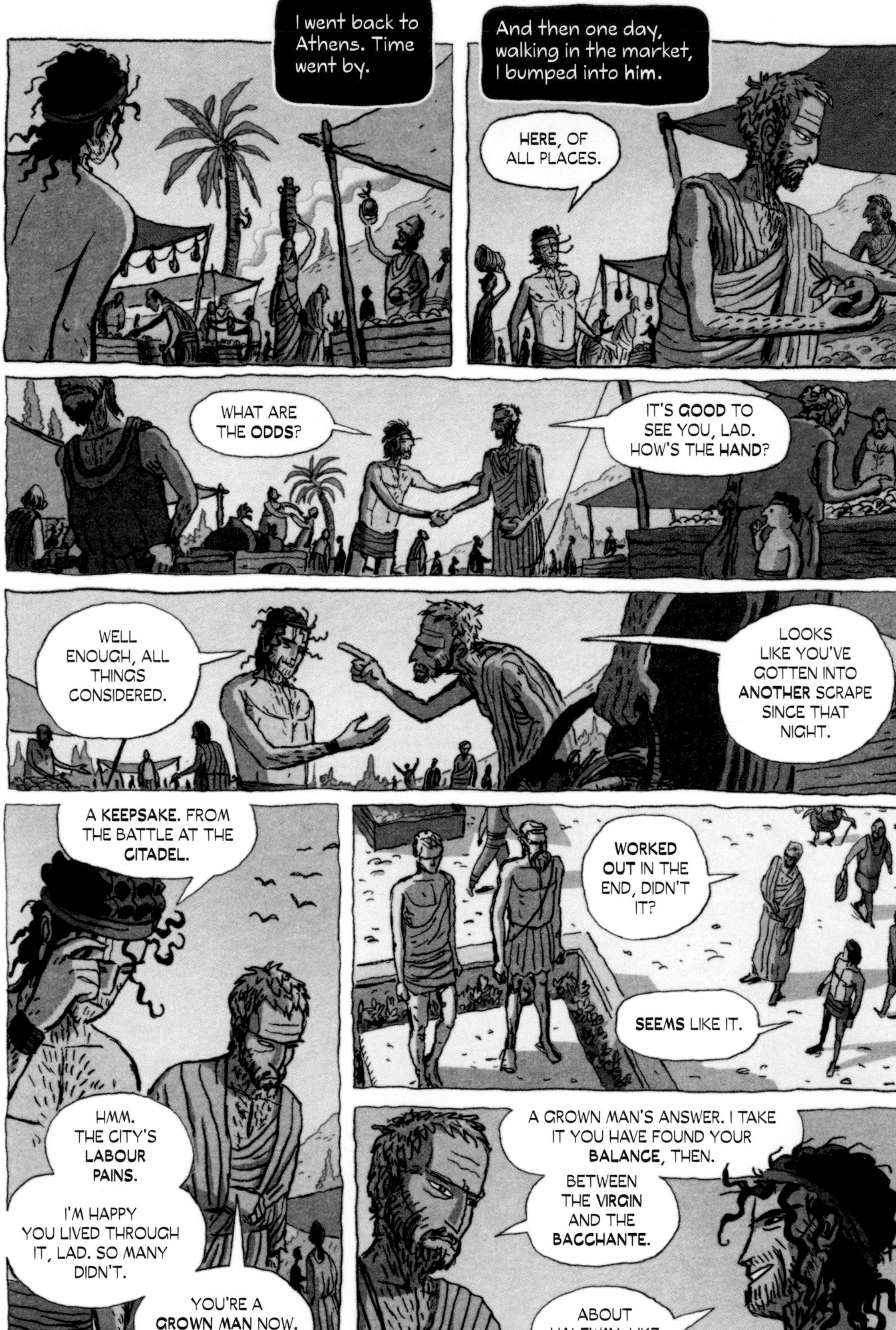
I went back to Athens. Time went by.
And then one day, walking in the market, I bumped into him.
HERE, OF ALL PLACES.
WHAT ARE THE ODDS?
IT'S GOOD TO SEE YOU, LAD. HOW'S THE HAND?
WELL ENOUGH, ALL THINGS CONSIDERED.
LOOKS LIKE YOU'VE GOTTEN INTO ANOTHER SCRAPE SINCE THAT NIGHT.
A KEEPSAKE. FROM THE BATTLE AT THE CITADEL.
HMM. THE CITY'S LABOUR PAINS.
I'M HAPPY YOU LIVED THROUGH IT, LAD. SO MANY DIDN'T.
YOU'RE A GROWN MAN NOW. CHERISH THIS.
WORKED OUT IN THE END, DIDN'T IT?
SEEMS LIKE IT.
A GROWN MAN'S ANSWER. I TAKE IT YOU HAVE FOUND YOUR BALANCE, THEN.
BETWEEN THE VIRGIN AND THE BACCHANTE.
ABOUT HALFWAY. LIKE YOU DID.

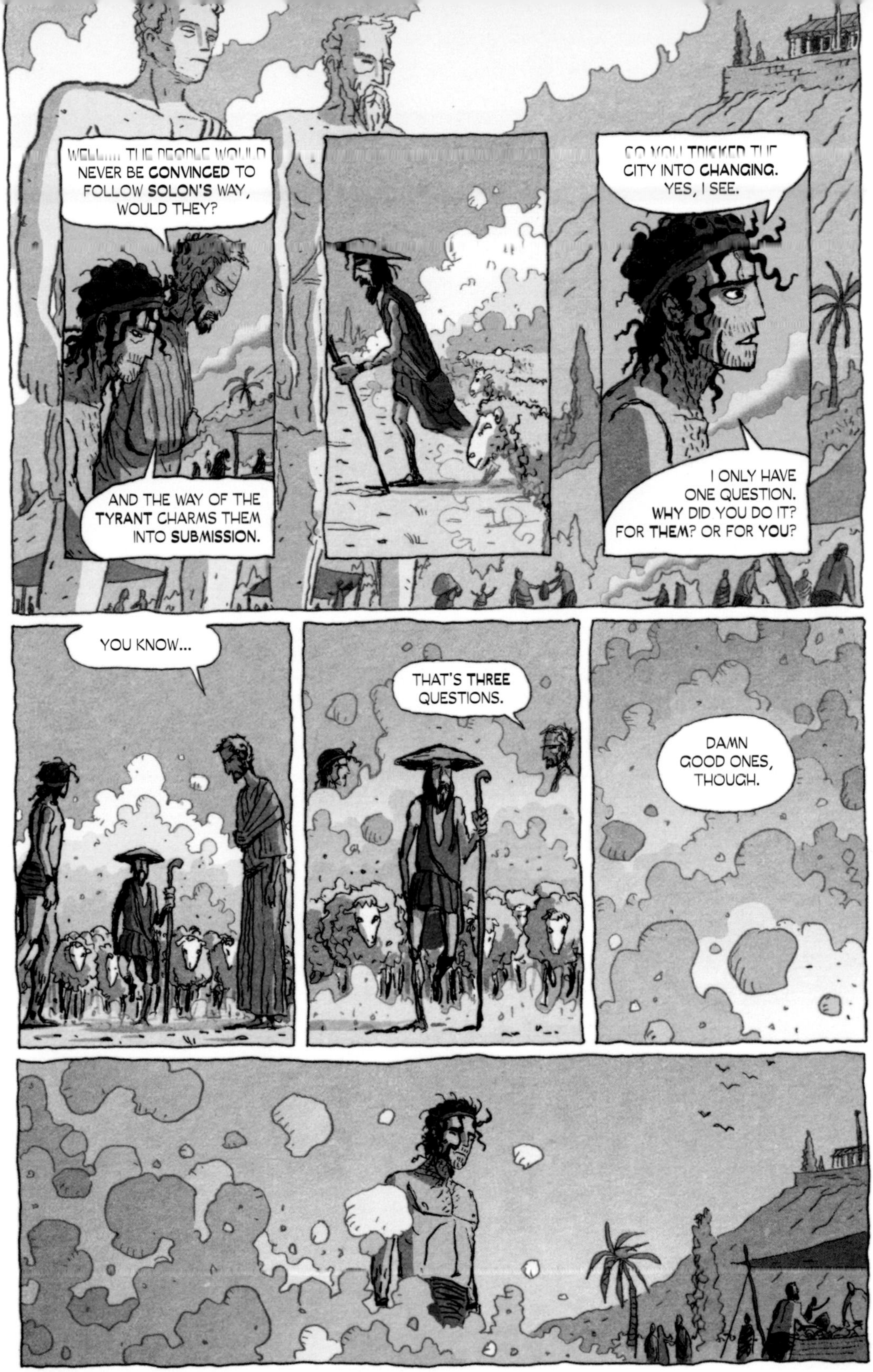
WELL... THE PEOPLE WOULD NEVER BE CONVINCED TO FOLLOW SOLON'S WAY, WOULD THEY?
AND THE WAY OF THE TYRANT CHARMS THEM INTO SUBMISSION.
SO YOU TRICKED THE CITY INTO CHANGING. YES, I SEE.
I ONLY HAVE ONE QUESTION. WHY DID YOU DO IT? FOR THEM? OR FOR YOU?
YOU KNOW...
THAT'S THREE QUESTIONS.
DAMN GOOD ONES, THOUGH.

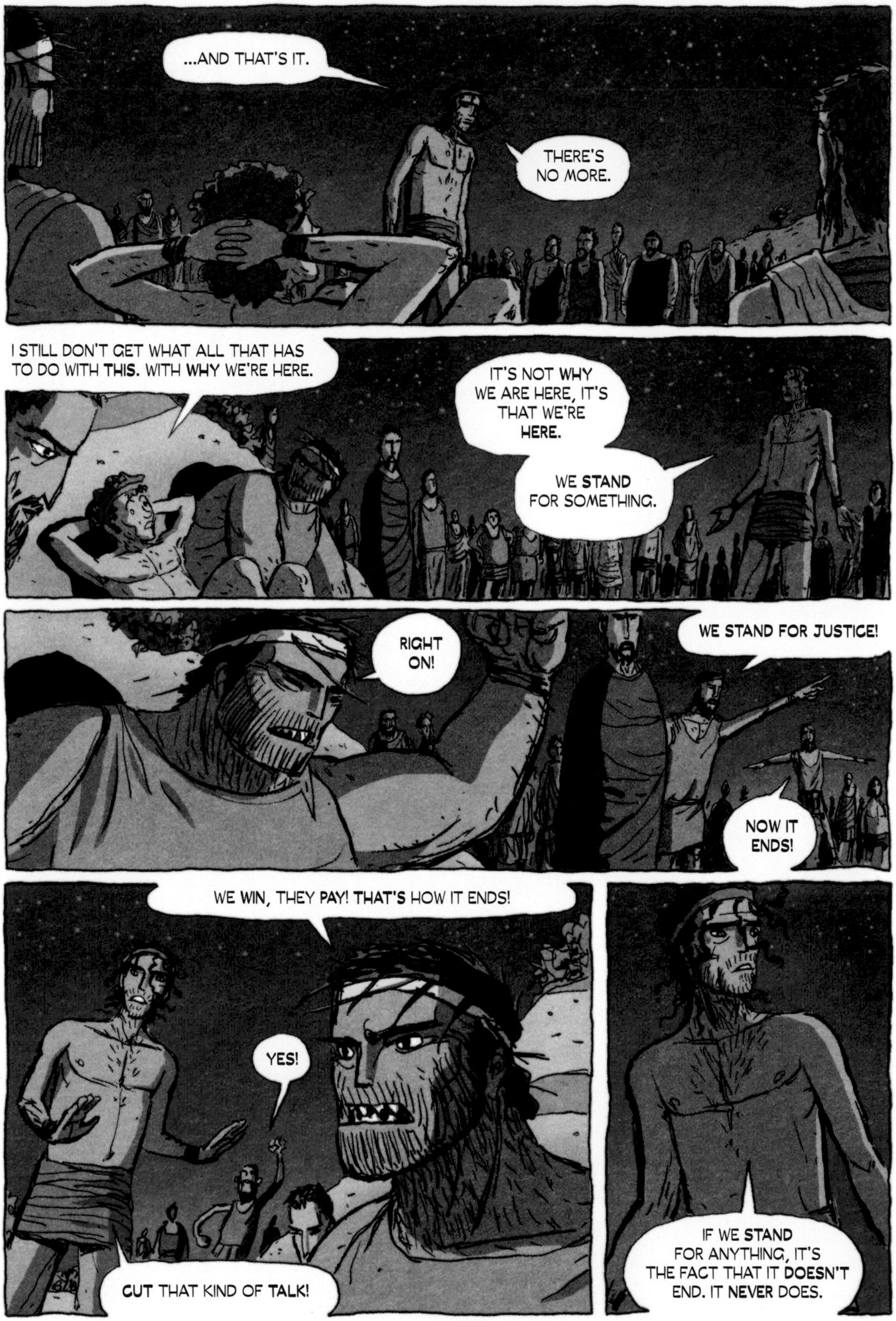
...AND THAT'S IT.
THERE'S NO MORE.
I STILL DON'T GET WHAT ALL THAT HAS TO DO WITH THIS. WITH WHY WE'RE HERE.
IT'S NOT WHY WE ARE HERE, IT'S THAT WE'RE HERE.
WE STAND FOR SOMETHING.
RIGHT ON!
WE STAND FOR JUSTICE!
NOW IT ENDS!
WE WIN, THEY PAY! THAT'S HOW IT ENDS!
YES!
CUT THAT KIND OF TALK!
IF WE STAND FOR ANYTHING, IT'S THE FACT THAT IT DOESN'T END. IT NEVER DOES.

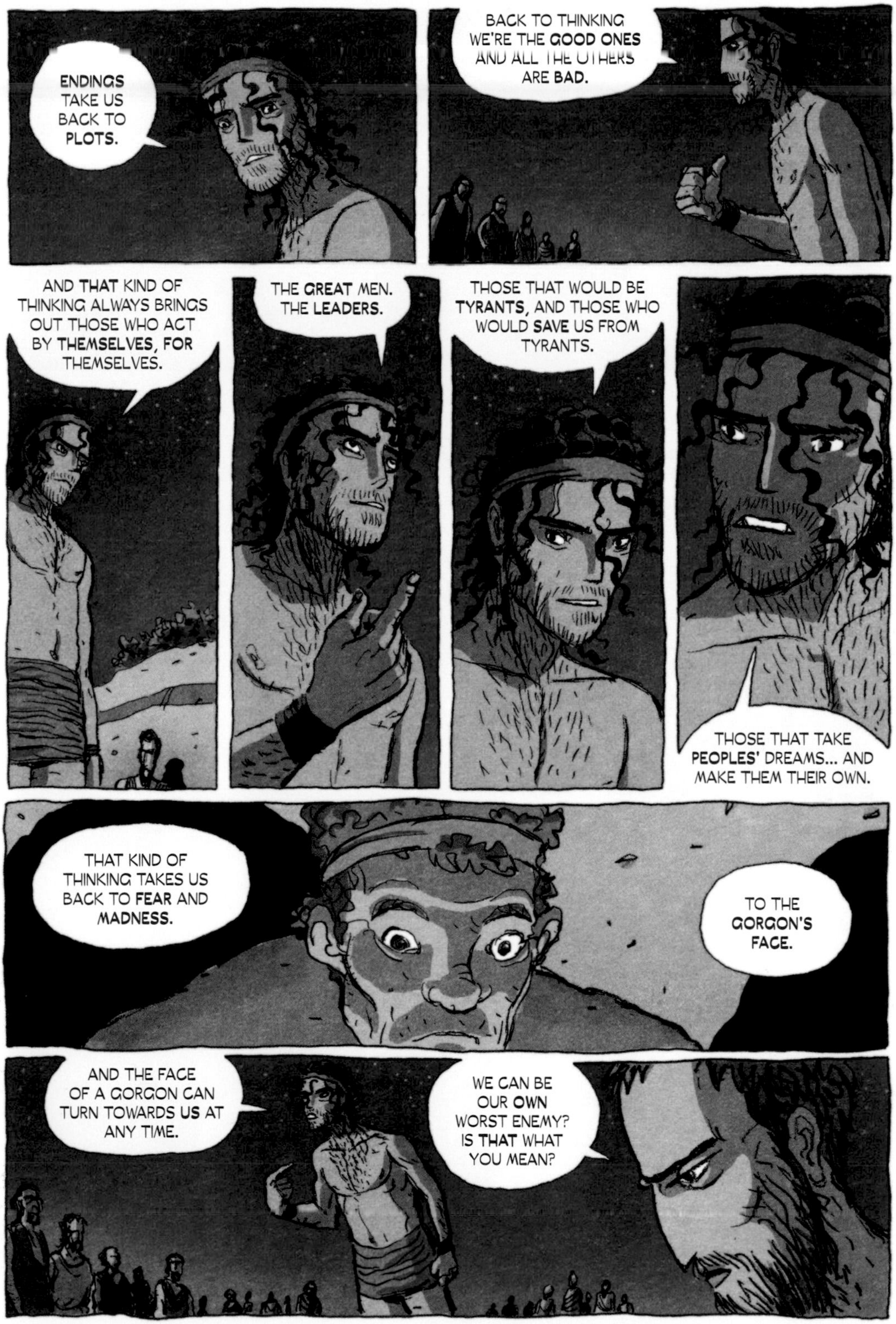
ENDINGS TAKE US BACK TO PLOTS.
BACK TO THINKING WE'RE THE GOOD ONES AND ALL THE OTHERS ARE BAD.
AND THAT KIND OF THINKING ALWAYS BRINGS OUT THOSE WHO ACT BY THEMSELVES, FOR THEMSELVES.
THE GREAT MEN. THE LEADERS.
THOSE THAT WOULD BE TYRANTS, AND THOSE WHO WOULD SAVE US FROM TYRANTS.
THOSE THAT TAKE PEOPLES' DREAMS... AND MAKE THEM THEIR OWN.
THAT KIND OF THINKING TAKES US BACK TO FEAR AND MADNESS.
TO THE GORGON'S FACE.
AND THE FACE OF A GORGON CAN TURN TOWARDS US AT ANY TIME.
WE CAN BE OUR OWN WORST ENEMY? IS THAT WHAT YOU MEAN?

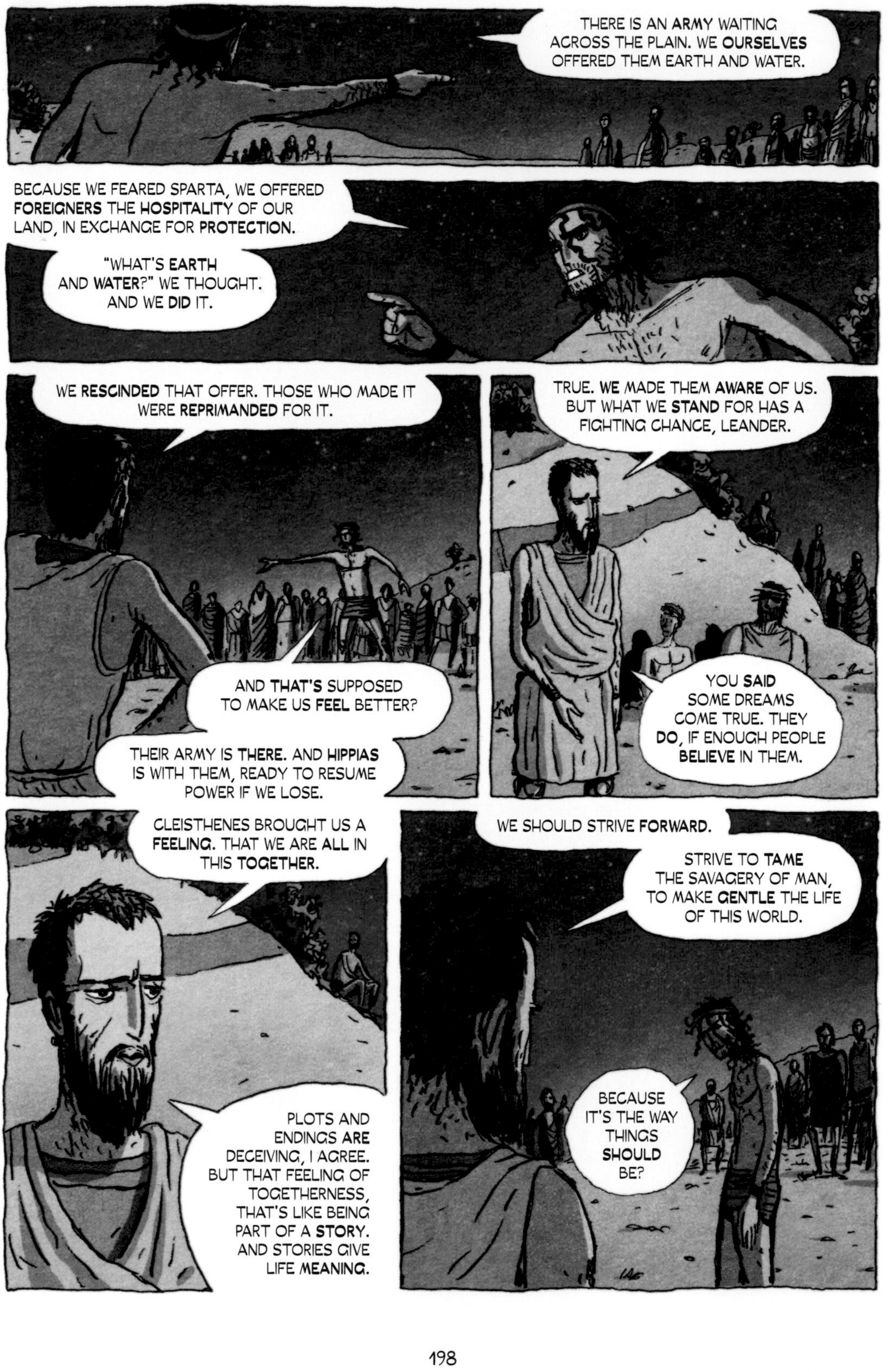
THERE IS AN ARMY WAITING ACROSS THE PLAIN. WE OURSELVES OFFERED THEM EARTH AND WATER.
BECAUSE WE FEARED SPARTA, WE OFFERED FOREIGNERS THE HOSPITALITY OF OUR LAND, IN EXCHANGE FOR PROTECTION.
"WHAT'S EARTH AND WATER?" WE THOUGHT. AND WE DID IT.
WE RESCINDED THAT OFFER. THOSE WHO MADE IT WERE REPRIMANDED FOR IT.
AND THAT'S SUPPOSED TO MAKE US FEEL BETTER?
THEIR ARMY IS THERE. AND HIPPIAS IS WITH THEM, READY TO RESUME POWER IF WE LOSE.
TRUE. WE MADE THEM AWARE OF US. BUT WHAT WE STAND FOR HAS A FIGHTING CHANCE, LEANDER.
YOU SAID SOME DREAMS COME TRUE. THEY DO, IF ENOUGH PEOPLE BELIEVE IN THEM.
CLEISTHENES BROUGHT US A FEELING. THAT WE ARE ALL IN THIS TOGETHER.
PLOTS AND ENDINGS ARE DECEIVING, I AGREE. BUT THAT FEELING OF TOGETHERNESS, THAT'S LIKE BEING PART OF A STORY. AND STORIES GIVE LIFE MEANING.
WE SHOULD STRIVE FORWARD.
STRIVE TO TAME THE SAVAGERY OF MAN, TO MAKE GENTLE THE LIFE OF THIS WORLD.
BECAUSE IT'S THE WAY THINGS SHOULD BE?

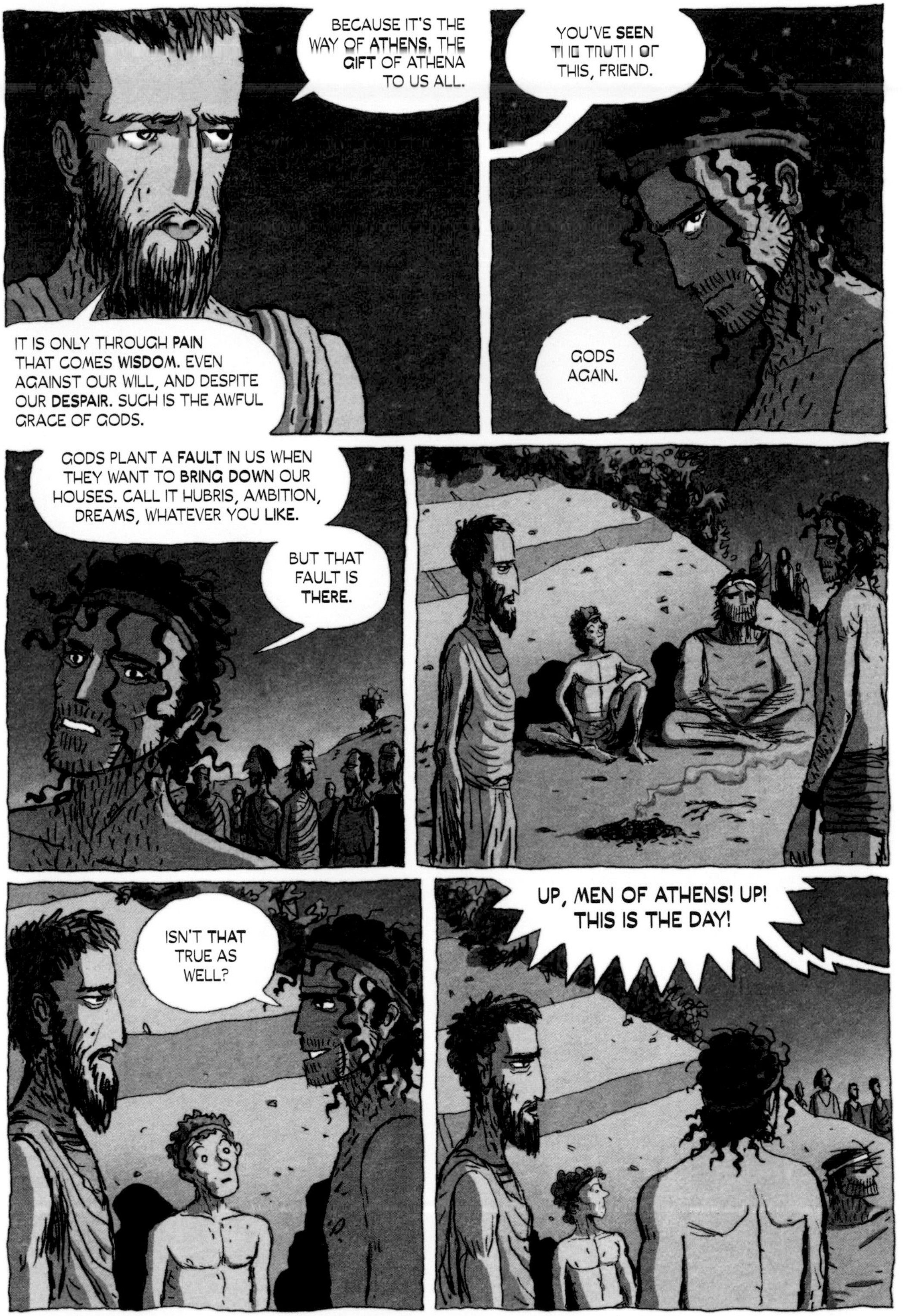
BECAUSE IT'S THE WAY OF ATHENS, THE GIFT OF ATHENA TO US ALL.
IT IS ONLY THROUGH PAIN THAT COMES WISDOM. EVEN AGAINST OUR WILL, AND DESPITE OUR DESPAIR. SUCH IS THE AWFUL GRACE OF GODS.
YOU'VE SEEN THE TRUTH OF THIS, FRIEND.
GODS AGAIN.
GODS PLANT A FAULT IN US WHEN THEY WANT TO BRING DOWN OUR HOUSES. CALL IT HUBRIS, AMBITION, DREAMS, WHATEVER YOU LIKE.
BUT THAT FAULT IS THERE.
ISN'T THAT TRUE AS WELL?
UP, MEN OF ATHENS! UP! THIS IS THE DAY!

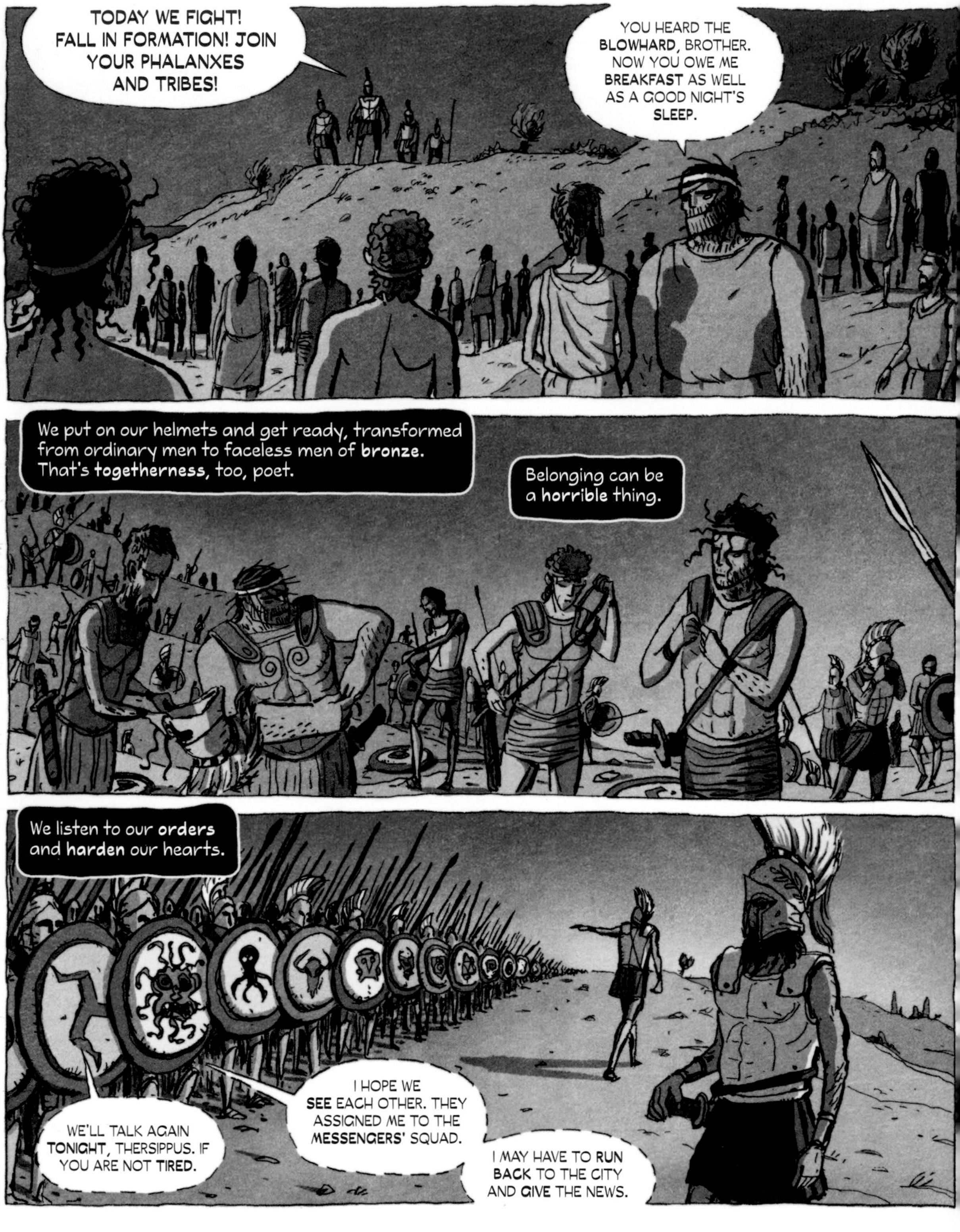

TODAY WE FIGHT! FALL IN FORMATION! JOIN YOUR PHALANXES AND TRIBES!
YOU HEARD THE **BLOWHARD**, BROTHER. NOW YOU OWE ME **BREAKFAST** AS WELL AS A GOOD NIGHT'S **SLEEP**.
We put on our helmets and get ready, transformed from ordinary men to faceless men of **bronze**. That's **togetherness**, too, poet.
Belonging can be a **horrible** thing.
We listen to our **orders** and **harden** our hearts.
WE'LL TALK AGAIN **TONIGHT**, THERSIPPUS. IF YOU ARE NOT **TIRED**.
I HOPE WE **SEE** EACH OTHER. THEY ASSIGNED ME TO THE **MESSENGERS'** SQUAD.
I MAY HAVE TO **RUN BACK** TO THE CITY AND **GIVE** THE NEWS.

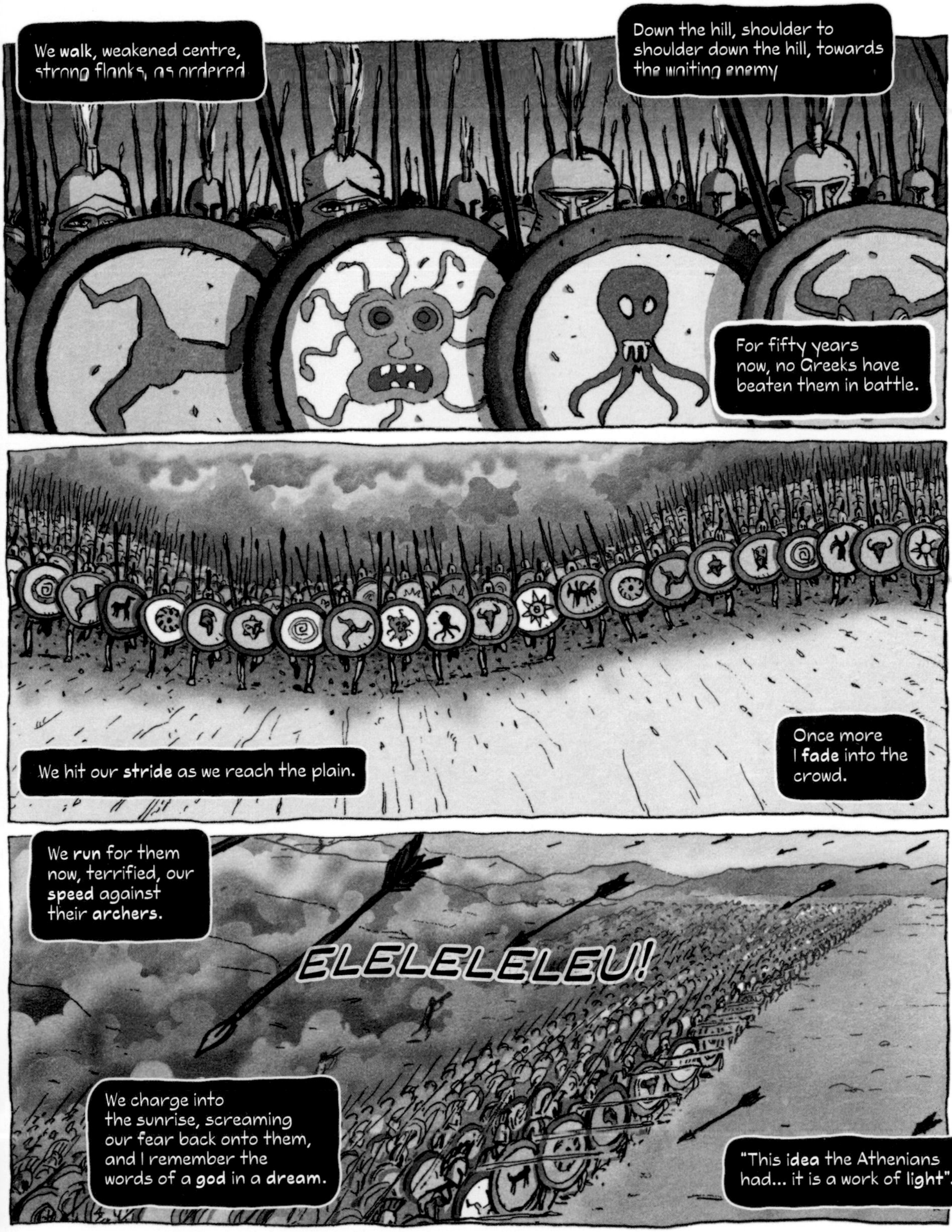
We **walk**, weakened centre, strong flanks, as ordered
Down the hill, shoulder to shoulder down the hill, towards the waiting enemy
For fifty years now, no Greeks have beaten them in battle.
We hit our **stride** as we reach the plain.
Once more I **fade** into the crowd.
We **run** for them now, terrified, our **speed** against their **archers**.
ELELELELELEU!
We charge into the sunrise, screaming our fear back onto them, and I remember the words of a **god** in a **dream**.
"This **idea** the Athenians had... it is a work of **light**".

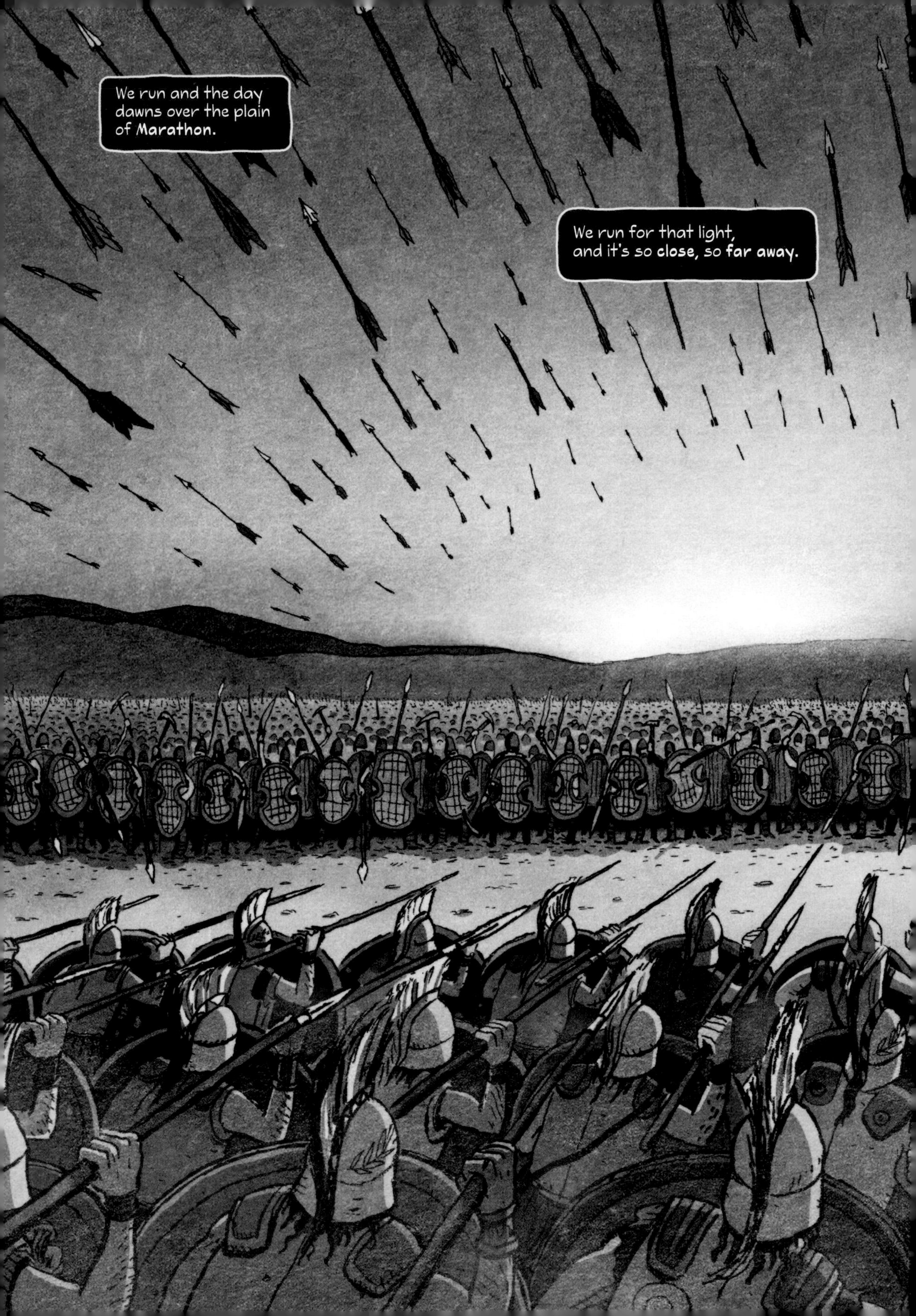
We run and the day dawns over the plain of **Marathon.**
We run for that light, and it's so **close,** so **far away.**

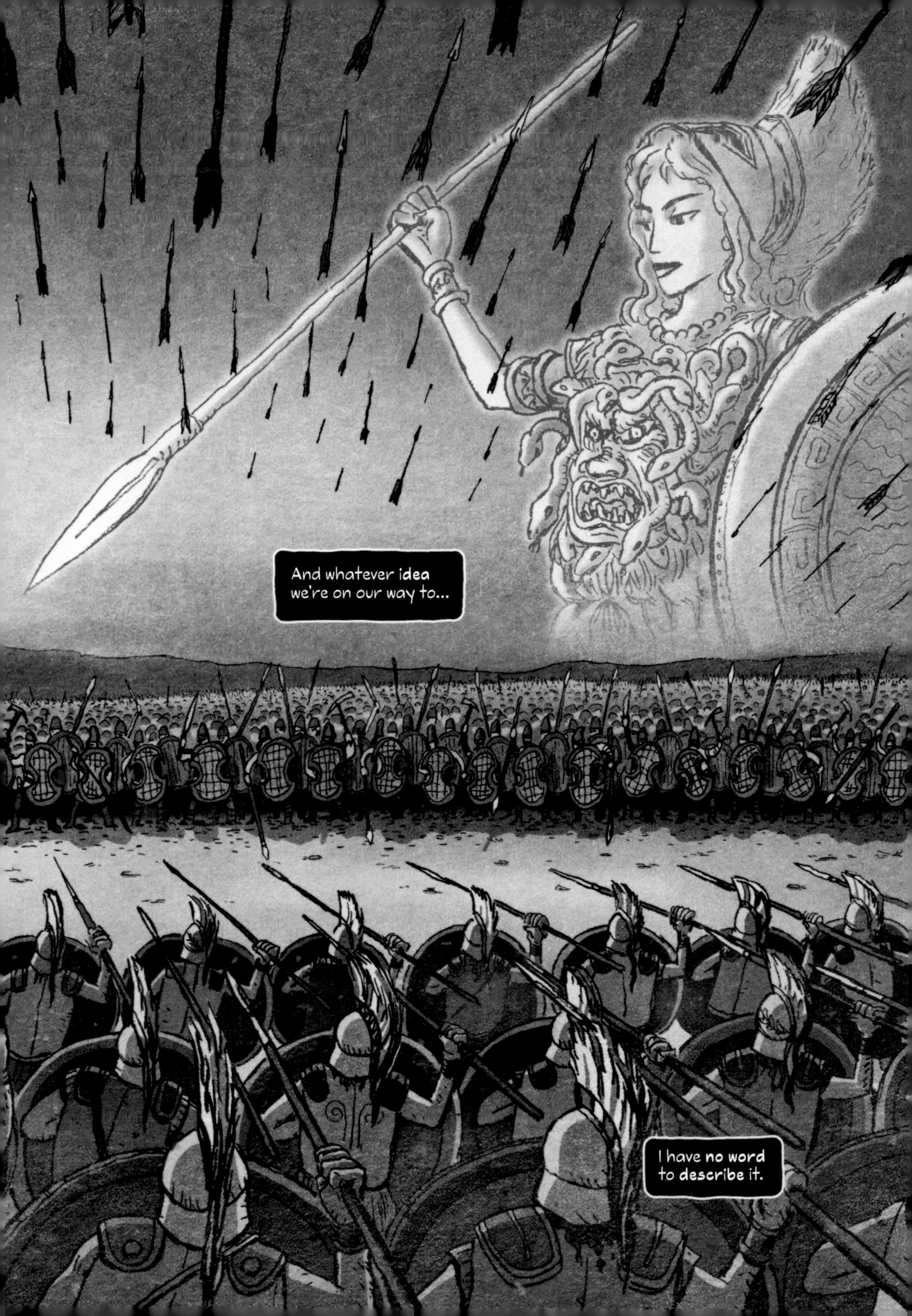
And whatever idea we're on our way to...
I have no word to describe it.

Thank you:
To Apostolos Doxiadis, for friendship, support, and helping Leander draw things on the ground.
To Georgia Kawa, for planting seeds and watching them grow.
To Iraklis Papadatos and Henri Di Donna, for their strength and warmth.
And to Io and Kimon Papadatos, for their encouragement and great patience.
To Despoina Syrtadiotou, for lighting up the dark.

To Giorgos Mavrogordatos, Eliza Sioumpara, Nasos Themos, and Panos Valavanis, for expert opinions.

And to Christophe Devaux, Stavros Kaplanidis, Manolis Kapnisakis, Christine Lacour, Michèle Marin, Nathalie Meunier, Panos Sebros, Nikos Soulakis, Photis Syrtadiotis, Nancy Syrtadiotou, Thomais Syrtadiotou, and Andreas Thomopoulos, for being so unconditionally there.

Drawing from History

So... how much of it was true, you ask?

Well, there's a wise saying storytellers use, and it's certainly useful in our case: "Based on a true story".

In most cases, authors use this saying to add legitimacy to fictions, but it has a double edge. *Based* and *story* are words laden with an implied departure from the truth, and they outnumber *true* by 2 to 1. This is the deep, dark secret of all "true" stories, even more so in the case of fictions set in the 6th century BCE.

In crafting *Democracy*, we worked under the same circumstances as Leander working on his vase - with little more than glimpses of the actual people, motives and ideas that gave birth to the Athenian Democracy. Like our protagonist, we struggled to make sense of conflicting accounts and biased interpretations of -literally- ancient history. Herodotus' *Histories* (written somewhere between 450 and 420 BCE), Thucydides' *History of the Peloponnesian War* (written somewhere between 430 and 397 BCE) and Aristotle's *The Constitution of the Athenians* (written somewhere between 330 and 320 BCE) are the closest thing we have to a primary source, and even these were written long after the fact(s), and are far from uncontested. In some cases, ancient historians reminded us of contradictory media news reports: one's facts were another's unsubstantiated rumours, and vice versa.

Inevitably, to gain a deeper, more detailed perspective on the period, we had to rely on the works of contemporary historians. These works we found to be perceptive, profound, and challenging, and *Democracy* owes them all a great deal. But the perspective they offered was no less fractured than what we gleaned from the primary sources. Like their predecessors, contemporary historians don't always see eye to eye on what happened and why.

In other words, the truth of history remains as elusive as the truth of fictions. Yet rather than let this deter us, we used it.

The thing about *Democracy* is that it is not just a historical novel. One of the reasons we didn't pick a known historical figure as our protagonist was that we did not want to interpret the events in an authoritative, "that-was-the-way-it-was" manner. By telling the story of the men that fathered the Athenian Democracy, we would have imposed just one, "official" version of that story. Instead, we wanted to tell the story of people like us, who, throughout history, have to face the tidal waves brought on by such cataclysmic events - and make sense of them. So we opted for a common man, a young man who embodies timeless human feelings about the democratic ideal. For the story of democracy is not one of the past, but an ongoing, everyday struggle.

Feelings about democracy can be both positive and negative. Like so many people in today's political climate, Leander feels frustrated, manipulated by forces he cannot control or influence. He struggles against social injustice and corruption, but also, privately, against his own uncertainties and failings. He strives towards an ideal he can't even name, a concept that is ambiguous, flawed, fragile - yet it is also something of hope; a light in the dark.

And the truth of what happened? There are some versions of it in *Democracy*, as many as we could fit in, and they're presented to Leander, each with its own claim to validity. As Hero would say, he is asked to choose. We ask our readers to do the same.

Abraham Kawa
November 17, 2014

Commentary

While you can enjoy *Democracy* just as well without them, these brief comments offer some further insight on the people, places and events of our story. Eagle-eyed readers may have noticed a couple of 'Easter eggs' hidden throughout the tale, so here seems as good a place as any to confirm your suspicions. A name, place name or term in **BOLD CAPITALS** means that there is a separate entry for it.

AGAMEMNON

The legendary warlord of the Greeks during the Trojan War. A controversial figure, both in Homer's *The Iliad* and in a number of Greek tragedies, Agamemnon chose to sacrifice his daughter Iphigenia to the gods, so that they would grant the Greek fleet safe passage to Troy across the Aegean Sea. This act sparked a horrific cycle of blood and revenge: after the 10-year war, upon his return, Agamemnon was assassinated by his wife, Clytemnestra, who had never forgiven him for killing their daughter - and later yet, Clytemnestra herself was killed by her own son, Orestes, who could not forgive her for killing his father. Haunted by the Furies, the goddesses of guilt and retribution, Orestes fled across Greece till he came to **ATHENS**, where he was tried for his crime and finally acquitted, thanks to the intervention of the goddess **ATHENA**. The story has been endlessly retold both in ancient Greek works and later versions, but one of the earliest and best was the *Oresteia*, a trilogy of plays written by none other than the **POET** of our tale.

AGORA

Before the establishment of assemblies and councils in Ancient Greece, the agora was the place where citizens gathered to listen to announcements and proclamations made by the city's ruler. In later times, the agora maintained its status as a place for gathering, but it also became a hub of commercial, political and religious activity. In **ATHENS**, the tyrant **PEISISTRATUS** established the central position of the city's agora by removing private dwellings from the area and by adorning it with fountains and a temple. Its site was bound to be the city's centre anyway, since it intersected with the large main road of Athens, the Panathenaic Way. In modern Greece, *agora* is still the word for *market*, especially an open-air one.

ARKTOS

The Greeks measured the day in twelve hours. *Arktos* was the hour after dark,

the time of stars and magic. The word, which means *Bear* in Greek, refers to the constellation later known as Ursa Major. Greek astronomers imagined the sky as an enormous hunting ground, where legendary beings stalked each other: other than the Bear, these included Scorpio, Sirius the hound, and Orion, the great hunter.

ASSEMBLY OF CITIZENS

Known as *Ekklesia* in Greek ("*gathering of the summoned*"), it was one of the Athenian state's three main governing bodies (the others were the **CITY COUNCIL** and the *Areopagus*). Our story focuses on the Council, so we show the Assembly only once towards the end, but it was an institution that dated back to the 7th century BCE. When **SOLON** set down his laws and reforms, he made the Assembly open to male citizens of 18 years of age or over, and took care to admit even those citizens who were basically serfs with only a small amount of property. As a body, the Assembly had a measure of control over city policy, including the election of chief magistrates. Still, its power was less concrete than that of the Council, since only the latter body had the privilege of fixing the agenda of topics and motions to be discussed in the Assembly. Votes in the Assembly were taken by a simple show of hands. Though there were such Assemblies in many Greek **CITY-STATES**, the majority of historical data available concerns the Athenian Assembly. The institution survived - and thrived further - after the reforms of **CLEISTHENES** and the Age of Pericles, continuing well into the Hellenistic period, but the Roman occupation of Greece resulted in a slow, inexorable siphoning of its powers.

ATHENA

The Greek goddess of wisdom and the arts, Athena was both the patron of

ATHENS and the personification of its values. According to Plato, her name originates from the Greek word *Theonoa* ("*She who has the mind of god*"), which further posits her as a symbol of moral intelligence. In fact, from a psychological point of view, it may be argued that Athena, as well as the other Greek gods, functioned as personifications of the ancients' thinking process. In that respect, Leander's encounters with Athena are internal dialogues with that part of his psyche that drives him to move on and to overcome his limitations. The Serpent and the Owl, the goddess' sacred animals, further personified her function as both a protector of man (who, like the serpent, was thought to be a child of the earth) and a bringer of enlightenment (since Athena saw through the darkness of the soul, just like the owl can see through the night). Within our story , Athena and the gods represent an older order of things, a darker age of religious and social ritual that is about to transform into the more anthropocentric "Golden Age", the heyday of Athens and its democracy. It is proof of her closeness to humanity, however, that Athena sides with the way of enlightenment and acts as a bridge between the old age and the new.

ATHENS

In the 6th century BCE, Athens was one of the two most powerful **CITY-STATES** in Greece. It dominated the province of Attica as well as areas such as the northern Greek colony of the Chersonese. While it had not yet achieved the superpower status it had during the 5th century, Athens at the time was bustling with development. Ships sailed from its small, yet busy port to a multitude of destinations, grand temples were in construction, and the city's markets were crowded with farmers, prostitutes, grocers, potters, and sellers of textiles and spices. Its population was composed of artisans, landowning aristocracy, and peasantry, as well as poor unskilled workers, slaves (an analogy of two for every free man) and seedy lowlifes, all thrown together in a melting pot. The regime of the tyrant **PEISISTRATUS** had already made Athens financially robust, and the legislative innovations of **SOLON** had created institutions such as its **CITY COUNCIL.** Yet perhaps more importantly, the Athenians prided themselves on their being the inhabitants of a city that was lawful, on having the patronage of one of the principal Olympian deities, **ATHENA,** and on being cultured and indomitable. These qualities,

coupled with historical circumstance, facilitated the fall of the corrupt regime of HIPPIAS and HIPPARCHUS and brought about the birth of democracy.

AULOS

An ancient wind instrument, usually double-reeded, with a sharp, persistent, bagpipe-like sound that was difficult to combine with lyrics. Its mythical origins are pretty much as **APOLLO** tells us, though the god understandably omits the incident of his contest with the satyr Marsyas. According to legend, the unfortunate satyr picked up the *aulos* after **ATHENA** threw it away, and brazenly challenged Apollo to a musical duel. He lost, and the god punished his gall by flaying him alive. While popular in some cities, the *aulos* gradually lost favour in others, especially in **ATHENS.** The Athenian statesman Alcibiades famously refused to play it, and the philosopher Aristotle interpreted Athena's rejection of the *aulos* as an ethical rejection of an instrument which adds nothing to wisdom. The association of the aulos with DIONYSUS comes from Plato, Aristotle's Athenian teacher, who heard an enthusiastic, passionate quality in its music that befitted the cult of the god.

CITY COUNCIL

A council of citizens charged with running the affairs of a Greek **CITY-STATE.** Its name, *Boule*, after the Greek word for *will*, is still used as the name for the

Greek parliament. As established by the lawmaker SOLON during the 6th century BCE, the Athenian Council was more reminiscent of a parliament than a senate; it gave voice to a considerable portion of the citizenry, even though its 400 representatives were chosen from the privileged classes of property-owning citizens. Crucially, the Council acted as a counterweight to the *Areopagus*, the governmental body that had predated Solon's reforms and whose membership was restricted exclusively to those who had held the high office of *Archon* (Chief Magistrate). When **CLEISTHENES** created the new **TEN TRIBES** in order to weaken the political influence of aristocratic families and to give the people a share in government, he changed the number of representatives to 500, with 50 members from each tribe. In this way, he promoted local representation rather than hereditary oligarchy, and laid the foundations for the development of a democratic government.

CITY-STATES

Rather than being a unified country, Greece in the 6th century BCE was a land divided into various areas of influence, defined and ruled by independent city-states. One might imagine alliances between these cities were fragile: today's ally could quickly become tomorrow's enemy. Politically speaking, these cities were run by coteries of variably oligarchic nature, with governing systems ranging from hereditary monarchies (as was the case with the militaristic city-state of **SPARTA**) to tyrannies, where a statesman usurped and held power without having any right to it by law (such as that of **PEISISTRATUS** in the city-state of **ATHENS**). So, understandably, Greece at the time was always at the brink of several wars. More importantly, it was difficult to unify this collection of rival states against the danger of the greatest military force of the then known world – the PERSIAN EMPIRE of king Darius the First. That the outcome of the Greco-Persian Wars was not utter defeat for the Greeks was nothing short of miraculous, and more than two millennia later, battles such as those fought at **MARATHON** and Thermopylae still stand as testaments to bravery, courage and a just cause versus brute military might.

CLEISTHENES

Widely considered as "the father of democracy", Cleisthenes was also, in historical terms, a riddle wrapped in a mystery inside an enigma. So little is known about him, in fact, that the year of his birth is only estimated as being somewhere around 570 BCE, and his life after his reforms is completely undocumented. Some historians paint him as a selfless reformer, others as a manipulative opportunist, yet everyone agrees on his status as a revolutionary statesman and one of the most influential figures in world history. Interestingly, Cleisthenes was an ancestor of both Pericles, who is recognized as the most charismatic leader of the Athenian state, and Alcibiades, who gained notoriety as the city's least scrupulous politician. It seems a fitting legacy for someone so controversial.

CYNEGEIRUS

A celebrated hero of the battle of **MARATHON**, Cynegeirus is more famous for his death and his kin than his life. A native of the small Attican town of Eleusis, he perished valiantly during the routing of the Persians, when he grabbed hold of the stern of a Persian ship and was cut down by the blow of an enemy axe. The Greek historian Herodotus tersely relates that the fatal blow cut off Cynegeirus' hand, allowing us to presume that he died of excessive haemorrhage or an infected wound. The Roman historian Justin, however, embellishes his demise to super-heroic proportions, claiming that, after losing his hand, Cynegeirus grabbed the fleeing vessel with his remaining one, and when that hand was mutilated in turn, he kept hanging onto the Persian craft by his teeth. The tale has granted Cynegeirus a status comparable to that of the **TYRANT SLAYERS**. On the 2500th anniversary of the Battle of Marathon, a memorial to him was erected in his native town of Eleusis. As for his kin, they include two brothers who fought beside him: Ameinias, who went on to distinguish himself at the battle of Salamis, as well as the **POET** of our tale, none other than the great tragedian Aeschylus.

DELPHI

While not a city-state per se, Delphi stood out in Ancient Greece as a different locus of power. Considered to be the *omphalos*, the navel of the earth - and thus the centre of the known world - Delphi housed the most famous Oracle of ancient Greece, the Oracle of the Temple of **APOLLO**. The continued status of Delphi as a centre of worship is indicative of its importance as a political player. Having the Oracle of Delphi deliver a favourable omen - or a bad one - could decide the fate of governments, since these proclamations were seen as nothing less than the will of the Gods. Naturally, this meant that the priests of Apollo could be influenced or bribed. Herodotus tells us that this was exactly what happened when **CLEISTHENES** persuaded the Oracle to goad **SPARTA** into a war against the tyrant of **ATHENS**.

DIONYSUS & APOLLO

Dionysus, the god of drunken merriment and ritual madness, may seem like an odd god to pair with Apollo, the god of light, truth and music, but we are far from the first to do so. The two gods shared the sacred site of **DELPHI** in antiquity, complementing each other, while in more recent times they have come to symbolize the split in the human psyche between rational order (Apollo) and irrational chaos (Dionysus). This dichotomy, first theorized about in Friedrich Nietzsche's *The Birth of Tragedy*, is present within every important human endeavour, including, of course, democracy - a regime where our propensity for chaos confronts our need for order. On the one hand, these gods can be seen as representatives of the ancient order of things, which is about to be replaced by an age of men in our story. Yet their complex relationship marks chaos and order as an ongoing, timeless presence in human affairs. Humanity evolves only through a mutual understanding of the two, as personified by the wisdom of **ATHENA**.

EARTH AND WATER

A symbolic offering of submission to a conqueror. The offering of earth symbolized the surrender of the conquered people's land, while the gift of water meant that the conquered were also ceding all rights to the resources of their land. According to Herodotus, the giving of earth and water was a standard demand made by the **PERSIAN EMPIRE** to the Greek **CITY-STATES** in the lead-up to the Greco-Persian wars of the 5th century BCE. The historian records that some cities refused, most famously SPARTA, whose citizens threw the Persian envoys down a well and told them mockingly to dig out earth and water for themselves. It must be said, however, that in the shifting geopolitical climate of the day, rivalries between the Greeks could cause some cities to respond otherwise. In fear of the Spartans' continuing efforts to establish **ISAGORAS** as tyrant of **ATHENS**, the Athenians actually sent ambassadors to Persia to request the Persian Empire's aid. When the Persians asked for earth and water, the ambassadors initially *agreed* to the demand, and the offer was rescinded only on their return to Athens, where they were sternly reprimanded for their action.

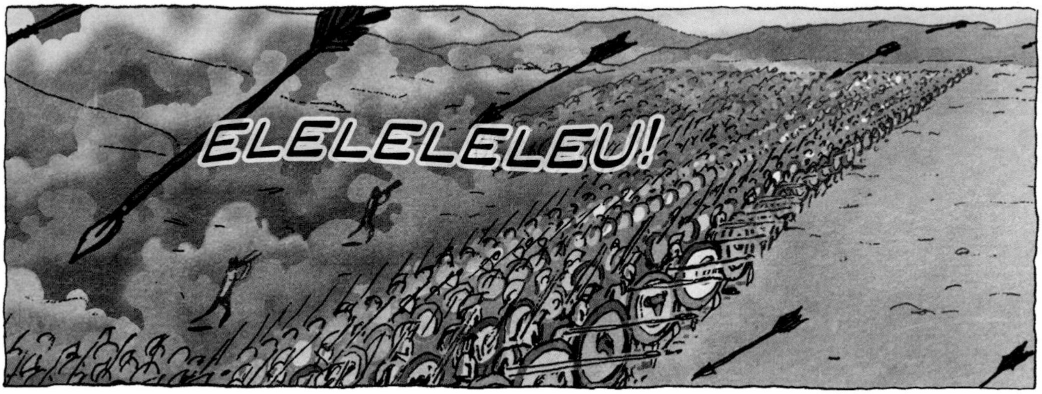
ELELELELELEU!

ELELELEU

A war cry intended to strike fear into the hearts of the enemy. No account survives of its precise meaning, and it is usually believed that it is onomatopoeic in nature, i.e. an imitation of the sound of the war cry rather than a word per se. Aristophanes records the cry as "*elelele*u" in his play *The Birds*. As for how such a war cry actually *sounded*, there is a variety of opinion; some writers compare it to Russian battle cries or the Confederate "rebel yell", while others call it an ululation comparable to those common in the Middle East. One notion we found particularly interesting was that war cries such as "elelele*u*" and "alala" are connected to the goddess **ATHENA**, since they are interpreted as attempts to mimic the chilling cry of the owl. But what is perhaps the most exceptional description comes from the play *Agamemnon*, where the **POET** compares the Greeks' battle cry to "the cry of vultures whose nest is plundered".

GO TO THE CROWS

A very strong curse in Ancient Greece. To say it to someone basically means you wish them dead, and their unburied corpse devoured by carrion birds.

GORGON

A legendary monster of antiquity, one of three snake-haired sisters, so "hated of mortal man", as the **POET** writes in *Prometheus Bound*, that "none may behold and bear their breathing blight". Her name comes from the Greek *gorgos* (horrifying), but her actual name was *Medusa* (guardian). Early Greek art and poetry indeed presented her as so hideous that all who saw her turned to stone, but later artists and writers infused her with a terrifying beauty. The Latin poet Ovid, in fact, went as far as to posit that Medusa was a gorgeous girl who was raped by the god Poseidon inside a temple of **ATHENA**, causing the angered goddess to turn her into a monster (an unfair punishment, to say the least). After the Greek hero Perseus slew Medusa, he offered her severed head to Athena, who had it mounted onto her breastplate, for even in death, it had maintained the power to petrify those who looked into its eyes. This head, called *Gorgoneion*, has both a symbolic and a literal function in Greek art. On the one hand, it is a mask-like emblem worn by the goddess in paintings and sculptures or used in temple pediments, antefixes and shields, where it plays a similar role to a gargoyle or an Asian ritual mask, acting as a guardian that wards off evil. On the other hand, it is also supposed to be - literally - a monstrous female head on Athena's breastplate, poised and ready to petrify anyone who displeases the goddess. Every time Leander is afraid to look at his goddess, it is because he is afraid what he will see won't be the emblem, but the Gorgon's head itself.

HERO AND LEANDER

We readily admit that the presence of this legend in our story is somewhat of an anachronism, since its earliest appearance as a poem occurs in Ovid's *Heroides*, in the 1st century CE. But arguably, the story of Hero and Leander, like a lot of the myths Ovid worked on, could have been much older than that. In our tale, the legend serves as a reminder of the power of stories and ideas to inspire - or to hinder. The Athenians needed to believe in Cleisthenes' vision in order for that vision to grow roots in reality, just like our Hero and Leander needed to believe in their love in order for it to grow beyond a retelling of a tragic myth.

HETAIRA

Scholars define the *hetairai* as the Ancient Greek equivalent of female escorts, but it must be said that they were also their day's career women. The word is the female form of *hetairos* (companion, associate), and this definition hints at the complexity of the services provided by them. A *hetaira* had to be educated and sophisticated enough to participate in a symposium (unlike most women at the time), and her views would both be listened to and valued. She had to be an accomplished entertainer, well versed in dancing and music-playing, and capable of holding her own in any debate. Unbound by the laws that kept other women in their homes, she was free to engage in public life and concerns. *Hetairai* were also unique among women because they were financially independent; indeed, they were taxed, like any other citizen. Depending on her associations, a *hetaira* could become vastly influential. Aspasia, who was greatly esteemed by the prominent philosophers of her day, became the consort of Pericles; while Phryne, who modelled for the famed sculptor Praxiteles, was deemed so divinely beautiful that she was acquitted of a charge of impiety just by baring her breasts before her judges.

HIPPARCHUS

According to Thucydides, it was Hipparchus' violent death, and not his actual status, that branded him a tyrant. Historians tend to agree with this, assigning him a minor political role and painting **HIPPIAS** as the actual successor to **PEISISTRATUS**. Little else is known about him, in fact, other than that he was considered a patron of the arts, having lured to **ATHENS** some of the most important lyric poets of the age, such as Anacreon of Teos and Simonides of Ceos. His reputation as amorous seems to come from his ill-fated wooing of Harmodius rather than any record of his conquests, but it has stuck through the ages.

HIPPIAS

Together with his brother **HIPPARCHUS**, the tyrant Hippias ruled **ATHENS** between 527 and 510 BCE. They assumed control of the city after the death of their father, **PEISISTRATUS**, who had managed to remain in power for something close to three decades. Historical sources tell us Hippias was a charismatic politician, far more inclined to be the head of state than his younger brother, who was more disposed to the sponsoring of poets. Though both Thucydides and Aristotle confirm that the tyrant's rule became much more oppressive after the assassination of his brother in 514 BCE, they differ in their accounts of how Hippias dealt with the conspirators. Thucydides tells us that Hippias had the men who marched in the procession of the **PANATHENEA** searched for concealed daggers, and that out of them he selected those who he thought were part of the conspiracy. Aristotle, however, directly contradicts this claim, stating that the tyrant had no evidence of a conspiracy at first, and that such evidence was provided by the **TYRANT SLAYER** Aristogeiton under torture. While we have compressed events for the sake of spectacle - there is no evidence of a mass massacre of presumed suspects like the one shown in our story - both sources go on to say that Hippias slew and banished a great many citizens as a consequence of the assassination. It was during that time, when Hippias was searching for a possible asylum in the event of a revolution against him, that he had his daughter married to the son of the tyrant of Lampsacus, a city in Asia Minor which was allied with the **PERSIAN EMPIRE**. This move did indeed facilitate Hippias' access to the court of the Persian king Darius, and Hippias fled there after he was ousted from power. Both the Spartans and the Persians, judging a democratic Athens to be a threat to their interests, made attempts to have Hippias reinstated. As Herodotus relates, when Darius decided to wage war on Athens in 490 BCE, Hippias led the Persian forces to **MARATHON**, despite a bad dream he had that the Persians would be defeated there. After that, there are no accounts of his fate.

HOLY ONES

While ancient sources reveal precious little on the roles assigned to the personnel of the Oracle of **DELPHI**, we know that the Holy Ones were five in number, chosen from reputable local families, and appointed for life. Their duties varied from assisting the priests in the performance of religious rites to being present in the opening and interpreting of prophecies. The vagueness of their function, as well as references to secret sacrifices that they carried out, have led some scholars to surmise that they were priests of **DIONYSUS** rather than **APOLLO**, which lends them a certain air of mystery.

ISAGORAS

A scion of a noble, yet otherwise obscure family, Isagoras was deemed by some sources a partisan of **HIPPIAS** and **HIPPARCHUS** while the tyrants were in power. After the end of the tyranny, he became the chief political rival of **CLEISTHENES**. In this, Isagoras had the support of **KLEOMENES**, the king of **SPARTA**, with whom he had been on friendly terms from the time the Spartans campaigned against the tyrants. The rumour about Kleomenes being a little too familiar with Isagoras' wife comes from Herodotus, and whether based on fact or not, it does suggest that the ancients were suspicious about the shady dealings between Isagoras and the Spartan king. Their actual plan was to replace the Athenian **CITY COUNCIL** with Isagoras and three hundred of his partisans, effectively handing the city over to a new tyranny controlled by Sparta. Herodotus assures us that, unlike his followers, Isagoras managed to escape from the city along with Kleomenes. Indeed, the Spartans later attempted once more to establish Isagoras as tyrant, but this second effort failed as well.

KLEOMENES

While historians are not sure about the date of his birth, they tell us that Kleomenes was king of **SPARTA** from 520 to 490 BCE. His intervention in the affairs of **ATHENS** is also well documented, setting him apart from his predecessors, who tended to limit their forays to the immediate vicinity of Sparta and the peninsula of the Peloponnese. This is one of the reasons why Kleomenes is a divisive figure to most ancient historians, yet Herodotus' treatment of him borders on character assassination. In the *Histories*, Kleomenes was depicted as treacherous, sacrilegious, mentally unstable and verging upon madness. According to Herodotus, he died a shocking death, cutting himself to pieces with a knife while imprisoned by his own kin. He was succeeded by his half-brother, Leonidas, the warrior king who later perished at the Battle of Thermopylae with his famous 300 Spartans. (And yes, dear readers, that is the young Leonidas arguing with Kleomenes during the siege at the Citadel. There is no historical evidence of Leonidas accompanying his half-brother and liege to Athens. We made it up. But it *could* have happened.)

MARATHON

The name of a plain roughly 25 miles from **ATHENS**, famous as the site of The Battle of Marathon. Fought in 490 BCE, it turned out to be one of the greatest victories won by the Athenians against the might of the **PERSIAN EMPIRE** during the Greco-Persian Wars of the 5th century. While the Persians were vastly superior in number, the Athenians, joined by a small allied force from the city of Plataea, charged them against all odds and managed to rout them back to their ships. Historians have offered few (and conflicting) explanations as to why the Athenians chose to attack without waiting for reinforcements from other cities (such as **SPARTA**, which had promised its aid, yet was conspicuously late in delivering it). One possible reason could have been that the Persians had dispatched their navy to the undefended Athens, leaving their infantry at Marathon to pin down the Athenian army, and that the Athenians had to attack, both because they had to defend themselves and because they had to march back to Athens and protect their city.

As the Persians were intent on reinstating the exiled tyrant **HIPPIAS**, the significance of the Battle of Marathon is manifold. It was the first true test of the Athenian democracy; the event that proved this new, unprecedented political system was a successful concept worth fighting for—and capable of winning. Within our story, we chose to refer to Marathon by name only at the very end, and not just to preserve a modicum of suspense. We feel that this battle for democracy is still taking place - and we needed to imply that it is taking place anywhere and at any time, not just on a plain full of fennels in 490 BCE.

The victory at Marathon was also the origin of the long-distance athletic race of the same name. According to some historians of later antiquity, a runner was dispatched from Marathon to Athens in advance of the returning army, in order to give the news of the victory. The distance of

the modern race corresponds to that covered by the Athenian messenger, and the race itself was conceived in commemoration of his legendary
run.

PANATHENAEA

The Festival of All Athenians, held every four years in honour of **ATHENA**, the
patron goddess of **ATHENS**. Known as The Great Panathenaea, it lasted for
eight days during the month of August. While great importance was given to
religious rites, including abundant sacrifices to the goddess, the festival also
included athletic events, music and poetry contests, and most famously, a
lavish procession to the city's citadel and the temple of the goddess. During this procession, a splendid saffron veil (or dress, according to others),
especially weaved for the occasion, was carried to the temple and laid on
the knees of the goddess' statue. Though the festival was believed to be an
ancient event, dating from the time of king Erechtheus, it was reorganized
and shaped in its known form by the tyrant **PEISISTRATUS** in 566 BCE. The
festival procession has been immortalized in all its splendour in the Parthe-
non Frieze, a monumental work by the sculptor and architect Phidias. Cur-
rently, the frieze is in pieces, cut up and removed from its place on the goddess' temple. Fragments are held in London's British Museum, the Acropolis
Museum in Athens, and six other museums around the world, waiting to be
reunited.

PEISISTRATUS

It is not known when the great tyrant of **ATHENS** was born, but he seems to have died around 527 BCE at a great old age. He ruled the city from 561 to 555, was exiled for a period of 3 to 6 years, and then was restored triumphantly to power, only to be ousted again for something close to a decade before he returned once more, this time to rule until his dying day. His legacy was both grand and controversial. Aside from his organizing of the **PANATHENAEA**, he is known for being a populist and champion of the poor, often in direct confrontation with the interests of the aristocracy. He was a bitter political rival of Megacles, who was the leader of the party of coastal landowners (and father of **CLEISTHENES**). The business with the lookalike of Athena is recorded as a true incident, representative of Peisistratus' political shrewdness. In fact, historians tell us that Peisistratus first seized power by way of another shrewd trick, when, after wounding himself, he claimed his rivals had tried to kill him and managed to secure a large cortege of armed bodyguards. He then used this cortege to seize the citadel and, subsequently, the reins of power.

Trickery aside, what cannot be contested was that Peisistratus was a popular, widely supported, enterprising ruler. Other than boosting the city's exports and economy, he invested in building projects such as fountain houses aqueducts, and was a patron of the arts. Herodotus tells us that his regime maintained the ancient laws and operated more like a constitutional government than a cruel dictatorship. The Athenian democracy was, in many ways, as much an offspring of the rule of Peisistratus as a result of the reforms made by **SOLON** and Cleisthenes.

PERSIAN EMPIRE

Branching out from the Iranian plateau sometime during the 6th century BCE, the Persian Empire encompassed the majority of the Asian continent and stretched beyond it, from the Indus Valley all the way to Egypt, Thrace and Bulgaria. It was the greatest military power of its time, ruling over fifty million people, which was equivalent to almost half of the population of the known world. Its government was centralised, with all authority over its vast territories given to its king. In fact, as Herodotus tells us, the Persians shunned political systems such as oligarchy and democracy, believing the former would lead to dissention amongst those in power, while the latter would result in anarchy. Even though king Darius' attack against the Greeks was a response to their supporting rebel colonies under his rule, he was clearly averse to the Athenian democracy, especially since his "solution" to the problem was to restore **HIPPIAS** as tyrant of **ATHENS** and to demand the allegiance of the entire Greek mainland. To the ancient Greeks, a war with the Persians must have seemed as imminent as it was to European countries in early 1939.

POET

One of only three ancient Greek tragedians whose plays survive in a complete form, the poet Aeschylus has long been considered the father of tragedy. Born in 525 BCE, he was an innovator of dramatic art as well as a multiple award-winning playwright during his lifetime. While earlier dramatists had only one actor responding to the chorus, Aeschylus increased the number of actors to two: by having two characters interact on stage, he actually introduced the concept of dramatic conflict. (Needless to say, writers throughout history owe the man *a lot*.) Innovations aside, however, Aeschylus' plays are celebrated - and performed - to this day, and this longevity is due to their worth as dramas in themselves, rather than their historical value. His seven extant plays - *The Persians, Seven against Thebes, The Suppliants, Prometheus Bound,* and *The Oresteia* trilogy - are all wonderful treatments of timeless themes: human arrogance and conceit, divine providence and interference, the social importance of the democratic state, and the struggle of law and reason versus revenge and chaos.

Ancient sources confirm that Aeschylus fought in the Battle of **MARATHON** alongside his brother **CYNEGEIRUS**. The inscription on the poet's gravestone, in fact, reads that "of his noble prowess the grove of Marathon can speak, and the long-haired Persian knows it well", while it omits any reference to his status as a playwright. The chance this gave us to include the man and his values within our story was too good to miss, especially since he was a great influence on *Democracy*. Aeschylus did not win his first award as a dramatist until 484 BCE, six years after Marathon, so he really was a "minor" poet at the time. It would have been a little heavy-handed to identify him explicitly, so we didn't call him by name. But we had fun peppering his debate with Leander with notions inspired by the plays he would go on to write, so look for stuff from *The Oresteia* and a quote from one of his "lost" works, *Niobe*.

SACK OF TROY

A lost epic poem about the end of the Trojan War, specifically the successful ploy of the wooden horse used by the Greeks to gain entrance within the walls of Troy and the massacre that followed. It was believed to have been composed sometime during the 7th century BCE by the Miletian poet Arctinus. Only a tiny fragment of it survives, but descriptions of its storyline indicate that it must have been an action-packed piece with a high body count – hence Leander's innuendo that **CYNEGEIRUS** would probably have appreciated it more if his story had been bloodier.

SCYTHIANS

The name was used widely through ancient Greece to describe the nomadic peoples that dwelled in the Caucasus region and around the Black Sea. They were renowned as being great riders and archers – Scythians in ancient Greek art are always depicted with a bow and arrow - and dressed in distinct caps, jackets and trousers. Not all historians agree that there were Scythian archers policing ATHENS in the 6th century BCE, since their presence is not explicitly documented. We do have evidence that **PEISISTRATUS** employed *Thracian* mercenaries as a police force, and during the 5th century there were indeed Scythian policemen in the city, though they were slaves of the state rather than mercenaries. that Peisistratus employed Scythians was put forward by some historians in order to explain the frequent appearance of Scythian archers on Athenian vases from about 530 to about 500 BCE. One piece of evidence that further supports this theory is a marble statue of a rider on the Acropolis, dating from the late 6th century and dressed in the characteristically brightly coloured trousers of a Scythian.

SOLON

Long considered one of the "Seven Sages", the most eminent thinkers of ancient Greece, Solon was a true polymath. During his long life (born in 638 BCE, he died in 558 BCE, at the age of 80), he was a statesman, lawmaker, poet, traveler, and reformer. Born to an aristocratic family descended from the last kings of **ATHENS**, Solon became chief magistrate of the city in 594 BCE. His wisdom in running its affairs led to his being granted special powers and tasked with resolving the economic, regional, and class rivalries that divided the people. What Solon enacted was nothing less than a full constitutional reform. He redefined the concept of citizenship so as to give a larger percentage of the people the right to participate in the **ASSEMBLY OF CITIZENS**, and he made the magistrates accountable to the people. Along with the **CITY COUNCIL** (a creation of Solon's), the Assembly became the foundation of the later democracy. Before Solon, only the nobles had control of the government, and class was determined by birth. Solon replaced traditional nobility with an aristocracy based on wealth. Coupled with an aggressive policy that encouraged trade, foreign commerce, the cultivation and exportation of olives and olive oil, and the competitiveness of Athenian products, this innovation boosted the city's economy to a tremendous degree. But perhaps the most celebrated of his reforms was the "Lifting of Burdens", a law that prohibited creditors from forcing those debtors unable to pay to become their serfs and slaves. This reform not only saved farmers from the indignity of surrendering owner-ship of their land and giving their produce to their creditors, but also put a limit on the acquisition of property, preventing the excessive gathering of wealth by a select few. So adamant was Solon on maintaining these re-forms, in fact, that he left Athens and travelled the world to avoid being compelled to repeal them.

In our story, **CLEISTHENES** says that Solon's reforms failed, but that has more to do with our character's irreverent, confrontational outlook than with actual historical fact. What failed was Solon's overall effort to bring about a consensus between the rival classes, not the reforms themselves. The "Lifting of Burdens" remained in place as a state law for centuries, and even **PEISIS-TRATUS** and his sons kept the Council and the economic system Solon cham-pioned, if for no other reason than to ensure a smooth running of the state.

Historians say that, towards the end of his life, Solon returned to Athens, where he tried - unsuccessfully - to oppose Peisistratus. In our story, their rivalry is also presented as symbolic, serving a purpose similar to that be-tween **APOLLO** and **DIONYSUS**. The lawgiver and the tyrant represent the opposing pulls of idealism and pragmatism on the common man. The road to democracy was paved through the struggle between the two.

SPARTA

Throughout the 6th and 5th centuries BCE, Sparta and **ATHENS** were the two major powers in Greece. Their relationship anticipated subsequent pairings of world powers, such as England and France, or the United States and the Soviet Union. As detailed in our story, Sparta did influence the shift from tyranny to democracy in Athens, and did so in ways both subtle and brutal. The reasons behind this have as much to do with the geopolitics of ancient Greece as with the nature of Sparta itself. An unashamedly militaristic and oligarchic city, Sparta featured no splendid temples or state edifices other than those dedicated to the training of its warriors and its strictly observed religious rites. The sole occupation of this culture was war, and its sole motivator was fear. The structure of the state was based on serfs and slaves, whose menial work supported the Spartan lifestyle, but whose existence filled the Spartans with the constant dread of a potential revolt. To stave off that revolt, Sparta had to keep strong, and to keep strong, it had no choice but to conquer. What Sparta represents in our story is a different system, a way of running a society directly opposed to the path that Athens took - which goes a long way to explain the feud between the two cities.

TEN TRIBES

As detailed in our story, **CLEISTHENES** did indeed mix, match and reorganize the citizens of **ATHENS** into ten groups. The actual tribes were: 1) the *Erechtheis*, named after Erechtheus, the serpent-king and foster son of **ATHENA**; 2) the *Aigeis*, named after king Aegeus, father of the great hero Theseus; 3) the *Pandionis*, named after Pandion, during whose reign the cult of **DIONYSUS** came to Athens; 4) the *Leontis*, named after Leos, a pious man who sacrificed his three daughters to the gods when he was told by the Oracle of **DELPHI** that this would save the city from famine; 5) the *Acamantis*, named after Acamas, a hero of the Trojan War; 6) the *Oineis*, named after Oeneus, the king who organized the epic hunt for the Calydonian Boar; 7) the *Kekropis*, named after Cecrops, another half-serpentine king who introduced reading, writing, and the customs of marriage and ceremonial burial to Athens; 8) the *Hipponthotis*, named after Hippothoon, a hero associated with the teachings of the arts of agriculture; 9) the *Aiantis*, named after Ajax, the great hero of the Trojan War; and 10) the *Antiochis*, named after Antiochus, son of the hero Heracles.

THERSIPPUS

In modern times, it has become accepted that the runner sent from **MARATHON** to **ATHENS** to give the news of the Athenians' victory ran the full 26 miles in armour, hot from the battle, then collapsed and died as soon as he uttered the words "We won". Tradition names the runner as Pheidippides, but that was not always the case. Herodotus does credit Pheidippides with an epic 2-day, 152-mile run from Athens to **SPARTA** *before* the battle, when the Athenians asked the Spartans for their help - but he has Pheidippides survive that run. The historian makes no mention of a run from Marathon to Athens, and the first mention of such a run - along with its tragic climax - was made much later by Plutarch, who gives two possible names for the runner, Eucles and Thersippus. Over the centuries, these two (three?) runners have been collated into one, Pheidippides, and both feats are credited to him. Since we thought it cool to feature the runner of Marathon as a character, we went back to naming him Thersippus in order not to spoil his identity, and we hint at his destiny only at the end.

TREASURIES

While the remains of the treasuries of **DELPHI** - the reconstructed Athenian treasury in particular - gave us a pretty good idea of what these build-

ings looked like on the outside, there is little information as to how the votive offerings were laid out on the inside. So we chose not to come up with
a design, but a feeling - one similar to that which permeates the neoclas-
sical paintings of Johann Zoffany: a sense of multiple objects stacked in a
space too small for them. It seemed appropriate, since the ancients used
the treasuries both to store these offerings and to display them, not in the
clear, linear way of museum displays, but as a hoard offered to the gods.
Moreover, as the offerings represented the pride, devotion, and essence of
the cities they came from, they encapsulate the spirit of ancient Greece:
the balanced contrast of war and peace, harmony and chaos, reason and
madness. One work that captures this spirit in all its awesome complexity
is Homer's description of the Shield of Achilles in the *Iliad*, so our treasuries
are also a sort of homage to it.

TYRANT SLAYERS

The lives of Harmodius and Aristogeiton before their
"celebrated deed", as Aristotle calls it, are mostly undocumented. What we do have are accounts of the back-
ground behind the assassination of **HIPPARCHUS**, and
both Aristotle and Thucydides agree that the murder
was a personal matter. According to them, when Hipparchus' amorous ad-
vances were repelled, he set out to insult Harmodius. He did that by inviting
Harmodius' young sister to be the carrier of a basket of sacred offerings
in the procession of the **PANATHENAEA**, only to reject her as undeserving of
such honour (implying either that the girl was not a virgin, or that she was
unworthy by way of her association with a brother who led a "loose life"). It
was this insult, as the ancient writers point out, that finally prompted the
two companions to action. In the aftermath of the murder, Aristogeiton was
tortured in order to reveal the names of those friends of his that knew of
his plan - and had perhaps conspired with him and Harmodius in execut-
ing it. Tradition maintains that both he and Leaena, a **HETAIRA** he was ac-

quainted with, refused to talk, and were put to death for their defiance.

Regardless of the precise details, both ancient and contemporary historians agree that the murder started a domino effect that led to the ending of the tyranny and the establishment of democracy. The Tyrant Slayers spawned a cult of personality comparable to that of today's ultimate pop revolutionary, Che Guevara. **CLEISTHENES** did use Harmodius and Aristogeiton as propaganda tools when he commissioned a statue of them to be erected in the **AGORA.** It was paid for by the city - a significant first - and became a sacred site.

On its base was written the following commemoratory inscription: "A marvelous great light shone upon Athens when Aristogeiton and Harmodius slew Hipparchus".

It was composed by the poet Simonides, who, ironically, had first been brought to the city by Hipparchus.

Acknowledgments

This novel would have never come to be without the histories of Herodotus, Thucydides and Aristotle, so all due credit should go to them. Out of the other ancient sources we looked at, Plutarch's *Parallel Lives* and "On the Glory of the Athenians" proved most helpful. In grappling with the material these writers put down, both Alecos and I must acknowledge our debt to some scholars we found essential. Tom Holland's *Persian Fire: The First World Empire and the Battle for the West* was a work we consulted throughout our writing process, and so was Josiah Ober's *The Athenian Revolution: Essays on Ancient Greek Democracy and Political Theory*, as well as his *Mass and Elite in Democratic Athens: Rhetoric, Ideology, and the Power of the People* (to which we could add a long list of Professor Ober's essays on the matter of Athens). We were also helped immensely by Jacqueline de Romilly's *Problems of Greek Democracy* and *The Democratic Impulse in Ancient Athens*, W.G. Forrest's *The Emergence of Greek Democracy*, Gustave Glotz's *The Greek City and its Institutions*, Simon Goldhill and Robin Osborne's *Rethinking Revolutions Through Ancient Greece*, Dimitris Kyrtatas' *Lessons of Athenian Democracy*, and Pierre Lévêque and Pierre Vidal-Naquet's *Cleisthenes the Athenian: An Essay on the Representation of Space and Time in Greek Political Thought from the End of the Sixth Century to the Death of Plato*.

Also instrumental in crafting the ambiance of our tale were such diverse works as Danielle S. Allen's "Punishment in Ancient Athens," Antony Andrewes' *Greek Society*, Hilary J. Deighton's *A Day in the Life of Ancient Athens*, Edith

Hamilton's *The Ever-Present Past*, Julian Jaynes' *The Origin of Consciousness in the Breakdown of the Bicameral Mind*, Claude Mossé's *Archaic Greece from Homer to Aeschylus*, Maria Sakalakis' *Deceit in Archaic Greece*, Ingeborg Scheibler's *Greek Ceramic Art*, and Jean-Pierre Vernant's *The Origins of Greek Thought* (along with his *Mortals and Immortals* and *Myth and Religion in Ancient Greece*, and his and Marcel Detienne's *Cunning Intelligence in Greek Culture and Society*).

In addition, I'd be remiss if I didn't mention some key influences from fiction and the arts: Aeschylus' *The Oresteia* figures large in this respect, of course, but inspiration came also from Nikos Kazantzakis' *Zorba the Greek* and *The Last Temptation*, Michael Cacoyannis' "Greek Tragedy" film trilogy, Walter Hill and David Shaber's *The Warriors*, John Boorman and Rospo Pallenberg's *Excalibur*, Ray Harryhausen, Desmond Davis and Beverley Cross' *Clash of the Titans*, Sidney Lumet and Paddy Chayefsky's *Network*, the comics of Alan Moore, Jim Steranko's *Nick Fury*, Hugo Pratt's *A Midwinter Morning's Dream*, and the music of Manos Hadjidakis. Last, but not least, I'd like to acknowledge my debt to Robert F. Kennedy's 1968 speech on the death of Martin Luther King, which quotes both Aeschylus and Edith Hamilton to timeless, devastating effect.